Haynes
Restoration Manual

MGB (2nd Edition)

Lindsay Porter

Dedication

Paul Skilleter is to blame for encouraging me to start writing about cars and the First Edition of this book was dedicated to him. This new edition carries the same unqualified thanks, especially since the original idea for the book was his. As always with Paul, the idea was a good one and his generosity in allowing me to use it is typical of him.

First published by G. T. Foulis & Company as *MGB Purchase and Restoration Guide* in1992
Reprinted with revisions, February 1994
Reprinted 1994, 1995, 1996 and 1997
Reprinted by Haynes Publishing as *MGB Restoration Manual* (with new cover and minor text amendment) in 1998
Reprinted 1999, 2000, 2001, 2002, 2003, 2004, 2006, 2008, 2009, 2010, 2011, 2012, 2015 and 2016

A catalogue record for this book is available from the British Library

ISBN 978 1 85960 607 0

Library of Congress catalog card No. 92-64083

Haynes Publishing,
Sparkford, Yeovil, Somerset
BA22 7JJ, UK

Tel: 01963 440635
Int. tel: +44 1963 440635
Web site: www.haynes.co.uk

Haynes North America, Inc.
861 Lawrence Drive, Newbury Park, California 91320, USA

Printed in the UK.

Other Haynes Publishing titles of interest to MGB enthusiasts:

MGB Owner's Workshop Manual (III)

MGB: The Illustrated History (2nd Edition) by Jonathan Wood & Lionel Burrell
(ISBN 0 85429 948 3 now out of print)

The Classic Car Bodywork Restoration Manual by Lindsay Porter
(ISBN 978 1 84425 829 1)

Jurisdictions which have strict emission control laws may consider any modification to a vehicle to be an infringement of those laws. You are advised to check with the appropriate body or authority whether your proposed modification complies fully with the law. The publishers accept no liability in this regard.

While every effort is taken to ensure the accuracy of the information given in this book, no liability can be accepted by the author or publishers for any loss, damage or injury caused by errors in, or omissions from, the information given.

Contents

Foreword by Roche Bentley

When the original edition of this book was published I was honoured and delighted to write the foreword. I anticipated that Lindsay's book would be a success and congratulated him on the comprehensive tips on buying an MGB and on the detailed descriptions of restoration. Ten years on, and with tens of thousands of copies sold, the first edition has been appreciated by new and existing MGB owners for its excellent coverage, and this second edition covers the developments and changes which have since occurred.

Buying a poor MGB and making a hash of a restoration is easy, as unfortunately so many can testify. The recent hype in classic cars, with a sharp upswing in prices followed by a slump, has left MG and other classic car enthusiasts confessing to being bewildered by the dramatic changes. However, in the case of MGs, especially MGBs, MGB GTs and MGB GT V8s, the values of the better maintained and well restored cars have continued to increase.

The introduction of new MGB and MGB GT bodyshells has also had a very beneficial effect on the MG scene, and Rover Group's Heritage project was brilliantly conceived and carried out. MG owners completing DIY restorations at home found that Heritage's decision to sell bodyshells complete with wings, doors, bonnet and boot meant that much of the difficult work had been done.

Buying and restoring an MG is something that most of us want to do properly and with guidance. Lindsay Porter's excellent book, with its detailed descriptions, is an essential guide, and one which the MG Owners' Club thoroughly recommends.

Roche Bentley.

Using this Book

The layout of this book has been designed to be both attractive and easy to follow whilst carrying out practical work on your car. However, to obtain maximum benefit from the book, it is important to note the following points:

1) Apart from the introductory pages, this book is split into two parts: Chapters 1 to 8 dealing with history, buying and practical procedures; appendices 1 to 9 providing supplementary information. Each chapter/appendix may be subdivided into sections and even sub-sections. Section headings are in italic type between horizontal lines and sub-section headings are similar, but without horizontal lines.

2) Photograph captions are an integral part of the text (except in Chapters 1 and 2) - therefore the photographs and their captions are arranged to 'read' in exactly the same way as the normal text. In other words they run down each column and the columns run from left to right of the page.

Each photograph caption carries an alpha-numerical identity, relating it to a specific section. The letters before the caption number are simply the initial letters of key words in the relevant section heading, whilst the caption number shows the position of the particular photograph in the section's picture sequence. Thus photograph/caption 'DR22' is the 22nd photograph in the section headed 'Door Repairs'.

3) Figures - illustrations which are not photographs - are numbered consecutively throughout the book. Figure captions do not form any part of the text. Therefore Figure 5 is simply the 5th figure in the book.

4) All references to the left or right of the vehicle are from the point of view of somebody standing behind the car looking forwards.

5) Because this book majors upon restoration, regular maintenance procedures and normal mechanical repairs of all the car's components, are beyond its scope. It is therefore strongly recommended that the Haynes MGB Owner's Workshop Manual should be used as a companion volume.

6) We know it's a boring subject, especially when you really want to get on with the job - but your safety, through the use of correct workshop procedures, must ALWAYS be your foremost consideration. Appendix 1 attempts to give a good grounding in basic safety techniques, but please remember that safety is your responsibility: check correct safety procedures with manufacturers of products and equipment supplied, and you are strongly recommended to seek some kind of training from your local evening school, where available.

7) Whilst great care is taken to ensure that the information in this book is as accurate as possible, neither the author, editor nor publisher can accept any liability for loss, damage or injury caused by errors in, or omissions from, the information given.

Introduction & Acknowledgements

First Edition

With MGB production finished for good, and even Abingdon razed to the ground, some say that there can never be another real MG sports car. Whether they are right or not, it is indisputable that there will never be another new MGB. Or will there...? Let's say you took an MGB, one that has seen better days, took the wings off, repaired the body and rebuilt interior and mechanics. You'd make it as good as new! And, really, that's what this book is all about; it's a guide covering every stage in the purchase and restoration of an MGB so that, if the work is carried out properly, you could end up with the next best thing to a brand new car. You'll be maintaining one of the inevitably dwindling numbers of the last of the real sports cars; the last Abingdon MGB. The fine traditions embodied in every one of them can, now, only be upheld by the restorer - which is why there is a chapter on the history and the heritage that lies behind the cars - and it is hoped that every owner, whether carrying out a minor repair or a full-blown rebuild, will remember to include something of the proud spirit of Abingdon in his tool kit. There are so many to thank for their help in the preparation of this book, but there is no question as to where to start. Without the help of my wife, Shan, the book would never have been. Her talents as typist, sub-editor, critic and especially as researcher sans pareille have been greatly in evidence throughout the months of preparation, and as a consequence there is a lot of 'her' woven into its pages.

My good friend Paul Skilleter is to be thanked for having given a great measure of help and assistance, while Nigel Rogers, friend and neighbour in the best Herefordshire tradition has been invaluable in his preparation of my own MGB during its restoration for many of the shots used in this book. Pearl and Derek McGlen provided the very best advice to be had anywhere on the MGC, (and a number of pictures, too) and Peter Laidler was similarly helpful with V8 material. Steve Glochowsky, President of the American MGB Association, supplied American pictures and much data on US cars, and Ken Smith was also most helpful in this respect.

Prompt, helpful darkroom work of the highest quality was supplied by Alan Wood, while cartoonist Mick Martin was a real 'find' from the days when I edited Practical Classics Magazine's Club News pages. Peter Franklin, ex-Abingdon Personnel Manager gave an insight (literally!) into the last days at Abingdon, and Roy Brocklehurst (Syd Enever's successor there) kindly gave his forthright 'on-the-record' views on the demise of the MGB.

Many other owners and DIY enthusiasts have given of their advice and time, and to all of them I am most grateful.

In the United States, John H. Twist of University Motors, Michigan, spent many a winter's evening preparing his notes and photographs, and it quickly became obvious that there could be no one more knowledgeable about the mechanics and electrical systems of the MGB than he: it is a privilege to share his knowledge here.

Perhaps the best thing to have come out of this book, for its author at least, is that every one of the people mentioned here has been not just a source of expert information but has become more of a personal friend than could ever have been imagined. My grateful thanks are due, and gladly given, to them all!

Second Edition

This virtually all-new Second Edition reflects the fact that you can now recreate your own 'new' MGB in one of two ways: you can use the latest tools and equipment available to the home restorer to rebuild your faithful car; or you can start afresh with an all-new, almost original Heritage bodyshell.

We bought a Heritage shell as the basis of a project car for this book and we purchased a running but ratty donor vehicle through the classified ads in the MG Owners' Club's excellent magazine, Enjoying MG. Moss Europe, the British end of the world's largest MG parts company, Moss Motors, of California, supplied almost all of the MG dedicated parts and an incredible amount of knowledge and expertise. Parts man, Martin Smith, must have microchips where others have brain cells, and Graham Paddy, Adam Blackaby and Tim Becket were frequently instrumental in making things 'happen'.

In my office Catherine Larner did a wonderful job of sorting and using the photo archive, obtaining fresh pictures and so on, while Zoe Palmer and Kath Tickle typed and organised the final draft in their usual cheerful and efficient ways.

There are just too many others to single out – but you'll find them all in these pages!

Two people do come in for a special mention, however. One is Graham MacDonald who carried out almost all of the work on the project car – and no one has found fault with a single thing that he has done. Normally, after a rebuild, there is the 'shake down' period where faults have to be fixed. In the case of our project car there were precisely – none! Not many production line new cars can boast that. Thanks Graham!

Left until last but most important to me, of course, is my wife Shan. It was she who insisted that I got on with this new edition, and she who gave her inimitable and invaluable support to the whole project – as well as taking very many of the photographs you see in this book. After twenty years of MGBs (and others!) in various stages of undress cluttering up our garage, our garden and our lives, she has become – well, stoical.

Chapter 1
History

In the Beginning ...

When the last MGB rolled from the sudden emptiness of Abingdon's redundant production line on 22 October 1980, it ended an era of sports car motoring which could be said to have begun there some eighteen years and four months earlier when the first production MGB was built but which, in truth, had its roots at least as far back as the early 1920s.

In 1910 William Richard Morris opened a retail garage, known as The Morris Garage, in some old stables which he owned in Longwall Street, Oxford. At about the same time, however, he began to build cars at nearby Cowley under the auspices of a company which later, in 1919, became known as Morris Motors Ltd.

This latter activity so fascinated the volatile 23-year-old Morris that he became more and more involved in motor-car production until the point came where he had to entrust the expanding and successful 'The Morris Garages' (as they had become) to a general manager.

In 1921, Cecil Kimber, a man whose name has since become of revered importance to MG enthusiasts, was appointed as Sales Manager to The Morris Garages. He was enterprising and immediately successful - so much so that when the General Manager took his own life in 1922, Kimber, then 34 years of age, was asked to fill the vacancy.

Kimber's obvious drive and immediacy of action set in motion a chain of events which are beyond the scope of this essentially restoration orientated book to unravel, but which led to the metamorphosis from which MG emerged as manufacturers of motor cars in their own right. As in all the best stories, this one is surrounded with mystery, myth and controversy, but the 'facts' which underpin the tale seem to be that:

- Kimber arranged to build rebodied versions of the Morris Oxford with a tourer body known as 'Chummy', lowered suspension and up-market appointments. It was never sold as an 'MG'.
- In 1923, production was transferred from Longwall Street to Alfred Lane, Oxford.
- Also in 1923, Kimber's own Chummy was modified and entered in the Land's End Trial. He won one of the many gold-medal awards, but preferred an optional pair of cufflinks!
- In late 1923 or '24, six Cowley chassis were fitted with bodies made by Raworth. Some consider these to be the first MGs, but they do not seem to have been referred to as MG at the time.
- The MG emblem was seen, enclosed in an octagon, for the first time in an advertisement in May 1924.
- From 1 September 1924, the 'MG Super Sports' was offered with three body variations based once again on the honest but uninspiring Morris Oxford, in addition to the continuation of a range of closed bodies on the same chassis.
- Through 1924 and 1925 a hybrid sports car using a Hotchkiss engine, one-off chassis modifications and a body by Carbodies was built at Longwall Street. It was entered by Kimber in the 1924 Land's End Trial and he again qualified for a gold medal. This car was subsequently 'adopted' as the first MG by the Nuffield Group's publicity department (in spite of evidence to the contrary) and christened 'Old Number One'.

Production of Cowley-based MGs continued at an increasing pace over the next few years and, in 1928, The MG Car Company was registered in its own right. In the same year the Company introduced, at their first independent Motor

Show stand, both the large, fast and prestigious 18/80 Six and the Morris Minor based M-type Midget with quite startling performances for its day and its size. The Midget was based on Morris' new 'baby' car, the overhead camshaft Morris Minor, whose engine had been acquired as part of the Nuffield Group's takeover of Wolseley. They, in turn, had developed the diminutive but powerful engine unit from a Hispano-Suiza aero-engine design and, in fact, when used in the Minor family saloon, the engine was a detuned version of that fitted to the MG

The first MG Midget was the most significant car to have been produced by the Company, at least in terms of the marque's evolution, and was highly successful, with over 3,200 being made. Its significance lies in the fact that it was truly a recognised Sports-Car, being sporting in performance and not merely 'Sporting' in appearance as had been the case with most previous offerings. Moreover, that performance was achieved with the use of proprietary, largely unspecialised components mildly rearranged in such a way that their achievement as a whole exceeded the sum of their parts. This theme is important in that it was to be seen running throughout all successful MG production for the next half-century.

M-type Midgets were produced until 1932 amongst a splendid profusion of other Midgets and six-cylinder Magnas, none of which matched the M-type for sales, but some, such as the C- type, chalked up satisfactory track successes.

In 1932, upon the demise of the M-type, a new Midget known as the J-type first saw the light of day. Although with basically the same mechanical layout as its predecessor and consequently a similar

performance appeal, the J-type, perhaps more than any small MG before it, contrived to combine a great degree of visual appeal with speed borne of efficiency and lightness. From this point on, the profusion of growths was pruned back a little with the effect of strengthening and more readily defining future development. A succession of six- cylinder cars in both open and closed forms were developed, culminating in the WA whose production was ended in 1939 by the onset of the Second World War, while the Midget line, that with which we are most concerned here, evolved by 1936 into the legendary TA Midget.

Just one year after MG's Nuffield masters enforced their departure from the motor sport scene, a larger-engined, larger-bodied Midget appeared, known at the time as the T-type. Gone was the stretched version of the original M type 'Wolseley' engine, and in its place was found another implant from the same firm. The Wolseley 10 engine of 1292cc was tuned and fitted; mated to a synchromesh gearbox (except for the earlier cars) and made to power a car of softer suspension but better roadholding than its predecessors. Hydraulic brakes replaced the Kimber- favoured cable-operated variety. These 'modernisations' outraged purists of the time in much the same way that motoring generations later, the MGB was to upset the motoring 'masochists' of the Sixties.

The Autocar of 1936 praised the new car's roadholding abilities by saying: 'General handling is good, for although the springing is a shade softer, and hydraulic shock absorbers are now fitted all round instead of at the back only, the Midget can be put into a fast curve confidently and be swung around an acute turn with a most satisfactory feeling

of security.' The road test went on to describe the innovation of 'a green-tinted lamp [which] is illuminated as long as the car's speed remains below 30mph.' But reservations were cast, and the article added archly that: 'It is understood that the necessary modification has already been incorporated.'

The TB Midget hardly had a production run at all before war erased all attempts at creating motor cars, but it did herald the introduction of an engine with reduced stroke compared to that of the TA, which was subsequently fitted to the post war TC. This car was a widened version of the TB and began another thread which was to run unbroken through the remainder of MG history, for, in 1947, for the first time, more TCs were sold abroad than in Britain...

MGB Parentage

The story so far has attempted to put into context the circumstances in which the MGB can be regarded as a classic sports car; that of a heritage which is second to none in its singlemindedness of purpose, and supreme in its success in building simply exciting sports cars. From late 1949, with the introduction of the MG TD, specific components which were eventually to be incorporated into the MGB began to be fitted to the MG cars of the day.

Though the TD was later said by The Autocar to have 'lost pretty well all the endearing starkness of its predecessors', it was probably this very 'loss' that enabled it to be the first MG to become at all well-known in America, for while it retained the trusty 1250cc engine, it benefited from a new box-section frame

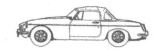

upswept over the rear axle, a wider body and independent front suspension. This suspension set up had been designed by none other than Alec Issigonis (later Sir Alec, designer of two of the most significant landmarks in British motoring - the Morris Minor and the Mini) and was destined for use in a new Series E Morris 8-based MG saloon. (Which, in the event was not introduced until 1947 as the rather hybrid MG YA.)

The suspension, however, was used two years later in the TD where its efficiency gave both increased comfort and improved roadholding. In effect the system comprised a kingpin about which the steering operated, suspended by a pair of 'wishbones' - one at top and bottom - the bottom one of which bore upwards against a coil spring while the top, acting as the top face of the moving parallelogram, was also the link to a hydraulic shock absorber. Steering was by rack and pinion.

For a while the TD was a runaway sales success, but as the design began to age and competition from such cars as the Triumph TR2 increased, it became increasingly obvious that a replacement was necessary.

In the early Fifties three events took place which had a bearing, either direct or indirect, upon the evolutionary process with which we are concerned. First, a special bodyshell was prepared at Abingdon and mounted upon an MG TD chassis in order that a private entrant could enter Le Mans in 1951. This bodyshell, designed by Abingdon's Chief Designer, Syd Enever, is so very like that of the MGA to come that no shred of controversy can exist as to that car's bodily origins.

Second, at the start of 1952, MG already a part of the Nuffield Group, became a component within the British Motor Corporation when the Nuffield and Austin giants merged to become the world's fourth largest automobile producer, after the USA's 'Big Three', the significance of which would soon be felt at Abingdon.

And third, in 1953, the MG Magnette was announced to replace the YA/YB series of pre-war designed cars. That this last is significant can be no more than interesting speculation but it must be noted that the Magnette, derived as it was from Gerald Palmer's Wolseley design, was the first unitary-bodied car to be built at Abingdon and was still under production there when Abingdon's own design team was beginning to crystallise its first thoughts on the MGB, and it could well have been at the back of the designers' minds when they decided upon unitary construction for the MGB.

The other two developments were significant in more empirical ways, however. The 1951 Le Mans body had been developed by 1952 to the point where Syd Enever and John Thornley (by now MG's General Manager) could offer the BMC management a genuine TD replacement. Unfortunately for MG, a decision had already been taken to produce an Austin-Healey, the '100' model, leaving no resources available for the new MG. As a result of a fall in TD sales a stop-gap model called, unsurprisingly, the TF was introduced with 'modernised', more rounded, bodywork and a sales curve which showed that an increasingly discriminating public were not to be fobbed-off. In a desperate throw the TF was given the Magnette's 1466cc engine which, it was felt by many, should have been fitted in the first place. This increased power but not sales, especially and crucially in the United States where the TF was regarded as no more than a slap in the face by those expecting more from a new model of MG. The development of EX175 was sanctioned at last by the management.

If the new car, to be called the MGA, took on the body and chassis of the 1952 prototype, its engine and drive train were radically different in a way which adds another important piece of the jigsaw puzzle of our story. BMC were embarking upon a policy which, in conjunction with many other political and economic factors in British life, was to have a devastating effect upon the variety of motor cars and components on offer. The term used was -and still is - that of rationalisation, and its effect was to ensure that Fifties cars as disparate as the A40 range, the Morris Oxfords, the MG Magnette, many commercial vehicles and then the MGA, were all fitted with basically the same engine and gearbox. The engine, known as the B-series, had three main bearings, twin carburettors (for the MGA) and, it must be confessed, sat happily within the MGA's chassis rails, and went rather well. The gearbox was originally designed for column-change use but had been converted to stick-shift, and in the MGA was fitted with an extension which meant that a short gear lever fell nicely to the driver's hand.

The rear axle was of the 'banjo' type (this referring to no more than the rounded shape of the central part of its one- piece casting) and was a three-quarter-floating hypoid-bevel unit, also commonised with much of the BMC range.

This move away from the Midget tradition was probably wise in view of the bad feeling engendered by the TF, and reactions to this fresh start were excellent. In terms of production figures, the

Abingdon workforce did themselves proud. In 1956, the figure exceeded thirteen thousand, and in 1957, twenty thousand. In that year alone, more cars were produced than had been made in all the years before the war, and thanks for that were mainly due to the instant appeal generated by the MGA in the United States.

The Autocar test achieved a 'best' of 99mph from the car, found that the acceleration was 'very good' and that, 'long winding hillside roads are a joy to traverse.' It is perhaps significant, though, that the car was criticised for 'raining in' and dampening the driver's right leg - a situation that would have been considered part and parcel of sports car ownership a few years previously but not, it seems, in 1955.

The swooping curves of the MGA's production figures were more or less sustained by a policy of development which led to the introduction of improved interior appointments, the fitting of front disc brakes and the uprating of the engine to 1588cc, a unique capacity which could not be tolerated for long by BMC and finally became 1622cc in common with other cars fitted with the B-series engine at the same time.

The MGA Twin-Cam, which appeared in 1958, was something of an enigma - it might have taken Abingdon in a direction which could have greatly influenced the MGB still to come, but in the event, it did not.

Although excitingly equipped with a race-orientated twin-overhead-camshaft engine (which left no room under the bonnet for the sensible positioning of such components as the distributor - there were access hatches behind both front wheels) and disc brakes all round, when measured against the reliable, everyday use to which the 'standard' MGA could

be put, the Twin-Cam was something of a failure. An interesting footnote to Twin-Cam production is that it would seem that customers were able to order a Twin-Cam (with disc brakes, special wheels and all) but with standard engine, throughout its production run. However, when Twin-Cam production ended, the last week or so was taken up entirely with the construction of these now-rare cars which were known, but never catalogued, as the 'MGA De-luxe'.

The 1588cc Twin-Cam engine, although perhaps briefly considered, was never reliable enough for use in the MGB, and instead, in the short-term it bequeathed its engine capacity to the MGA.

First Born

Like all good things, the MGA had to come to an end. In 1962 the radically different MGB was introduced and, in a letter of that year sent to Road & Track magazine, Mr Tony Birt, Advertising Manager of Hambro Automotive Corporation, MG's US distributor claimed that: 'everything is new [of the MGB] but the octagon.' In view of the marque's history, it is instructive to look back and see just how much of the MGB was indeed brand new. The body was, without a shred of doubt, all-new. The tail bore a strong resemblance to the Abingdon-produced Austin-Healey Sprite Mk II/MG Midget Mk I and the front wing door line, door handles and rear bumper could be seen to have strong antecedents in Abingdon's late Fifties design project, EX 205/1, but the MGB's sensational profile and dramatic front-end sculpting were all its own. The radiator grille brilliantly combined the appeal of the

traditional MG radiator shell with a modern, aggressive touch. In short, the MGB's styling, without being in the least brash or blatant was, and is, a masterpiece of design suggesting all the effortless speed that it was in fact capable of producing.

What is more, the MGB's new body was not only aesthetically brilliant, it was technically superb too. The new car was three inches shorter in both wheelbase and overall length than the MGA, and two inches wider, and within that framework included greatly increased cockpit space, wind-up windows, more leg room and far more luggage space. While both cars shared an identical volume at 262 cubic feet, the MGB provided a lot more car for its size, and yet without any increase in weight over its predecessor. The answer, of course, lay in the adoption of unitary construction such as that which had already been used on the Magnette and the Sprite/Midget. However, while the Sprite's lighter structure had been relatively easy to build and was suitable for a smaller scale production run, that of the MGB was complex and demanded the use of sophisticated and expensive tooling, needing a lengthy production run to pay for the high initial setting-up costs - a requirement that must have been met three times over!

The car's designer Syd Enever had been accused of erring, if anything, on the side of caution and excessive size in his design of the MGA's chassis, and he was clearly determined that the MGB would be no less sturdy. In practice, he was so successful that the MGB is only significantly weakened by quite advanced corrosion. Front twisting loads are transmitted along vestigial front chassis rails and complex inner-wing structures, back into a quite massive double bulkhead,

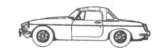

between which is a plenum chamber carrying air for the heater. Even the radio speaker support is a structural member helping to tie-in part of the bulkhead to the strong gearbox tunnel. Sills - vital on an open car - are three-section members, containing an enclosed vertical membrane sandwiched top and bottom between the other two, and the rear parcel shelf-cum-battery box adds to the car's lateral stiffness at the rear. Also new was the car's interior, with improved - though still leather - seats, well trimmed doors and a new dashboard layout, albeit with several familiar looking instruments.

But what of the MGB's mechanical arrangements? The engine was larger than that of the MGA by 11%, an increase necessitated by a frontal area which was 2% greater and a drag coefficient which was worse by a more significant amount. Therefore to push the same weight of car through increased wind resistance would have resulted in a slower car if the same size engine had been used. The MGB's 1798cc engine was still a 'B'- series unit but it had come a long way from its MGA days, and even further, through 1622, 1588 and 1489cc from the days when it had been used in 1947 in 1200cc form in the Austin Devon. This final engine stretch had necessitated the elimination of the water jacket between the central cylinders and between the central exhaust ports in the head but the technique, known as 'Siamesing' was far from new, having been instrumental in successfully powering three million Model A Fords, and has given absolutely no problems to half a million MGBs either. The first MGB engine's bottom-end was similar to that of the 1622cc engine with three main bearings and, apart from the weakness which time was to

expose in this area, the latest engine was a great success and a great improvement giving 95bhp (86bhp - MGA 1600 Mk II) and 110lb ft of torque (97lb ft).

The gearbox was essentially the same as that of the MGA, although with improved synchromesh, and the banjo rear axle was unaltered save for a slightly lower ratio to compensate for the difference in gearing caused by a 1" reduction in road wheel size to 14". Front suspension, with its oldest antecedents of all, was virtually unchanged and as successfully effective as ever, while steering was marginally lower geared.

Put to the Test

While it is clear that many of the MGB's mechanical components were far from new, Tony Birt's letter was in essence true because the car as a whole was quite unique. Motoring magazines on both sides of the Atlantic, and both sides of the world, were quick to pass judgement on the car, among the first being Autocar who reported on it in September 1962. They were impressed in their usual sober way and felt that it was 'a forward step in that the car is faster than the previous model, and yet more docile and comfortable. Moreover, from any angle it looks good ... and it should be as big a success in home markets as it will surely be abroad.'

Motor were a month later in getting to grips with the 'B. They, too, liked the car in most respects, commenting that: '... there is, in fact, almost every modern saloon car amenity, except for a back seat and courtesy switches to operate the map-reading lamp when a door is opened.' But, in

common with most owners, they did not like the hood. 'Raising and lowering the hood was, however, a slow process,' they said, 'at least for anyone not well-drilled in the procedure, suggesting its suitability for California's reliable climate rather than for Britain's erratic weather, and hood frame joints close to passengers' heads looked potentially dangerous.'

Road & Track confined themselves to a technical exploration of the MGB's qualities, not at that time having one available for road test, it seems, and in Australia it took a year before Wheels got its hands on a 'B in August 1963. They found a problem which has often plagued owners since, causing annoyance even when no positive damage has occurred: 'Developing 94bhp at 5500rpm the engine has an 8.75 to 1 compression ratio which does not agree with local fuel mixtures. We encountered running-on problems almost every time the engine was closed down, but there was never a trace of pinging.' Also, perceptively, Wheels noted that: 'Pedal placement is not particularly satisfactory for the sporting driver since it is not possible to heel-and-toe when braking and changing down simultaneously,' and then: 'Some confusion can occur when operating the electrical switches at night.' Presumably being in New South Wales they had little cause to be confused by the amazing illogicality of the heater controls! Although no eulogy this, the magazine liked all the points praised elsewhere, such as comfort, space, roadholding and speed.

Car & Driver's test, reported in the last month of 1964, made one keep looking at the photographs to ensure that they were talking about the MGB at all. 'There are a number of full-sized domestic cars that will get through a fast, rough

corner with less bother than the MGB .... The operation [of the folding soft-top] can hardly be described as difficult ... cockpit ventilation ... is virtually non-existent.' But their prophetic powers were faultless when they concluded: 'Detroit pressures, in the form of all-synchro transmission, whopping horsepower and proper handling for relatively meagre amounts of money - and of course the potent new Sunbeam Tiger - may ultimately force MG into developing a more powerful engine, a new suspension and an improved transmission.' With the sad and singular exception of the latter, they could not have been more correct ...

Car & Driver's test car was still fitted with a three main bearing engine but, in fact, in October 1964, an engine with a redesigned bottom end and five main bearings was fitted. This modification was made because, in spite of an oil-cooler having been fitted as standard to export cars, and as an option to British cars, 3-main-bearing cars had been slightly prone to crank-whip under the extremes of use for which the car was, of course, designed. As a consequence, engines which were hard pressed had a life as low as 60,000 miles or so and, if used after the evidence of bottom-end rumble had presented itself, could destroy their rear oil scroll which was a fixture in the rear of the crank/block assembly, which invariably and expensively - although it rarely happened - meant a scrap engine. To be fair to BMC, the engine was modified before any customers complaints could have been received and as soon as possible after the problem was perceived. Moreover, 3-main-bearing engines which have completed over 120,000 miles without a crank regrind and are still showing good oil pressure are not unheard of. It was just

that the 5-main-bearing engine was as solid and unburstable as the car's body and, unless drastically neglected, was virtually impossible to wear out at much less than 100,000 miles. To add a belt to the braces, an oil cooler was fitted as standard in Britain from the same time.

At around this stage, BMC were working on prototypes, in conjunction with Healeys, for a large-engined addition to the MG range. The first fruits were not to be borne until 1967.

In the meantime, the MGB proper was to gain an addition to the family which would make a lasting impact. In October 1965, the MGB GT was announced, which was a virtually unchanged Roadster up to the waistline - except for the front wings which no longer had cut-outs through which the Tourer's windscreen supports could pass - but which was fitted with a permanent roof and a large, estate car-like, rear door which transformed the use to which the MGB could be put. The soft overall outlines of the 'B were topped with a relatively angular superstructure which has a close affinity to BMC's 1100 of the time and which looked very much as though it had been designed to go there in the first place. And when one considers the 1959 prototype EX 205, it no doubt had, in concept at least. The MGB GT was officially described as 2+2 for a long time, but in reality the '+2' had to be a very small pair indeed to squeeze themselves onto the padded perch provided behind the front seat. However, the car's load carrying capacity was greatly increased, visibility was improved through the deeper screen and, because the rear glass was far less prone to 'misting' in damp weather than the Roadster's rear screen, all in all, the car provided a far more comfortable method of travelling on a typical English day, which stands a one in three chance of being a rainy day.

Performance-wise, the weight penalty incurred brought some surprising results. The Roadster's stiffness was already good for an open car, but the GT's was even better and, allied with a better weight-distribution and the anti-roll bar, which was fitted as standard to all cars two months after the GTs launch, the GT cornered marginally better than the Roadster - but it must be emphasised that the difference was marginal. Naturally, acceleration was slightly down, but top-speed was maintained because of the better aerodynamics involved. The GT also incorporated a modification which was not to be applied to the Roadster until some eighteen months later, in April 1967; that of a Salisbury tube-type rear axle.

Also in 1967 two of Car & Driver's predictions came true almost simultaneously. Firstly, the MGB was fitted with a new sturdier 4-synchromesh gearbox and was also offered with an automatic option which was very much liked by Autocar, but the new MGB variant from which these stemmed was the real star of the show. Unfortunately for the new car, appropriately named the MGC, it was more a first-night flop than a true star. Fitted with a redevelopment of the old Austin-Healey 3000 engine, which had proved too heavy and too tall for the standard MGB and which thus enforced a redesign of the car's under-the-skin front end, the MGC should have been a winner in terms of the sheer performance that many enthusiasts, particularly those in the USA were looking for, but instead it was a relative failure. Undoubtedly, the car lacked the raw acceleration that had been expected from its redesigned engine; undoubtedly it understeered due to the excessive weight up front, though not disastrously. One motoring journalist of the day put much of the 'Cs failure

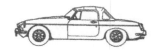

down to another factor: 'BMC were in a terribly demoralised state at the time of MGC's launch, and this was shown in what virtually amounted to contempt for the motoring press, which naturally responded, if not consciously, with a sort of "well blow you" attitude.'

Standard MGBs, as well as receiving the widely welcomed new gearbox, were also fitted with reversing lights as standard, a negative earth alternator which improved the charging rate immensely - a vital factor to a car where voltage drop from the twin-battery connections can cause starting problems in damp weather unless batteries are in tip-top condition - and American cars were fitted with a 'wall-of-padding' safety orientated dashboard, energy absorbing steering column and dual circuit brakes. In addition the first emission control equipment was fitted to US cars, forming the thin end of a very fat wedge!

In many ways this was the golden era of the original- style of MGB motoring, one which lasted until October 1969. Cars were still fitted with a choice between a second and third-rate soft top, but the car appeared very much as it had in its original, unsullied form. The dashboard was changed slightly so that the light switch became easier to find, the seats reclined (when opted for) after pulling a lever - instead of having to take a spanner to a pair of nuts and bolts on the seat backs - and the car's electrics were improved. The gearboxes on offer were first class, the leather on the seats really was leather, emission equipment was not too intrusive, and all was well with the world of the MGB. Except the sales!

Adolescence

After the bumper year of 1966, when GT sales took-off, sales had fallen back gradually until 1967 and 1968 Roadster sales were at their lowest since launch. In 1969 the year of the launch of the first facelifted MGB, sales rose again quite dramatically and continued to surge forward in 1970. The 'new' MGB (for little but a few significant details were changed) had a typical adolescent's lack of respect for convention and, to the horror of those purists who became enraged to the very point of writing a letter to Motor Sport magazine, the traditional MG grille was dropped. In its place was a recessed black grille with a chrome surround and, in keeping with the new image, Rostyle (magstyle) wheels were fitted in place of the standard MG pattern disc wheels. Over-riders were finished with black rubber inserts, and the traditional leather seats were supplanted by those of a black vinyl covered variety, but recliners were now the standard offering, and most testers found the new seats more supportive than the old. Front wings were fitted with blue B.L. badges which were generally disliked and it was with some delight that an American customer reported that his badges had had the decency to drop off during shipment!

The difference in production figures between the post- October 1967 period, when real technical improvements were made to the car, and the post-October 1969 period, when changes were purely aesthetic is, perhaps an apt comment in itself upon priorities of the buying public at that time.

The unorthodox 'B was given useful detail improvements in September

1970 and again in October 1971 when a new facia with face-level air vents was fitted.

In October 1972, the appeal of the 'B reverted very much to an 'as-you-were' stance with the reappearance of the traditional radiator more in keeping with MG tradition than its predecessor's had been, but apart from a few internal trim changes, very little seemed different. Perhaps that is why sales were on a downward trend between 1972 and 1975.

The US magazine Popular Imported Cars reported in their 1973 road test on the new model that, while weight and price had risen, 'not everything had gone up. At 78.5, horsepower is down 12.5 compared to that developed by the original 'B.' The reasons for a lack of interest in developing the car around this time can be found not at Abingdon but elsewhere. A combined effort between Triumph and the Austin engineers at Longbridge produced, by the early Seventies, an experimental car known as 'The Bullet' which was to enter production in 1975 as the Triumph TR7. It is probable that by 1972, The Bullet was being considered as a direct MGB replacement so that an expensive MGB update would have been ruled out. In the event, that prediction was partly true because only one month after the introduction of the TR7, which was then available only in closed form, the MGB GT was withdrawn from the American market after only a handful of raised ride height 'rubber bumper' 'Bs had been shipped. There was a story in circulation at the time that the GT was withdrawn because it was too heavy! The story went that when a car was certified for exhaust emission, it had to be driven on a rolling road with a built in inertia setting to match the weight of the car. Therefore the heavier the car, the higher the setting

and the harder the car had to work. At this higher work load, it was said, the Roadster just passed muster while the GT failed to make it and there were thus no 'Federalised' single carb GTs in the USA. The one month gap between the demise of the American market GT and the introduction of the far from successful TR7 cannot be seen by many as pure coincidence, however!

Far more sensational than the potpourri TR7, and yet even more of a failure in numerical terms, was the MGB V8. In the mid-60s, the Rover company, later to become part of the same B.L. group as MG, acquired the rights to a Buick V8 engine which no longer had a place in Buick's range. It was first used by Rover in 1967 but was then bought from Rover in small numbers and put to sensationally good effect in a new, long-bonneted, 130mph Morgan called the Plus 8. Also in 1969, Rover offered the engine as an option in their new saloon, and in 1970 they introduced a kind of cross between the Jeep-style Land-Rover and a medium- sized up-market saloon called the Range Rover. This all-terrain vehicle was equipped with a detuned, but still powerful, version of the ex-Buick engine, giving 137bhp against the standard unit's output of 150 or so.

In 1970 an independent engineer by the name of Ken Costello began experimenting by fitting an MGB with the Rover V8 unit. Weighing in at around 320lb, the aluminium engine was barely heavier than the standard cast-iron MGB unit, and the car was a tremendous success, except that the exceptional power of the engine was such that gearboxes, rear axles and rear springs were often up to or beyond their tolerances. In 1971 and 1972 and with a 'Thank-you' to Costello for doing much of the development work that was

so quiet that nobody heard it, BL developed their own, 'official' MGB V8. It was introduced in 1973 in the GT form only, to take advantage of the GT's inherently stiffer body shell, and fitted with the lower powered Range Rover engine. In 1975, the V8 was caught up in the standard MGB revisions (which was hardly surprising since their body shells and much else besides were absolutely identical) and was then offered with rubber bumpers. In spite of its tremendous performance, and fuel consumption that was scarcely worse than that of the four-cylinder cars, the MGB V8 sold to only 2,591 customers in its four years of production, for reasons which one can only guess at. One of the principal reasons was undoubtedly that the V8 was never offered in the United States, partly because the hassle of developing the car for emission control regulations was never thought worthwhile.

However, the V8's cult-status in Britain, and almost mythical standing in the USA, are hardly borne out by road tests of the time. Autocar summed up the car by saying: 'Good performance with remarkable economy .... Smooth fuss-free engine with good torque but little engine noise. Perennial MGB faults. Too expensive.' And this latter point was probably the most convincing reason of all for the lack of sales. In 1974 it was possible to buy a 3-litre Ford Capri with almost equal performance, four genuine seats and greater comfort, plus a Mini for shopping, for the cost of a V8!

Both the MGB and V8 shared bulkhead and flitch panel pressings, these modifications being virtually the only structural ones necessary to enable the V8 engine to slot into the existing bodyshell. In September 1974 modifications of a more visually startling and

technically demanding nature were carried out to all cars, to the undoubted near-apoplexy of those who had been upset in 1969.

The Final Facelift

The huge, black urethane covered bumpers, fitted to all MGB's from the 1975 model-year on, made a dramatic difference to the car's appearance and camouflaged a couple of hundredweight of supporting steelwork and a raised ride height. Roy Brocklehurst, Syd Enever's successor, later claimed that these modifications involved the factory in, 'the equivalent of a major model facelift with a hell of a lot more engineering integrity behind it.' The modifications not only made a difference to the car's appearance but, lacking the anti-roll bar at the rear which was to be fitted from mid-1976 and yet with the newly increased body height and extra crash-resistant weight, the car rolled rather badly. Autocar's sober 1975 assessment of the car concluded that: 'The 1 1/2" increase in ride height... seriously increases roll and makes the car roll-oversteer too readily, and it is therefore somewhat twitchy even under public road conditions.' However, the English owner's compensation that: 'the car is usually faster in both acceleration and maximum speed', reaching a maximum in one direction of 109mph, was not shared by owners in the States. There, emission control regulations meant that the 'Bs breathing arrangements were dramatically altered, making it asthmatic and downright sluggish. A single 1 3/4" Zenith carb meant that the American cars would never use the last

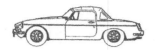

quarter of their 120mph speedometers and could be out-accelerated by MG Midgets and Triumph Spitfires. In California the situation was even worse with the compulsory fitting of a catalytic (cataclysmic?) converter adding a further twist to the garotte on performance.

In fairness to BL, these quite devastating changes to the character of the car were not entirely of their own choosing. From 1968-on Abingdon had found itself caught in a rising torrent of enforced, legislative changes to engine, interior and bodywork, largely emanating from the United States in which to survive involved working harder and harder at carrying out modifications which nominally increased the safety of their cars but which, in practice, often meant that car's primary safety attributes were diminished. A first class example of this was the increase in ride height to enable the MGB to comply with American laws regarding bumper and headlight height. The modified car certainly met the letter of the law, but could a car which took longer to brake because of increased weight, which took longer to overtake, at least partly for the same reason and which, worst of all, lost a significant amount of its cornering ability be considered inherently safer? There has even been controversy over whether raised bumpers actually caused greater injuries in the event of collision with pedestrians. Is a pedestrian safer being thrown up and onto the bonnet from impact with a low bumper line rather than being pushed down and under the vehicle from a high bumper? Whatever the strengths of the arguments here, it seems probable though ironic that such legislative pressure actually increased the production span of the MGB in the short term; 40 development

engineers working full-time from 1968-on just to keep the car legally on the road left insufficient effort to spare for the development of a replacement.

During the early months of the 'Rubber Bumper' reign, British Leyland decided to celebrate the 50th Anniversary of MG by issuing a limited number of MGB GT's. Seven hundred and fifty cars were built and were standard in virtually every respect except that they were fitted with every option then available such as overdrive, tinted glass and head restraints, but in addition gold-painted V8 wheels and tyres were fitted, and the bodywork was painted in British Racing Green with a gold stripe.

Just one more version of MGB was to evolve and this was little different from that which had gone before. In 1976, in addition to the fitting of the rear anti-roll bar already mentioned, the car was given a small range of alterations which took the car in the only logical direction which was by now open to it - that of increased comfort, away from the out and out sportiness which had been its goal for so long. Seats were covered in 'deckchair' striped fabric, V8-style instruments were employed incorporating an electric clock, carpets were to be found on the floor and lower geared steering complemented the use of a smaller steering wheel. To all intents and purposes, this was it; the final MGB which saw the name of MG through to the final month of production in October 1980.

However, during that month only, the once-proud Abingdon workforce set about producing a small last testament to all that MG had stood for. The last one thousand cars to roll from the production line were known as the 'Limited Edition' model and were painted in Pewter

(Roadster) or Gold (GT), and were offered with distinctive alloy wheels, or wires as alternatives. It was the end, in spite of efforts to save the MGB, and in spite of earlier, much earlier proposals for a replacement. Why? Clearly the general world recession and the trans-Atlantic credit cutting duette which Britain and America were playing together up to and during the time of the car's demise, had the effect of making it more expensive for people to buy cars generally, but the views of Roy Brocklehurst, one time Chief Designer at Abingdon, were given in early 1981 by which time Roy was a leading British Leyland executive.

He said that the ever faster moving treadmill of US safety and emission regulations was a positive disincentive to sell any car there, and that an ever more complex spider's web of product liability lawsuits were being brought about by litigation-happy individuals in which every defence, even the majority of successfully defended cases, produced another strand in the web of case histories in which the manufacturer was almost bound to find himself trapped at some time in the future.

As far as an MGB successor was concerned, BL had to invest where they could see the greater returns accruing. 'In a sense you could say that it was a choice between a successor for the MGB and putting Metro (BL's highly successful new Mini) back several years. Given that the costs for the development of any new volume car are astronomical - on top of which the engineering effort needed just to keep the car 'afloat' on the US market, which any sports car needs, means that the financial targets necessary to realise a satisfactory return on that astronomical investment are forever receding

in front of you.'

Finally, he made the most telling point of all, and one which the British people – British Leyland's shareholders – would no doubt agree with. 'We have to keep reminding ourselves that we are not in business to make cars but to make money.'

Making money was certainly not something that the MGB was doing at the end. The last two years of production showed a rapid drop in output and an even faster drop in sales – so much so that in the spring of 1981, six months after production had ended, there were enough cars still in American showrooms for a whole year's sales, while in England, John Hill of the MGB Centre found himself still able to order an MGB Roadster to the colour and specification he wanted in August of that same year.

However, if the demise of the MGB can be seen as inevitable, the disclosure and subsequent disposal of the factory at Abingdon, Oxfordshire, which was the site of the first MG production in its own right and where the last car to be produced was the last MGB, can only be described as rather hard faced on the part of the BL management. The story is best summarised by Roche Bentley, Secretary of the MG Owners' Club, writing in the June 1981 edition of the Club magazine, Enjoying MG. Under the heading of 'Final Death of Abingdon', Roche wrote: 'A few weeks ago BL held an auction of memorabilia and office effects at the MG factory at Abingdon. I personally did not attend and frankly I was disgusted at the whole affair. I consider that BL should have distributed the items worth having to the now redundant MG workforce in the form of a free lottery. Thus the men could have obtained souvenir

hand tools, plaques and things like fireman's helmets fairly and at no cost, and the important, valuable items such as the original MG flag and Cecil Kimber's desk could either have been given to Cecil Kimber's family or donated to BL Heritage Limited. The remaining items such as racking and old typewriters and chairs could have been sold to a local trader. But to have hundreds of people picking through the last remains of fifty years of Abingdon was, to my mind, morbid and sick. I will never forgive BL for the way they announced the closure of Abingdon and the redundancy of the 1100 workforce via the media on the day following the MG Abingdon celebrations and I think that their latest method of disposing of the last relics was heartless.

'By the way, not many people realise that the failed sale of the MG factory did not come about at a reported £30,000,000 and that a few months ago BL sold the complete factory and all the surrounding space for a bargain £5,000,000 to an insurance company. I'm sure that Aston Martin's consortium and MG Owner's Club could have raised that price from public subscription to maintain MG in a workable form.'

How sad and how unnecessary that a great name in motoring should end its days among such controversy with Roche Bentley's feelings being echoed by most enthusiasts who attended the final sale – and what infertile ground in which to plant seeds for the Metro MG.

The Aston Martin plan to save Abingdon had failed. A few minor concerns, and also the MG Owners' Club, tried marketing new MGBs in lowered, chrome bumper form, or with V8 engines, but none made an impact. It was left to

restorers to 'Save The MGB', and this was why this book was written.

Later Developments

Unbelievably, it was 1981 when I wrote the first edition of this book, and how things have changed! The bitterness, quite transparent in the last few paragraphs, has given way to a feeling of greater optimism. The Rover Group (currently owned by BMW) is fully behind the efforts of their subsidiary, Heritage, to supply new MGB parts and the new bodyshell off the original tooling, and the MGF has proved that there *is* a future for the British sports car!

Since writing the first edition, I discovered a little more about the amateurish management that sank both the MGB and its supposed successor the Triumph TR7, and almost brought down a company. This little story is like taking a slice out of something rotten and is best appreciated by understanding that no matter where the dissection had taken place, similar rot would have been found...

In September 1972, British Leyland decided that the new O-series engine (in reality a radical OHC evolution of the B-series unit) would have to be fitted to the MGB as a 'critical' matter in order to meet impending US emission restrictions. In October of that year, the company decided to scrap the MGB! In November, the car was reinstated with projected sales of 600 per week. In December (the same year, remember!) the Triumph TR7 launch was formally accepted, and projected MGB sales were downgraded to 450 cars per week. Fine!

In 1973, plans were set in motion to 'Federalise' O- series for the MGB. Sales were re-

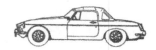

forecast to one thousand cars – per year!

In 1974, they decided to continue B-series in the MGB to 1975 and to fit the O-series first to the US Marina sedan. By December, US Marina was cancelled.

By January 1977, inertia had led to the 'Federalisation' of the MGB engine – which could be why it was so slow and inefficient; it was never properly planned for. It was decided to fit O-series to the MGB in 1980 and the development programme was restarted.

Of course, MGB never made it that far, and so BL decided to fit O-series to the TR7 in place of its own unique and unnecessary 2-litre unit. Needless to say, TR7 was scrapped in October 1981 without ever receiving the new engine.

It was small wonder that so many BL employees felt disillusioned! However, what was remarkable was the incredible loyalty they felt to 'their' cars, despite the atrophied abilities of many of their senior managers. From around 1980, BL took the first steps in a massive clear out: unwanted models, management and machinery. As was inevitable, some of the good went with the bad. But when Abingdon was dismantled, the MG spirit lived on. While Triumph presses and machine tools were being scrapped. MG's were being quietly, furtively salted away. For what? Nobody knew, but it was an extraordinary act of faith that was to have an extraordinary outcome.

In the late 1970s, British Leyland approved the formation of British Motor Heritage Limited and the Heritage Trust. The job of the latter was and is to assist in the preservation of British classic cars, and it was formed as a registered charity

operating from its headquarters at Studley Castle in Warwickshire. It is supported commercially by the Covenant of profits from British Motor Heritage Limited. Heritage Limited is a commercial operation selling everything from parts to specialist information, and is mainly concerned with cars descended from BMC and British Leyland.

In the mid-1980s, British Motor Heritage Limited, under the direction of its Managing Director, Peter Mitchell, and his Assistant Managing Director, David Bishop, set about investigating whether it would be possible to re-manufacture the MGB bodyshell – a feat never before attempted by any motor manufacturer in the world, let alone by a small subsidiary with limited resources.

By searching back through the archives David was able to discover which panel pressing tools were required, then all he had to do was find them! This task alone entailed numerous visits to pressings plants, interviewing people who had been at the plants when the bodyshells were in production and then identifying correctly pieces of metal which had been out in the elements for between nine and fourteen years. I remember meeting David just after the launch of the new bodyshell and I don't think I have ever met anyone looking both more exhausted and more content! But then David had a good deal to be contented about.

Having found most of their tools and having discovered that they still worked, the project was given the go-ahead during the autumn of 1987. David brought together a team of ex-Abingdon, Pressed Steel and other employees who had been involved in the manufacture of the original cars and set up production in a

relatively small unit in Faringdon, not a million miles from Abingdon, in Oxfordshire. It was one thing to bring these various production lines pieces together and quite another to make them operate on the small scale envisaged. One of the problems was that, because of the build specifications that the body has to meet, BMH had to use some of the original factory spot-welders which are so large and heavy that they have to be suspended from an overhead gantry. Using just one of these machines would have devoured so much electricity that it would have melted the local electricity sub-station! A 400bhp twin turbo-charged diesel generator was installed, along with the plant's own industrial electrical distribution system, and another seemingly insoluble problem was overcome.

The introduction of the new bodyshell, and the GT shell that followed it, has made it possible to get nearer to producing a brand new MGB than at any time since the car was discontinued. However, the existence of the plant within the Rover Group has led to all sorts of further speculation, including the cover story in Car magazine in August 1991 where it was predicted that the MGB would be relaunched by Rover wearing slightly modified bodywork and fitted with the much loved and respected V8 engine. Slated for 1992, the new MGB will undoubtedly be built and that will be thanks, first and foremost, to the almost incredible energy and persistence of David Bishop and his team, and also the Heritage-approved suppliers who have invested so much of their own money in having original MGB parts put back into production where the Heritage tools have no longer been available or

where they have simply run out of capacity.

Thanks to the enormous enthusiasm felt for the MGB from drivers, owners and restorers right through to the MG specialists, and Heritage themselves, the ending of this Second Edition's first chapter is very different from the First Edition. Where, then, I wrote about 'Saving the MGB', it's now possible to proclaim, with joy and enthusiasm, 'The MGB Lives!' ...

H1. A sad sight - the Abingdon factory coming under the demolisher's hammer. (Picture: Courtesy Peter Franklin) ➡

H2. The phoenix! The author takes the Heritage-bodied Project MGB on its first test drive.

Chapter 2
Buying

Buying a 'B is easy! Buying the right one, however, takes a little patience, a little knowledge and - often - no little time. Even a car such as the MGB, with its justified reputation for reliability and longevity, is prone to faults and weaknesses due to the ravages of corrosion, wear and, all too often, downright neglect. On the other hand, the car's ever-growing popularity means that unscrupulous sellers are presented with an ideal opportunity to gloss over weaknesses in a problem car and pass it off as a good example of the marque. This chapter aims to provide the prospective purchaser with a sequence of checks on a car under consideration, which should be virtually foolproof in ensuring that a car is as good - or only as bad - as it seems. It should also provide the owner, who is in the process of deciding whether to rebuild his or her car, with the information necessary to make an estimate of the total amount of work - and thus expenditure - required.

Take Your Pick

First of all, the prospective owner has to make a decision on which model of 'B to buy. Although the 1962 version of the car was derided as being 'soft' by MGA enthusiasts (it often still is, in fact!), the owner of a 1980 car would instantly know that he had stepped back in time if driving positions were swapped with the owner of an earlier model. Some idea of the changes that took place is given in Chapter 1, while the appendices detail the technical and numerical background to the developments. On the whole, changes were made by stealth rather than obviously and dramatically.

It is possible, however, to place the MGB's evolution into era, although the manufacturer's own model changes do not necessarily reflect these. The first covers the early, 3 main bearing-engined cars with simple, uncluttered appearance and few refinements - even the heater was an optional extra! Because of the difficulty in obtaining spares for these cars (and exchange engines have not been available for many years) they really come more into the 'Collectors' category than any other MGB. In practice most remaining early cars have been 'modernised' with 'wrong' engines, axles and gearboxes, doors and door fittings and even seats, so an original one in good condition would be well worth having.

5-main-bearing engines, available from October 1964, are much longer-lived units, the earlier 3-bearing units being subject to crank 'whipping' and relatively rapid wear, although carefully cared for examples are capable of quite prodigious mileages without the slightest bother. Although the improved 'tube-type' rear axle was fitted to Tourers from April 1967, the next true era begins in October 1967 (2nd Series MGB) when a greatly improved and all-synchro box was fitted with an under rated and little bought automatic option. Tidy looking reversing lights were standard, battery charging was improved by the substitution of an alternator for the old-fashioned dynamo and a sensible array of safety and emission control modifications were made, although to US cars only. A British or American 'B of this era, which carried through to October 1969, especially if fitted with reclining seats, wire wheels and overdrive, is

probably the most desirable 'pure' MGB of all. Unspoiled by so called 'styling' or corporate badges, unfettered by well-meaning but often counter-productive safety regulations, still with leather upholstery; this MGB above all is clean, efficient and real fun to own.

From October 1969, 3rd Series MGBs (or 5th Series if you illogically include MGAs in the serial run, as did the manufacturers) were presented with exhaust emission controls and a 'sharper', more modern appearance. British models 'go' just as well as their predecessors. It simply becomes a matter of taste as to whether a black grille is preferred to chrome, and vinyl seats to leather. Although there were trim changes made, this era carries on to late 1974, when purists were knocked reeling by Abingdon's answer to the problems posed by US safety legislators.

'Black-bumper' MGBs were not only given a face-lift, but a body lift, too, causing handling to deteriorate badly. These cars were much heavier than their predecessors, weighing in at over the ton! Yet more emission control 'refinements' caused a further cutback to power to American cars which then gave a miserable 65bhp (DIN). However, many US enthusiasts have since 'de-Federalised' their cars. 'Black-bumper' 'Bs until August 1976 must, surely, be the MGBs to avoid, because after that date anti-roll bars were added which put back most of the lost cornering ability, and also detail modifications were made taking the car to its by then logical and well-equipped conclusion.

Final note must be made of the Abingdon 'Specials'. In 1975 750 MGB GTs were built to commemorate BL's own version of MG's 50th Anniversary. Unfortunate, in that they included the worst mechanical features of the cars of the time,

these MGB GT Jubilee model cars were different in little but trim from their standard counterparts except for the V8-style road wheels and 175-section tyres. The Limited Edition MGBs were rather different in that they were, genuinely, the last 1,000 MGBs ever made. The last Tourer and the last GT were kept by BL themselves while the remaining 579 GTs and 419 Tourers were sold - and sold within a very short time of their announcement. These cars had trim changes such as body stripes, and were distinctively painted and badged. Without a shred of doubt these are going to remain the most valuable and prestigious of MGBs, a sad but proud testament to a great workforce and a great car.

Where to Look

Half-a-million MGBs were built. In rough terms, one third stayed at home, one third went to grace California, while the rest of the world (but mostly the rest of the USA) had to share the remainder of the cars.

Consequently, British and Californian owners will find a reasonable number of MGBs advertised in the local press while everyone else has to look that bit harder. The two most important clubs for 'B owners (AMGBA in the States and MGOC in the UK) carry a 'Cars for Sale' column in their magazines. The British club's magazine, is published monthly and always offers a very wide range of MGBs.

In the more highly MGB populated areas, the everyday car auctions sometimes have MGBs on offer but time and the opportunity to check the car over can be severely limited. Very low mileage cars, or those with an interesting history, are

sometimes offered by the 'quality' auction houses such as Sothebys - but be prepared to pay! Another approach, and one which has been used with great success by the author, is to find the most popular medium for selling MGBs in your area, be it the local press or the club magazine, or even the publications of a neighbouring area, and place a series of advertisements stating 'MGB Wanted' with some details of what is required. Unfortunately some newspapers - those in Paris being an example - refuse to accept such advertisements, but the technique is quite common and highly successful in the UK.

John Twist of University Motors, Michigan, USA writes: 'In the US the best way of finding an MG is through the local newspaper want ads. Other means include: bulletin boards in foreign car shops and parts outlets; various club publications; several of the major collector magazines such as: Hemmings Motor News; Cars and Parts; Road & Track - these are monthly publications offering For Sale and Wanted columns. In addition there are two MG magazines now in print - MG Magazine, which is obtainable from 2 Spencer Place, Scarsdale, NY 10583 and Abingdon Classics, from P O Box 233, Mulberry, Florida 33860.

'When a potential purchaser of an MG enters University Motors and wants an impression of the MG he wants to purchase, we first look in the files (we have a cross-reference for chassis numbers) and can give an idea of any previous work performed on it. Other shops may be able to carry out this paperwork inspection, too. It's important that if the seller says that the MGB has recently been "tuned" or "rebuilt" (or some such other term meaning twenty different things) that the buyer call the shop where the

work was performed and ask about the extent of the work completed and their impression of the car.'

'B-ing Sure

Checking over a prospective purchase not only can be but should be very time consuming if the 'right' car is to be bought rather than a glossed-over heap of trouble. What follows is an elimination sequence in three separate parts, each one taking longer and being more thorough than the last, this approach having the virtue of saving the purchaser both time and embarrassment. It is always easier to withdraw at an early stage than after an hour spent checking the car over, with the aid of the owner's comments and mugs of coffee! Thus, Stage A aims to eliminate the obvious 'nails' without having to probe too deeply; Stage B takes matters somewhat further for cars that pass the first stage; while Stage C is the 'dirty hands' stage, the one you don't get into on a snowy February evening unless you are really serious.

Toolbox

Old, warm clothes (if the ground is cold). An old mat or a board if the ground is wet. A bright torch. A pair of ramps. A screwdriver or other probe. Copies of the following pages and a notepad. Pencil. A bottle, trolley or scissors jack. Axle stands.

Safety

Safety should be carefully considered and any necessary steps taken. In particular, when inspecting a car, don't forget safety. NEVER rely on the handbrake to hold a car that is on a slope or up on ramps. Ensure that the wheels are chocked when using jacks or ramps. Use axle stands if you have to inspect the underside of the car. Do not use a naked flame or smoke when inspecting the underside of a car battery box or engine bag. Never go beneath a car supported by a jack.

Using the Checklist

The checklist is designed to show step-by-step instructions for virtually all the checks to be made on a car offered for sale. After each check, the fault indicated is shown in brackets. e.g., the instruction:

'Look along wings, door bottoms, wheel arches and sills from front to rear of car' is followed by the fault, shown in brackets, as '(Ripples indicate filler presence/crash damage. £££)'. The pound Sterling signs require some explanation. They are intended to give a guide to the cost of rectifying the fault if it exists. £ indicates that the cost is likely to be less than the cost of a new tyre, £££ stands for the cost of a new set of tyres, or more, while ££ means that the cost is likely to be between the two. The cost guide relates to the cost of the component(s) only, other than in the case of bodywork - allow more if you have the work done for you.

When examining a car you are advised to take this book (or copies of the relevant buying checklists) and a notebook with you. As each item is checked, a record can be kept in the notebook. You may wish to record a running cost total for necessary repairs as faults are discovered - this could be a useful bargaining tool at the end of your examination.

It is strongly recommended that the repair and restoration sections of this book and also Haynes MGB Workshop Manual are examined so that the checker is fully familiar with every component being examined.

Stage A - First Impressions

1.　Is the car 'square' to the ground, and are bonnet, bumper, grille, door to hinge-pillar gaps even and level? (Closed-up door gaps and rippled front wings usually indicate poorly repaired crash damage. £££+)
2.　Look along wings, door bottoms, wheel arches and sills from the front and rear of the car. (Ripples indicate filler presence. £££)
3.　Check quality of chromework, especially bumpers. (Dents, dings and rust. ££)
4.　Turn on all lights, indicators and reversing lights and check that they work. (Sidelights/marker lights rust in their sockets. ££. Rear licence/number plate lamps earthing/grounding problems plus other specific component problems)
5.　'Bounce' each corner of the car. (Worn shock absorbers allow the corners to feel springy and bounce up and down. Each damper - £)
6.　Check visually for rust - gain an overall impression at this stage. (From cosmetic, to dire! £ to £££+ - see following sections)
7.　Check for damage in rubber bumpers if fitted. (Rips and other damage. ££)
8.　Examine general condition of interior at-a-glance. (Rips, dirt, parts missing. ££ or £££)
9.　If car advertised as 'unrestored', check rear

wing/panel seam, which will be visible in unrestored cars. (Genuine cars may be worth much more. £££)

10. Check fit of curved part of rear chrome bumpers. (Accident damage. Possibly £££)

11. Check hood for: fit around windows, rips and clarity of screen. (Hood replacement. £££)

12. Quality of paintwork. Does it shine when dry? Are there scratches beneath the shine? Is it chipped? (Neglect and poor-quality, cover-job respray. £££)

13. Do the seller and his/her surroundings look like those of an enthusiast? (Maintenance. £££)

Stage B - Clean Hands!

If a car doesn't match up to requirements after Stage A, don't be tempted - reject it! There are always more cars to be seen. Stage B decreases the risk of making a mistake without even getting your hands too dirty!

Check hard for body corrosion in all the places shown below. Use a magnet to ensure that no filler is present - magnets will only 'stick' to steel. Work carefully and methodically.

Bodywork - Checklist

1. Front apron, beneath grille. (Accident damage, corrosion, cheap repair. ££)

2. Front wing Headlamp area. (Corrosion. Filler. £££ if severe)

3. Lower front wing - continuation of sill line. (Corrosion. Filler. Damage. £££, if severe because hidden corrosion indicated)

4. Vertical line a few inches back from front wheel arch.

(Corrosion. Filler. £££)

5. Sills. (Corrosion. Filler. Damage. £££ to replace)

6. Door bottoms. (Corrosion. Filler. ££ or £££)

7. Door skins below window/ 1/4 light vertical dividing strip. (Splits. Filler gives only a temporary repair. ££)

8. Measure door fit along rear, vertical edges. (Open at bottom, closed at top means sagging bodywork - virtually terminal. £££+)

9. Rear wheel arch. (Corrosion. Filler. £££)

10. Open door. Lift up and down and note 'looseness'. (Hinge wear. £ Corroded door. £££)

11. Check the area along the length of the chrome strip. (Corrosion around trim clips. Unless severe, usually cosmetic. £)

12. Check the bottom corners of the windscreen glass - GTs only. (Corrosion. £££)

13. Check the base of the tail lights - GTs especially, but Roadsters prone too. (Corrosion. £££)

14. Look for cracking at the left side of the boot/trunk lid of later cars where the support connects to it. (Fatigued steel requires welding, possibly plating and boot/trunk lid respray. ££ or £££)

Interior

1. Examine seat and backrest. (Worn, thin or split covers. Leather £££, Cloth/ Plastic ££)

2. Tip seat forward. Check for damage. (Scuffing and tears. Leather £££, Cloth/ Plastic ££)

3. Check dash. (Cracks, tears or scratches. 'Wrong' instruments. £ to £££)

4. Check condition and cleanliness of hood/headlining. (From £ if dirty to £££ for replacement)

5. Examine steering

wheel/gearknob. (Correct parts fitted? £/££)

6. Test inertia reel seat belts, if fitted. (Should hold when tugged sharply. £)

7. Check door trim and door/window handles. (Wear and scuffing at bottoms, buckling of hardboard backing, broken handles. £ to ££

8. Ensure that the seats fold forward, that the 'paddle' allows different backrest positions (where fitted) and that they slide and lock. (Failure to slide easily, especially on the driver's side, is often an indication that the floor is weak. £££)

9. Wind both windows up and down - there should be no restriction. (Usually lack of lubrication. £)

Mechanical

Ask owner to start up engine. Let it idle - thorough warming-up takes quite a while on the road - this will help. (Does he/she let it idle on choke? Harmful practice!)

1. Pull and push the steering wheel and attempt to lift and lower at right angles to steering column. (Clonking indicates: wear in column bush, loose column connections. £. Wear in steering column U/J. £)

2. Pull bonnet release. Is it stiff? (Seized mechanism or cable. £)

3. Open bonnet. Check for non-standard air cleaners, rocker cover, etc. (if originality is important. £-££)

4. Is oil cooler in place? NB: Not standard on very early, UK cars. (Sometimes removed when leaking. Replacement £. Potential engine damage in hot climates £££)

5. Check engine/engine bay for general cleanliness and presence of oil. (Leaking gasket/lack of detail care. Probably £)

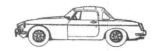

6. Listen to engine. Tappets should be audible. Bottom-end rumble, timing-chain tinkle - non-adjustable - should not. (Worn engine. Timing chain and sprockets ££. Worn crank. £££)

7. Is paint peeling around clutch/brake cylinders? (Carelessly split fluid strips paint. £, plus time)

STOP ENGINE AND LEAVE FOR A FEW MINUTES

8. Remove radiator cap SLOWLY with rag, and beware of spurting, scalding water. Inspect coolant level and its general cleanliness. (Orange indicates rust and a long time since it has been changed. NB: For 1977-80 models the coolant in the overflow tank is not a good indicator of the actual cooling system. Remove the cap at the top of the thermostat with a spark plug socket, bearing in mind safety. Check for oil on top of water. Remove dipstick. Check for water droplets in oil. (Head gasket problems. Probably £££)

9. Remove engine oil filler cap. Look for yellow or brown slimy sludge or foaming. (Severe bore/valve guide wear. £££) Look for white foaming or 'goo' inside cap. (Faulty ELC - Evaporative Loss Control system. £)

10. Car out of gear. Handbrake off. Push car backwards and forwards for a few yards. (Creaking wire wheels indicate need for rebuild or replacement. ££ each)

11. Inspect the fins of the radiator. (Newer MGBs have greater problems with oxidation than older cars. Exchange radiator. ££)

12. Examine engine mountings for signs of previous removal. The engine mounts should have fine thread bolts, nuts on the underside, lockwashers on all nuts. The top starter bolt - 1968 and newer - should carry the gearbox wiring loom and/or the engine-to-gearbox bolt just to the top of the starter should carry the loom on its rear side - under the bolt head. (Previous engine removal is not necessarily bad but it would be interesting to know why!)

13. Jack both front wheels off the ground together. Turn steering wheel from lock-to-lock. (Roughness indicates wear in steering rack. Replacement or overhaul. ££-£££)

Road Test

If you, the tester, are driving, ensure adequate insurance cover. Otherwise, simulate the following tests with the owner driving.

1. Start up. Is starter noisy on engagement? (Worn starter dog. £)

2. Is it difficult to engage first gear? NB: Expect a long, heavy clutch pedal. (Worn clutch and/or worn selector mechanism. £££)

Drive for three or four miles to become familiar with the car and to warm the engine.

3. Drive at 30mph. Brake gently to a halt. A: Does car 'pull' to one side? B: Do brakes rub or grind? (A: Worn pads or shoes. £. Seized callipers. ££. B: Worn pads or shoes. £, but more if discs or drums ruined.)

4. Drive at 30mph in 3rd gear. Apply then release accelerator four or five times. Listen for transmission 'clonk'. (Worn universal joint. £. Worn differential. £££. Worn halfshaft/driveshaft. ££. Worn wirewheel splines. ££)

5. Drive at 40mph. Lift off accelerator. Listen for differential whine. (Worn differential. £££, if severe or unbearably noisy.)

6. Accelerate hard in 2nd gear to 40mph then lift off. Listen for engine knocking. (Worn engine bearings. £££), also -

7. - does gearbox jump out of gear? (Worn internal selector mechanism. £)

8. Drive as in 6./7. above but lift off in third gear. Does gearbox jump out of gear? (Worn internal selector mechanism. £)

9. Drive at 50mph in 4th gear. Change into 3rd gear. Does gearbox 'crunch'? (Worn synchromesh. £. Faulty/worn clutch. ££)

10. Drive at 30mph in 3rd gear. Change into 2nd gear. Does gearbox 'crunch'? (Worn synchromesh. £. Faulty/worn clutch. ££)

11. Do front wheels flutter or shake at 40mph? (Wheels out of balance. £. Worn front suspension. ££)

12. When cornering, does the steering wheel attempt to return to the 'straight-ahead' position. (If not, probably indicates tight kingpins. Renewal. ££)

13. In second gear at about 30mph accelerate hard, then decelerate hard, don't brake. (If car veers to left or right, the rear axle is loose or the springs are faulty. New axle U- bolts. £. New rear springs. ££)

14. At low speed, brake and listen for front-end clonks. (Loose wire wheels. Retightening is free! But worn splines on wheels and hubs. £££)

15. When stationary, operate the brake pedal. Apply light pressure in repeated strokes. (If the pedal slowly works its way to the floor - even over a minute, the master cylinder is faulty. This problem is more common to dual circuit systems. ££)

16. Operate the red brake-warning light, or ensure that it illuminates when the key is turned to the 'Start' position (1975- 80), then push on the brake pedal as hard as possible. (If the light illuminates, the rear brakes probably leak. Replacement wheel cylinder. £. Sometimes only adjustment is required.)

17. Accelerate from about 1000rpm in top gear, full throttle. (Pinking/spark knock

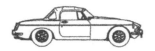

probably indicates maladjusted timing. Can cause piston damage over a long period. ££ or £££)

18. 1975 cars on. Accelerate to 4,000rpm then change up to second. ('Popping' through the exhaust indicates faulty emission controls - US cars - or over-rich carburettor setting.)

19. At highway speeds climb a slight hill with a very light throttle. (Hesitation, coughing, snapping or spitting indicates over-lean carburettor setting. Can cause valve damage over a long period. ££)

20. Does overdrive flick in and out promptly in 3rd and 4th? NB: Early vacuum-operated overdrive switches only switch 'out' with throttle depressed. 1977-80 cars only have overdrive on 4th. (Slowness indicates worn solenoid switch. £. Possibly more severe overdrive wear. £££ could be low oil level)

21. Stop car. Apply parking brake firmly. Engage 2nd gear. Gently let out clutch - but depress again as soon as car shows any signs of distress. (If car pulls away, worn rear brakes. £. Oil in brake drum. ££. If car remains stationary but engine continues to run - worn clutch. ££+)

22. Switch off engine. Does it 'run on' or 'diesel'. NB: Quite common with all 'Bs before 1973. (Revs less than 800 on tickover. Probably carbon build-up in cylinder head. £ + time. Revs more than 800 on tickover, probably idling adjustment requires slowing down. 1973-on models with anti run-on valve - the ELC system is faulty. £-££) You may have to retard the ignition. See Haynes Manual or consult your Specialist

Boot/Trunk Inspection

1. Is the spare tyre inflated and with a good tread? (Replacement. £ - obviously!)

2. Does the jack work? (Replacement. £, or lubrication)

3. Is there a hammer for wire wheels - all wire wheeled cars - and a spanner - 1968-80 wire wheeled cars? (Replacement. £)

4. Is there a key for the boot/trunk lock? (Replacement key if right number can be found, or even replacement lock. £)

5. Does the boot/trunk light illuminate - if fitted? (Switch, bulb or wiring fault. £)

Stage C - Dirty Hands

This is the level at which the car - by now being seriously considered - is given the sort of checks that make as sure as possible that there are no serious hidden faults which could still make the purchaser change his or her mind. It might also throw up a few minor faults to use as bargaining points with the seller!

While Stage A took only a minute or so, and Stage B took quite a while longer, Stage C involves a lot more time, inconvenience and effort. But, if you want to be sure, it's the most vital stage of all.

Safety

Ensure that wheels are chocked when using jacks or ramps. NEVER go under a car supported only by a jack.

1. Jack rear wheels off ground, one at a time. Grasp wheel, twist sharply back and forth - listen for 'clonks'. If wire wheels fitted, do wheels move relative to brake drum? (Worn splines on hubs/wheels. £££)

2. Jack up front wheel at wishbone, partially compressing front suspension. Spin wheel and listen for roughness in wheel bearings. (Imminent wheel bearing failure. £)

3. Grip roadwheel top and bottom - ensure car weight cannot fall onto hand - and rock in the vertical plane. (Play indicates: wear in wire wheel splines. £££. Wear in wheel bearing. £. Wear in kingpin. ££)

4. From beneath car, examine rear of rear brake drums and insides of wheels for oil contamination. (Failed oil seal/blocked differential breather. £)

5. Lift carpets, check floor for rusting, particularly adjacent to inner sills in footwell. (Significant corrosion. Possibly £££)

6. Feel inside front inner wings for corrosion at tops of wedge- shaped box sections. (Severe corrosion. £££)

7. Remove mud, if present, from around rear spring hangers. Probe for presence of corrosion with screwdriver. (Significant corrosion. £££)

8. Examine and probe around inside of rear wheel arches and area inside boot/trunk in line with rear wheels. (Corrosion. £££)

9. Sniff around fuel tank from beneath and look for evidence of fuel staining, especially from front of tank and from around the sender unit. (Tanks corrode from above, from outside. Replacement ££)

10. Probe around jacking point, crossmember and under-sill area with a screwdriver. Check visually for distorted jack tube and support. (Severe corrosion. £££)

11. Examine insides of front apron, particularly at ends. (Corrosion. ££)

12. Examine insides of rear apron, particularly at ends. (Corrosion. ££)

13. Inspect the engine for oil leaks. NB: There will almost invariably be some! Check: Front seal on timing chain cover. (Not common but usually caused by blocked

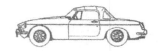

Evaporative Loss Control system.)
Check: Rear seal, leaked oil usually comes through gearbox bellhousing drain hole. (Sometimes gearbox oil leak to blame. £. Otherwise rear oil seal on 5-main-bearing engines. £. Or, badly worn oil scroll on 3-main-bearing engines caused by severe crank whip. Scrap engine or heavy rebuild costs from professional engineers. £££)
Check: Side covers - tappet inspection plates - on left side of engine. (Very common on single-carburettor, US models. The heat is so high at the catalytic converter that the gaskets fail. £)
Check: Around the oil filter. (Spin-on canisters can come loose, as can bolt-mounted type. Badly fitted rubber seal on bolt-mounted type. £)
14. Examine the front of the rear axle for oil leakage and oil thrown onto the body. (Slight leakage not uncommon. Heavy leakage suggests a faulty seal, clogged vent or overfilled differential casing. £)
15. Grasp each shock absorber linkage in turn and shake them. (Worn bushes, linkages or shock-absorbers. £ each).
16. Look for evidence of grease on grease points. (Lack of servicing. £ to £££)
17. Condition of exhaust system and exhaust mountings. (Replacement exhaust ££)
18. Check brake discs for deep scoring. (Replacement discs. ££)
19. Check, visually, condition of battery/batteries - from above - and battery mountings - from below. (New battery/batteries. £-££. Corroded mountings. ££)
20. From under the bonnet, grasp the throttle shaft - twin carb models only - and attempt to shake it at each end. (Excessive movement results in an uncontrollable idle, and vacuum leaks. Exchange or replacement carbs. £ to £££)
21. Determine the freeplay of the clutch pedal. (If more than 1 inch or so, the clevis pin in the pedal/master cylinder pushrod is worn. £) NB: Springs should be attached to both pedals. Move the pedals from side to side. (More than slight movement indicates worn pedal bushes, or the bolt holding the pedals is loose. £)
22. Check the steering wheel for excessive freeplay by attempting to rotate it lightly with the car stationary and the front wheels on the ground. More than 1" at the circumference of the wheel is excessive. If freeplay exists, grasp the steering universal joint (under the rear air cleaner on left-hand drive cars) and feel for looseness in joint, while someone else twists steering wheel back and forth. (Replacement universal joint. £. But often caused by worn front shock absorbers, in which case. ££. 1968-80 cars - US - but later cars in UK with collapsible steering systems - fault lies in play between the two portions of the inner column. ££)

Notes for American Purchasers

by John Twist of University Motors, Michigan

Ensure that there is a title plate on the MGB (front right inner fender 1963-1969) and on the top of the dash (can be seen from outside the car) and on the door sill from 1970-80. These numbers MUST correspond with the numbers given on the title - and all but 1980 models begin with GHN or GHD. (We've seen some MG 1100 titles passed along with MGBs!) Don't pay for and receive the MGB without getting the title. The title is your protection that the car is legally yours!

There is little protection for you if the car has been stolen - you can always call the local police and have a title check made to see if the car is 'hot'.

Most states require, prior to licensing, that a 'safety check' be made by the local police if the car comes from out of state. The common items checked are: lights, brakes, Vehicle Identification Number, wipers, washers - and in some states the exhaust and other items have to be inspected. It's foolish to show up for the inspection knowing that a certain item is not working - call first to find out what is required.

The banks, savings and loans and credit unions will lend money on MGBs, but only to the amount shown in the 'Blue Book' or National Automotive Dealers Association (NADA) monthly report. These listings only go back ten years or less and the loan values are often well below that which the purchaser may believe is proper for the car - but that is the way it is! There are only a few exceptions - but you can attempt to 'beat the system' by having several appraisals of the car done by dealers of reputable shops, affording the bank a better idea of what they are loaning the money for.

Whatever faults are found, remember that all faults are repairable. If you want the car, use the cost of repair for leverage when agreeing the final price with the owner. Any MGB will require some repair and maintenance immediately after purchase - plan on at least the amount indicated by the £££ symbols used here for a complete lube and tune. (Author's note - probably only ££ in the UK.)

Whatever the budget is, don't spend it all on the car, leaving yourself shy of the money needed to do the repairs. Remember MG's motto - Safety Fast! - and make sure you can afford to run your MGB safely as well as fast!

Buying an MGC
by Pearl McGlen

To begin with, a glance down the classified columns of most motoring magazines and, indeed, Club publications such as the excellent Enjoying MG of the MG Owners' Club, will show a very wide divergence in the prices being asked for MGCs. This difference can, in some cases, amount to an astonishing amount for what appear - on the surface at any rate - to be almost identical cars in what sound like identical condition! Be very careful - all too often a car will be advertised as having undergone a total 'rebuild' when it would probable be truer to say 'new door skins, an oil change and a quick blow over in cellulose'! Take my word for it, a totally rebuilt MGC, if the work was done properly, has cost a great deal of money, and there is no way that you are going to buy such a car for the ridiculously low prices sometimes temptingly quoted in advertisements.

To begin with, the MGC is a horse of quite a different colour from the well-known and recognised MGB. Outwardly they may appear very similar, inwardly there are few similarities at all, with the exception of the actual interior trim and the body from the bulkhead back.

The MGC has, however, become something of a legend through its extreme longevity. There are still C's about, at the time of writing, with well over 100,000 miles on their clocks (some can even boast twice that figure!) and in the main these cars are still solid, reliable and suffer from few of the ills that would beset a less robust car of similar vintage and mileage.

MGCs suffer very few problems in the engine and gearbox department. They are not generally prone to overheating, excessive oil consumption, gearbox or axle problems. The engines, when properly maintained, are good for at least 100,000 miles, and many go a lot further without recourse to any rebuilding. The gearboxes, too, are excellent and, probably because the C is something of a 'lazy' car, are not beset by the sort of problems you would expect from a V8, for instance, which develops a great deal more torque and thus puts much more strain on the gearbox. Like the gearbox, the back axle rarely gives much trouble in MGCs.

Probably the C's most problematic mechanical area lies in the front suspension, i.e. the kingpin/torsion bar system which is quite unique and is not shared with any other MG. However, make no mistake about it, there is nothing weak about this suspension set up. In fact, it is very strong indeed, and the problems which do arise only occur because of lack of maintenance. If the kingpins are not regularly greased they wear, and the result is, at best, extreme wheel wobble at speed and, at worst, dangerous steering and front wheel tracking completely out of alignment which, if not already failed by the MOT (in Britain), could cause a serious accident. Brand new kingpins are no longer available for the MGC but it is possible to have your own reconditioned, provided, of course, that they have not been allowed to get to the stage where they have actually seized up. Mind you, in Britain, no MOT testing station should ever allow a car to get to this point as it is not something which occurs overnight.

When you go to view an MGC bear in mind that a good, clean, original car is far preferable to one which has been 'messed about'. By this I mean a car which has had lots of undesirable non-standard equipment put on it. Beware of the C which has had fibreglass flared wings, and non-standard large wheels and tyres, fitted. Often the engine has also been 'souped up', not always by experts, and the resultant car can be worth a great deal less than a nice original example, even if the latter does not look so potent!

At the same time, you have to bear in mind that there were a handful of MGCs which were expertly tuned and modified, some from new, such as University Motors' Specials and Downton tuned cars. These particular MGCs, provided that they are really genuine, are very desirable and collectable indeed, but BEWARE! Far too many people have tried to jump on the bandwagon of success enjoyed by Downton and University Motors cars, and there are a lot of 'hybrids' around with rather dubious ancestry!

Chassis numbers can play an important part in assessing whether a claimed UM Special is genuine or not as it is fairly safe to say that there were no UM Specials prior to 1970, and it would be a very rare car indeed which was a genuine UM and had a chassis number any lower than 7,000+. Genuine UM cars usually had their suspension modified, normally to Koni shock absorbers all round, which was sufficient to improve the cars' handling quite considerably, but some 'improvements' carried out were merely cosmetic.

Apart from those UM Specials which were Downton modified (producing more torque and greater horsepower whilst still retaining excellent flexibility and economy) Downton also converted several privately-owned MGCs, and these were done over a period of years from early 1968 to as late as early 1975. The majority of these cars have invoices from Downton Engineering to back

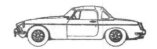

up the work which was carried out on them, but occasionally the paperwork can go astray and then it is important (if the car you are viewing is claimed to be a Downton) to check that the cylinder head is suitably engraved with the Downton head number and various tuning information. The owner should be able to point this out to you. If not, be suspicious that the car is not genuine. It is quite possible that the car in question has been tuned, but by someone else, and - surprising though it may sound - very few, if any, other tuning firms have had the same astonishing success with the MGC as did Downton Engineering under the auspices of Dan Richmond. Most tuners can make the MGC go a great deal faster, as it is a very rewarding subject to tune, but almost without exception they produce a less flexible, rougher running machine with an unquenchable thirst and an owner probably wishing he or she had left well alone!

Moss point out that some UM Specials had rear seat conversions and batteries positioned in the well behind the rear arches.

Always try to get the most desirable optional extras on your car if you can, i.e. wire wheels, overdrive, sunroof - if it is a GT - and, if you are also lucky enough to have the choice, go for one of the later models which can be distinguished readily enough by the all-black, later type reclining seats which took over from the non-reclining, coloured piping variety. These cars are usually denoted by a G or H registration in Britain. The later cars also had their axle ratios raised numerically which decreased them in practice, thus giving a car which is more rapid through the gears although not quite so long-legged and economical as the earlier, high ratio-axled cars.

One of the most vital parts of the MGC body is the bonnet. No other Abingdon MG has such a distinctive bonnet with its large power bulge and smaller, distinctive 'tear drop' necessary to give clearance to the carburettors. By far the majority of these bonnets were produced in aluminium, which is good news, but there were a few made in pressed steel and today, although it is impossible to buy a brand new alloy bonnet, it is possible to buy a new steel one. These are extremely expensive, however, and it is therefore desirable to try to purchase a car which has a good bonnet, free from dents and damage. Alloy bonnets are notoriously 'soft', and dent easily, but on the credit side they do not rust, although some corrosion can occur along the line of the stainless steel strip which decorates the front of the large power bulge, caused by an electrolytic reaction between the steel nuts which hold the strip in place and the alloy itself. It is well worth removing this strip and replacing and well-greasing the tiny nuts and bolts in order to prevent this corrosion from progressing too far.

Another important point is that, to preserve the highest possible value, a car should be kept in its original paint livery. A list of the actual colours used for the MGC is available in the appendix of this book and the only deviations from the list should be on genuine University Motors Specials, many of which were resprayed in a different colour to suit either the whims of their new purchasers or University Motors themselves. Some of these were rather bizarre, bright orange and two tone yellow and blue being two examples, and no one could be blamed for wishing to revert to the cars original paint scheme if they purchased such a car! Fortunately, quite a few UMs were left in their original colours and simply had extras added to them.

A heated rear screen is a useful extra to have. This was fitted as standard equipment to the CGT and it is an added bonus in originality to have the genuine rear heated screen and not one of the later type as fitted to MGBs.

Although wire wheels are always more attractive, and possibly may add a few pounds to the price/value of a car, steel wheels can and do look very smart with their huge moon-like chrome discs, and they have the added bonus that they do not go out of balance as easily as wires, are much stronger and easier to keep clean and rustfree.

Overdrive is obviously a very desirable extra in these days of high fuel costs and, on a lengthy journey, can be of great benefit. However, if your car is not going to be used regularly for long distances, it will still be found to be quite economical without the benefit of overdrive, and one added bonus will be that it is one thing less to go wrong!

It must also be mentioned that the big, straight six engines fitted to the MGC were also fitted in one other car only, and that was the Austin 3-Litre limousine. However, there were essential differences, such as a slightly lower compression ratio, different thermostat housing, milder cam, and the oil dipstick situated on the opposite side of the engine. The engine numbers are also slightly different and, therefore, it is not too difficult to spot an MGC which has an Austin 3-Litre engine fitted. Having said this, much of the Austin engine can be used as a straight replacement for that of the MGC. In practice, though, the 'C engine is so long-lived and disinclined to give trouble that there is little demand for replacements, whether from the Austin 3-Litre or elsewhere!

Oil pressure when hot should be approximately 15lbs on tickover and at least 50lbs running, while a good engine will often read 70lbs plus when running. In any case, this engine is very easy indeed to work on, being easily accessible and very straightforward. Probably its greatest disadvantage is its sheer weight, which calls for special equipment should you need to remove it.

Condition of the interior of the MGC you wish to buy is also important unless you want to dig deep into your pocket for the cost of re-upholstering.

In my view, the MGC is one of the greatest 'characters' ever built at Abingdon. It's a gentle giant which is getting rarer as each year passes - if you want to travel by 'C, check the bodywork as for the MGB and the specific mechanical areas I mention here. Most mechanical repairs rate £££ in this buying guide's parlance.

University Motors Specials: How to Spot One

A total of 141 cars were bought in by the London, England, firm of University Motors at the end of production, and all of these should have chassis numbers from 7000 onwards. Of this total only 23 cars were Roadsters.

Although it is impossible to be accurate, as no records exist, it is believed from reliable sources that only an approximate total of 21 MGCs were actually modified by University Motors and made into official 'Specials'. The remaining cars were simply sold as standard 'Cs. Of the 21 genuine Specials, only a handful had the very special 'Slatted' black grille which replaced the standard item. This was often linked with a matt black bonnet bulge, vinyl roof and sun roof. Badges varied; some were supplied with a distinctive and attractive heavy, round, chromed badge in the UM colours of red/white and blue, whilst others had a smaller, rectangular badge attached to the wings. One or two had their headlights replaced with square versions (and subsequent reshaping of the wings), some were resprayed in different colour schemes (one or two were two-tone) and the majority of the actual 'Specials' also had the powerful Downton- tuned engines, the most popular seeming to have been the Stage 2 (No 43 conversion) which retained the twin carbs, but one or two even rarer models had the very powerful Stage 3 (No 45 conversion) fitted with the triple carb set up.

All UMs appear to have had Koni shock absorbers fitted all round, all had Motolita steering wheels and a certain amount of chroming in the engine bay. Some have flared wheel arches and larger (wider) wheels and tyres, but it is hard to establish whether these were fitted by UM or at a later date. Many had special alloy wheels fitted, especially those with steel wheels, and Cosmic wheels were apparently popular, although there are again one of two very rare cars with the magnificent J.A. Pearce Magnesium knock-off wheels fitted.

All genuine UMs with Downton conversions would obviously carry identifying cylinder head numbers.

Replacement parts for Downton tuned cars are still readily available from firms such as Maniflow (the staff are ex- Downton), Peter Wood at Westwood Portway Group, and the MGB Centre at Redditch, but they are expensive.

Buying an MGB GT V8
by Peter Laidler

When I go to buy, for myself or another, I take a long hard look at the seller. Whether you agree or not, I believe that if the seller and his garage look like a tip, then there is every chance that the car is going to be one as well. Additionally, let us make no bones about it, the MGB GT V8 is an expensive car to maintain even if you do do it all yourself, and even more so if it is maintained by a garage. So, if the seller looks as though he can't even afford a Mini, then it's certain that he can't afford to run the V8, and it will have been poorly maintained and neglected.

The next thing is to ask yourself: 'What do I think of it at first glance?' (i.e. first impression). Looking further, do not be fooled by the car that has about 20,000 miles on the clock and looks like a real old dog. Accept the fact that the youngest V8's were built in 1977, although the great majority are older than that, and anything with less than 50,000 miles on the clock is a rare bird and should be treated with suspicion. There are such cars, but in the main they are now quite well known within the regular V8 club circles.

Now, let's have the figures. There were only 2,591 genuine MG-built production V8s, all were GTs and have chassis numbers on a plate near the oil filter starting at GD2D1 numbers 101 to 1,956 for a chrome bumper car and from 2,101 to 2,903 for the rubber bumper car, but excluding numbers 2,633 to 2,699 inclusive. There are the Costello versions and, more recently, the growing number of non-standard conversions to roadsters and GTs. Have an engineer check before you buy one of these, for quality of workmanship and ensure that

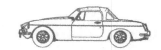

the 1800cc car's diff has been uprated to one with an MGC/V8 ratio, otherwise the car will be virtually undriveable.

The Bodywork

This aspect is well documented elsewhere. What applies to the 'B also applies to the V8 as, apart from minor bulkhead and nose alterations, they are virtually identical to the 'B.

The Interior

The V8 only came out with 4 colours of interior trim, except for the very last two which had black and silver striped trim. These colours were black, navy blue, 'ochre' (a bright yellow colour) and 'autumn leaf' (a mid-brown colour). New replacements are available from the leading Specialists such as Moss. The seat covers can be carefully removed from the frame and washed in warm soapy water, as can any dirty trim pads.

The Engine

The V8 engine is, in the main, a clean engine so beware of one that is covered in oil. While the engine is running slowly, listen for any tapping noises coming from the rocker covers or from within the centre of the engine, deep within the inlet manifold. Any tapping or rattling is sure to be the hydraulic cam followers. There are 16 of these and they last about 50,000 miles, in my experience, along

with the rocker shafts. These should really be replaced in sets. It is not difficult to do but the cost of parts is more than £££ in the book's price-check symbols.

The water pump is also subject to failure and this can be felt by rocking the nose. It sounds like a dull rumble when it is worn. Take the car for a drive and, when it is thoroughly warmed up, check the oil pressure. It is rare for a V8's oil pressure to climb over 40lbs per square inch, and when idling and warm it sometimes only just flickers around the 10lb mark. What is important, though, is that the pressure should be constant. If, during a good hard run, the pressure stays at, say, 30lbs then I would say that it is good enough, so long as it is a CONSTANT 30lbs. The V8's is not a high pressure system but a high volume system (which is also the reason why the oil level should be carefully maintained). The question of losing oil is another subject, and any V8 with oil thrown all over the engine is suspect. The Thames Valley Police V8s were sold with about 150,000 miles on the clocks, and they were not using any oil! Thus, oil consumption on a sound V8 should be negligible, but it should be regularly changed (say, every 3,000 miles along with the filter). In my opinion, dirty and thick oil carbons-up the cam followers and rocker shafts and ruins them - I have seen it all too often! All of the major components for the V8 engine should be readily available for many years to come. With such a gem of an engine on their hands I doubt whether Rover Group will drop it from their inventory.

The Running Gear

This is, to all intents and purposes, identical to the 1800 'B. There are differences in the suspension settings, but this is about all. The brakes are similar but with wider discs and callipers to match, and both are readily available. The kingpins and bushes are identical, the rear axle is similar, but beware of one that has anything more than the slightest clunk, as the complete axles and the special crownwheel and pinion are now 'no longer available'. (Footnote: Try your specialist supplier – as they may have been put back into production.)

The gearbox has always been the biggest drawback of this car. The cruel fact of life is that the gearbox is at the limit of its torque capacity in the V8, and the special laygear that gives the V8 its remarkable, and some say perfect, gear ratios is not conducive to sheer strength. For those who practise traffic light racing, the laygear and first gear simply tear themselves apart (£ and ££ respectively in this buying guide's price-check symbols). The annoying part about this problem is that 'it just happens' - there is no warning except perhaps the quietest clicking noise and then bang! It's gone! All the parts that make the V8 gearbox special are available at time of writing, except for the main casing.

The Exhaust Manifolds

Much has been said about these items in the past. If they are split at the 'Y' junction then it is certain that they have been bolted up too tightly. They are available from Rover Group, and the latest bunch are of an

apparently higher quality than the earlier type. If they are cracked, then negotiate a suitable reduction from your dealer, if you can, as they are now priced in the £££ range. The old ones can be cast welded, but for the work to be done properly it is a job for a coded welder with correct cast rods. Most enthusiasts now have export Range Rover gaskets between the manifold and the heads to eliminate metal to metal contact.

The Wheels

By now the chrome might be in poor condition on neglected cars. The only people Dunlop, the original makers, are said to suggest to strip, polish, re-chrome and assemble are Motor Wheel Repair Service at Shepherds Bush, London. However, they have now been put back into production.

Summing-Up

In general, there are V8s of all types from poor to mint. A poor example will take many hundreds of pounds to bring up to good condition, and perhaps thousands to bring up to mint condition. There is no hard and fast rule as to prices; you simply get what you pay for. I know some people think that any old V8 in poor condition is worth a fortune, but the truth of the matter is that a poor example is not worth much more than the price of a poor 1800 'B. After all, to bring the body up to scratch costs the same, but the remainder, the engine and gearbox, costs a small fortune. [Author's note: There are, however, far fewer V8s, and

their sheer scarcity is bound to mean that prices of all V8s will rise faster than those of equivalent 1800 'Bs.]

There are some parts that are now 'No Longer Available' from Rover Group but these are, in the main, the parts that other manufacturers have bought up in order to make their own V8s. These parts don't wear out and are confined to the special inlet manifold and adaptor, oil pump base and a few other things. The good news, of course, is that these same car builders have solved their own problems by having these parts made and that they are usually for sale and available to the V8 owner.

Having decided to buy a V8, I would always use the criterion my father used. He said that it is always better to buy just better and just more expensive than you want to. That way you always feel that you have done well for yourself. How true! Remember that the V8 is an expensive car to maintain, but not to run. I think it prudent to comment that most of the people that I know who are intent on keeping the car 'forever', have got a small second car as well. With so few V8's having been made it's far better to wear out your Mini first!

When you have got yourself a V8, here is a list of publications without which it will be virtually impossible to properly run the car: Workshop Manual (AKD 3259), Workshop Manual Supplement (AKD 8468), The Parts List MGB V8 (AKM 0039), User Handbook MGB V8 (AKD 8423). The Moss Parts Book will also prove invaluable.

Buying - In Conclusion

Having examined a car in this sort of depth, it is likely that the

prospective MGB/C/V8 owner will be confronted with an almost frightening array of faults. Although the price check symbols will help in determining the most expensive faults, the following notes will help to provide some sort of perspective to those faults now all too clearly on view.

Body rot and underbody corrosion are far and away the two worst enemies of the MGB range. Although the car is sturdily constructed, any rot found should be viewed on the iceberg principle; for every spot of corrosion evident on the outside, things will certainly be ten times worse on the inside, and that includes that critical, vertical membrane invisibly contained within the sill sections. The chapter on sill replacement will give some idea just how vitally important the sill areas are, containing as they do, most of the car's longitudinal strength, particularly in the case of the Tourer.

Upholstery used to be a problamatical area but nowadays almost every aspect of cloth, vinyl and leather trim is available from the leading MG specialists.

However, the prospective owner who is determined to own a first class example of the marque can find him or herself in a real dilemma. Is it best to buy a rough but complete example and restore it to show standards, or would an 'original, low-mileage' example be preferable? In practice both alternatives have their disadvantages. A complete body restoration can cost a great deal of money if the work is carried out by a top-class firm - making the commercial restoration of all but a few cars an uneconomic proposition - but then of course that is where this book comes in! The only way to be sure of getting rid of rust is to restore the bodywork, and the only way to make

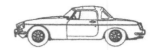

economic sense out of the project is to do it - or to do much of it - yourself.

Popular myth has it that little-used cars are the best buys but, unless it has languished in California's sunny climes, the older car with absolutely no rust inside its inner panels is so rare as to be almost non-existent. Even the lowest mileage examples are found to have some inner corrosion - invariably to the amazement of their owners if they are unfortunate enough to require crash damage repair.

Whichever option the enthusiast finally decides upon,

there can be no doubt about which car should be avoided like the plague, and which can be detected using the procedures shown in this chapter. This is the average-to high priced MGB, with glossy paint and chrome spinners shining seductively in the spring sunshine, effectively blinding the would-be purchaser to the artificially smooth, plastic filled body and the endless expense and heartache to come.

Choose well to start off with - and enjoy years of motoring in one of the last of the simply, enjoyable sports cars.

B1.   MGC engine compartment.

B2.   Whether buying for rebuild or just to use, a car with original equipment is a definite 'plus'. Replacement of small but, to the purist, vital parts can often be infuriatingly difficult. This photo shows an early MGB engine compartment.

B3. Early GT interior. Note the white piping on the leather seats.

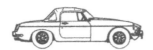

B4. Early 1969 Tourer interior. Replacement leather is very expensive.

B5. Later models had face-level vents and a centre console, plus more comfortable seats.

B6. US dashboard 1977-80 (Picture: S. Glochowsky).

B7. Post 1975 saw a single carburettor and other strangulations fitted to US cars. Some owners have reverted to twin SUs (Picture: S. Glochowsky).

B8. Latest engines in the UK had increased space in an engine bay designed to accept the V8. Electric fan was standard.

B9. This is a severe case, but the buyer should feel inside the wing of the car under consideration and take a careful look through the adjacent holes in the inner flitch panels, under the bonnet.

B10. Doors and sills can rot badly - including the lower wings in line with the sills ...

B11. ... and this shows what it was like with the outer sill removed. Inner members are ALWAYS worse than expected.

B12. MGCs are little more difficult than MGBs to restore, but engines are much heavier (Photo: Pearl McGlen).

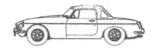

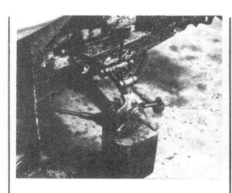

B13. MGC front suspension parts are unique to that car and in very short supply, so check carefully. Here the telescopic damper has been removed. (Photo: Pearl McGlen).

B15. The beading between front wings and the top bulkhead panel can deteriorate.

B17. Wings frequently rot around the headlamp surround, behind the sidelight and at the ends of the apron, behind the bumper. (Picture: S. Glochowsky).

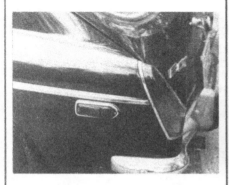

B14. Rear bumper alignment provides a clue to any past accident damage. (Photo: S. Glochowsky).

B16. Note the seam between the filler cap and reversing light. This is usually filled in during restoration and is thus a clue as to whether an excellent early car is really 'unrestored and original'.

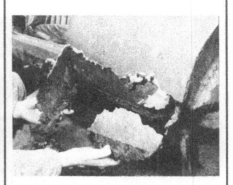

B18. Even severe corrosion can be camouflaged with plastic filler. This wing base looked quite presentable until 'attacked'. The magnet test is crucial here - see text.

B19. BL badges on a pre-October '69 car probably mean that it has been fitted with later wings. Another rot spot, incidentally, is a vertical line to the right of this picture. The mud-shield behind it should also be checked carefully, especially at its base.

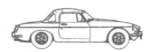

B20. Other favourite rot-spots are: Inner sills, check underneath carpets and/or rubber mats.

B21. Jacking points and under-sill areas, and ...

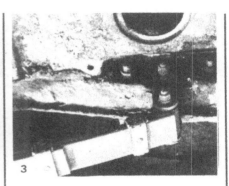

B22. ...rear spring hangers. Probe the latter two with a screwdriver.

B23. Most 'desirable' options, value-wise, are overdrive, wire wheels and reclining seats (on earlier cars). These non-standard chrome-plated wire wheels require constant attention if they are to look their best. ←

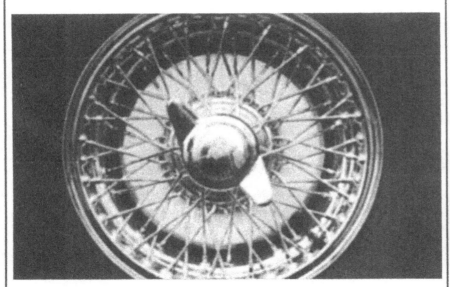

B24. Engine mountings on 'V8 body-shell' cars (with forward mounted, electrically-cooled radiators) are prone to breakage. Check carefully. ↑

B25. In England, any form of 'customising' is likely to lower the value of an MGB in the eyes of most enthusiasts, but in the US work was often carried out by the dealer as in the case of this 1978 Roadster which was pinstriped before it was put in the showroom. (Picture: S. Glochowsky). ←

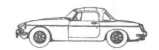

UK Tax Exemption

Cars built before 1 January 1973 are exempt from UK vehicle excise duty ('car tax'). The important point here, especially for cars first registered in early '73 or later imports, is that the relevant date is the build date, *not* the date of first registration. If you provide MG with the chassis number (VIN), they will give you the evidence you will need to claim tax exemption from your local Driver Vehicle Licencing Centre.

Classic Car Insurance

If you own a 'classic' MGB, you can save money and ensure that you aren't caught in the 'old-car-not-worth-much' insurance trap.

Classic car insurance is usually cheaper than private motor insurance. This is because classic vehicles are generally used less than the main family vehicle and with extra care, making them a good risk as the likelihood of a claim is lower.

Naturally, enough, most insurance companies will set some restrictions to qualify for this. Models considered to be 'classics', are usually supported by an owners' club. In addition, insurers specify that the car must be above a certain age, in most cases 15 years old, though other companies have different age limits. In addition, the car must not be the main vehicle or be used for more than a specified annual mileage. To an extent you can choose the mileage that suits you, but the lower this is the lower the premium.

Above all, there is a cardinal rule that must be remembered when insuring your 'classic'

MGB. Make sure you can agree the value of your vehicle with your insurer. It's the only way to protect your investment, should the worst come to the worst.

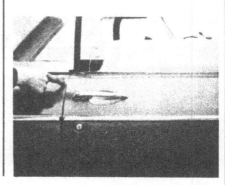

B26. If the top door gaps have closed up, the car has 'sagged' in the middle. Measure the gap, top and bottom.

B27. Roadster hood rear 'windows' become clouded in time. Light clouding can be removed by polishing with metal polish, but it usually means a new – expensive – soft-top. If the rest of it is in sound condition the 'window' can be cut out and a new one stitched in by a high-class upholsterer at a fraction of the cost of a new hood.

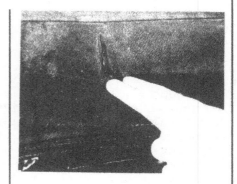

B28. Soft-top rips are unsightly and can never be patched satisfactorily. Soft-top fabric can rot where it clips down to the bodywork. Lift it up and take a look. You could be in for a surprise!

One thing is for sure. If your vehicle is eligible, you really should consider an agreed value classic car insurance policy.

Chapter 3 Bodywork
Part 1: Restoration

This book covers both the restoration of an existing bodyshell and the use of a new Heritage shell and, for that reason, this bodywork section has been split into two parts. Bodywork Part 1 deals almost entirely with the restoration of an existing shell although, inevitably, some of the information found in here will be useful to the restorer using a Heritage shell. Bodywork Part 2 deals with rebuilding a car around a new shell, and will also be of benefit to those retaining their existing shell. For instance, the sections on fitting new panels to the Heritage shell will also apply to a large extent to the restorer of the existing shell.

Bodyshell - Restore or Replace?

Most people believe that the restoration of an MGB around a new Heritage bodyshell reduces the time required to restore the car. We have not found this to be the case. Certainly, the business of cutting out rot and replacing it with sound metal is a time consuming one if it is done properly, but just think about this. With a new Heritage shell you take delivery of a complete bodyshell - complete in terms of sheet metal certainly, but *sans* everything else. The time you save in not having to carry out bodywork repairs will probably be spent twice over in having to fit a new wiring loom, having to ensure that every captive nut is in place and in fitting the screen, the dashboard and every single one of the hundreds of clips, grommets, catches and screws to be found in a shell. We started with one of the early Heritage shells and the fit of components has undoubtedly improved since that time. It is now impossible to start, as we did, with a shell bare of front wings, bonnet, doors and boot lid. These will all have been fitted for you at the factory, and that represents a very considerable saving in time. On the other hand, you will have to remove all the panels for thorough painting and you will still have to drill every hole for the chrome trim and for the hood fixings; you will have to work out where the handbrake cable, the bonnet pull, and many other minor items will have to go - but at the end of the day you will have a brand new bodyshell and in my view, there is nothing that compares to that! You won't have a bodyshell that is exactly original to any particular age of MGB, however. The Heritage shell is an amalgam of several different era of MGBs and, although the differences are only slight, they may matter if you are looking for pure originality.

In the end, the decision may come down to the condition of the donor car or the car being restored. Only you can make the decision as to whether you think your car is restorable, whether you want to retain its original bodyshell or whether you would rather go down the Heritage route.

In many ways, this section of the book is the most potentially useful one to the restorer. At the time of writing, MGB bodywork restoration has been covered in no other book, and yet it is the most crucial area of the car. Poor bodywork reduces the life, safety and value of the MGB, while restored bodywork (in conjunction with a suspension rebuild) puts back the joyously taut handling which the car possessed when new.

Those enthusiasts without welding equipment have several courses still open to them (quite apart from the obvious and most costly one of leaving it to the highly

expensive - and completely uninvolved - professional). It is possible to hire electric arc welding equipment in most large towns, although this type of welding equipment is usually found to be too fierce for outer body panels even in the most experienced hands. For 'chassis' work, for tack-welding inner wings or door skins, however, arc welding is fine. In the UK, most Technical Colleges and Evening Institutes run evening classes where beginners can learn the rudiments of arc or gas welding.

Incidentally, brazing can also be carried out with an arc welder with the addition of the appropriate accessory.

Brazing cannot be used for structural repairs because it is considered that brazed repairs are not as strong as welded ones, and brazed structural repairs in the UK will cause the car to fail the annual MOT test.

Gas welding is far more versatile than arc welding, at least as far as thin-gauge metal is concerned, but gas bottles are harder and more expensive to obtain and are far less safe to store and use. In the UK, British Oxygen sell a pair of mini-bottles called a 'Portapak' - the cylinders can be exchanged at any one of 120 BOC Gas Centres throughout the UK - and similar gas welding kits are available in the USA, Australia and elsewhere. Cheaper gas welding sets, often using disposable canisters are sometimes bought by enthusiasts for restoration work but they are not recommended. The quality of the equipment is generally poor which makes welding difficult to carry out satisfactorily, and the disposable canisters are very expensive if anything more than a few minutes welding has to be carried out.

The most popular form of welding available for the DIY enthusiast is now MIG welding, which is a form of arc welding, albeit one that is far less likely to burn through the steel as you are welding it and which produces a higher quality of weld with less distortion than any other type of welding.

The subject of car body repairs is sufficient for a book in itself. Which leads me on to The Car Bodywork Repair Manual written by this author and published by Haynes Publishing Group. It contains over 300 pages and over 1,000 illustrations showing how to carry out all the skills covered in this section, which is as well because there certainly isn't room to go into the mastering of specific skills in this book.

Tools and Equipment

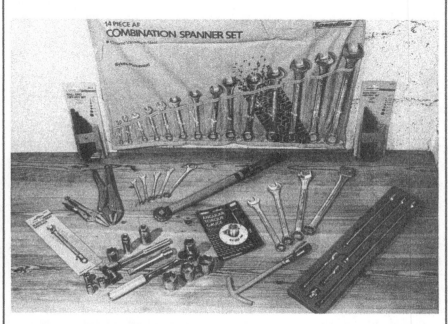

T&E1. A good selection of hand tools will prove invaluable. Buying the cheapest tools is a false economy and you would be well advised to invest in a good-medium range such as those from Sykes-Pickavant.

T&E2. Obtain a suitable fire extinguisher for workshop use. Dry powder may be best; water-filled is unsuitable where an electrical fire may be concerned. Contact Chubb Fire for advice on which type to use. (Courtesy Chubb Fire Limited).

T&E5. More useful hand tools from Sykes-Pickavant; this is the bench folding tool which enables you to make accurate folds when constructing steel panels; two pieces of steel clamped together would do the same job although in a far more long-winded way.

T&E3. Only used now and again but a godsend when it's needed, this is the Sykes-Pickavant ball joint splitter.

T&E4. SP also produce this range of toolboxes and lockers to enable you to keep your hand tools in an orderly style. ➡

T&E6. Two more sheet metal bench tools from SP are the bench wheeled guillotine and the flanging tool which places a shoulder on the edge of a piece of metal, enabling two pieces to be lap-jointed, giving a flush finish on the outside. ⬆

T&E7. The Monodex sheet metal cutter allows distortion-free sheet metal cutting, albeit at the expense of an aching hand! ⬅

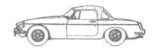

T&E8. There's no competition when it comes to domestic-sized gas welding kits. This is the BOC Portapak ...

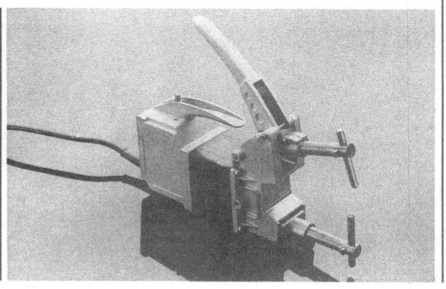

T&E9. ...the kit and exchange cylinders are available from BOC cylinder centres throughout the UK, and similar establishments are to be found in Australia, the United States and most other countries.

T&E11. For factory-finish welds, you will need a spot welder. It cannot be used, of course, when there's no access for the welding tips.

T&E10. MIG welding is probably the most versatile of all for car bodywork repairs. This is the stylish and efficient SIP Migmate Super.

41

T&E12. Very upmarket are these two SIP plasma cutters. They enable you to cut out sheet steel quickly, cleanly and without distortion, and the smaller models, the Plasma 25 is about the same price as mid-range MIG welders.

T&E13. If you're going to carry out your own respraying, you will need a compressor. The SIP Airmate range has the right combination of performance and affordability, and the cost would be recouped on the first job you carried out.

T&E14. The same company also produce a full range of spray guns, right up from the least expensive DIY model to the full-size professional gun. ⬇

T&E15. This Clarke random orbit sander enables you to rapidly sand filler and primer during the respray process without the scratches and marks that would be left by ordinary electric-type sanders. It is ideal for use with the larger DIY compressors.

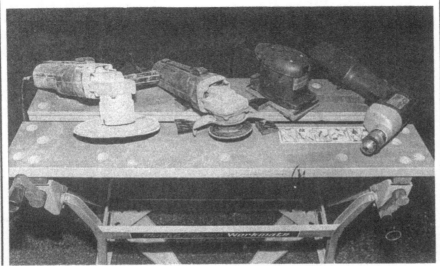

T&E16. A range of electric hand tools will be absolutely essential. Shown here from left to right are the following Black & Decker tools; random orbit sander; mini-grinder; electric sander; rechargeable electric drill which enables you to get into odd spots around the car without having potentially dangerous cable trailing along the floor.

T&E17. Machine Mart, a company with retail outlets throughout the UK, sell a huge range of workshop equipment, such as this Clarke engine stand. Only useful if you carry out a lot of such work, an engine stand may nevertheless be available from your local tool hire centre. ◄

T&E18. One tool you will definitely need is this Machine Mart two ton trolley jack, carrying the name Jack King.

T&E19. Another invaluable set of tools are these Machine Mart axle stands. Some owners make do with old bricks, oil drums and the like, but it is most important that you do not do so! Bricks can crumble; cans can topple and the results of a car falling on you could be very terminal indeed. ◄

T&E20. Part of your preparation should be the purchase of as many nuts, bolts, washers and clips as you think you might need. We obtained packets of Namrick fixings - all of them of bright zinc-plated steel, except for those that we purchased for use in the most vulnerable parts of the car which were made of stainless steel. **Nuts and bolts associated with suspension should be of original specification because of the specified tensile strength required. Non-specified bolts may shear and cause a component to fail.** Many MG specialists can supply fitting kits (nuts, bolts, washers and clips) for fitting many components ◄

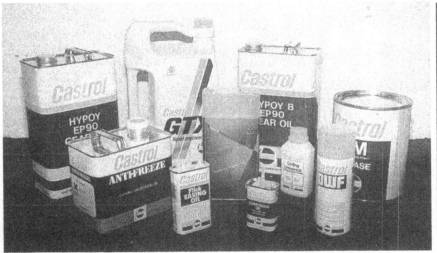

T&E21. You will also need a comprehensive range of lubricants. Castrol (UK) Limited's Technical Department can supply full information on MGB lubrication requirements.

T&E22. Having completed the restoration of your pride and joy you will want to prevent any future corrosion. Machine Mart sell workshop dehumidifiers, such as this Clarke unit, which keep the humidity level down in the workshop and thus dramatically reduce the incidence of corrosion.

T&E23. The Car Bodywork Repair Manual, also by Lindsay Porter and published by Haynes, contains over a thousand illustrations and covers every aspect of car bodywork repair techniques, including detailed information on welding, panel beating and spraying.

Safety Equipment

In many parts of this book, various items of safety equipment are specified. Obtaining them must take top priority for the health and safety of the user and those around you. To start off with, purchase safety goggles, industrial leather gloves, cotton overalls, and ear plugs for use with noisy power tools.

'Toolbox'

At the start of many sections, a 'Toolbox' section appears, listing most of the tools and equipment needed to enable you to carry out the work. No list of 'essential' workshop tools is presented here, but simply the advice that it is safer and cheaper in the long run to always buy (or hire) the best tools available.

'Safety Notes'

At the start of every section is a 'Safety' note. Naturally, safety is the responsibility of each individual restorer, and no responsibility for the effectiveness or otherwise of advice given here, or for any omissions, can be accepted by the author. 'Safety' notes are intended to include useful tips and no more. Some more

useful information on workshop practice and general safety measures is given as an Appendix 1. You are strongly advised to read this appendix before starting any of the tasks detailed in this book.

It is also essential that you obtain all safety information available from manufacturers and suppliers of tools, equipment and materials that you may use in the course of restoring your MGB so that you can find out the correct safety procedures and apply them.

Before carrying out any major body repairs, it makes good common sense to drain and remove the fuel tank to a place of safety. The remaining fume-filled tank is especially dangerous, so consider having it properly cleaned out during any extended restoration. Never drain a fuel tank indoors or where the highly flammable vapours can gather, such as over a pit. Store petrol drained from the tank in safe, closed, approved containers. If the empty tank is to be stored, have it steam cleaned to remove the petrol vapours. Place a damp rag into any openings and keep the tank out of doors for very short-term storage. Keep all sparks and flames away from the fuel system whilst working on it.

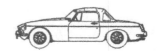

Chrome Bumper Removal

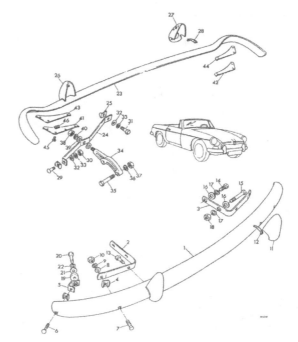

CBR1. The front bumper is removed after unbolting it from the bumper brackets and the outer edges of the front valance.

CBR2. Similarly for the rear bumper, but remember to detach the number plate lights. Foot power works well on the invariably seized mounting nuts but soak them in releasing fluid otherwise the cast mounting bracket may snap.

CBR3. The chrome bumper components. Items No. 2 and No. 34 are the bumper brackets that bolt to the chassis. ⬆

CBR4. The impact-absorbing front bumper assembly fitted to the last of the US-spec. chrome-bumpered cars. ⬇

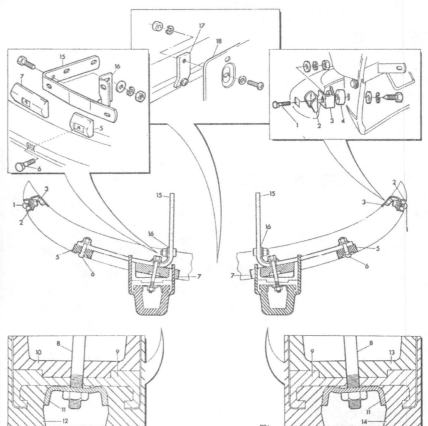

CBR5. The components of the latest US-spec. chrome bumper models. ➡

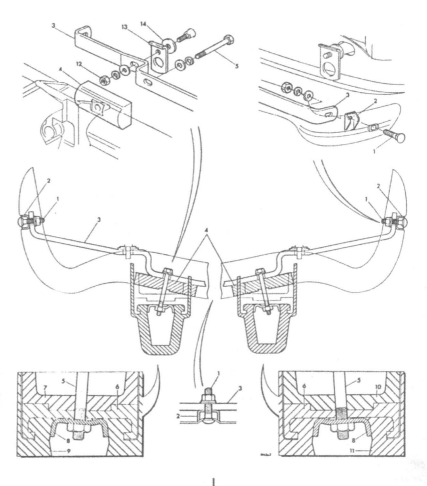

Rubber Bumper Removal

RB1. Disconnect the front bumper's lamp wiring with the bonnet open.

RB2. Remove the four nuts and eight washers from the bumper inner mountings and the four bolts and eight washers from the outer locations.

RB3. Lift the bumper away.

Roadster Screen Removal

Toolbox

AF socket or ring and open-ended spanners. Rags and white spirit to remove old mastic (sealer).

Safety

If the screen is broken, cover the cockpit with an old sheet to catch the glass splinters should the glass fragment. Wear thick gloves.

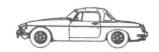

RSR1. The two chrome bolts which hold the central screen tie rod have to be removed. It will be found necessary to slacken them and then to lift the screen before they can be completely undone and removed. Alternatively, start by removing the tie rod from the top of the windscreen. ➡

RSR2. The screen itself is held in place by two bolts on each side which pass through the holes shown here. Remove the dashboard for best access; a minimum of glovebox removal will be required.

RSR3. Lift the screen up and forwards and away - note the 'dog-leg' shape of the support legs. Cover the screen and store it somewhere safe.

GT Screen Removal and Replacement

Toolbox

A sharp craft knife and a cup of soapy water. A length of stout twine. New screen rubbers. Blunt screwdriver. Tube of screen sealing mastic.

Safety

You may have to hit the glass quite hard to get it in and you stand a chance of breaking it when getting it out so wear stout leather gloves and goggles and cover the screen and dashboard with old blankets.

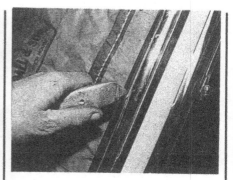

GTS1. DON'T attempt to lever out the old trim strip - it will distort and become useless. Dip the blade in the soapy water (this enables it to slip through the rubber) and cut the rubber away ...

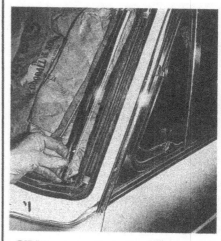

GTS2. ... so that the trim can be lifted out.

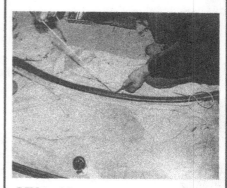

GTS3. Use a new rubber when refitting. Bed it on to the screen with mastic then push the twine into the gap around the rubber where it will fit into the screen aperture in the car's bodywork.

GTS4. More sealing mastic being applied.

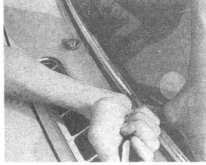

GTS7. The new rubber will be soft enough to enable you to ease the bright sealing strip around the outside of the screen.

Door Stripdown

Before a door can be re-skinned, or when a new door shell is to be fitted, the old door has to be stripped of all trim and fittings. (New Heritage doors are supplied bare of any fittings whatever, incidentally.)

Toolbox

Crosshead screwdriver. Impact screwdriver and suitable hammer. Small straight-point screwdrivers. Long-nose and engineer's pliers.

Safety

No real problems - apart from pinched fingers! Wrap door glass in a large cloth and store in a safe place.

GTS5. Ensuring that the twine stays in place and is overlapped, lower the screen into place in the aperture.

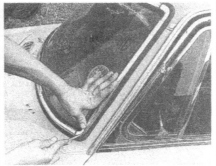

GTS8. Finish it off with the last upright, having ensured the corner pieces have gone in first.

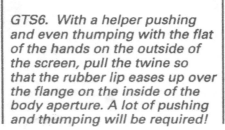

GTS6. With a helper pushing and even thumping with the flat of the hands on the outside of the screen, pull the twine so that the rubber lip eases up over the flange on the inside of the body aperture. A lot of pushing and thumping will be required!

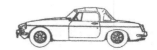

DS1. Start by removing the trim rail at the top of the door (2 crosshead screws at each end), then remove the single screw which holds the window winder in place.

DS4. Remove door speakers if fitted.

DS7. Open wide. This won't hurt!

DS2. Unscrew the two crosshead screws holding the door pull in place (lift the fold-down handle on earlier models).

DS5. The door trim clips forwards and off. Take care, if the trim is an old one, to lever near to the spring clips.

DS8. Carefully screwdriver off the spring clip which holds the latch release rod in place ...

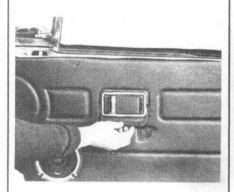

DS3. Door catch bezels 'break' in the middle - they clip apart then slide out.

DS6. The protective plastic sheet should be carefully removed and reused later if not damaged.

DS9. ... and the one which holds the locking lever.

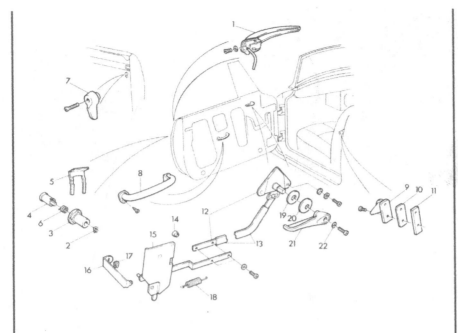

DS10. Pull them forwards and out of location with the latch.

DS11. Take out the screws holding the latch unit in place.

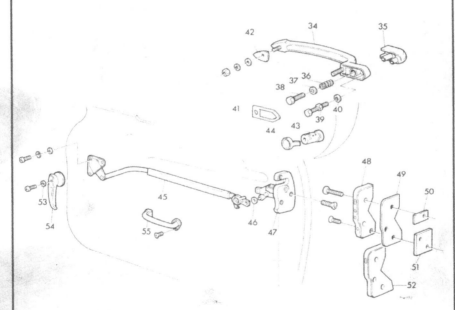

DS12. Remove the latch unit.

Figure 1. Earlier (GHN3/GHD3) cars used one of two simpler locking systems which were more straightforward to remove and replace. Their components are shown here.

Items 1 to 22 apply to earlier sports-tourer only, with pull-out exterior door handles.

1	Outer door handles	9	Striker	17	Spring clip	44	Retaining clip
2	Spring clip	10	Packing	18	Tension spring	45	Remote control link
3	Lock housing	11	Tapping Plate	19	Fibre washer	46	Anti-rattle washer
4	Lock barrel	12	Remote control lock	20	Finisher	47	Lock
5	Lock retaining clip	13	Anti-rattle sleeve	21	Inner door handle	48	Striker
6	Self-centring spring	14	Outside door handle buffer	22	Spring washer	49	Shim - 0.003 in or 0.006 in (0.08 mm or 0.16 mm)
7	Inner locking Knob	15	Lock	34	Outer door handle	50	Tapping plate (upper)
8	Door pull	16	Operating link	35	Pushbutton	51	Tapping plate (lower)
				36	Spring	52	Striker lock
				37	Shakeproof washer	53	Spring washer
				38	Set screw	54	Inner door handle
				39	Set screw with locknut	55	Door pull
				40	Shakeproof washer		
				41	Fibre washer		
				42	Fibre washer		
				43	Lock barrel		

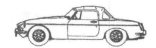

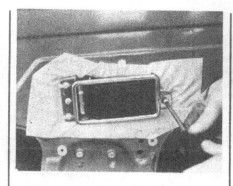

DS13. Remove the four screws holding the latch pull in place ...

DS16. Unbolt the bottom of the runner, either inside the door ...

DS19. Remove the regulator securing screws. Slide the rollers out of the bottom of the channel fixed to the bottom of the window glass.

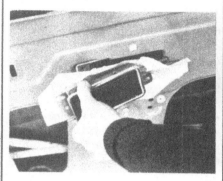

DS14. ... and remove it.

DS17. ... or from outside, removing the bracket as well. Leave the runner loose, inside the door.

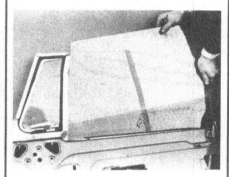

DS20. Lift the glass up and out of the door.

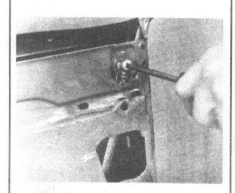

DS15. Take out the window runner top screw.

DS18. Remove the window regulator extension screws.

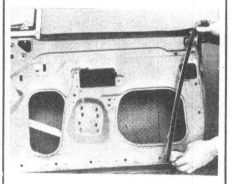

DS21. Lift the rear glass channel out of the door.

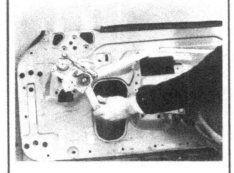

DS22. 'Persuade' the regulator assembly out of the holes in the door.

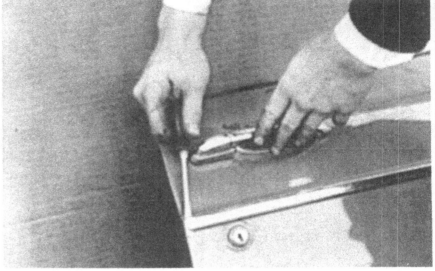

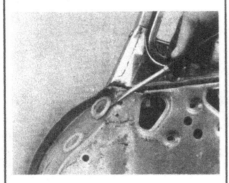

DS23. Lever the front grommets out of their holes in the front of the door.

DS25. Undo the two nuts which hold the front window channel (an extension of the quarterlight).

DS27. The chrome trim clips forwards and off (be very careful not to distort it), the door push is held by two nuts - two screw threads protrude from the handle, backwards through the door skin - and the lock is held by a spring clip which slides into a groove in the lock, tight against the inside of the door skin. ↑

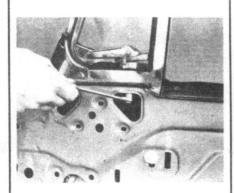

DS24. Remove the two nuts which hold the quarterlight from beneath, and the one which holds it from the front of the door.

DS26. Lift the quarterlight assembly out of the door.

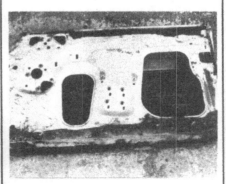

DS28. Voila! The now denuded door skin is ready for whatever work is to be carried out.

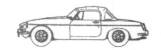

Door Repairs

Now that brand new Heritage doors are available, we would generally recommend that you don't re-skin a rusted-out door but replace it with new. Fitting a new skin in such a way that completely avoids distortion in the door frame is a very skilled operation and you may find that all your efforts come to nought. However, it is significantly cheaper to fit a new door skin than to fit a new door so, if you want to try your hand, here's how to go about it.

MGB doors are prone to giving trouble in two different areas and, although both problems can be prevented by careful maintenance, repairing either of them is a largish job. The first and, apparently, smallest problem is that of door splits which appear in the upper panel of most Roadsters, sooner or later, just below the quarterlight. These splits, or stress- cracks are caused by the construction of the doors which incorporate frameless windows supported vertically only by the rear of the quarterlight frame.

When the door is shut, the pressure of the quarterlight against the screen pillar sealing rubber and the glass itself against a hardtop, when fitted, is fed into the most vulnerable point of the doorskin, the quarterlight frame. The only cars which stand a chance of avoiding this problem are those whose door striker plates are set in such a way that when the door pull button is depressed, the door does not spring out against the force of the sealing rubber. In practice, this means that the door tends to protrude very slightly along its trailing edge, instead of shutting flush, but that is the lesser of two evils.

Door splits can be repaired simply by welding along the line of the fault, but this is no more than a short-term remedy. The weld itself will never break, but the heat treatment unavoidably given to the surrounding area makes the metal prone to splitting again within a relatively short time, in a line parallel to that of the original split.

The only answer is to 'let-in' a piece of steel sheet, rather like a patch on a pair of jeans, the only difference being that when the patch is fitted, it is used as a template which is placed over the split area of the door panel. It is scribed around, the split section is carefully and accurately cut out, and the new piece tack-welded into its place before being filled or leaded over prior to refinishing.

On the other hand, if the door base is also rusted, it would be far easier to reskin the door. MGB doors are highly prone to rusting out along their bases due to the ingress of water in spite of the sealing strip along their window apertures. John Hill's door skins and door base repair sections enable the vast majority of doors to be repaired, saving the owner a good deal of money, but some doors are just too far gone and have to be replaced. If the latter is the case, follow the instructions for stripping and refitting a door and for bodywork finishing.

If tackled early enough, severe corrosion is a preventable problem. Doors should be annually injected in all their vulnerable internal sections with a rust preventative such as Waxoyl - a small chore which can save a lot of problems - not forgetting to clean out drain holes in door bottoms, too.

Toolbox

AF socket spanners. Pliers. Medium and large points of crosshead screwdrivers. Angle grinder with flexible pad (can be hired from tool-hire stores).

Hammer. Hacksaw. Impact screwdriver or wrench. Wooden-topped bench, or large sheet of timber on the floor. Welding equipment. Tin snips.

Safety

Clear protective goggles. Protective gloves. Follow usual safety procedures when either electric or gas welding. Remember that cut edges or slivers of steel sheet can be razor sharp.

DR1. *With a crosshead screwdriver, remove door handle, window winder handle, door pull, door trim and padded waist rail. Place smaller parts in a labelled plastic bag. Remove plastic liner (where fitted) from behind door trim panel by peeling it away from the door. Keep for later use.*

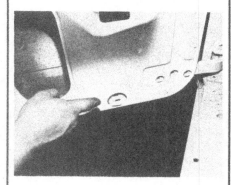

DR2. *Remove quarterlight by unscrewing, with a crosshead screwdriver, the two screws securing the quarterlight frame at the base of the door.*

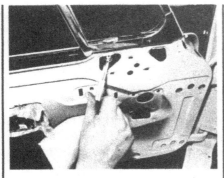

DR3. Undo the two nuts situated beneath the quarterlight through the apertures shown.

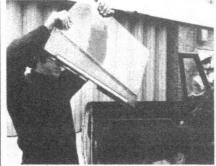

DR5. The glass can now be tilted and lifted high out of the door. Wrap it in a cloth and store it safely. ⬆

DR6. Here John Hill has chosen to leave the quarterlight in place until after the door has been removed. Undo the three crosshead screws holding each hinge to the door, using a large point screwdriver. They are usually stubborn, and John uses a wrench to gain more purchase on his screwdriver. ⬆

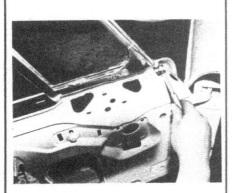

DR4. Remove the plastic grommet and undo the nut securing the quarterlight found there. Undo the four bolts holding the winder mechanism in place (Fig 2, item 2) and the four bolts holding the winder mechanism extension (Fig 2, item 5), slide the steel wheel found on the end of the regulator arm out of its runner on the bottom of the window glass. Lift the glass by hand and remove the winder mechanism. (Let it lie in the bottom of the door, if working alone, and remove it later.) Disconnect the rear channel (Fig 2, items 7 & 8).

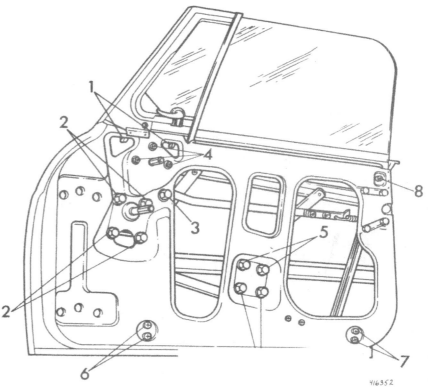

Figure 2. Early Roadster door interior.

1 Ventilator securing nuts
2 Regulator securing bolts
3 Regulator arm stop
4 Door lock remote control securing screws

5 Regulator extension securing set screws
6 Front door glass mounting bracket securing screws
7 Rear door glass mounting bracket screws
8 Door glass channel securing screws

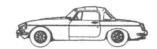

DR7. Another alternative is to use an impact screwdriver which, when struck with a hammer, imparts a twisting force upon the stubborn screw which is virtually irresistable. Ensure that the screw head is clean before use.

NB: The hinges are best left fitted to the door pillars. In addition to the four visible screws holding them in place, they are each also secured by a large nut only accessible by someone with very long arms from inside the wings after the mudshields have been removed! ➡

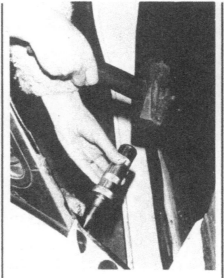

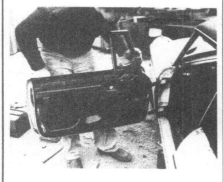

DR8. The door is drawn off the hinge straps by pulling it outwards and away from the hinge pillar.

DR9. The door skin is held on to the body of the door by a simple fold, rather like an elongated version of the flap on an envelope. This runs down both sides and across the bottom of the door. Using a mini-angle grinder (or a sharp file and plenty of elbow grease!) grind the edge of the fold. ➡

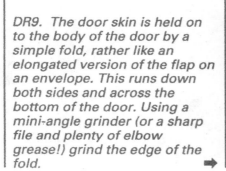

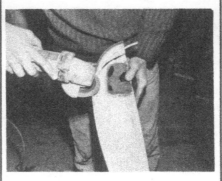

DR10. Continue up each side and then, wearing heavy gloves, strip off the redundant flange.

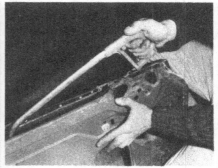

DR11. The only place where the door skin is welded is across the quarterlight fixing area. Simply cut straight through the middle with a hacksaw.

DR12(A). Quite often, the bottom of the door is sound. If not, mark out the rusted area so that it can be cut away.

DR12(B). Door base repair sections come complete with curved end-pieces welded in place.

DR13. A strong oxidising flame on a welding torch will make a surprisingly neat cut, especially if cleaned up later with the angle grinder. Otherwise use a Monodex-type cutter or power jigsaw with metal cutting edge. A cold chisel would probably distort the door frame.

DR14. This is the door skin and base repair panel as offered by John Hill. The base panel includes both bottom corners, but if a little more of the door has rotted it can be built up from flat sheet steel.

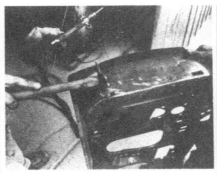

DR16. It is important to ensure an accurate fit. The panel should be lightly tack-welded and tapped back into position as it distorts, before being fully welded up.

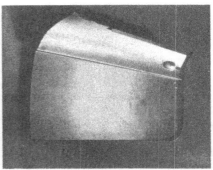

DR18. The door skin is placed upon the floor, flanges upwards ...

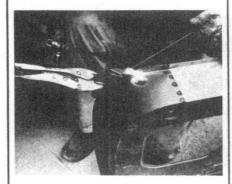

DR15. The repair panel is firmly clamped into place (or held with pop-rivets or self-tapping screws) and welded onto the existing door mainframe.

DR17. The opportunity should now be taken to paint the inside of the main frame (after removing any existing surface rust) and the inside of the new door skin, too.

DR19. ... the door frame is placed on top, and the whole assembly placed upon a wooden board. Tap the upright flange inwards a few degrees all the way round.

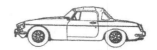

DR20. The fold should be continued a little at a time, going around the whole length of the flange, time and again. If the folding process is not done as evenly as possible, the metal will stretch, with a real risk of kinking taking place.

DR21. To achieve a really tidy looking fold, free of hammer marks, finish off with a piece of wood, as shown. Note how the door should been tipped during the whole process in such a way that the part being hammered is always in contact with the board beneath it.

DR22. The skin only requires welding at the position of the quarterlight mountings. Note how even this small area has been clamped to avoid distortion. If the door frame has been accidentally distorted, or if the folding has not made the door quite rigid enough, there is no reason why the replacement skin should not be tack-welded in three or four places inside the folds. ➡

DR23. The repaired door can now be refitted to the car. Hinge screws should not be fully tightened until the door gear has been fitted, so that correct door and quarterlight alignment can be ensured.

DR24. MGB doors rust from the inside-out. Even doors as badly rusted as this one, in the foreground, can be brought back to the condition of the one fitted to the 'B behind it.

DR25. Door splits cannot be repaired with filler! All that happens is that the filler is pushed straight back out again within a day or two. Fitting a door mirror which bolts through the panel can help to cut down the risk of splitting - those that are fitted with self-tapping screws won't help, though.

Having repaired the door it would be advisable to seal out as much water as possible by fitting a new window sealing strip.

The new door skin will have to be drilled to match the holes in the new strip which is simply pop-rivetted into place. See the relevant section in Chapter 4 for information on repainting and how to refit the chrome strip. It would be advisable to paint the door before refitting it if its rebuild is not part of a total restoration.

While fitting a new door

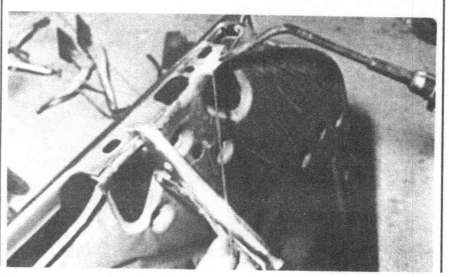

skin is not incredibly complex or expensive it is, of course, fairly time consuming. You can avoid ever having to do it again by religiously following the advice on anti-corrosion treatment given elsewhere in this book.

GT Tailgate and Mechanism

GTT1. Start by disconnecting one end of the prop mechanism and then, with an assistant holding the door open, unscrew the hinges. It will be heavy and cumbersome and is best lifted away from the car by two people. (Courtesy Moss Parts Catalogue) ➡

GT Rear Quarterlight

GTQ1. To remove, unscrew the window catch (1) from the body. Ease away the door seal in front of the quarterlight and take out the screws retaining the finishing strip. Unscrew the hinges (2) from the door pillar and lift away. ➡

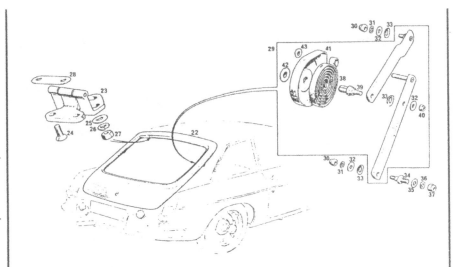

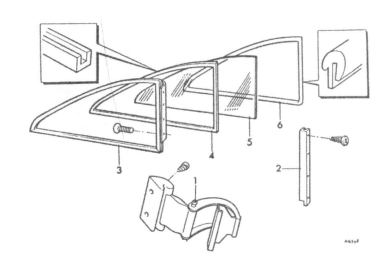

Boot and Tailgate Locks

BTL1. The lock itself is held to the boot or tailgate with these two screws ... ⬅

BTL2. ... and these. Use a crosshead screwdriver. ➡

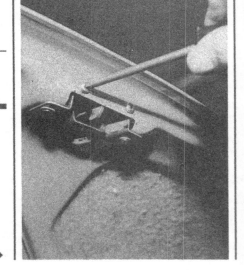

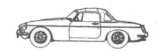

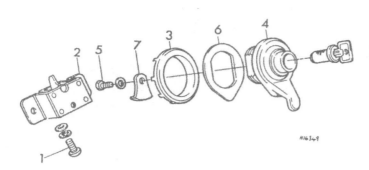

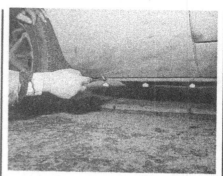

BTL3. The push button assembly is held to the lid by a threaded retaining ring (3). The catch screwed to the closing panel is held with slotted holes so that it can raised and lowered to align the lock with the latch. When refitted, it might need to be forcible bent forwards or backwards so that the boot lid or tailgate shuts and seals correctly. ⬆

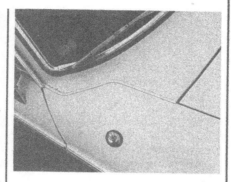

FWR1. The GT front wing differs from that of the Roadster. This is where it fits against the front scuttle panel.

Front Wing Removal

Toolbox

A range of AF sockets, ring and open-ended spanners. Releasing fluid. Welding torch or blow lamp - to help release seized nuts. Crosshead screwdriver, electric drill and possibly mini-grinder with goggles and gloves. Impact screwdriver. Hacksaw.

Safety

Basic workshop procedure - see Appendix that pays special attention to use of the mini-grinder, and beware of jagged metal.

FWR2. The mounting bolts can be found inside, behind the dash.

FWR3. The Roadster front wing differs in as much as the top surfaces have a hole through which the windscreen mounting legs must pass. The screen must be removed before the wings can be taken off. ➡

FWR4. The bottoms of the front wings are held in place by three cross-head screws. They invariably become 'welded' with rust, or they may have been wrongly fitted with bolts, or even with a welder. Try an impact screwdriver; try a drill with a sharp bit; resort to the mini-grinder if you have to.

FWR5. Behind the facia panels, the wing tops are held by three bolts. Removal is not easy - realignment when the wing is being replaced is even harder. Retrieve any spacers that you may find behind the wing and top panel.

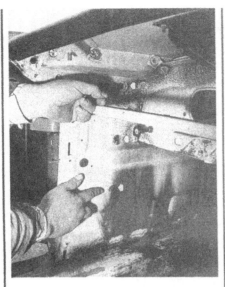

FWR6. Four more easily-accessible bolts are situated behind the footwell trim panels. ⬅

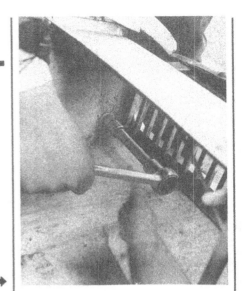

FWR7. Two bolts hold the fronts of the wing to the inner panels. ➡

FWR8. Three more bolts hold the front wing to the front apron. Unscrew, cut, drill or grind them away as necessary. ⬅

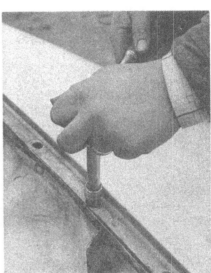

FWR9. It is not only noble, it is also easiest to leave until last the line of bolts that runs down the channel in which the bonnet closes. First, remove the lock nuts which hold the radiator steady and the bonnet release. ➡

FWR10. Taking care not to damage the surrounding bodywork and, especially, the leading edge of the door, lift the wing free. ⬅

FWR11. Before fitting a new wing, clean all the threads with the correct size tap. ➡

Front Inner Wing Repair

Toolbox

All necessary repair sections; welding equipment; tin snips; sheet metal cutter; hacksaw; bolster chisel and hammer; mini- grinder; goggles and industrial gloves.

Safety

The usual safety precautions should be taken when welding and when cutting ultra sharp sheet metal. Move anything flammable from around the area being welded, and remember to protect fuel lines from flames and heat.

FIW1. Many restorers find the front inner wings a real 'Shock! Horror!' area when rebuilding their MGB. They budget in time and money for a straightforward front wing renewal only to find that the rust bug has been nibbling away where he likes it most, in dank, dark unseen crevices. ⬇

FIW2. All rot must be cut out. Here, the top flange has also deteriorated. The vertical plate holding the fuse box has been separated by carefully drilling out the spot-welds and then equally carefully chiselling it free and bending it out of the way. At this stage, all trim, wiring and other flammables have to be moved out of the way. ➡

FIW3. All of the leading MGB specialists sell repair sections for corroded top flanges.

FIW4. An especially common repair section is the one shown here for replacing the trumpet shaped box on the MGB. It's a different shape on the MGC.

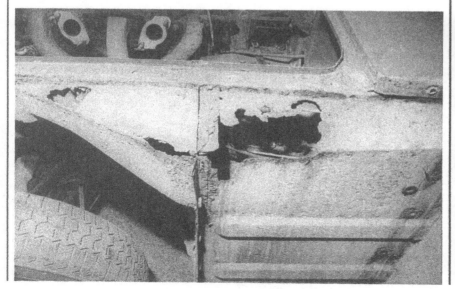

FIW5. Correctly attired with full face shield and with heavy industrial gloves, a new trumpet is welded into place with the MIG welder. All steel surfaces have to be really clean!

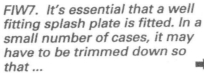

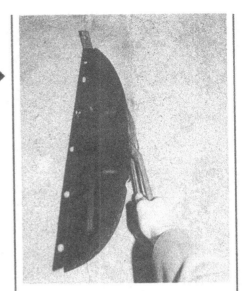

FIW7. It's essential that a well fitting splash plate is fitted. In a small number of cases, it may have to be trimmed down so that ... ➡

FIW6. More repair sections for common rot spots.

FIW8. ... when the sealing rubber is pushed on, the splash plate fits beneath the wing. ⬅

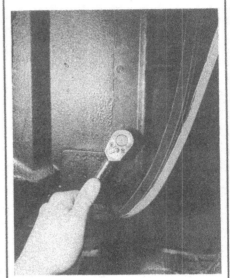

FIW9. A line of bolts holds the splash plate to the inner wing ➡

FIW10. ... and one more bolt is found right at the bottom where you can hardly get at it with a spanner. These are some of Namrick's stainless steel bolts being used in an especially vulnerable spot. ⬅

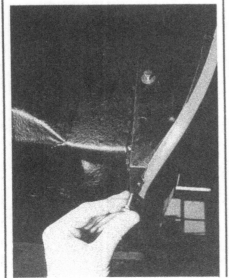

FIW11. Be sure to fit the sealing rubber to the top part of the splash plate before the wing is fitted otherwise you won't get it in. Also, seal around the edge with mastic. If you don't seal off properly, mud and salty water will get past, settle at the bottom of the front wings and cause more corrosion. ➡

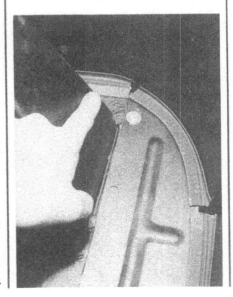

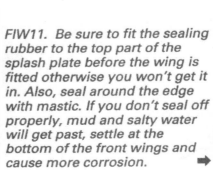

Front Valance Replacement

Toolbox

Releasing fluid; socket set; patience and - if the worst comes to the worst - drill and bit for drilling out sheared studs.

FVR1. A dozen machine screws hold the front valance to the bottom of the front wing and the front bodywork. Soak the old captive nuts in releasing fluid for a couple of days before beginning work, to reduce the risk of shearing off. The front bumper and support bracket will have to be removed first. ➡

FVR2. This is the new front valance being fitted to the project car with bright zinc-plated bolts and washers purchased from Moss.

FVR3. This 'Rubber Bumper' front valance was fitted from new with crosshead screws. You may have to use an impact screwdriver. You may have to say your prayers! ➡

Radiator Duct Panel

RDP1. Built on the original equipment, and available ➡ through Heritage suppliers such as Moss, the duct panel, which fits beneath the oil cooler, is available complete. Great for crash repairs, but if your 'B has corroded so badly that this panel is needed, consider using a new bodyshell!

Rear Wing Repair and Replacement

Changing the rear wings involves a little more skill, a good deal more time and a heck of a lot more patience than replacing an MGB's front wing, because you've first got to cut off the old wing in the right places, clean up all the wing mounting areas, cut out and repair any rust that you may find in the inner panels, and then stitch on the new rear wing. On the other hand, the rear wing takes up about two fifths of the length of each side of the car, so when you've finished the job you can rest safe in the knowledge that a fair proportion of the car's outer panels have been replaced and

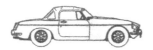

made sound for many years to come.

Toolbox

All necessary repair sections; welding equipment; tin snips; sheet metal cutter; hacksaw; bolster chisel and hammer; mini- grinder; goggles and industrial gloves; Monodex-type cutter or other non-distorting panel cutter; mini-angle grinder (available from tool-hire firms); thin or electrician's bolster chisel; medium-heavy ball pein hammer; tin snips; electric drill; self- tapping screws or pop-rivet equipment.

Safety

The usual safety precautions should be taken when welding and when cutting ultra-sharp sheet metal. Move anything flammable from around the area being welded, and remember to protect fuel lines from flames and heat. Beware cut edges in sheet metal, especially thin slivers of metal - wear heavy industrial gloves. Always wear gloves and goggles when using an angle grinder. Always remove the fuel tank when welding around the rear of the car. Watch out for welding 'splatter' when working beneath the car or inside the rear wheel arches. Note the usual safety points regarding working on a car raised off the ground.

RW1. It will be obvious that a GT's rear wing is slightly different from that of the Roadster wing being fitted, and you'll certainly have to remove the trim from around the rear windows in order to be able to fit it properly, but fitting a wing is fitting a wing and the directions shown hereafter should guide you in the right direction.

RW2. Here's a prime example of someone cutting the surplus metal away a section at a time, rather than tearing into it and trying to remove all of the wing in one go.

RW3. It's essential that you hold the wing or repair panel against the rusty panel before doing any cutting so that you can see exactly which flanges and mounting points to leave in place and how far back to cut. This is a full wing, of course.

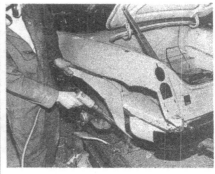

RW4. Using a professional air chisel the rearmost part of this part of the wing has been cut away ...

RW5. ... ready to be cleaned up with an angle grinder later on.

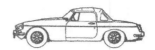

RW6. Actually, if you are doing the work at home, it's best to cut carefully and neatly, and not to leave yourself with too much cleaning up to do.

RW7. And here the rear wing lower repair panel is held up against the existing rear wing showing how much more cleaning up needs to be done. These panels can be very prone to distortion but, if you wish to use them, ensure that you get the type with a top flange on the repair panel which gives it a great deal more rigidity and resistance to distortion from the heat of welding. This type of panel is actually far easier to fit than a full wing, but of course, you've got to place a weld half way up the panel where the manufacturers never put one, and you won't have had the opportunity to replace the rust-prone moulding strip along the top of the wing. If you want to do an absolutely pukka job there's only one thing for it, and that's to replace the full rear wing.

RW8. If fitting a wing repair panel, avoid distortion by using a nibbler or mini-grinder - don't chisel!

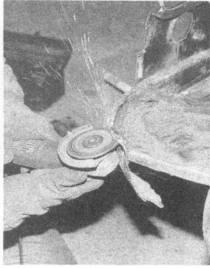

RW9. Final cutting away of unwanted metal - note gloves which must be worn!

RW10. And here, the old rear wing has been removed completely. Very often the tray situated to the rear of the inner wing and the inner wing itself have corroded. In this case there appeared to be a smidgen of corrosion in the outer edge of the inner wing. ➡

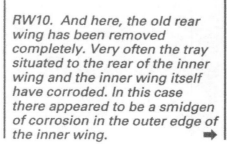

RW11. This GT inner wing was more obviously in need of replacement.

RW12. It's absolutely crucial that all the mounting flanges are cleaned back to bright metal, but it's also important that the sanding or grinding disc doesn't make the metal excessively thin. It's best to use a 40 grit sanding disc on a rubber backing pad. You really should wear thick industrial gloves and goggles to protect your eyes from sparks.

RW13. And here's what to do if the outer section of the inner wing is also rusty - cut it off! Once again, refer to the fit of the replacement panel before doing any cutting back.

RW14. The replacement inner wing panel comes with a flange around its inner edge which slots neatly into the inner part of the inner wing. All the old underseal must be removed from that part of the inner wing before (a) the fitting can be properly carried out or (b) the welding can be done. When you try it, you'll note that MIG-welding is particularly sensitive to the cleanliness of the metal on which it's being used. If the metal is greasy, painted, rusty or dirty, the weld quality will be terrible!

RW15. Before doing any welding, the rear wing (this is a complete panel) will have been clipped, screwed, and clamped in place to ensure that it fits properly. Then, when you're sure of the fit, you can MIG-weld the joint in place. ➡

RW16. The ideal way of holding the wing flange to the inner wing is by using a spot-welder. This is an SIP 'spot', and if you're doing a full restoration, it could be a worthwhile investment since the quality of the welds produced is equivalent to those carried out by the manufacturer. If this is a one-off job, however, you could try hiring a spot welder, but make sure that you get the right type of arms to enable you to carry out welding in a confined space, such as this one.

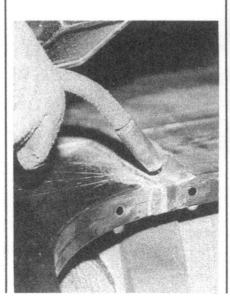

RW17. This welder, being something of a traditionalist, chose to run braze-weld along the MIG tack-welding he had carried out on the rear panel. He prefers the way in which the braze flushes into the joint, sealing it completely. On the other hand, a properly executed MIG-weld makes an equally good seal.

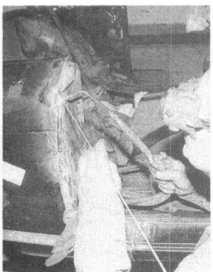

RW18. He also flushed some braze into this joint, adjacent to the B-panel. It's essential that all brazing flux is scrubbed off with hot soapy water after the braze has been completed, otherwise the caustic nature of the flux can allow corrosion to take place beneath the paintwork.

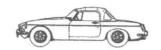

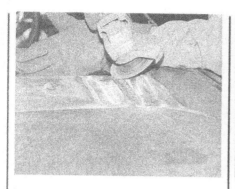

RW19. When all the brazing was completed, the excess braze was sanded off with the mini-grinder.

RW22. An alternative would be to make up your own repair section for the lower part of the B-post, especially if the area is particularly small. This part of the work is best carried out before the replacement rear wing is fitted.

RW20. Some specialists sell the inner wings in separate sections which makes them easier to fit if, for whatever reason, the outer wing is sound whilst the inner wing is being replaced.

RW21. Adjacent to the rear wing is the B-post closing panel. The original Rover unit is still available, and a small repair section for the lower end can also be purchased from Moss.

Sill Replacement

As everyone knows, the MGB was, if anything, over-designed and offers massive strength for a car without a chassis. Consequently, although it does rust badly if not protected against the ravages of the elements, it takes an awful lot of rust to make an MGB unsafe. There is, however, one area that

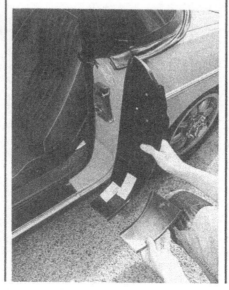

is more critical than most and which, moreover, tends to show up as being rusty only when its safety has passed the point of no return, and that is the sills area.

The MGB's sills are constructed in the form of a square-sided box section (the box-shaped part covered over by the rubber or carpet at each side of the floor) while the flat part under the door (the kick-plate area) and the curved body panel that is so much prone to stone chipping is little more than a cover. Consequently, it is never enough to replace only the outer part of the sill unless the sill has collision damage and is otherwise sound inside. What is more, whenever rust shows through the outer sill, or through the bottoms of the front or rear wings adjacent to the sills, you can guarantee that the crucial load bearing inner sills will be corroded.

Fortunately, all repair sections are available to restore MGB sills to as-good-as-new, including the jacking point which is all too often seen pressed upwards into a weakened sill structure.

Do remember, to support the car's bodyshell on a level surface, at the points where the car's roadwheels impart their thrust into the bodyshell, to reduce the risk of distortion, and remember also that quite apart from the finished job having to be sound (and if in doubt, get a pro to do the final welding at each stage) it will be judged by most people on its appearance. Check carefully at each stage that everything fits properly, and be prepared to spend a great deal of trouble getting the sill lined up correctly with the door aperture. Only take apart one side of the car at a time to retain as much rigidity as possible, but also to give a reference as to how things ought to look - it's surprising just how much can be forgotten once the job is taken apart!

Be prepared to end up doing more work than you originally bargained for. Not only is the car always more rusty after it has been taken apart than the world's worst pessimist would ever have suspected, but if the sills are bad why shouldn't the front and rear inner wings, front floor - and more - be equally afflicted? And it will be no good expecting to be able to ignore rot in adjacent areas. No one has yet perfected a technique for welding steel successfully to fresh air! However, if all this sounds too pessimistic, you can have the consolation that all your effort will result in a car which is as sound as Sid Enever, the designer, intended it and undoubtedly sounder than the 'original, un-rebuilt' MGB down the road - because you will know what the insides are like!

Toolbox

At least a 2 1/2lb hammer (a heavy hammer used lightly gives more control than a light hammer used wildly); a sharp cold chisel, preferably of the 'bolster' pattern; a number of self-grip wrenches; pop-rivets or self-tapping screws and appropriately sized drill bits; welding equipment and angle grinder (both of which can be hired); tin snips and/or Monodex cutter; metal primer; repair sections as needed.

Safety

Never work under a car that is supported by jacks or piles of bricks. Always use proper axle stands and ensure that the supports do not wobble before going underneath. Securely chock the two wheels remaining on the ground. Always wear really strong industrial gloves when working with sheet metal, and wear goggles of an approved type when sanding, grinding or

chiselling. Ensure that all tools are in good condition and follow the usual welding safety rules against 'flash' from arc welding, and fire risks, including the provision of a good quality fire extinguisher. Always remove the fuel tank and batteries before welding near the rear of the car. Remove all flammable materials (including underseal and soundproofing) from *both* sides of panels adjacent to the weld area.

SR1. If chrome over-sills have been fitted, you have to take them off first. My advice is to leave them off! They could cover a multitude of sins.

SR2. The sill on the left is what you see, and the sill in the middle is what you get. If you replace only the middle bit, you will do nothing for the strength of the car. Around half the length of the factory sill extends behind both wings, while the 'cover' sill is no more than cosmetic.

SR3. Section through a 'cover' sill cut out of a scrap car. This shot shows the basic structure of the sills and also the uselessness of the flimsy cover sill. They should be banned!

SR4. If the rubber of carpet from the inner sills is to be reused, peel it off carefully. Scrape out the flammable sound-proofing adjacent to the sills, and also remove the footwell trim panel, seat belt and any wiring or pipe work which may have been routed in this area. Have a proper powder-type, workshop sized fire extinguisher handy. Consult your supplier or Chubb (see address in Appendix) for correct type - welding fires can be very difficult to put out.

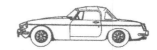

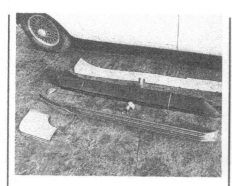

SR5. These are the basic repair sections to be used for a thorough job.

SR8. ... but a mini-grinder will also enable you to cut cleanly between the rear wing and B-post.

SR11. Here, the completely rotten sill has fallen away after chiselling along the top flange. The razor-sharp edges show clearly why gloves should be worn!

SR6. The sill extends behind the rear wings. If the rear wings are sound you can get away with cutting off the lower portion and fitting a repair panel. Use the panel as a guide for scribing a cutting line.

SR9. Cut straight through the sill and B-post joint; and here a hacksaw is ideal.

SR12. You will have to cut carefully between the rear of the sill and the rear inner wing using a bolster chisel and later cleaning up with a mini grinder.

SR7. You could use a hacksaw to cut a clean, straight line ...

SR10. If the surrounding panels are also to be repaired, you could use the sharp bolster chisel but do wear gloves!

SR13. It will also be necessary to cut the sill from around the bottom of the A-post.

SR14. Having cut the sill away from the top sill flange, drill out each of the spot-welds and carefully chisel what remains of the flange away. It will be very sharp!

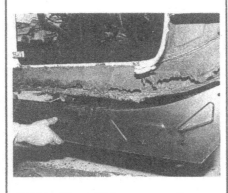

SR15. The sill inner membrane is normally invisible, but is essential for the integral strength of the sill. Offering it up shows you just how much of the old inner membrane has to be cut away.

SR16. You can now cut the old inner membrane away using, once again, the sharp bolster chisel.

SR17. The old castle section, the bottom part of the sill, can also be cut away and the remaining edges and flanges cleaned up carefully with a sanding disc on the mini-grinder.

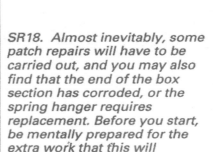

SR18. Almost inevitably, some patch repairs will have to be carried out, and you may also find that the end of the box section has corroded, or the spring hanger requires replacement. Before you start, be mentally prepared for the extra work that this will entail!

SR19. Use clamps or self-tapping screws to hold repair panels in place while they are soundly MIG-welded.

SR20. The base of the A-post is almost certain to need attention. If necessary, remove the bottom door hinge, cut out the rot and weld in new steel, complete with flanges, to take the new sill.

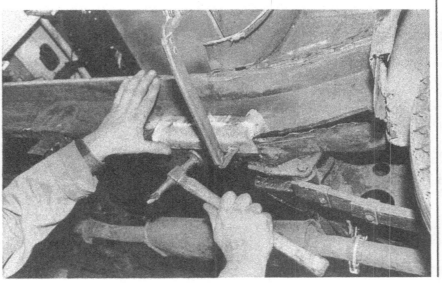

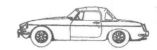

SR21. The new castle section of sill-base being offered up to check for fit.

SR22. It's best to only tack-weld it in place at this stage until, with reference to the inner membrane and the outer sill with the door fitted up, the shape of the sill and the car's bodywork can be properly determined. ⬇

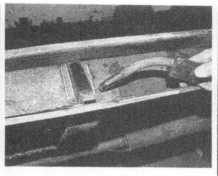

SR23. Don't forget the jacking point reinforcement plate that has to be welded above the crossmember before the inner membrane is fitted.

SR24. Assuming that the crossmember is sound, and that the jacking point has corroded, a new one can be fitted up at this stage.

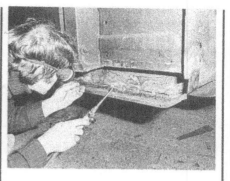

SR25. Here, a series of gas-welding tack-welds are used to soundly fix the castle section into place.

SR26. Zinc-rich primer is being used to paint any exposed metal inside the sills. Some of it will burn off when the next stage of welding is carried out, but much of it will stay in place and provide a useful barrier against rust. You will obviously inject Waxoyl when the job is complete but not before; it's highly flammable!.

SR27. The new membrane is offered up to the new castle section and the cleaned up top flanges.

SR28. A spot-welder is the ideal tool for welding the membrane to the castle section and to the top flange in the door aperture.

SR29. MIG is best for welding the top part of the membrane in place.

SR31. ... which is then completed by clamping and welding in the new jacking point.

SR33. The new outer sill section is offered up and tried for fit. Note that this car is supported on a cradle which enables it easily to be returned to the horizontal for checking alignments. The DIY repairer is recommended to work on the car in its normal position but raised, safely and securely, to a suitable working height. ⬆

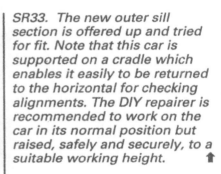

SR30. In this case, small repair sections have to be made to the end of the crossmember (they can be purchased new) ...

SR32. It cannot be over-emphasised that before the inner membrane, already described, and the outer sill, to come, are fitted, the door must be refitted to the car and the car lowered to its wheels. You can then check the door-gap top and bottom to ensure that the car has not sagged or opened up. If you allow movement to take place at this stage and then weld in the new sill sections, you will lock your MGB into a new, incorrect, shape. Not a good idea! ➡

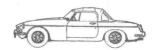

SR34. The sill is carefully clamped in place and, once again, the door refitted to ensure that the sill alignment is correct. It can be tack-welded to the A-post and then fully welded when all alignments are correct.

SR35. The top flange will now consist of three pieces of steel, and they must be dressed so that they are in close proximity to one another ...

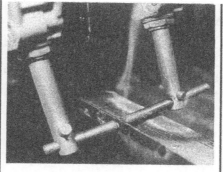

SR37. A line of close spot-welds will provide the strongest possible joint. You could seam-weld along the top edge, although it might later prove difficult to fit the door seals.

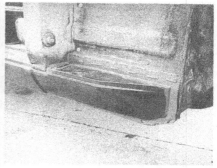

SR39. This shot shows how the height of the inner membrane is slightly above that of the sill, thus giving a good surface for welding to.

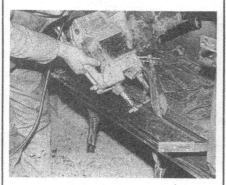

SR36. ... in order that they can be spot-welded together.

SR38. More seam-welding will allow the sill to be welded to the top of the inner membrane. Note that you should always wear gloves when MIG-welding.

SR40. At the rear of the sill, the rear wing repair panel can now be fitted. It seems like a lot of work to have to replace part of a wing that had nothing wrong with it, but it's the only way of fitting a new sill.

Floor Repair

Toolbox

All necessary repair sections; welding equipment; tin snips; sheet metal cutter; hacksaw; bolster chisel and hammer; mini- grinder; goggles and industrial gloves; Monodex-type cutter or other non-distorting panel cutter; mini-angle grinder (available from tool-hire firms); thin or electrician's bolster chisel; medium-heavy ball pein hammer; electric drill; self-tapping screws or pop-rivet equipment.

Safety

The usual safety precautions should be taken when welding and when cutting ultra-sharp sheet metal. Read carefully supplier's safety instructions with everthing you use before commencing work. Move anything flammable from around the area being welded, and remember to protect fuel lines from flames and heat. Beware cut edges in sheet metal, especially thin slivers of metal - wear heavy industrial gloves. Always wear gloves and goggles when using an angle grinder. Always remove the fuel tank when welding around the rear of the car. Watch out for welding 'spatter' when working beneath the car or inside the rear wheel arches. Note the usual safety points regarding working on a car raised off the ground.

FR1. Specialists such as Moss can supply a complete floor pan - infinitely preferably to cutting and patching unless there are only small areas of repair to consider. ➡

FR2. Invariably, there will be adjacent areas or corrosion which will need replacement after cutting out the old floor. Cut well beyond the rot to good, sound metal.

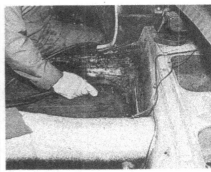

FR3. The new floor can be MIG-welded all the way around the edge ...

FR4. ... but take care when welding inside the footwell since MIG fumes can be toxic in a confined area. This work should be undertaken out of doors. In my view, the trim that can be seen in place here should have been removed before the job was carried out. (It was not done in my workshop!) Note the way a jack has been used to hold the floor 'down and in place' while the welding is carried out. Gloves should also be worn. ⬅

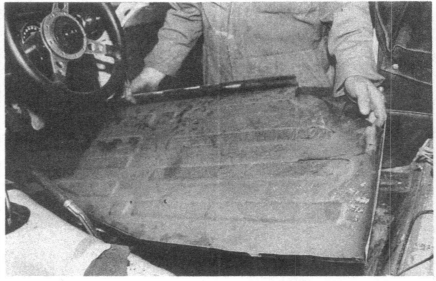

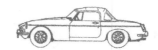

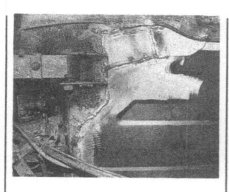

FR5. This shows how the floor repair has been cut to fit around the sound rear spring hanger. In many cases, this will have to be replaced separately.

FR6. The floor also has to be welded to the crossmember and then sealed all the way around the edge with seam sealer to prevent the ingress of water.

Boot Floor Repair

Toolbox

All necessary repair sections; welding equipment; tin snips; sheet metal cutter; hacksaw; bolster chisel and hammer; mini- grinder; goggles and industrial gloves; Monodex-type cutter or other non-distorting panel cutter; mini-angle grinder (available from tool-hire firms); thin or electrician's bolster chisel; medium-heavy ball pein hammer; electric drill; self-tapping screws or pop-rivet equipment.

Safety

The usual safety precautions should be taken when welding and when cutting ultra-sharp sheet metal. As notes on page 74. Move anything flammable from around the area being welded and remember to protect fuel lines from flames and heat. Beware cut edges in sheet metal, especially thin slivers of metal - wear heavy industrial gloves. Always wear gloves and goggles when using an angle grinder. Always remove the fuel tank when welding around the rear of the car. Watch out for welding 'splatter' when working beneath the car or inside the rear wheel arches. Note the usual safety points regarding working on a car raised off the ground.

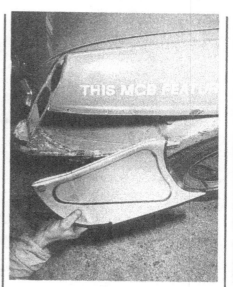

BFR1. Complete Heritage boot floors are available and, once again, it's often best to replace rather than repair. The most common corrosion area is covered by these repair sections which sit just behind the rear wing. The procedure is similar to that for the previous section. Once again, ensure that everything flammable, including fuel tank and batteries have been removed before beginning work.

Chassis Member Repairs

Toolbox and Safety are the same as for 'Boot Floor Repair'.

CR1. Strictly localised chassis corrosion can be cut out, going straight back to sound metal and letting in a repair section which can easily be fabricated in the vice. Usually, however, corrosion like this is not localised other than at the outer extremities.

CR2. As often as not, a patch repair like this is no better than a sticking plaster on a broken leg. What is really needed is for the complete area to be cut out and replaced. This is often a far bigger job than is at first apparent. ➡

CR3. Corrosion in the main crossmember should be met by replacing the whole section, although how you would stop at the crossmember and not have to replace the floors and the sill I can't imagine! Going this far is really a job for the experts in order to ensure that the crucial body structure does not become distorted. ⬇

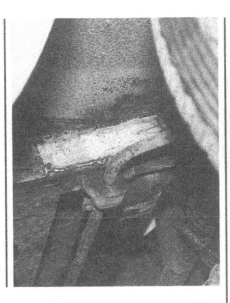

CR4. On the subject of the extremities, the rear end of the chassis rails, where the spring hangers bolt through, are prone to corrosion, and Heritage repair panels are available from specialists such as Moss. Replacement of these outer panels is certainly viable for the careful DIY repairer ...

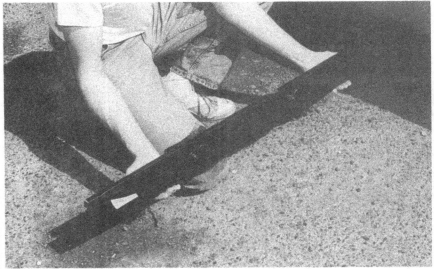

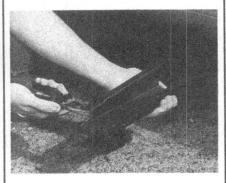

CR5. ... as is the replacement of the outer ends of the crossmember. These are non-Heritage panels and therefore they may need just a little fitting. In this case, the outer mounting flanges were cut but not bent, although a simple tweak with a pair of pliers did the job. ⬆

CR6. The front end of the spring hangers seen in the floor replacement section are available as accurately made Heritage parts; although, if they are corroded, they would need to be mounted on a much wider repair than is included in this section. However, this is the vital part, and the floor repairs that surround it are relatively straightforward to fabricate. ⬅

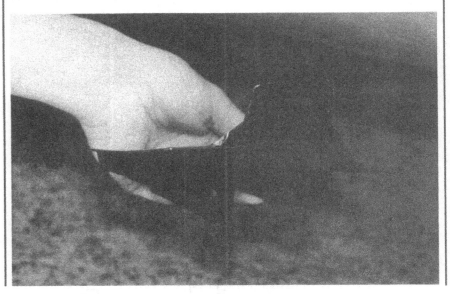

Chapter 4 **Bodywork**
Part 2: The Heritage Shell

This chapter concentrates on what is involved in building-up the bodywork on a Heritage bodyshell. Most of it also applies to the restoration of an existing shell, once the structural work described in Chapter 3 has been attended to:

The first few dozen Heritage shells were bare of front wings, doors, bonnet and boot lid. They also had a reputation for having one or two dimensional quirks! Problems occurred at fitting-up stage, and some very advanced 'tweaks' to the shell were called for. As Moss Europe's Peter Beadle put it in Moss Motoring magazine: 'The "brute force and ignorance" method of alteration has long been used by assembly staff at Abingdon and elsewhere around the world

with great success.'

Nowadays, all Heritage bodyshells come 'preassembled' with wings, doors, bonnet and boot already fitted, which reduces such problems dramatically. We purchased one of the early shells - which at least allows us to show here the problems that might be encountered when fitting all new panels to an existing shell.

Building-up the Bodyshell

HS1. Before and after! You, too, can go from a rusted bodyshell, such as this one on the left, to the partly built-up project car behind it. ⬇

HS2. A complete bodyshell, examined by Heritage's knowledgeable foreman Jack Bellinger, awaits transport outside the Faringdon factory.

HS3. A full decade after MGB production ended, David Bishop assists with the construction of one of the prototypes of the brand new MGB bodyshell.

HS4. A small-scale production line, redolent in many ways of that of the Morgan factory, produces a steady stream of new MGB shells.

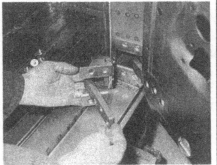

HS5. Heritage have put new door hinges back into production. They screw into the A-post with four crosshead screws into captive nuts ...

HS6. ... and on the other side of the A-post, behind where the wing will fit, the hinge is bolted into place with the aid of a large washer and a lock washer.

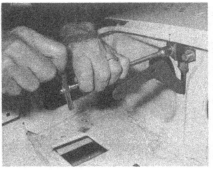

HS7. Next step is to fit the bonnet hinges. Two bolts into captive nuts inside the engine bay here ...

HS8. ... and two more inside the cockpit beneath the scuttle.

HS9. The bonnet fits to the hinges with nuts, bolts and washers, and there are slotted holes to allow adjustment.

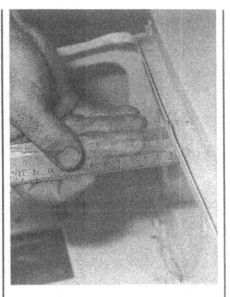

HS10. The distance by which the scuttle top protruded from the firewall varied from side to side which meant that the bonnet, in order to be fitted properly, had to be adjusted on the hinges.

HS11. The Heritage experts use flat steel levers to force the bonnet position and the bonnet hinges to take the required shape. When done skillfully, work of this sort is not a bodge! After all, you are only working with what were once flat pieces of metal; this is the process of bending them a little further in one direction or the other just as they used to do on the Abingdon production line.

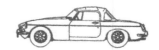

HS12. With the bonnet propped open, a new wing is offered up for fit. Needless to say, it doesn't!

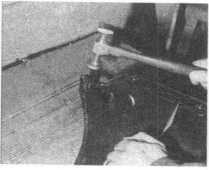

HS14. This was countered by panel-beating the wing shape to make it match that of the scuttle.

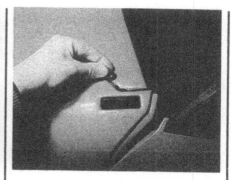

HS16. When fitting the front wing - shown in Chapter 2 - be sure to fit a spacing washer between wing and scuttle at the point of this bolt. The wing should not be pulled tightly against the scuttle. If you can't find the original, cut a new thick washer with a slot in it.

HS13. The rear end of the wing was found to be not quite the right profile.

HS15. The scuttle was also given the treatment to enable the wing to fit snugly against it.

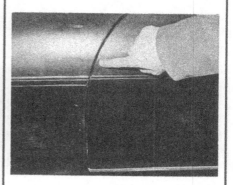

HS17. It's crucial to get the gap between the rear of the wing and the front of the door as accurate a possible. Door adjustments can be made of course.

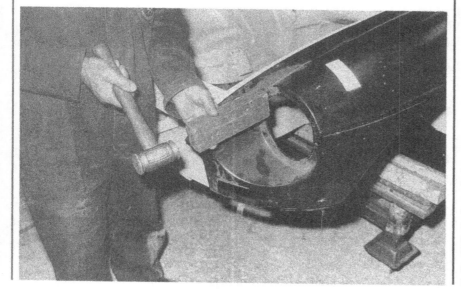

HS18. With the wing fitted but none of the bolts tightened up. The wing position can be altered by placing a wooden block in exactly the position shown here and tapping the wing backwards. Use the block anywhere else and you risk distorting the wing.

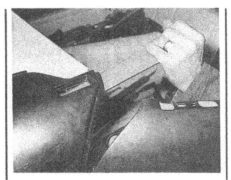

HS19. Another similar adjustment can be made to the shape of the back of the wing once the bolts have been tightened up ahead of this position or to move the whole wing forwards a touch.

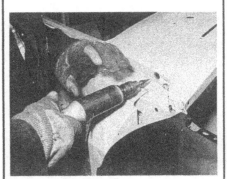

HS20. More movement will be afforded if the mounting holes in this position are opened out. This might or might not be necessary - it depends on the individual vehicle.

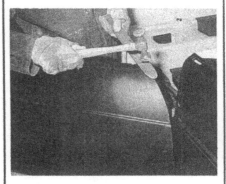

HS21. Don't forget that you can also adapt the shape of the front of the door to match the wing, although it's best not to hammer directly onto the door for fear of marking it.

HS22. It's crucial that the moulding that runs along the side of both wing and door are in complete alignment - check with a straight edge. ➡

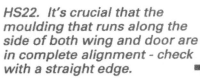

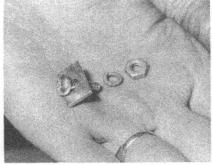

HS23. The bottom of the wing fits to the body with a small nut, bolt and washer, and a special square-shaped washer as shown.

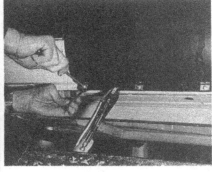

HS24. Clamp the wing in position and tighten all nuts and bolts in turn.

HS25. Where holes in the wing don't align with the holes in the body, you could grind away unwanted steel with a rotary cutter or remove the wing once again and file out the slot.

HS26. It's a good idea to put a tap through every hole to make sure that all the threads are clear.

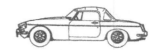

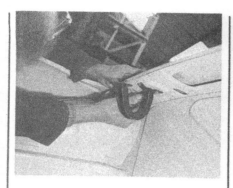

HS27. Boot lid hinges bolt simply to the inside of the rear bodywork.

HS28. The hinges themselves may need some adjustment in order for the boot lid to shut in the correct position. You can place in the vice and squeeze in order to close them up, as shown (measure carefully at each stage to ensure that you don't overdo it); or to lengthen the hinge, find a suitable piece of wood with a diameter larger than the V of the hinge and hammer it into the hinge opening. ➡

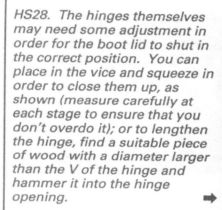

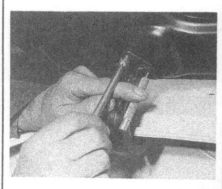

HS29. Using an odd length of steel to align the holes, start with the first screw and fit the boot lid to the hinge.

HS30. Fit all the bolts, but before tightening any of them, check boot lid fit.

HS31. Once the limits of adjustment have been reached on the hinges, extra movement can be gained by levering the boot lid as with the bonnet in HS11.

HS32. A car park of new Heritage bodyshells awaiting collection at Moss Europe's HQ in London ...

HS33. ... and the complete GT Heritage bodyshell, which also comes completely fitted up with all outer panels, thereby avoiding all the problems referred to in this section! ⬇

Donor Car Stripdown

When buying a donor car for a Heritage shell rebuild, you should aim to buy one with the specification that you want to end up with, and a car that is complete rather than in good condition. You could re-use the chrome trim and interior trim and, although they may look quite acceptable on the old car, when you come to build up the new one you will invariably find that the excellent condition of the new shell means that you simply can't live with the old components! You would be well advised to budget for purchasing as much new trim as you can possibly afford. It almost goes without saying that it would be false economy not to recondition as many of the mechanical parts as possible as you build them into the new shell.

DC1. Stripping down the old bodyshell will be a lot of fun and shouldn't take too long.

DC2. Even when you think you've finished stripping everything off the old shell, don't throw it away! You'll be surprised at the number of tiny components that you will need to retrieve later on. Keep the old shell, if you have room, until the work is complete. ➡

DC3. Parts will generally be a lot worse after you have taken them off than you thought they were beforehand. This heater unit looked to be re-usable until it was stripped out of the car.

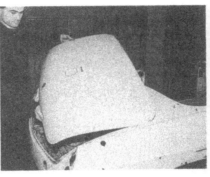

DC4. This boot lid would have been good enough to use again had it not been that we were carrying out a complete Heritage re-shell.

DC5. One front wing was good; the other in poor condition. The former was one of the items sold to recoup some of the cost of the project.

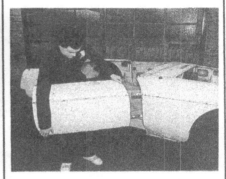

DC6. You could take the doors off the car and then store them inside, in the dry so that the components can be removed when you want them.

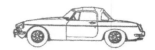

DC7. It's actually quite tricky to remove the screen by yourself and it's best to have a helper to assist in lifting the screen forwards, up and away.

DC8. As many parts as possible can be left on the engine at this stage to be stripped off when the unit is reconditioned later.

DC10. This grille was deemed to be not good enough for the project car but was still able to be sold. Don't overlook this aspect of saving at least a small part of a Heritage shell project.

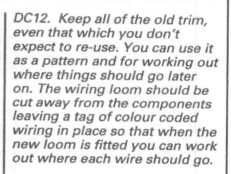

DC12. Keep all of the old trim, even that which you don't expect to re-use. You can use it as a pattern and for working out where things should go later on. The wiring loom should be cut away from the components leaving a tag of colour coded wiring in place so that when the new loom is fitted you can work out where each wire should go.

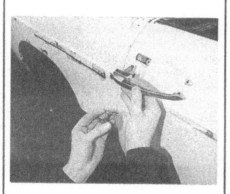

DC9. Door handles tend to last well and door locks may be perfectly re-usable provided that they operate satisfactorily.

DC11. Rear lamp units will often clean up well, and lenses benefit greatly from being washed in warm soapy water, both inside and out.

DC13. Door hinges do not always require replacement and can often be reused.

DC14. This small proportion of the parts taken from the donor car illustrates just how much room the stripped down car will take up. It would take more than the space covered by a single garage to lay out all the parts on the floor, so be prepared with plenty of racking or loft space in which to swallow the vast number of components. ➡

When stripping down the old bodyshell, take great care to label all of the parts as you take them off. You would also be well advised to invest in several rolls of colour film and to photograph every component before and after it is removed. You may well think that you will remember how much of the car goes back together but, believe me, you won't! The mass of detail will simply become a blur, and you'll be left having to work out for yourself how each individual item fits. Also obtain a roll of sandwich plastic bags and use a separate one for each collection of nuts, bolts and small fixings, labelling each one with a length of masking tape on which you can wrie with a felt pen.

Putting on the Paint

With the bodywork complete, the time usually comes when you have to decide whether to respray the car yourself or to have it carried out professionally. Quotes for professional resprays can vary widely from a low price for a quick 'blow-over', to thousands for a money-no-object 'Rolls Royce' finish. Quality has been known to vary and you don't always get what you pay for. Certainly, as the final shine (literally) on all your efforts in restoring the car's bodywork, the quality and value offered by the professional sprayer should be

carefully looked at. In the end the decision is down to personal choice, not forgetting available finances. Where you intend having a professional respray, it's always best to shop around and, better still, to use someone with whom you or other enthusiasts have had close contact.

Having said the above, it's certainly within the capabilities of most DIYers to undertake and achieve high quality spray finish at home. The key word is 'preparation'. Without a really good base on which to lay the paint, a good result just won't be achieved. A high gloss paint finish brings out even the smallest of surface imperfections. It is rather beyond the scope of this book to describe all the different techniques available, but attention to the points given below will enable a very satisfying result to be achieved. A much more in-depth treatment of home spraying, and car bodywork in general, is given in the author's book, The Car Bodywork Repair Manual, published by Haynes. Moss point out that as a rule of thumb you should allow at least four hours per panel preparation prior to painting.

Toolbox

Spray gun/compressor - hired, borrowed or bought - preferably high pressure, with a reservoir tank, but excellent results can be achieved with even basic machines, given patience. Sanding block and various grades of wet and dry paper. Though not essential, a random orbit, D/A (double action) sander reduces the preparatory elbow work considerably.

Nowadays, there are many different types of automotive paints available, including cellulose, synthetics and acrylics. More modern paints may be classed as having high gloss from the gun whereas, certainly with traditional cellulose enamel, some after-spray compounding will be regarded as the norm in order to achieve the final desired result. Again, different paints require different setting conditions, with some classed as air- drying and others needing a low temperature bake. This obviously makes the latter unsuitable for the home restorer. A further paramount issue to the home restorer is that of safety. Fumes from modern paints containing iso-cyanate, as implied by the name, can be deadly poisonous and should only be used in conjunction with

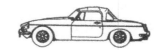

full air-fed breathing systems, usually well beyond the amateur, as outlined below. Hence, the only type of paint we can recommend for the DIYer to use is cellulose. Even with this paint a proper charcoal filter mask should be worn, and other general safety adhered to.

Safety

Cellulose paint

The spray is volatile and so are the fumes from the paint and thinners - keep away from all flames and sparks. Thinner dampened rags are also a fire hazard. The spray can cause you to lose consciousness if inhaled in a confined area. Always use a suitable filter mask (check with your paint supplier) and ventilate the work area. Simple cotton masks are just not good enough (handkerchiefs over the face are worse than useless). Protect your hands with barrier cream, or wear protective gloves when handling paint (ensure that any gloves are not themselves dissolved by the paint solvent). Keep well away from eyes. Do not use if you suffer from any alergic reaction or from any form of respiratory illness.

'2-pack' paint

Spray from this type of paint is toxic to the degree that it can be lethal! (The hardened paint on the car is not dangerous, of course!) Only use with an air-fed mask from a clean, isolated compressed air source (i.e. not from within the spray area) and never use this type of paint where the spray could affect others. It can also cause eye irritation, and eye protection should also be worn. Protective gloves should be worn when mixing and handling paint. Those who suffer from asthma or any other respiratory illness should have nothing to do with this (or

possibly with any other) type of paint spraying! There is also a fire risk with peroxide catalysts. In short, this type of paint can be seen to be totally unsuitable for DIY use and should be left entirely to the professional.

General

Don't eat, drink or smoke near the work area. Clean hands after the work is complete, but never use thinners to wash paint from the skin. Always wear an efficient particle mask when sanding down.

OBTAIN AND THOROUGHLY READ THE MANUFACTURER'S DATA AND SAFETY SHEETS BEFORE USING BODY FILLER, THINNERS, PRIMER OR PAINT. ACT UPON THEM AS RECOMMENDED.

The text in this section is in two stages. The first is taken from a series of drawings produced by Glasurit Paints, manufacturers of one of the most highly regarded brands of paint in the world, and showing the basics of how to go about respraying an MGB GT. The second covers the respraying of the project car by top-quality bodyshop, Sosna's of Hereford, who painted the

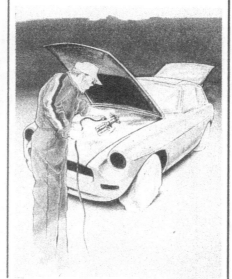

vehicle to show standards using, naturally enough, Glasurit paint. Major dings and blemishes in the bodyshell were first of all removed by Graham Macdonald in the author's workshop.

P1. Get rid of small blemishes in the bodywork before starting final preparation by using high quality body filler such as Plastic Padding. The company also produces an especially tough filler for use where lead loading would otherwise traditionally been used.

P2. Don't skimp on preparation - plan, in fact, to take several days over it, and then spray on the first coat of primer. A good deal of hand flatting followed by the application of a two-pack stopper should be followed by another coat of primer filler. ↑

P3. After another flatting session, the first coat of top coat can be applied. Go round the car painting all the tricky bits first. If you try to do them when respraying the whole body, you will invariably cause runs. ←

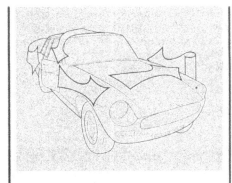

P4. Broadly speaking, this is the order in which to work, painting the roof first, followed by the back of the car and all the way around to the point where you first started.

P5. This painter has decided to start at the junction between front wing and door, although the rear corner would have been an alternative place. Note how at each stage everything is totally masked off. To avoid dust getting into the paint, you must remove the old masking and re-mask off before applying the top coat.

P6. After the first coat of finish has been applied, you will probably see lots more small blemishes, so be prepared to spend more time stopping and flatting where necessary.

P7. It is essential that the spray gun is held about a hand span away from the work piece and moved at right angles to it in strips until each panel is painted in turn.

P8. This is the order in which you should work. Do one side of the roof then skip round to the other and then if you like, you could start with an open door and work around the car in the order shown. Starting with an open door avoids the overspray that will be inevitable when you start and finish on a fixed piece of bodywork. ➡

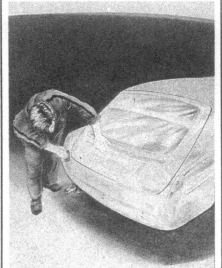

P9. You will need plenty of light in the work area to be able to see clearly the lower areas of the car bodywork. Otherwise you simply won't be able to tell how much paint you are putting on.

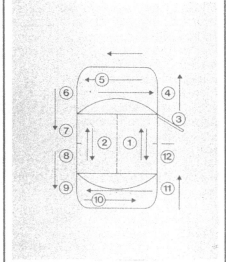

P10. After painting, you will have to polish and cut back the whole surface to remove paint overspray.

P11. In the home workshop, and using one of the less expensive guns, such as those made by Clarke or SIP, it's best to set the gun up by spraying at a piece of cardboard and using the adjustments on the gun to establish the right spray pattern and, as far as possible at this stage, spray density. ➡

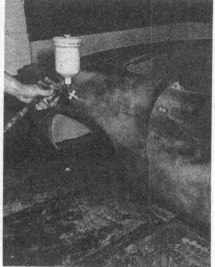

P12. Wearing a face mask, you can have several dummy runs on your piece of cardboard, but remember that the paint will not 'run' like it will on steel.

P13. Spend time thoroughly mixing the paint in the tin before starting to work with it. Spend several minutes if mixing by hand or, better still, use an electric drill with a mixer attachment.

P14. Wipe the whole of the car down with spirit wipe before attempting to spray it. This will remove any traces of grease and silicones that can devastate the paint finish.

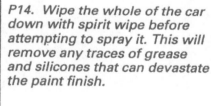

P15. Finally, and before spraying, wipe over the whole bodywork with a special sticky cloth called a Tak rag (available from DIY stores) in order to remove all traces of dust. Here Sosna's paint sprayer applies the air line at the same time to loosen any dust from cracks and crevices. Damp the workshop floor with a watering can to contain the dust. Keep the water off the car! ➡

P16. Sosna's invariably apply a guide coat before the paint proper. This is a very thin coat of a dark-coloured paint on top of the primer which, when flatted, shows any minor blemishes, enabling them to be stopped and filled before going any further.

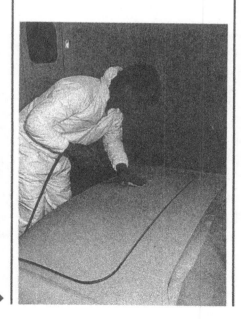

P17. After spraying the guide coat, it has to be flatted with rubbing down paper supported on a large block so that each of the hollows will be properly shown up.

P20. As described in the Glasurit section, P3, Sosna's sprayer, Mark Steadman, follows the same approach, starting with the areas around the boot lid aperture.

P22. Mark starts at the rear corners of the rear wing, getting down low where necessary as he moves forwards ...

P18. Before putting on the top coat, Sosna's sprayed a chip-resistant coat to the insides of the wings so that the finish would not be damaged by stones thrown up by the tyres. This chip-resistant primer can be over-painted with body colour and provides a really good-looking way of finishing and protecting the vulnerable areas of the car. ➡

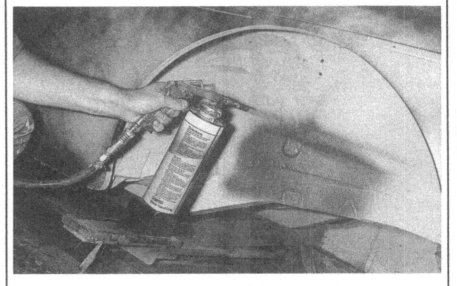

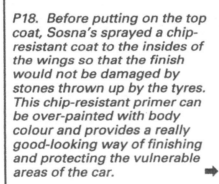

P19. Sosnas filter every last drop of paint before it is mixed, to avoid spraying dirt onto the workpiece. Filter papers can be bought inexpensively from your paint factors.

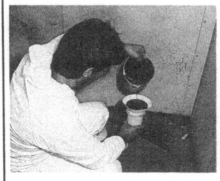

P21. He then sprays all the edges, nooks and crannies all around the car, such as at the bonnet opening.

P23. ... then, with door open, the aperture is painted ...

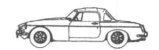

P24. ... and next the door itself.

P27. As he is moving around to the other side of the car, he pauses and does the front panels. Some sprayers would have preferred to have done this area first of all.

P30. ... Mark opens the door, using the inside of it to push it open with his hands to avoid causing any damage, and paints the rear wing, thus avoiding unnecessary overspray.

P25. The front wing is reached ...

P28. Then the bonnet is continued with front to back strips, and the right hand wing is sprayed in a continuous pattern.

P31. Then it's round to the back of the car again and the rear valance is painted ...

P26. ... and Mark works up from the bottom, so that when he reaches the bonnet he can keep going, spraying to the half-way point.

P29. After spraying the door in the closed position and painting the sill at the same time ...

P32. ... followed by the boot lid itself.

89

P33. The finished bodyshell is left for the paint to be hardened off in Sosna's extremely expensive low-bake oven which cures the Glasurit two-pack paint to an extremely tough, shiny and durable finish. The oven has also had extractor fans running while Mark was spraying, taking out as much of the over-spray as possible into a duct beneath the car to prevent too much of it falling onto the paintwork. This is something you simply cannot emulate at home. ➡

P34. Having a paint finish carried out to the fabulous standards achieved by Sosnas, using Glasurit 2-pack paint, was one of the keys in producing an MGB that would look like a showpiece but wear as well as any other 'new' car on the road. Take a look at the reflections and the shadow lines in this shot. This is a better paint finish than any that ever left Abingdon! ⬆

forming spider's webs of rust.

The only way of clearing rust that already exists is to cut it out in the case of sheet steel or to blast it off in the case of cast components.

Rust Prevention

The aim of rust prevention is to keep both moisture and oxygen away from the steel to be protected and, of course, the first line of defence must be correctly applied paintwork with a suitable etch primer such as that available from Glasurit. Etch primer bonds to the surface of the steel in such a way that any rust that does get through, for instance when the paintwork becomes scratched, is prevented from creeping underneath the paint and

RP1. The author and Graham Macdonald between them spent many hours with a sandblasting cabinet, loaned by John Fletcher, removing every trace of rust from under bonnet fittings, suspension components and the like.

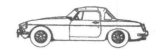

RP2. All of these components were first of all painted with Wurth zinc-rich primer, which is said to have the highest concentration of zinc of any paint primer available. This provides an excellent disincentive for rust to take further hold, especially when the components to be finished in black have been painted in Finnigan's Smoothrite, which gives an exceptionally hard and long-lasting finish. It also provides just the right shade of black for those under-bonnet components that should be painted in black. ➡

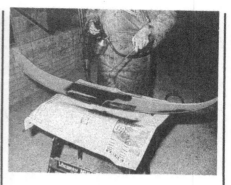

RP6. The inside of the front valance was also sprayed with Waxoyl prior to fitting it to the body.

RP3. Before applying rust prevention to the project car, Graham applied Wurth seam sealer to every single joint where water could find a way in. This involved some time crawling beneath the car and sealing off every access point.

RP5. Graham used the spray lance to introduce ordinary Waxoyl into the insides of the crossmember prior to having it fitted. Nicol Transmissions, who rebuilt the car's gearbox and rear axle had arranged for both the rear axle tubing and the crossmember to be plastic coated, which gives an exceptionally durable and attractive finish. ➡

RP4. The rust prevention kit consisted of a special spray gun, which comes complete with injector hose and spray lance (produced by SATA whose address will be found at the end of this book), and the excellent products produced by Waxoyl. All of the enclosed box sections and the bottom of the doors, as well as the insides of the framing in the bonnet and boot were, injected with conventional Waxoyl rust-proofing fluid - available in a yellowy wax colour or in black - and all of the exposed underbody areas were sprayed with Waxoyl under-body seal.

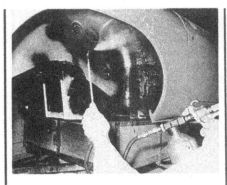

RP7. Beneath the wheel arches, Waxoyl under-body seal was applied. This never goes completely hard and is almost impervious to damage from stone chips. The sprayed-on appearance is quite attractive.

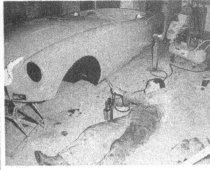

RP9. And the bottoms of the floor panels sprayed right up to the edge of the sills. Over spray was cleaned off later with plenty of rags and white spirit.

RP11. Parts of the insides of the rear wings could also be accessed through ready-made apertures - but beware! Waxoyl does tend to slide uselessly off shiny metal if you put too much on.

RP8. The rear of the under body was sprayed with the same under- body seal.

RP10. Access to the double skinned front bulkhead is easily found through various apertures cut beneath the scuttle top.

RP12. The SATA injector was used to inject fluid into all of the enclosed sections. Whilst many of them could be accessed through existing holes, some new holes had to be drilled, such as this one at the end of the toe boards - an easy spot to miss! Plug the extra holes.

RP13. All of the chassis rails and crossmembers will have to be injected of course. Access to the rear rails can only be obtained by drilling a hole at around the mid-point inside the boot. This enables the lance to reach full distance in both directions. The lance is inserted through the hole, and when it reaches the end of the chassis member the trigger is pressed on the gun. As the lance is withdrawn the inside of the box section is fully coated with Waxoyl which 'creeps' into all the seams.

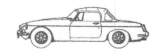

RP14. The tops of the wing beadings are prone to corrosion, but if they are sealed from above with paint and covered from beneath with fresh Waxoyl the problem should be deferred almost indefinitely.

If you are injecting Waxoyl into a car that has been restored or that is a good few years old, it may be best to mix the Waxoyl with 50% fresh engine oil. (Don't use old engine oil; the impurities it contains could cause rather than prevent corrosion). Engine oil will creep into existing rust far better than Waxoyl by itself, which can just sit on the top. Also, be sure to thin the Waxoyl down with white spirit in very cold weather so that it is runny. Standing the tin in a bowl of hot water before and during the work also helps

Don't regard rust prevention as a one-off exercise. It should be considered as part of body maintenance, and fresh Waxoyl or Waxoyl plus engine oil should be applied every twelve months, preferably after a long, dry summery period when all of the moisture is out of the car's bodywork. A cautionary tale from Moss: "Don't apply direct heat to a cold can, not even putting it on top of a radiator. It can and does, explode when hot! We know; we have done it!"

Roadster Screen Rebuilding and Refitting

The screen assembly on an MGB Roadster is a remarkably complex structure, and changing a cracked screen is time consuming to say the least! The aluminium frame has an anodised finish, and if you need to rub it down in order to remove scratch damage, refinish the aluminium with a suitable spray-on lacquer - wheel finish lacquer should be suitable. Cleaning the aluminium in this way should be carried out with a fine- or medium-grit emery cloth, followed by coarse then fine wet-or-dry paper, and finally with wire wool before using cutting compound and T-cut polish to give the finish shine. We obtained a new screen glass and rubbers from Mobile Windscreens of Worcester - find yours in Yellow Pages

RSR1. The full set of windscreen assembly components.

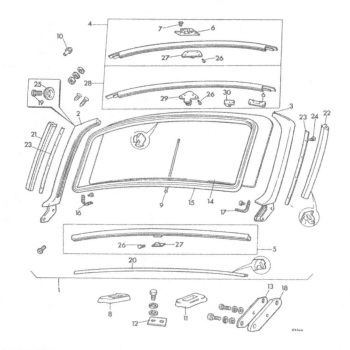

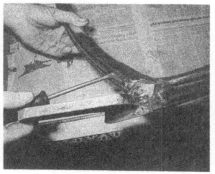

RSR2. Take apart the screen by removing all of the set screws that you will see at the ends of the top and bottom rails. The sealing rubbers will have to be pulled off first. Take as much time as you need to try to persuade obstinate screws to come free and, as a last resort, drill them out.

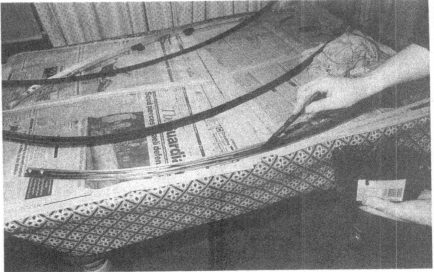

RSR3. Side rails can be tapped away using a rubber faced mallet.

RSR4. Strip all of the rubbers from the screen and screen frame assemblies. Don't even consider re-using them.

RSR5. These are the insides of the two screen pillars, showing the steel brackets that hold ➡ uprights to top and bottom rails. The brackets have been removed and in one case, where a snapped off thread could not be drilled out for fear of drilling into the aluminium, a new hole has been made and either a well fitting self-tapping screw can be used or, preferably, a new hole could be tapped for the correct size of screw.

RSR6. The plates that hold the top rail in place are themselves tapped. Drill out seized off screws with a small drill through the centre of the screw. This should enable you to screw out the remnants of the thread or to re-tap the hole. ➡

RSR7. A coat of Waxoyl inside the rails will help to protect the aluminium and steel plates against the inevitable corrosion that will take place there, and will also encourage the rails to slip onto the new windscreen rubbers more easily. ⬆

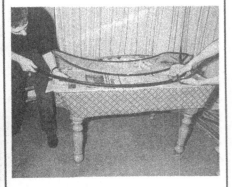

RSR8. Waxoyl helps a new sealing rubber to be slid into the bottom rail, the author pushing from one end with Graham pulling the other with a pair of pliers. It's not easy!

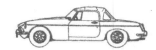

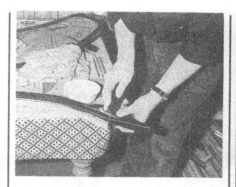

RSR9. The ends were cut off over-generously at this stage.

RSR14. The rejuvenated top (suitably Waxoyled) is pushed first of all into the top of the pillars ...

RSR10. The bottom rail was pushed onto the new windscreen rubber as far as it would go ...

RSR12. The rubber mallet was once again used to drift the pillars fully home.
Note that the sealing rubbers (Item 21, RSR1.) have been replaced at this stage. To get the old ones off, we had to cut down the line of the rubber and take out the screws (Item 24) holding the metal plates (Item 23) which reinforced the rubber. Conventional wisdom has it that these screws are born in place since no one we know has been able to tell us how they can possibly be fitted! The new rubbers were fitted without the benefit of the reinforcing strip and seem perfectly well located.

RSR15. ... and then the top rail pushed down and into place.

RSR11. ... and each of the upright pillars fitted, the steel brackets being inserted into the bottom rail. The screw holes at the end of each bottom rail have to be exposed in order to fit the screws, of course.

RSR13. New screws being inserted. Make absolutely certain that the new ones are no longer than the old, because otherwise there is a strong risk of screwing right through and breaking the new glass. Make a note when taking apart from where longer screws and shorter screws have been removed. ➡

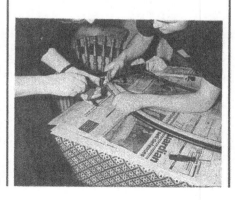

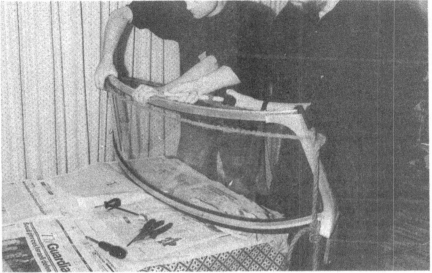

RSR16. It seemed impossible to pull the side pillars in far enough. We tied a rope around the top of the screen then made a tourniquet by twisting the handle of the mallet around and around until the rope pulled the sides in sufficiently to enable the brackets to be screwed into place. ➡

RSR17. Problem! If you're not careful part of the windscreen sealing rubber can get tucked under, which means that you will have to disconnect the frame and start that part of the operation again, just as we did!

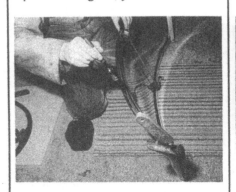

RSR18. If you've left fitting the bottom sealing rubber until this stage, now is the time to brush more Waxoyl into the slot where the rubber is fitted ...

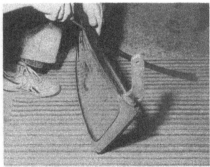

RSR19. ... before sliding the rubber in as shown previously - you may have to ease part of it in with a screwdriver - and cut it off exactly to length against the bottoms of the screen pillars.

RSR20. Back in the workshop, the newly rebuilt screen is offered up to the car.

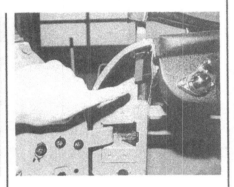

RSR21. Unfortunately, it was found to foul the slots in which it was supposed to fit.

RSR22. The Black & Decker Power File made short work of opening out the steel slot. Hand filing would be more time consuming

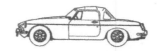

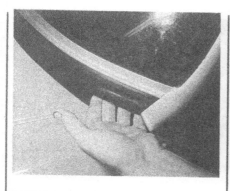

RSR23. As the screen is lowered down, lift the sealing flap along the base of the screen frame to prevent it from becoming trapped.

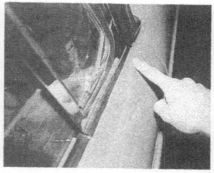

RSR26. In this case the quarter light had been moved as far as it could be against the hole in the door top.

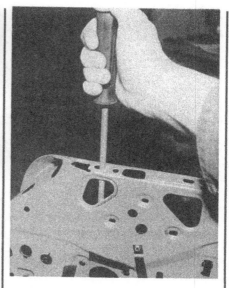

RSR24. It was necessary to fit the screen on and off several times, filing out the mounting holes so that the mounting bolts could be fitted and so that the screen could be moved to align with the door quarterlights. ➡

RSR27. A little filing out (followed by repainting with a brush) and movement in the bottom bracket in the quarterlight was all that was called for. In this sort of area Graham Macdonald proved himself a master of making things fit properly - essential if you are carrying out this sort of job.

RSR25. When fitting a new door, there may be some discrepancy between the position of the screen and the position of the quarterlight. ➡

RSR28. Aluminium spacers that fit between the legs on the bottom of the screen pillars and the bodywork should have been taken from the donor car. Make paper gaskets to fit between the aluminium spacer and the steel bodywork to prevent any risk of corrosion.

RSR29. *Behind the facia, the two mounting bolts on each side are inserted through body, through the spacer and into the threaded holes in the bottom of the screen pillars. Invariably, you have to pull hard on the screen to get it into position while someone else tightens up the bolts.* ➡

RSR34. *The fixing plate is screwed down to the dash top ...*

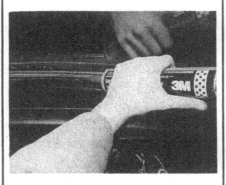

RSR30. *Before you go to the stage of seating the screen hard down on the scuttle, insert a bead of windscreen sealer both from inside ...*

RSR32. *The screen to quarter light sealing rubbers can be cut to follow the contour of the body at the bottom, slid down as far as they would go and cut off flush at the top.*

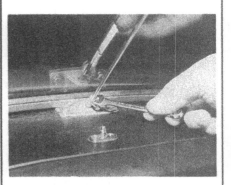

RSR35. *... and the tie-rod screwed into the fixing plate.*

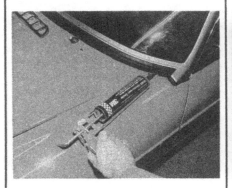

RSR31. *... and from outside the car.*

RSR33. *This is the tensioning rod that fits betwixt screen top and scuttle in the centre.*

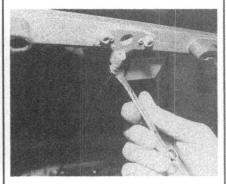

RSR36. *Similarly, it is screwed into the fixing plate on top of the screen.*

RSR37. *The rear view mirror bracket screws on to the top screen, providing a firm mounting point for the rear view mirror.*

Note that, although our 1969 MGB would not originally have had sun visors, we decided to fit them anyway as a desirable extra and one that was available on later cars. Also note that, ideally, you should fit the chrome finisher that goes over the end of the door seal, to the scuttle where the finisher has to go beneath the end of the screen. It is impossible to fit later - see Trim section for details.

The windscreen on the MGB is a most critical part of the car. It is an important part of the car's visual appearance, and its fit to the quarter lights is important both from the aesthetic point of view and that of water and draught sealing. You may, as we did, have to spend a very considerable time getting the screen frame to fit the car properly, but it will be time well spent. It is obviously best to trial fit the windscreen before painting the bodyshell. Don't assume as we did, that the screen would fit the bodyshell! Also remember that a new dashtop can only be fitted with the screen removed from the vehicle, see Chapter 5.

Quarterlights - Repair and Refit

At the time of writing, original

quarterlights are not available, and the only option is to refurbish the old ones or to use new 'repro' items that do not fit particularly well. Undoubtedly, in the fullness of time, new items will become available, although they're bound to be expensive. Keep in touch with your specialists, such as Moss, to check on progress.
STOP PRESS: New quarter lights became available just before this book went to press.

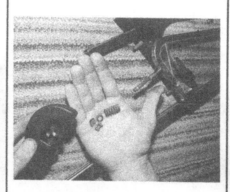

QL1. *The quarter light swivel passes through the bottom of the quarterlight frame and is held by a nut, washer and spring. The nut is almost always seized solid and the spring prevents you from cutting through it. We used a Sykes-Pickavant nut splitter to break the nut in two, freeing the spring and releasing the quarterlight from the frame.*

QL2. *With the nut out of the way, the quarterlight lifts up off the swivel and out of the frame.*

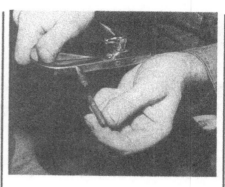

QL3. *As it happened, the swivel pin had rusted through and was redundant in any case. Typical! A repair was called for.*

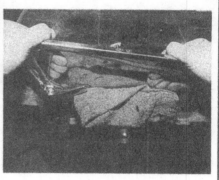

QL4. *First the glass had to be removed from the quarterlight frame. The glass was held in the vice with a rag to prevent damage, and the frame pulled from the glass and rubber.*

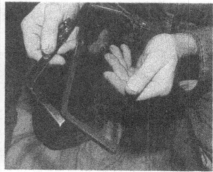

QL5. *The glass being removed totally from the frame.*

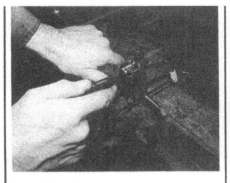

QL6. Graham used the junior hack saw to cut between the bottom of the frame and the stainless steel tube that surrounded the swivel pin.

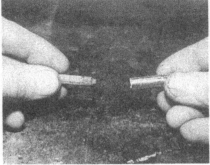

QL9. ... which released the remnants of the swivel pin and allowed it to be pulled out.

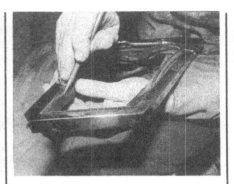

QL12. Graham Macdonald meticulously eases new sealing rubbers, as supplied by Moss, into the quarterlight frame.

QL7. This shows the head of the pin and the remnants of the swivel.

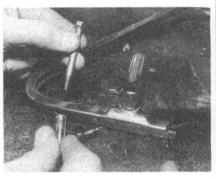

QL10. An ordinary steel bolt was used in place of the original swivel pin, and the stainless steel spacer tube was pushed over the bolt and held in place with a dab of epoxy resin glue.

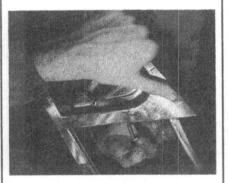

QL13. The quarterlight glass having been reassembled, the swivel pin was treated to a dab of Comma Copper Ease which would help prevent future corrosion.

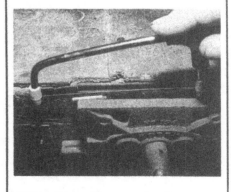

QL8. Somehow we had to re-use that distance tube, but we had no means of accurately drilling the swivel pin out of it. We compromised by cutting along the length of the tube ...

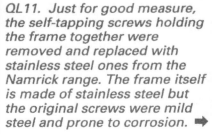

QL11. Just for good measure, the self-tapping screws holding the frame together were removed and replaced with stainless steel ones from the Namrick range. The frame itself is made of stainless steel but the original screws were mild steel and prone to corrosion. ➡

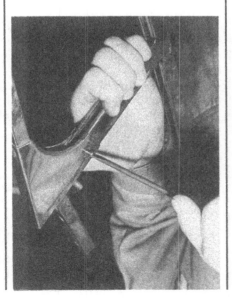

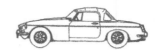

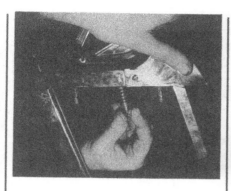

QL14. After some hunting, suitable size new springs were found and stainless steel washers and lock nuts fitted.

QL17. ... the specially remanufactured blanking plug into which the door window glass slides ...

QL20. New mounting plates were purchased - from Moss yet again! - and screwed to the bottom of the quarterlight frame and through the holes already provided in the door. These new items are now produced in bright zinc-plated form which proofs them against corrosion.

QL15. The lock nut was tightened sufficiently to provide enough friction to enable the quarter light to stay open.

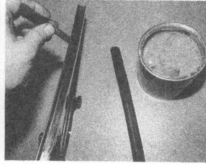

QL18. ... and the window channel seal which we glued into place.

QL21. We quickly found that the holes in the door did not align with the threaded holes in the quarterlight. ⬇

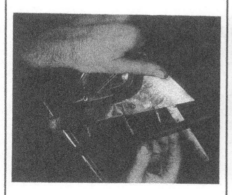

QL16. Moss once again came to the rescue with a supply of all the rubbers necessary for putting the quarter light back together, including the sealer at the bottom of the quarterlight frame ...

QL19. The quarterlight is simply slotted down into the top of the door.

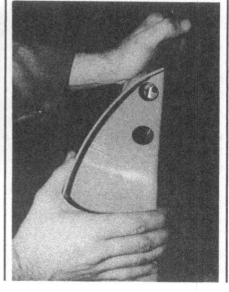

QL22. The quarterlight was lifted out, twisting it to get the bracket through the hole in the top of the door ...

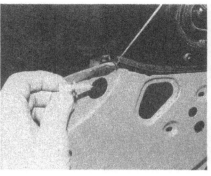

QL24. This is one of the special bolts used for securing the quarterlight to the door frame at the top.

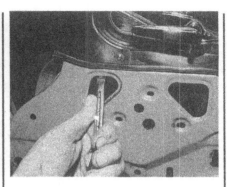

QL27. ... which can be reached through special access holes in the top of the door frame.

Door Locks, Latches and Alignment

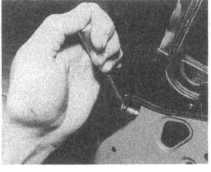

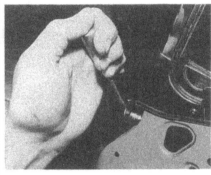

QL25. It can be reached through the access hole in the top of the door frame, although a little more filing out might be called for.

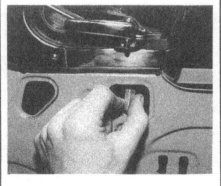

QL26. The two studs at the bottom of the quarterlight frame have to be fitted with these special nuts ...

DL1. The door latches are held to the B-post by means of these plated and threaded plates.

QL23. ... and the holes drilled out to give sufficient clearance.

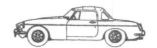

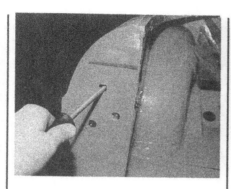

DL2. Once again, you may have to file out the holes in a new bodyshell to enable the screws to get through.

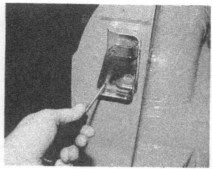

DL5. Crosshead screws go into threaded plates; the latch can be moved in all directions to give the necessary adjustment.

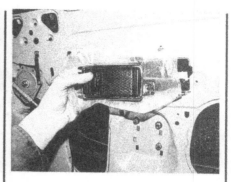

DL8. The internal door handle can be screwed into place, not forgetting to reuse the sealing plastic which is held in place with mastic.

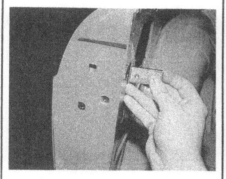

DL3. This is the top plate: both of them slot through the access hole provided on the inside of the body.

DL6. The striker plate is inserted through the holes provided in the door ...

DL9. The lock control rod, which links the internal handle with the lock mechanism, joins the latter by means of this metal and plastic clip.

DL4. Refurbish the old latches by sandblasting and spraying, or use new plated units such as those we obtained from Moss. Always fit a new gasket between latch and bodywork.

DL7. ... and screwed into the captive nuts already fitted.

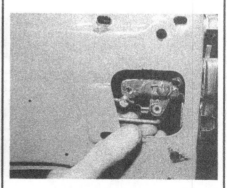

DL10. The clip is pushed into the lock assembly, and then the rod pushed into the clip.

DL11. The lock itself is inserted from the outside of the door, and the operating fork pushed over the relevant part of the locking lever on the striker plate. This is shown as Item 21 in DL19.

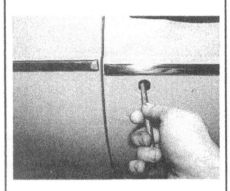

DL12. Surprise, surprise! The hole for fitting the lock had to be opened out with a file on the project car.

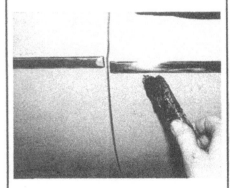

DL13. The bared edges were treated with Waxoyl.

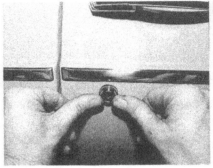

DL14. The lock can be fitted into place, but not forgetting to fit the rubber gasket between the lock and the door panel.

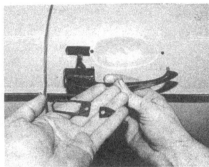

DL15. The external door handle also has to have gaskets between it and the paintwork ...

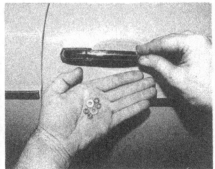

DL16. ... and is secured on the inside of the door skin with a plain washer, lock washer and nut.

DL17. It pays to carry out this part of the work before fitting any of the lock mechanisms. Graham physically twists the door shell to make it shut evenly against the B-post.

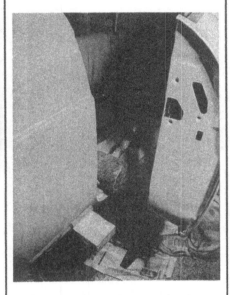

DL18. If the top of the door is protruding too far, place a rubber mallet on top of the sill and push the door hard along the top against the mallet. Take care not to dent the steel at the top of the door skin with the ball of your hand.

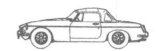

DL20. This is the anti-burst mechanism fitted to door units from GHN5 and GHD5 models, from vehicle number 294251. It is fitted to the door pillar, although provision may not be made on all Heritage bodyshells. ➡

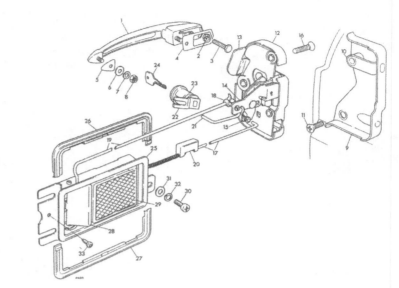

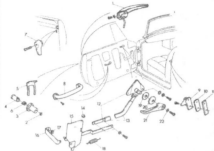

DL19. These are the handle, lock and latch mechanisms fitted to earlier cars.

Door Glass Channels and Window Winder

DG1. After fitting the quarterlight as shown in an earlier section, the window seal can be fitted to the door frame by first drilling holes, using the seal itself as a template ...

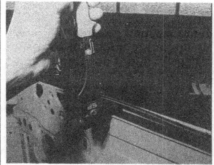

DG2. ... and then pop-riveting the seal in place.

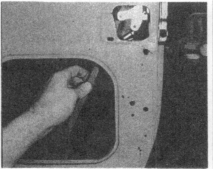

DG3. The rear window channel can be inserted into the door frame ...

DG4. ... the plated bracket is added - work out which way it goes! ...

DG5. ... and the retaining nut fitted with its large flat washer, but not yet fully tightened.

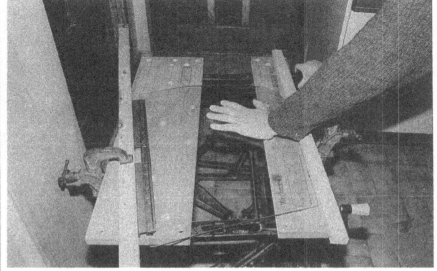

DG6. The top of the channel is secured with the crosshead screw and washer as shown. New channel inserts had already been added as shown in the section on Quarterlight Repair.

DG7. New rubbers were fitted to the window winder channelling: the rubber itself is available but, at the time of writing, new channelling is not. They will no doubt be put back into production at some time, but in the meantime good second-hand channelling can be found. ➡

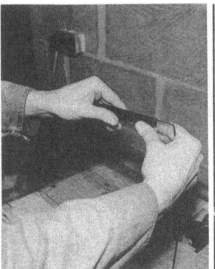

DG9. ... to use pressure. The versatility of the Black & Decker Workmate can be seen here. Throw a heavy cloth over the whole thing before tightening up to protect yourself against the risk of the glass shattering. ⬆

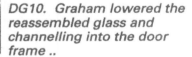

DG10. Graham lowered the reassembled glass and channelling into the door frame .. ⬇

DG8. The replacement channelling is held over the rubber and Graham Macdonald and I started to fit it by tapping with a rubber mallet. After a few heart-stopping moments we decided it would be safer ...

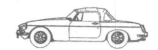

DG11. ... and with the rear channelling back as far as it would go, slotted the glass into place. You may find it necessary to disconnect the rear channelling altogether, in order to give sufficient clearance.

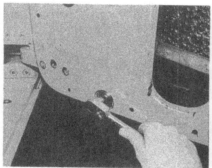

DG12. With the glass able to be pushed smoothly up and down, but without having excessive free movement, the bottom of the quarterlight and both ends of the rear channelling can be tightened up.

DG14. The regulator assembly is introduced into the door-casing, and the rollers are slid onto the channelling on the bottom of the window glass.

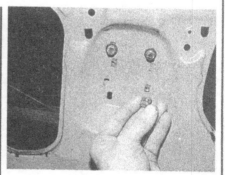

DG15. The regulator retaining bolts are fitted at this end of the mechanism ...

DG13. The window winder mechanism, known as the 'regulator' (Item 7) can be fitted next. Item 8 is a pad that fits behind the door trim and Item 6 a buffer - you may have to fabricate your own - against which the window stops when it is wound fully down. We used a pair of household rubber door stops available from a DIY centre.

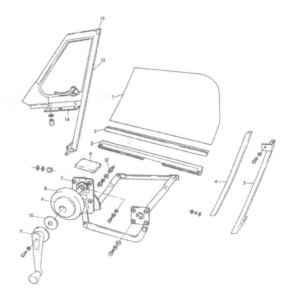

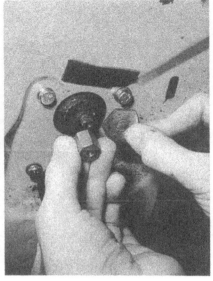

EW2. On later models, those
with plastic window winder
handles, a large hexagon is
fitted over the window winder
spindle. This has to be levered
off with a little bit of brute force
and a pair of large screwdrivers.
The Servoglide adaptor (left) is
held on with the screw
provided. ←

DG16. ... and at this end, too.
The extra holes in the new door
are to enable current MGB
doors to cater for all the various
types of lock, latch and window
winder mechanisms that have
been available over the years.

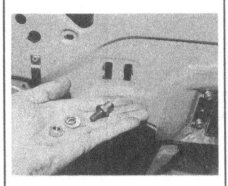

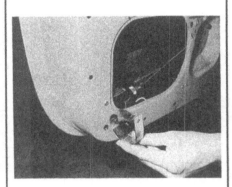

Safety

**Lucas advise that it is
dangerous to operate the
windows whilst checking or
adjusting any item in the door.
The motor is very powerful and
the mechanism could cause
injury.**

DG17. The top window stops
were missing from our donor
car (Item 12 DG13), but Graham
had the bright idea of pressing
into service a pair of spare
engine rocker box studs. They
do the job perfectly!

EW1. The Lucas Servoglide
electric window kit is a high
quality unit that adds an air of
modern luxury to your MGB.
Here's how we interpreted the
fitting instructions to suit the
peculiarities of the MGB. ↓

EW3. There is only one place
for the motor to fit satisfactorily,
and that is in the bottom corner
as shown, using the Servoglide
bracket provided.

Fitting Electric
Windows

Toolbox

Hacksaw; file; pliers; PVC tape;
centre punch; electric drill and
selection of twist drills; flat-
bladed and crosshead
screwdrivers.

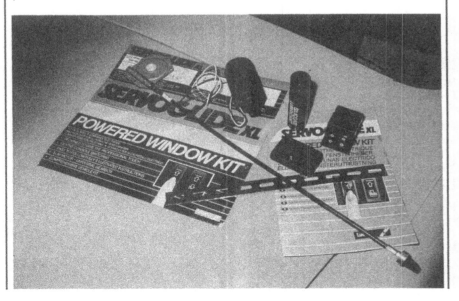

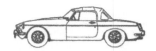

EW4. This enables the drive cable to reach the motor in the smooth sweep stipulated in the instructions. Allow the cable to run outside the door frame, and the necessary bulge in the door trim will be even from front to back, and will not be noticeable.

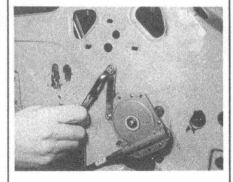

EW5. In order to prevent the gearbox from turning under the torque transmitted through it, this locating strap has to be fixed to the door frame.

EW6. A cut-out switch is screwed to the bottom of the door frame - screw position shown here - and has to be fitted so the window channel touches the operating lever on the micro switch just as the glass reaches the bottom of its travel. ➡

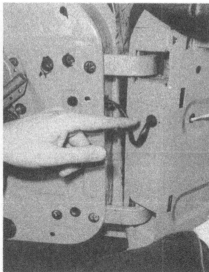

EW7. The wiring diagram provided in the Servoglide manual is extremely comprehensive. The grommets in the door and the A-post should be fitted so they do not directly line up, and this will enable the cable to tuck itself neatly out of the way as the door is closed. Bring the wiring into the cockpit of the car in the position shown.

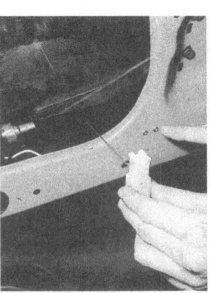

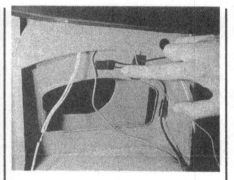

EW8. We decided to fit the thermal cut-out above the transmission tunnel and beneath the dash and thus well out of harm's way and away from heat from the car's heater.

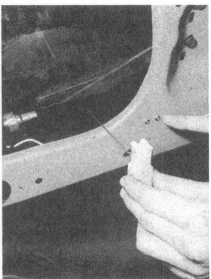

EW9. The pair of operating switches are wired as described in the manual. A housing is provided with the kit, but we decided to fit them to the switch holes in the console. The holes in the console were slightly too wide for the switches, and we had to cut two thin strips of plastic which were glued into the holes with great care using aircraft-modelling cement. Since the plastic we used was from another redundant console, the results were excellent.

EW10. *These plastic covers are fitted to the trim to hide the operating mechanism, and an emergency-use winding handle is provided as part of the kit.*

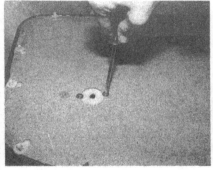

EW12. *The plastic covers have to be fitted to the trim after it has been removed from the door, and are held from the back by a pair of self-tapping screws.*

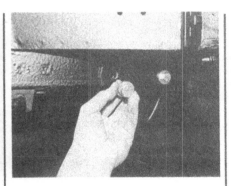

FRB2. *For the front bumper, the front-most bolt passes straight through the chassis with a nut and a washer on the other side, while the rear-most bolt screws into a captive nut.*

Front and Rear Bumpers

FRB1. *All six bumper brackets - two from the front and four from the back - were sandblasted and painted with Wurth zinc-rich primer and Smoothrite, and new zinc-plated bolts were obtained from Moss.* ⬇

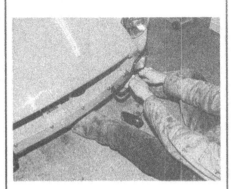

FRB3. *Graham found that the easiest way of getting the bumper brackets into shape was to fit them and then apply some brute force and ignorance.*

EW11. *We recoloured the plastic covers with Humbrol Krylon PVC paint so that they match the colour of the car's interior trim, but in the end we reverted to black covers because the colour contrast looked better.*

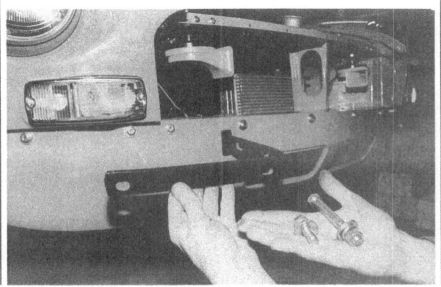

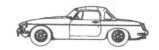

FRB4. Also from Moss came a complete set of bumper mountings, rubbers and chrome bumper bolts.

FRB7. The shaped spacers allow you to tighten up the bumper bolts, pulling the bumper against the mounting brackets without causing any distortion.

FRB10. ... before bolting the overriders in place at the prescribed position.

FRB5. The outer front bumper mountings bolt onto the front valance, utilising the rubber buffer as shown.

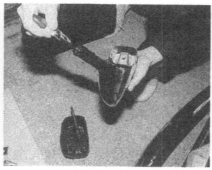

FRB8. Over a long period of time, overriders rust from the inside-out. We gave them the Waxoyl treatment ...

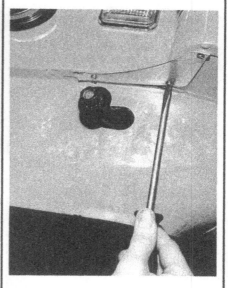

FRB11. At the rear end, the sandblasted and painted bumper brackets had already been fitted. It was also necessary to fit the finishing plates used to fill the gap between the curve of the bumper and the shape of the bodywork. Trial fit the bumper first, offer up the aluminium plates and mark their position with a felt pen, then drill and screw them in place - preferably with stainless steel self-tapping screws as shown.

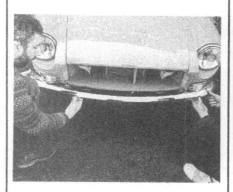

FRB6. Graham Macdonald and the author offer up the front bumper for trial fitting.

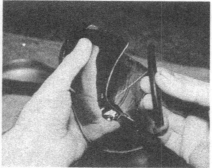

FRB9. ... and then fitted the new rubber fillet strips ...

FRB12. When offering up the rear bumper, it pays to have two people doing the job, otherwise there is a real risk of the bumper ends damaging the bodywork. Rover Group bumpers are now very expensive, although available new. We used Moss's own non-original bumpers, which are almost as good and a fraction of the price. It really is not worth considering having old bumpers rechromed since the cost would probably exceed that of buying new.

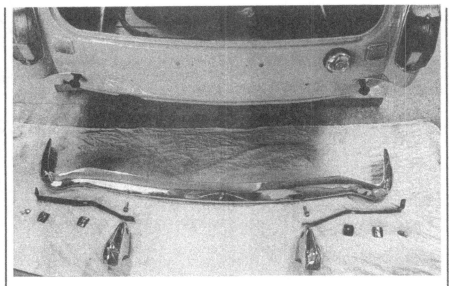

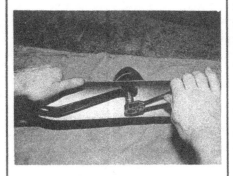

FRB13. Rear bumper brackets have to be bolted to the bumper along with the over-riders before offering the bumper up to the car ...

Bonnet and Boot Fixtures and Fittings

Surprisingly, the new bonnet did not come with a bracket for mounting the telescopic stay, and since we wanted to fit that type of stay rather than the older prop type, we had a choice between obtaining a new bracket or fabricating one. The original bracket is pressed with a reinforcing rib and so we decided to go for the former.

BB2. Two holes were drilled in the bracket and it was fitted to the new bonnet with a pair of self tapping screws.

FRB14. ... and two large nuts and washers hold the whole assembly in place.

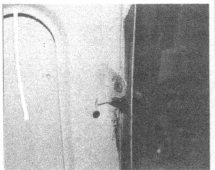

BB1. A scrap boot lid provided a stay mounting bracket. It was cut out with a chisel and then the spot welded and unwanted metal on the back of it ground away with a mini-grinder.

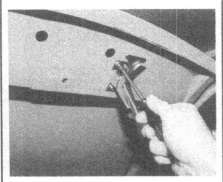

BB3. The bonnet safety catch is held on with three crosshead screws.

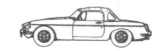

BB4. The lock consists of a threaded plunger, a large special washer and a spring to hold the washer tight against the head of the plunger. The plunger screws into a captive nut which is an integral part of the bonnet. ➡

BB8. We used this clamp to secure the bonnet release cable inside the engine bay.

BB5. The bonnet release catch (left) is fitted beneath the closing panel with the locating cup secured to the top of the panel with the same three bolts.

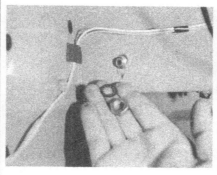

BB7. Viewed from inside the left hand footwell, the bonnet release cable outer is fitted through the hole provided and held with a lock washer and nut.

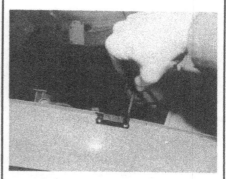

BB9. New bonnet stop rubbers are screwed down to the rain channel alongside the front wing tops.

BB6. The safety latch (bottom, right) is screwed down with two crosshead screws. At this stage, we had decided to repaint the components with silver Hammerite rather than with black. The bonnet pull cable is attached and clamped into position as shown. ➡

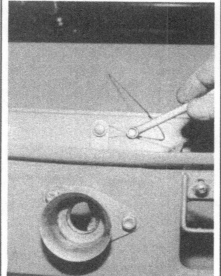

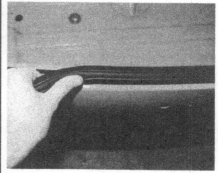

BB10. At the rear of the car, new boot seals are a push fit around the lip of the boot opening.

BB11. Use a fresh gasket when screwing the boot release handle into place on the boot lid.

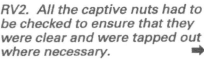

RV2. All the captive nuts had to be checked to ensure that they were clear and were tapped out where necessary. ➡

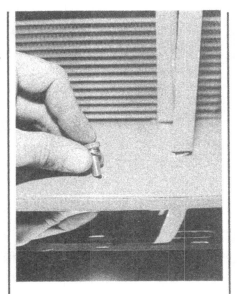

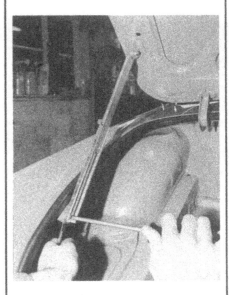

BB12. Lock nuts are used to secure the bonnet and boot telescopic stays so that they can be left loose enough for the stays to pivot on their catches without risk of them coming undone. ↑

Radiator and Ventilator Grilles

RV1. We originally intended to re-use the donor car's grille, but the finished result of the rest of the car was looking so good, we decided to go for new. ➡

RV3. The grille bolts down to the 'floor' ...

RV4. ... and three brackets hold the grille along its upper surface. The grille should always be trial fitted before spraying the car in case any adjustments have to be made to the grille aperture.

RV5. *The original ventilator grille was fine, but we obtained this insect screen accessory from Moss. Why was it never fitted as standard?*

Chrome Trims and Badges

The thought of the drill slipping whilst drilling a hole for new trim or badges in a freshly painted car is enough to bring you out in a cold sweat. You could drill all the holes before the car is painted but then you'll risk the panels having to be realigned and the chrome strips not lining up properly.

You could place a strip of masking tape along the panel to be drilled, mark out and drill carefully as before. The masking tape will help to prevent the drill from slipping. Alternatively, you can take your life into your hands as we did and proceed with care!

CTB2. *The special fixing washers come integral with their own pop-rivets.*

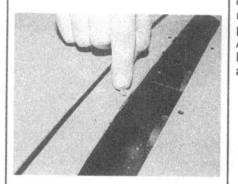

RV6. *Soft plastic bushes are pushed into the holes in the bodyshell ...*

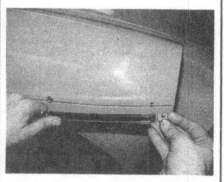

CTB3. *Graham applied a dab of grease to each one to provide extra corrosion resistance.*

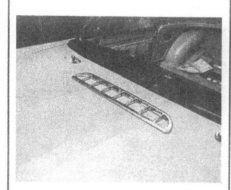

RV7. *... and the pegs on the bottom of the grille pushed through the mesh and into the plastic bushes.*

CTB1. *Measure accurately, line the holes up with a straight edge and a felt pen, use a sharp, fresh twist drill, and turn the chuck a few times by hand to get it started and so reduce the risk of slipping.*

CTB4. *These special clips push into the ends of the chrome trim. There's one for the front wing ...*

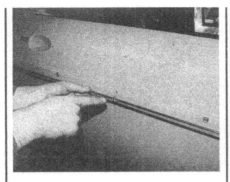

CTB5. ... one for the middle of the door trim ...

CTB8. The chrome trim is clipped onto the circular body clips...

CTB11. The position of the letters 'MG' were also marked on the template, and it was a simple matter to tape it down to the boot lid and drill through the positions indicated.

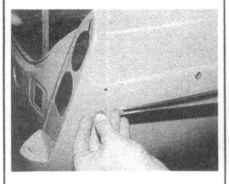

CTB6. ... and one for the back of the rear trim ...

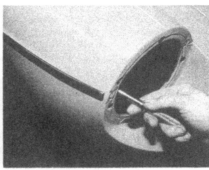

CTB9. ... and the three special clips lightly tightened - but take care not to snap the threads!

CTB12. All of the holes were dabbed with Waxoyl so that no bare metal was left untreated, and the surplus wiped off later.

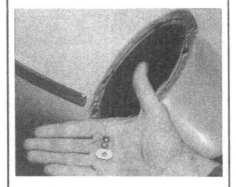

CTB7. ... and all are held with a large washer, spring washer and small nut.

CTB10. Chrome badges often break as they are removed, and the legs do not necessarily always appear in exactly the same place! We made a paper template from the new badges that we obtained from Moss, and we located the centre of the hexagon 44.5cm from the top of the boot lid. You should check this measurement for yourself!

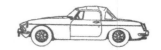

CTB13. The smaller 'MGB' badge only has to have two holes drilled, and the position of these was marked on a piece of masking tape.

CTB14. Each piece of the badge was carefully inserted through the holes ...

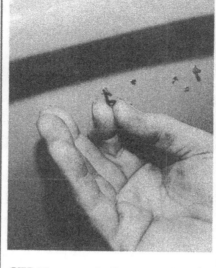

CTB15. ... and clipped on from the back with these tiny push-on spring clips. Don't be tempted to use the same sort of clips that are available for fitting the ventilator grille since they leave the badges standing proud, and can always be seen.

Door Mirrors

DM1. The door mirror mounting plate is used as a template for marking the positions of the fixing screws. ⬇

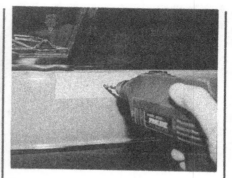

DM2. Masking tape provides a useful means of allowing you to 'write' on the door, and also helps to prevent the drill from slipping.

DM3. After treating the holes with more Waxoyl, the 'wall plugs' provided with the mirror are fitted into the holes.

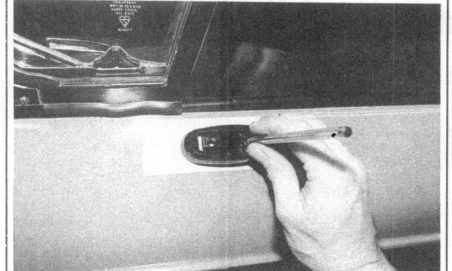

DM4. These allow you to screw the crosshead screws provided through the mounting plate and tightly into the door skin.

DM5. The mirror is held to the mounting plate with a single retaining screw. To be honest, it's a poor piece of design because the mirror drops off rather readily but there's no alternative if you want originality.

Number Plates

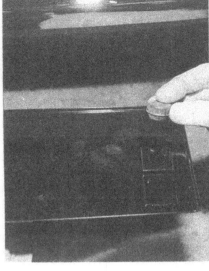

NP3. The rear backing plate includes brackets into which these rubber distance pieces are slotted.

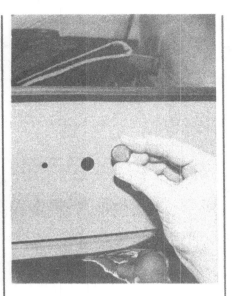

NP4. This redundant hole was filled with a grommet. The backing plate mounting holes can be seen to the left of it.

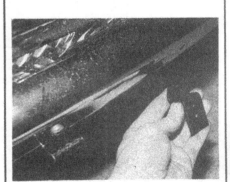

NP1. Front mounting brackets bolt directly to the holes provided in the front bumper.

NP2. After the steel backing plate has been screwed to the brackets, the number plate itself can be screwed to the backing plate. Our traditional style number plates were made by Serck Marston, who most people associate with the manufacture of MGB radiators and oil coolers. →

Chapter 5
Interior and Trim

Introduction

One of the great things about restoring an MGB is the availability of original parts simply not available for most classic cars. For instance, just about every variation of original trim can be purchased, and Moss Europe, run by Graham Paddy, has long been at the forefront of those companies involved in putting original trim materials back into production. With the project car we took a slightly different approach. We decided to go for comfort rather than originality as part of our drive to make the project car a true 'MGB for modern times'. There is no discernible difference between the techniques involved in fitting the modified trim shown in this section and fitting that of an original specification, and we have included information on how to retrim an existing seat with a new trimming kit.

I&T1. The project car was retrimmed at the Moss Europe workshop in London by two of Moss' ace mechanics: Alan Sinclair and Chris Redfern. A lot of trouble was taken to assemble every single piece of trim before beginning the work, which was completed in one long working day.

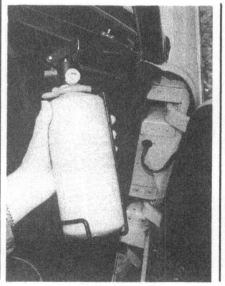

I&T2. Not strictly part of the trim, but the interior is where it went. This is the Chubb Conquest Fire Extinguisher that we selected to protect our pride and joy.

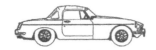

I&T3. The finished interior, complete with leather seats, looks fabulous, with lots of small details coming together to make a very luxurious and very comfortable MGB. ➡

Dash Top Trim and Vents

Safety

Read Appendix 1 on 'Fumes' when using volatile adhesives. Work in a well-ventilated area away from sparks, heat or flames. Don't smoke!

DTT2. The new trim is supplied in a long rectangle which has to be cut to fit. Use the old trim as a template or make a new one out of paper.

DTT4. Aerosol spray-on adhesive is by far the easiest to use but - IMPORTANT! - use only non-ozone damaging, CFC-free aerosols and only those whose solvent is non-injurious to health. Work in a well-ventilated area, away from flames. DON'T SMOKE! ⬆

DTT1. The vinyl trim on the dash top can only be replaced with the screen removed. Graham Macdonald began by masking off the surrounding area.

DTT3. A sharp craft knife can then be used to cut the trim to shape.

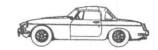

DTT5. The new trim can be positioned precisely on the dash top.

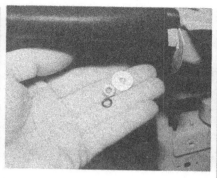

DTT8. The trim rail is placed on the front of the dash and the large washer, spring washer and nut provided fitted to each screw.

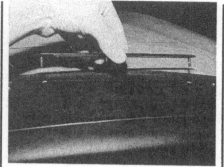

DTT10. The vent tops have a threaded screw at each end ...

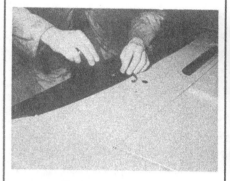

DTT6. With the surplus tucked between dash top and front wing, vent cut-outs can be made with the craft knife.

DTT9. Tighten each one lightly but don't over tighten.

DTT11. ... and the ventilator unit from beneath passes over these screws, and the whole lot is held together with spring washers and nuts.

DTT7. The trim material is wrapped around the front of the dash panel and the holes punched in the panel cut-out to accept the padded trim-rail mounting screws which are an integral part of the trim rail.

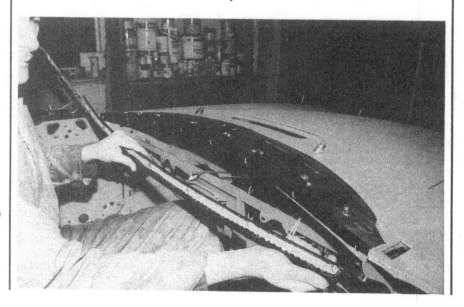

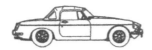

DTT12. Ventilator tubes tend to become old and brittle, so it pays to fit new at this stage. Note that the connecting elbows, joining the tubing to the air inlet holes in the bodywork, are obtained separately.

Dashboard - Standard

DB1. New dashboards are not available, but Moss will supply reconditioned ones on an exchange basis. The indicator light lenses had to be retrieved from the old one. Take yours off before sending in the old unit for reconditioning.

DB2. They're held to the dash with crosshead screws.

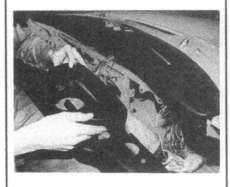

DB3. The instrument hood is also screwed to the dash panel with screws from the rear.

DB4. The first job was to offer up the reconditioned dash, and it was here that we discovered the biggest discrepancies with this early Heritage shell.

DB5. The right hand fixing bracket had to be slotted, in an attempt to make the bracket reach the captive nut provided. In the event the captive nut came free!

DB6. Since it was impossible to relocate, we fitted this part of the dash with a strong, hexagonal headed self-tapping screw. Later bodyshells are said to be much improved in this respect!

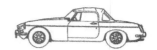

DB7. Another discrepancy came with the mounting points for the steering column, and here a little filing was all that was necessary to put matters right.

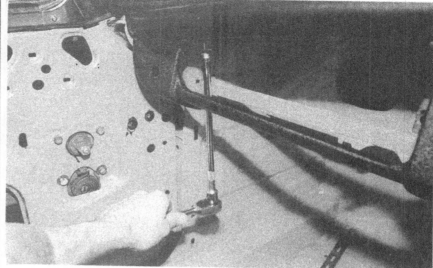

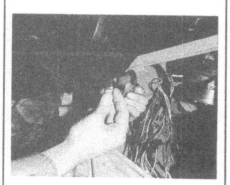

DB8. It is essential that the dash is correctly mounted at this point, since it forms the upper location for the steering column itself. The dash bolts through to the square tubular section crossmember.

DB10. ... with a long socket extension ... ⬆

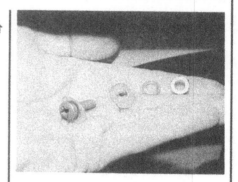

DB11. ... while the centre one is accessed through the radio aperture. ⬇

DB12. Lower mounting points consist of a bolt, two plain washers, a spring washer and a nut.

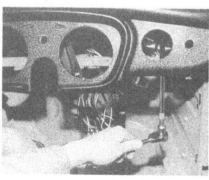

DB9. Outer dash bolts can be reached ...

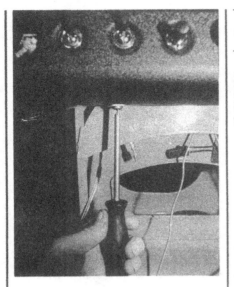

DB13. One of the central lower mounting points.

DB14. This is the arrangement of the components for the earlier MGB dash. Note the fixing plates (Items 2, 3, 4 and 6) and the blanking plates (Items 18, 19 and 20) used when no radio is fitted. ➡

DB15. This is the way the instruments are fitted to one of the later dashboards. More dashboard layouts, including those for the US market can be found in the Electrical section. ⬇

Glove Box Fitting

Refer to DB14 on this page for line drawing instructions on how the glove box goes together.

GB1. The glove box hinges are bolted to the bottom of the dash with two small nuts, bolts and spring washers per hinge. ➡

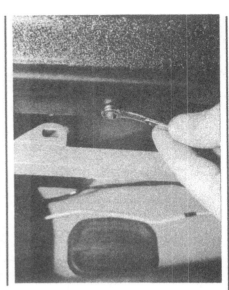

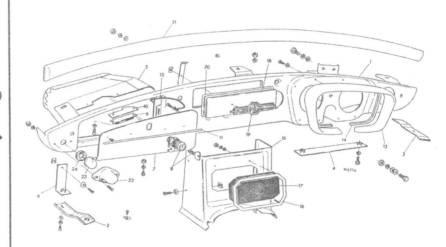

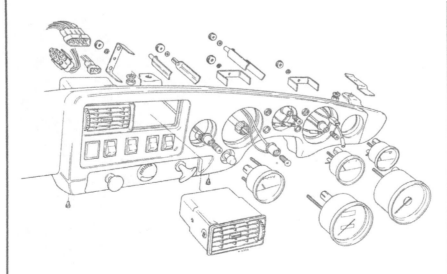

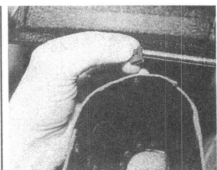

GB2. The glove box itself - made of fibre board and available new - has to be fitted with these spring clips to enable it to be screwed into place in the dashboard.

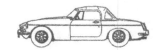

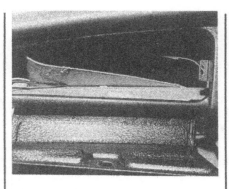

GB3. The glove box is slipped into place from beneath the dash, and the six self-tapping screws ...

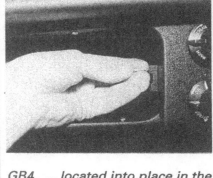

GB4. ... located into place in the six spring clips shown in the previous shot.

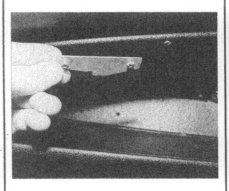

GB5. The glove box buffer and lock catch (Items 9 & 10) are screwed to the top of the opening.

GB6. Unless you fit the bracket to the rear of the glove box, the weight of items placed inside it will quickly cause it to break away at the front. ➡

GB7. The fitting of the wire check arm to the glove box lid is a bit of a Chinese puzzle at first ...

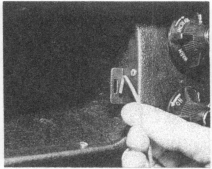

GB8. ... but when you figure out how it goes, it's obvious really!

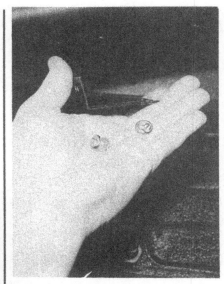

GB9. The glove box lock has to be disassembled in order that it can be fitted to the lid and then the locking latch refitted.

GB10. Don't forget to retain the chrome finisher strip from the old glove box, although new ones may be available.

Dashboard - Wooden Trim

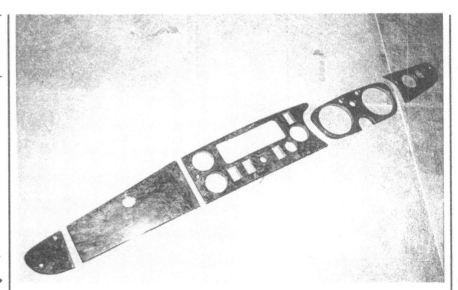

DWT1. *If you don't like the appearance of the standard dashboard, you can cover it up with wooden trim. Alternatively, a complete wooden dashboard can be purchased.* ➡

DWT2. *Each individual piece is offered up to the dash, and you then have the traumatic task of drilling holes ready to take ...*

DWT3. *... the self-tapping screws that hold the centre pieces in place. Be careful not to twist and break the wooden trim because it must be extremely weak across the short grain.*

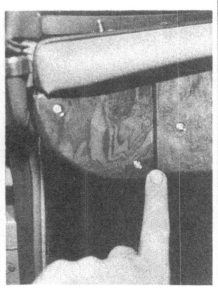

DWT4. *Take care that all gaps are even and true otherwise the job will look amateurish.*

DWT5. *Wooden dashes are available for a number of different dash options, including early left-hand drive models.* ⬅

Heater Components

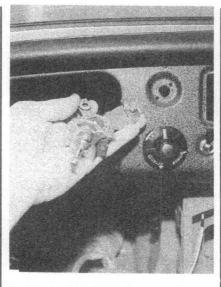

HC1. Heater controls are prone to wear and disintegration. We fitted new, and all are available 'off the peg' at Moss.

HC2. Control knobs push onto the controls until they click. They are removed by inserting a piece of stiff wire into the hole visible in the knurled part of the knob until the spring beneath is depressed, and then the knob can be pulled off.

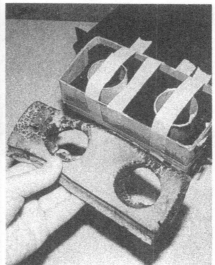

HC4. The heater casing taken from the donor car was so badly rusted below the 'water line' that it was not reusable. We found a second-hand one, and had it powder-coated to give an extremely tough and long lasting finish.

HC5. The base of the unit seals internally through a wedge shaped piece of foam rubber which is not, at the time of writing, available. We made a cardboard enclosure and taped it to the base of the heater unit to mimic the shape of the foam rubber.

HC3. MGB heaters are often poor because the heater radiator (Item 6) becomes clogged or internally silted. So, flush out the radiator or, if necessary, replace with new.

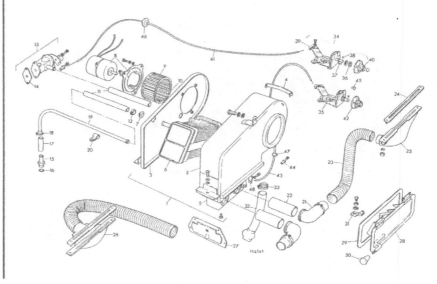

HC6. Aerosol foam was then fitted into the enclosure. Note that it is toxic, and you must also take steps not to get it on your skin; So, always wear gloves. Read the safety instructions included with the can with great care.

HC7. The foam bubbles and froths like a witch's brew until it sets hard ...

HC8. ... and can then be cut off level with the top of the enclosure with an old hacksaw blade. It is safe to touch at this stage.

HC9. The air intake grille was glued to the newly rebuilt heater casing ...

HC10. ... and lots of windscreen sealer applied to the casing where it would fit against the bodywork. The polyurethane foam proved not to be as durable as we would have wished, but it did the job with the assistance of extra windscreen sealer, and it was certainly better than nothing at all!

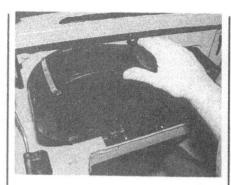

HC11. The heater casing was manoeuvred into position, inserting it at first at an angle ...

HC14. A selection of heater controls, cables and vents. ⬆

HC12. ... until it could be straightened up and bolted to the bulkhead at the top ...

HC15. With the air intakes provided in the Heritage shell bulkhead, it was possible to convert this early-style dashboard to take later-style face-level air vents. The radio would go in the console later. ➡

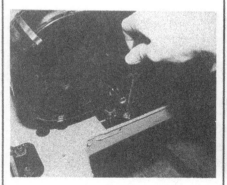

HC13. ... and screwed down at the bottom.

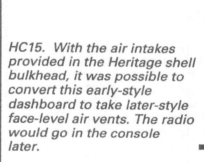

HC16. A pair of good second-hand vents were purchased ...

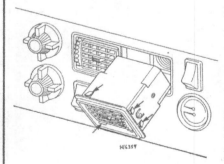

HC17. ... and these are the locating tags which clip into place as the vents are pushed home.

Footwell Vents

FV1. *On earlier models, there is a supplementary vent which allows fresh air to come directly into the footwells. This roller catch fits to the body ...* ➡

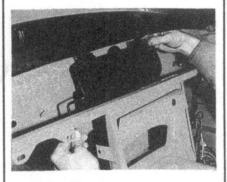

FV2. *... the vent door screws to the bulkhead and is held shut by the catch on the body.*

FV3. *The heater vent deflector plates screw directly to the transmission tunnel side walls.*

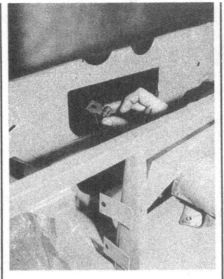

Steering Wheel Removal and Replacement

Safety

Before attempting to remove the steering wheel, disconnect the battery so that the horn and indicator components cannot be shorted out. Ensure that the fitting nut is retightened to the correct torque specified by the manufacturers - it is not sufficient to drift it home with a hammer and chisel.

Various types of wheel have been fitted, and accessory steering wheels are also often to be found. Where the wheel and boss are integral, remove the motif cap, either by removing the three grub screws from the side of the boss, or by prizing out the motif cap, depending on which type is fitted. On later cars, the steering wheel and hub are separate items. On some, you must first remove the motif, which is a press fit, and on later types remove the horn contact plunger. Lift the lockring tabs (integral with the lockring in early cars), and remove the bolts, lockring and steering wheel.

SW1. *This is the famous Moto-Lita wood-rim steering wheel - a popular accessory on sixties British sports cars, and still available new today. The boss is the component on the right, and it fits onto the splined top of the steering column.* ⬇

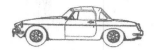

SW2. On this model the horn push and motif are removed and the horn wire disconnected.

SW3. The nut holding the steering wheel and boss in place is slackened but not removed.

SW4. It is unscrewed until it is flush with the top of the column, and then it can be struck with a soft-faced mallet while a helper pulls on the steering wheel. TAKE CARE! THE WHEEL CAN COME AWAY QUITE SUDDENLY SO DO NOT REMOVE THE NUT UNTIL IT HAS BECOME FREE ON THE SPLINES. ↑

SW5. The Moto-Lita steering ← wheel has been assembled to the boss, and it can then be tapped onto the steering column splines and the nut retightened. When the steering wheel is set so the spokes are symmetrically placed when the car is in the straight ahead position, re-tighten the nut, using a dab of Locktite to ensure it cannot come undone of its own accord. Tighten the nut to the torque specified in the workshop manual.

SW6. Moto-Lita produce various models of steering wheel, and this version was chosen to co-ordinate with the interior of our project MGB. Footnotes from Moss: 1) Avoid snapping the plastic pegs which hold the inner column away from the outer on collapsible column models. 2) It is better to try gently rocking the steering wheel from side to side to loosen it on the splines to resort to any form of hammering. ←

Sound-Proofing

Toolbox

Scissors; craft knife; contact adhesive; sound-proofing kit; spirit wipe.

Safety

Contact adhesive is highly flammable and also gives off dangerous vapour. Always work in a well-ventilated area. Keep away from children! Read Appendix 1 on 'Fumes' when using volatile adhesives. Work in a well-ventilated area away from sparks, heat or flames. Don't smoke!

The Acoustikit sound-proofing kit fitted here is made especially for the MGB and should not be confused with the cheaper brands of kit that consist of a roll of felt and a pot of glue! It is simplicity itself to work out what-goes-where with the comprehensive instructions enclosed.

SP2. Graham applied contact adhesive to the inside of the bonnet and to the sound deadening pad being fitted.

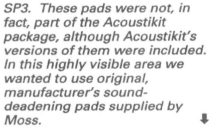

SP3. These pads were not, in fact, part of the Acoustikit package, although Acoustikit's versions of them were included. In this highly visible area we wanted to use original, manufacturer's sound-deadening pads supplied by Moss.

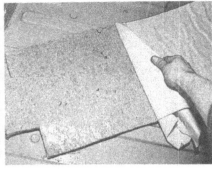

SP4. Many of the pads included in the Acoustikit package come with a self-adhesive backing which is exposed by peeling off the wax paper.

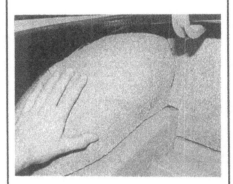

SP5. Each section is shaped to fit, such as this for the wheel arch inside the boot.

SP1. First job was for Graham to read the instructions and to follow the plan which shows clearly just where each numbered sound-proofing pad should be fitted.

SP6. The sound-deadening felt for the floor is shaped to fit between the seat runners.

SP7. Bitumen pads are available for fitting to the insides of the door skins. They are also self-adhesive and, as in the case of all self adhesive pads, the panel to which they are being fixed must be thoroughly cleaned off with spirit wipe to enable the adhesive to take a hold. In cold weather, it helps to play a hair dryer on the panel and on the pad itself. Otherwise, the adhesive might not take a hold.

Carpets

Toolbox

Craft knife; scissors; adhesive and spreader; carpet clips; electric drill; crosshead screwdriver.

Safety

Take note of the safety comments in the previous section on fitting sound-deadening kits.

C1. Full carpet sets are available for every model of MGB and GT in both the original material and in the plush version that we show being fitted here. (Courtesy: Moss Parts Catalogue). ➡

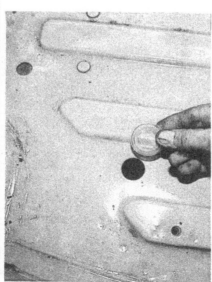

C2. Ensure that all grommets and bungs are in place and that the floor is fully seam sealed.

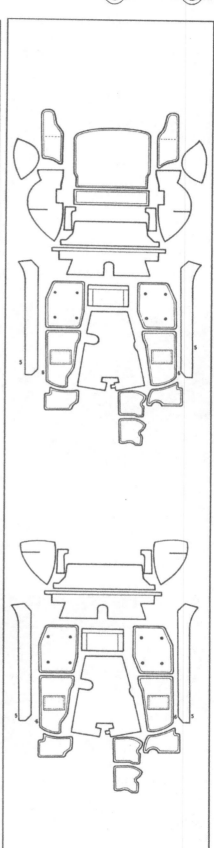

C3. When you buy a carpet set for your MGB ensure that it contains fully shaped sections, such as those available from Moss, because it is impossible to persuade a piece of flat carpet to fit the rear wheel arch successfully. Cheap carpet sets are simply not worth buying.

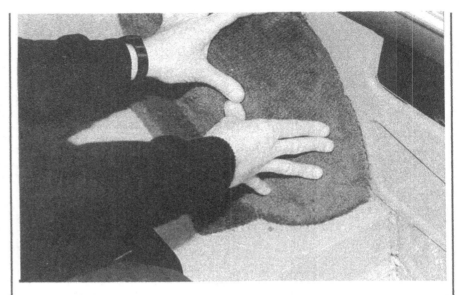

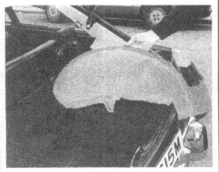

C4. Part of the GT carpet set is this beautifully moulded rear wheel arch liner. Imagine trying to form that out of flat carpet!

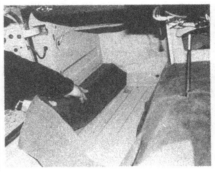

C6. ... before gluing down just the front end of the carpet.

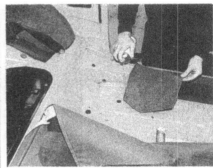

C8. Lastly, the rear of the sill section was glued down ...

C5. Alan Sinclair sprays aerosol adhesive to the inside of the carpet and onto the inner sill section ...

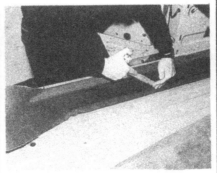

C7. He works his way back along the sill, using a hammer handle to force the carpet sharply into the joint between sill and floor.

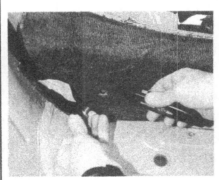

C9. ... and cut-outs made for the seat belt mountings.

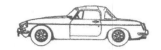

C10. Meanwhile, Chris Redfern was fitting the centre console carpet, and the one across the heel board.

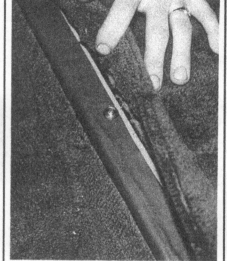

C13. ... and Chris lays the rear shelf carpet into place. ➡

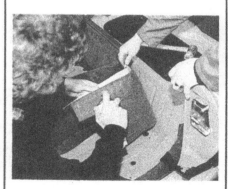

C11. More cutting out for seat belt mountings. Extra sound-proofing comes ready fitted to the back of this carpet.

C14. The top trim of the heel board carpet has been glued down, and the male part of a press stud has been screwed down through the heel board top.

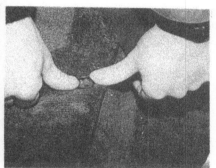

C16. The locking ring is pushed through the carpet from above ...

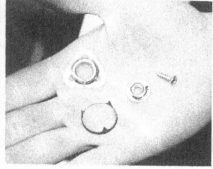

C12. Alan gives a hand to glue down 'his' end of the heel board carpet - note how each of these sections is fitted piecemeal - ...

C15. These are the components of each carpet press stud.

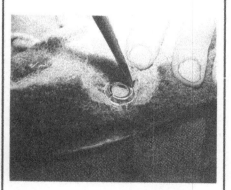

C17. ... and the female part pushed over the tabs which are then bent over, securing it into place.

C18. The cockpit footwells are finished off with ready-made and edge-bound trim boards, held in place with self-tapping screws.

C19. The floor carpets have holes already cut to enable the seat runners to be bolted down. The seats themselves hold these rear carpets in place. ⬇

C20. The front carpets have to be held with more press studs, drilled and screwed down to the floor. ➡

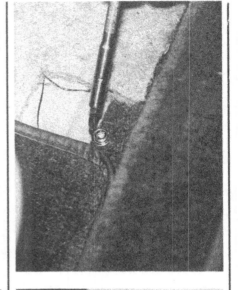

Centre Console

CC1. We built up the project car's centre console whilst out of the car. Only one of these three holes was used - for the cigarette lighter - while Moss's spares maestro, Martin Smith, searched high and low and came up with two chrome blanking plugs for the others. ➡

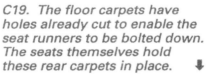

CC2. The interior light - another later-model improvement - screws to the top of the centre console.

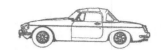

CC3. The catch that holds the centre console arm rest shut is prone to breakage - it usually happens when someone leans across the car to reach something from the other side - and if not replaced the hinge assembly at the other end of the arm rest breaks away. It is easy to replace and new ones are freely available and inexpensive. ➡

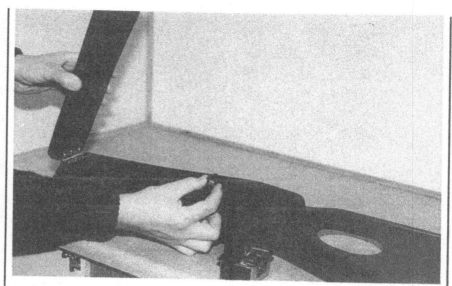

CC4. At this stage, the electric window switches have also been fitted (see Electric Windows section), and Alan and Chris are screwing the console in place to the brackets provided.

CC5. After fitting the gear-stick gaiter, the arm rest assembly can be clipped into place on the centre console.

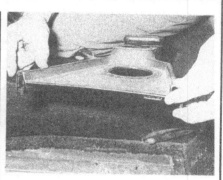

CC6. Careful examination of the ends of the arm rest will show that there are two tabs - being pointed out here by each index finger - which have to slot onto the plastic of the centre console as the arm rest is pushed into place.

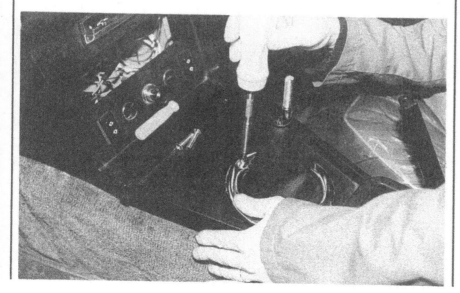

CC7. The chrome bezel around the gear-stick gaiter also holds the front of the console in place.

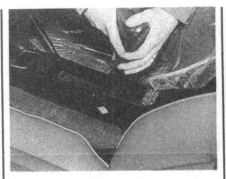

CC8. The rear of the arm rest has to be screwed down to the transmission tunnel after first drilling out a pilot hole ...

CC9. ... and then screwing in the self-tapping screw.

CC10. Just to finish the job off, Martin Smith came up with an attractive leather covered gear knob to match the car's new interior. ⬆

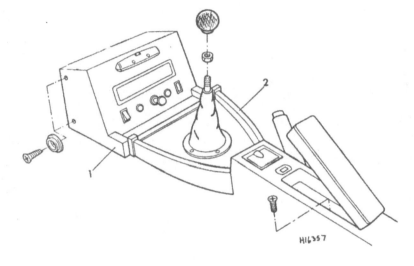

H16357

CC11. This is the earlier of the centre console units with integral arm rest. ⬅

H16358

CC12. The console assembly, GHN5 and GHD5 models from vehicle 410002. ⬅

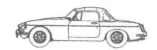

Door Trims and Seals

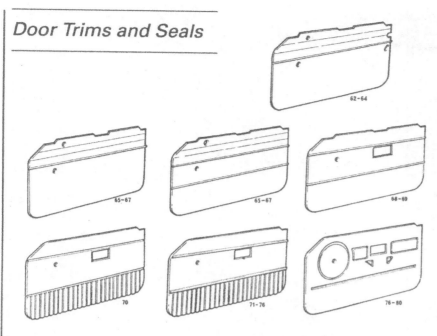

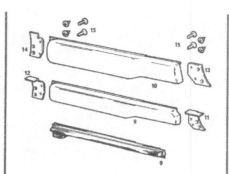

DTS1. These are the various styles of door trim available ready-made for your MGB. (Courtesy: Moss Parts Catalogue)

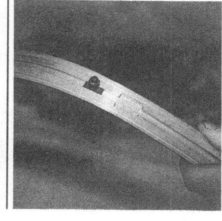

DTS2. Door seals are available in lengths for door openings - Roadster and GT - as are GT quarterlight seals. (Courtesy: Moss Parts Catalogue)

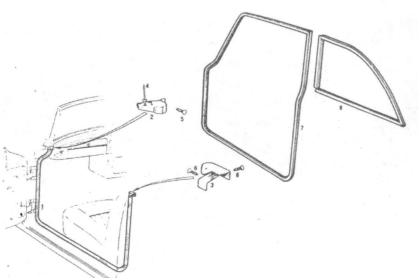

DTS3. Door top trims have to have the chrome-plated fitting brackets taken from the old and screwed to the new. They often rust and new ones are available. (Courtesy: Moss Parts Catalogue)

DTS4. Waist rail trim, that fits around the top of the rear cockpit, is held in place with special bolts that slide in a track on the rear side of the trim until they align with the punched holes in the rear of the body. Nuts and washers are fitted from beneath.

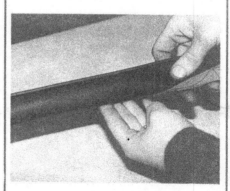

DTS5. Vinyl trim has to be glued to the aluminium extrusion with the piping carefully placed at the top edge so that it fills the gap between the trim and the car's bodywork.

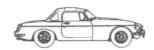

DTS6. After bolting on the waist rail trim, Alan Sinclair pushes the rearmost trim panel into place.

DTS7. The rear quarter trim panels are pushed into place, and then the door seals tapped on with a soft-faced hammer.

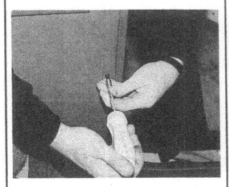

DTS8. This will establish the correct positioning for these trim panels, and they can then be drilled and fitted with screws and cup washers.

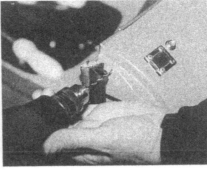

DTS9. After cutting the door seals off to length, holes can be drilled for self-tapping screws ...

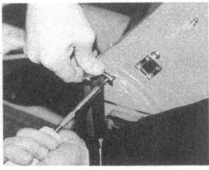

DTS10. ... to hold the trim finishers in place.

DTS11. The trim finishers that cover the front of the door seals can only be fitted before the screen is bolted down.

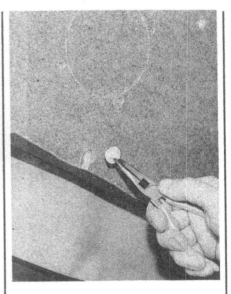

DTS12. Door trims are fitted with these plastic clips which are slotted into the ready punched holes in the hardboard and then twisted so that they fit tight.　　　↑

DTS13. Alan found that the door handles were too tight to the door for the new door trims to go comfortably behind them. He used plain washers placed between the handles and the door to pack them out sufficiently.　　↓

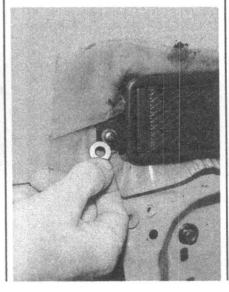

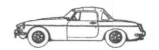

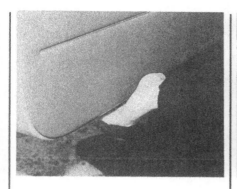

DTS14. The door trims were offered up so that the clips fitted into the holes in the door and then they were pushed in sharply with the palm of the hand.

DTS16. After using the new door pulls as a template to pierce the door trims, the door pulls were screwed into place right through to the plastic 'wall plugs' that can be seen in DTS13.

DTS18. Our old fixing plates for the door top trims had to be replaced with new ones ...

DTS15. Alan checks again that the door handles protrude far enough from these richly trimmed door panels.

DTS17. The plastic finisher strips that are slid between trim panel and door handle could have caused damage to the door trim and so Alan slipped a thin feeler gauge behind the finisher strips so that they could be pushed into place without causing any harm.

DTS19. ... which were screwed to the trim rails, and were then in turn screwed to the door tops.

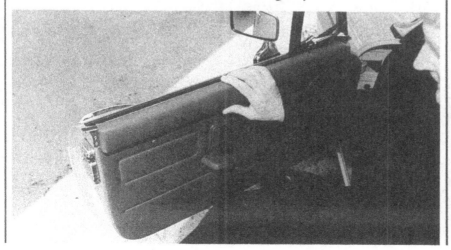

DTS20. Alan surveys the beautifully finished door trim panels - better than new! The grey finish trim was designed by Moss to match the grey leather seats - shown being fitted later on - and they have also had the door handles and finishers produced in a matching colour of grey plastic. All the parts are available off the shelf from Moss. ◀

Seat Removal and Replacement

SRR1. Moss Workshop Manager, Alan Sinclair, removes the seat runners from the donor car seats to which they had been fitted for the drive down to the Moss Workshop. ➡

SRR2. Graham Macdonald had previously sandblasted each of the seat runners, and then carefully painted each one in Wurth zinc- rich primer and Smoothrite silver aerosol paint.

SRR3. Alan carefully tapped out each of the mounting holes with this (somewhat unconventional!) tap wrench.

SRR4. Wooden spacers sit on top of the carpet, and aluminium ones give the seat runners something firm to clamp down onto. Our old ones had disintegrated, but more were discovered 'breeding' in the Porter spare parts bin. Moss have subsequently invested a susprisingly large amount of money in having them reproduced. ➡

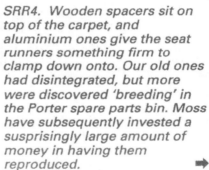

SRR5. Alan lowers the new Moss seat into place.

SRR6. The first bolts to be fitted were those at the rear, although it is most important not to tighten them down at this stage.

SRR7. The front bolts can be tricky to get in, and 'tricky' can become 'impossible' if the rear bolts are tight and the runners immovable.

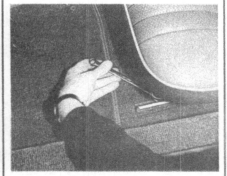

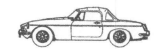

Seat Re-covering

Toolbox

Straight point screwdriver; crosshead screwdriver; soft-faced mallet; pop-rivet gun and long-head pop-rivets; sharp scissors; craft knife; contact adhesive; paint brush; pencil; light hammer; boxes for keeping clips and fittings in after removal.

Safety

Contact adhesive is highly flammable and also gives off dangerous vapour. Keep away from children! Read Appendix 1 on 'Fumes' when using volatile adhesives. Always work in a well-ventilated area away from sparks, heat or flames. Don't smoke!

Most people who work on their cars are quite at home with mechanical components, and are willing to tackle bodywork, but fight shy of any kind of re-upholstery work. Most upholstery jobs can be successfully carried out at home provided they are tackled methodically and carefully - just as though body panels are being worked upon, but with soft, deformable sheet materials being used rather than hard, stiff metal sheet.

The cost of having a worn seat retrimmed can be very high indeed, so this area is perhaps the most profitable for a beginner to develop and exercise his or her skills on.

The basic principles involved are the same no matter which type of cover is fitted. Re-upholstery kits are available for every type of seat, even leather (although these kits are, naturally, rather expensive) and even most of the original colours are now available.

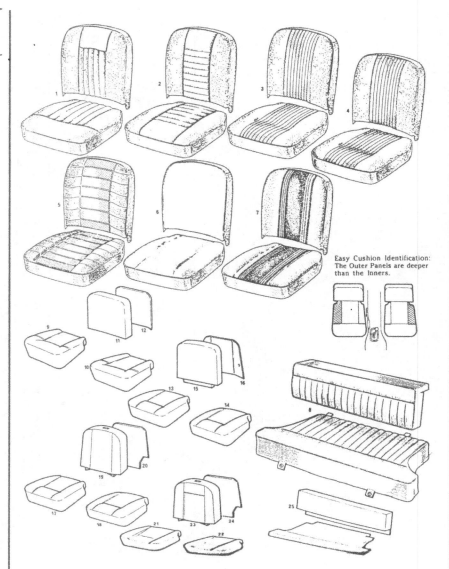

Easy Cushion Identification: The Outer Panels are deeper than the Inners.

SRC1. A selection of the seat coverings and rubber foam cushions now available for the MGB. Moss have invested a great deal of money in putting many of these parts back into production. (Courtesy: Moss Parts Catalogue) ↑

SRC2. Slide the seat to be re-covered back along its runners as far as it will go. A soft-faced hammer may be found useful! ➡

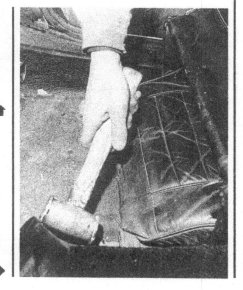

SRC3. Remove the screw in each runner holding them to the floor. Slide the seat to the foremost position in order to remove the equivalent screws at the rear. Lift out the seat, remove runners, and the various packing pieces left on the floor, for safe keeping. ➡

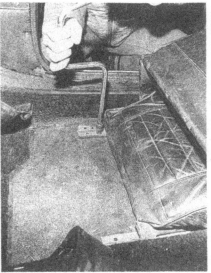

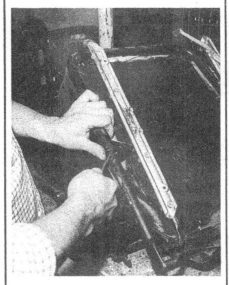

SRC4. Place the seat on a table or bench with its base uppermost, and begin removing the spring clips holding the upholstery to the frame tube.

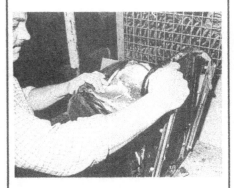

SRC5. With all clips removed - including those from the rear of the seat - the foam rubber squabs and cover can be peeled away from the base and removed.

SRC6. The rubber diaphragm is held to the frame tubing via spring clips. Short, thin steel rods are pushed into thickened edges of the diaphragm and these often slip out, allowing the seat to sag - a point worth checking if the seat feels a little bottomed-out.

SRC7. A rod should bridge the gap shown opened up here - it is through this gap that the spring clip fits. If the diaphragm is split, it will have to be renewed. ➡

SRC8. Unscrew the crosshead screw holding the seat reclining back-rest adjuster handle into place (where fitted). The handle is usually a tight fit and requires some 'persuasion' to remove.

SRC9. Remove the self-tapping screw which holds the side trim in place a few inches below the back-rest adjuster handle.

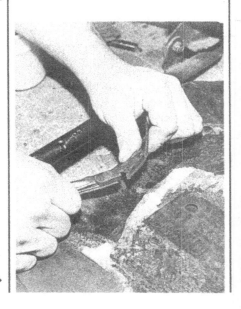

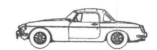

SRC10. Unclip the spring clips holding the back-rest back panel onto the frame. ➡

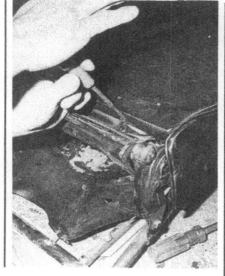

SRC11. Lift the bottom fold of the back panel out of the way and remove the spring clips holding the back-rest front panel onto its frame tube. ⬇

SRC13. Cut out the metal bezel set into the top of the back-rest through which the seat head-rest support is slotted (if fitted).

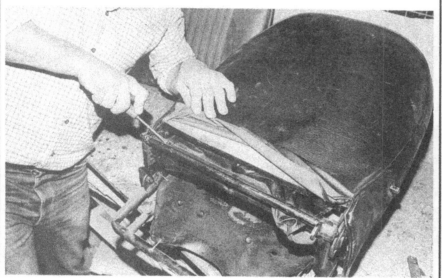

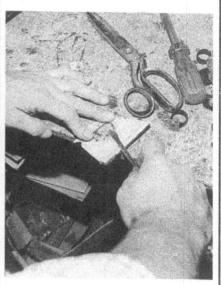

SRC14. Place the scrap of cloth with the bezel set into it onto the bench, turn it over and turn up the tabs which hold it onto its backing plate ... ⬆

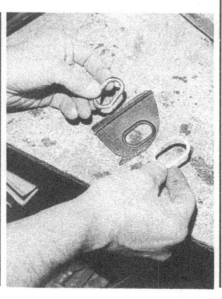

SRC12. Using a craft knife or scissors, cut out the old back-rest rear panel. ⬆

SRC15. ... leaving the three components as shown. The one in the centre is the now-redundant piece of cloth. ⬅

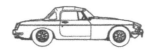

SRC16. Carefully peel the back-rest cover from its sponge rubber squab, easing the two apart so that they separate without tearing large chunks out of the squab. Then repeat the procedure with the seat squab and cover.

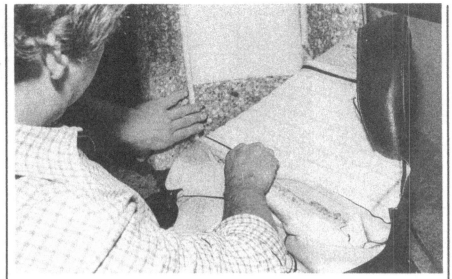

SRC17. Coat the outer couple of inches of the rear of the back-rest with adhesive ...

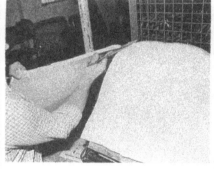

SRC19. Trim the foam to the shape of the back-rest. It is important to be neat, but engineering accuracy is not essential!

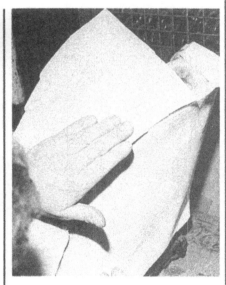

SRC20. Glue pieces of thin foam rubber to the edges of the back- rest, leaving a gap where the head-rest slots into place and down to the recliner shaft. ⬆

SRC18. ... cut out an appropriately sized rectangle of thin foam, paint the matching surfaces with contact adhesive and stick it in place covering the rear of the backrest.

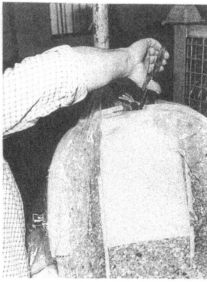

SRC21. Don't forget to leave that head-rest slot clear! Glue on some thin sheet plastic. ⬅

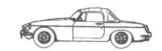

SRC22. Mark with a pencil on the new seat cover the position for the head-rest slot bezel which was removed from the old cover. Draw around the insides of the aperture taking care to locate the exact centre of the cover. ➡

SRC27. Cut out a piece of really thick card to fit snugly into each flap ...

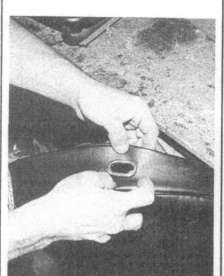

SRC23. Carefully and accurately snip out the oval shape you have marked out and push the bezel into place from above ...

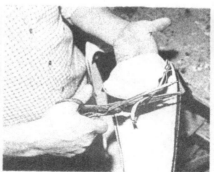

SRC25. ... place the backing plate over the tabs and lightly hammer them down, holding the bezel tightly in place.

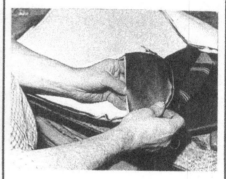

SRC28. ... and push and glue each one into place.

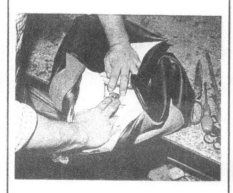

SRC24. ... turn the cover upside down, open it up like a shopping bag on the bench ...

SRC26. Turn the whole cover inside out and carefully trim off as much of the excess material outside the stitching around each of these flaps.

SRC29. Brush a strip of glue about 3 inches wide down each side of the central panel of the front of the back-rest.

SRC30. Brush two equivalent strips down the inside of the back-rest cover, but only on the inside of the front panel, matching those on the seat. This gives the cover the correct shape when fitted, and prevents it stretching straight across the backrest shoulders. ➡

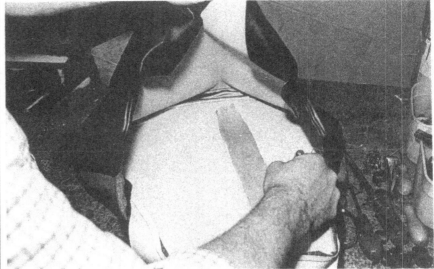

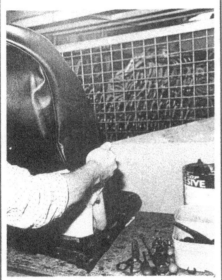

SRC31. Pull the cover onto the seat back.

SRC33. The back-rest back panel has a flap at the bottom which is shown here folded up inside like folding a flap into an envelope.

SRC35. It is folded smoothly around the pivot tube and held in place with spring clips.

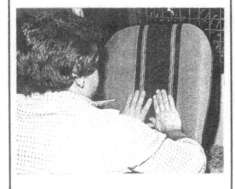

SRC32. Ensure that all wrinkles are pulled out. The plastic sheet previously fitted helps the cover to slide into place. Smooth the cloth down with both hands, starting from the top.

SRC34. The flap from the back-rest front panel is pulled tightly through, just in front of the rearmost tube.

SRC36. The excess is then pulled back out ...

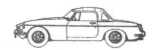

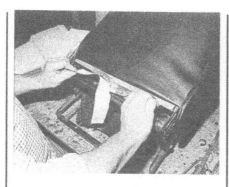

SRC37. ... and cut off with scissors.

SRC38. The back panel flap is then pulled back out and stretched slightly downwards - but not by so much as to cause stretch marks.

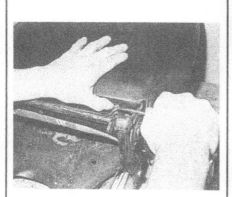

SRC39. This fold is held by spring clips to the innermost of the three tubes, and the excess trimmed off as before.

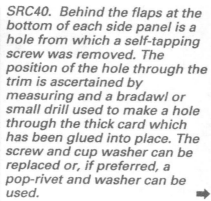

SRC40. Behind the flaps at the bottom of each side panel is a hole from which a self-tapping screw was removed. The position of the hole through the trim is ascertained by measuring and a bradawl or small drill used to make a hole through the thick card which has been glued into place. The screw and cup washer can be replaced or, if preferred, a pop-rivet and washer can be used. ➡

SRC41. The bracket adjuster shaft is found by feeling through the cloth, and is then lightly tapped with a hammer. This action neatly and accurately cuts a square out of the cloth exactly matching the shape and size of the adjuster shaft. ➡

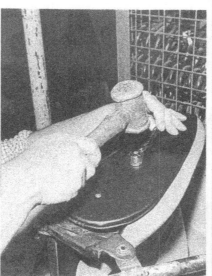

SRC42. The adjuster lever is then carefully driven back on with a soft-faced mallet, and screwed into place.

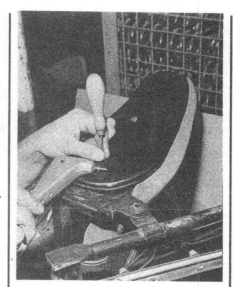

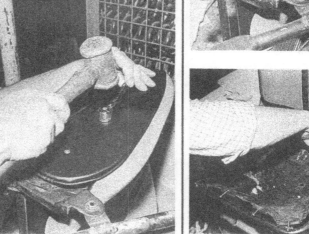

SRC43. With the back-rest complete, brush adhesive around the seat base frame, and around a corresponding area on the bottom of the seat squab, and glue the squab down onto the frame.

SRC44. *Cover the entire seat squab with thin foam in the same way as detailed for the back-rest. Ensure that the foam is glued down in such a way that it follows the contours of the seat base, and that the side pieces extend to the back of the seat.*

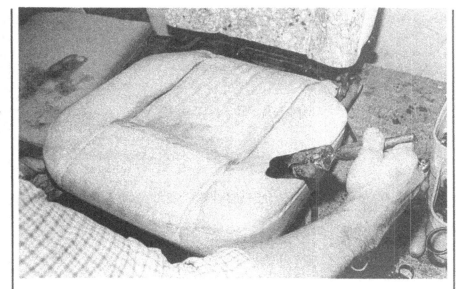

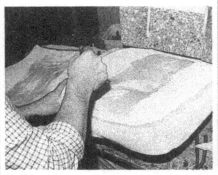

SRC45. *Apply adhesive to the centre panel of the seat base and to the corresponding area of the seat base cover, after first having turned the cover upside down and inside out.*

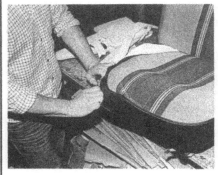

SRC47. *... and pulling forward one front corner and then the other, smoothing the edges down as the job is done.*

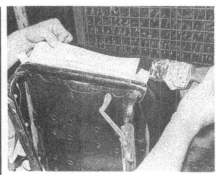

SRC49. *Apply adhesive to this section ... and fold it under to make a neat edge. This shot shows how long the first scissor cuts needed to be.*

SRC46. *Make absolutely certain that the cover is properly aligned all around before tucking in the rear flap ...*

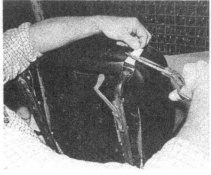

SRC48. *Snip the cloth in line with the outer edges of the base frame supports, and cut off most of the redundant centre section.*

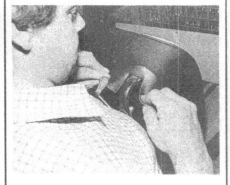

SRC50. *Work carefully here to ensure a neat finish.*

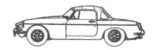

SRC51. Apply adhesive to the front flap and the front horizontal base tube, and glue the flap around the tube. Pull the front sufficiently taut to give a smooth, crease-free finish.

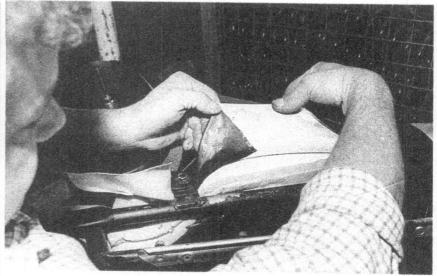

SRC55. This view is of the seat from below. The position of the cut in the side panel can be seen straddling the back-rest tilt pivot. The frontmost section of the side panel is neatly flapped and glued, as shown, before being clipped down to the side rail. ⬆

SRC52. Finish off by clipping the front edge down neatly.

SRC54. Push the back flap through and out of the way.

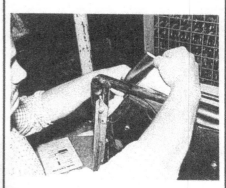

SRC56. The rear flap, protruding between back-rest and seat base (with the seat folded forward again) is again flapped at its ends, pulled taut and clipped down. ⬆

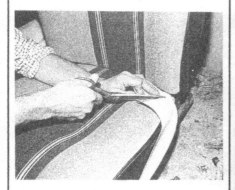

SRC53. Cut the side panel at its rear quarter in such a way that the cut is in line with the back-rest supporting the tilt pivot.

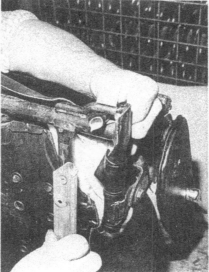

SRC57. Obviously the latch for the catch, which holds the seat back-rest in place (i.e. when not tipped forward for rear access) must not be covered over. The panel is cut, flapped from both sides to make a tube ... ⬅

SRC58. ... wrapped around the seat frame and neatly clipped down leaving the latch clear. ➡

SRC59. Steve Langdell, the man who carried out this particular job, looks highly please with the finished results. ⬇

SRC61. Old leather can be reconstituted. First, clean it with the foam (and as little water as possible) from saddle soap, applied with a sponge. Then treat the leather to several 'sittings' of hide food to restore suppleness. Leather can also be re-coloured with specialist Connolly kits. ⬆

SRC60. Replacement leather covers are so expensive that utilising leather panels from a scrap leather seat makes strong, economic sense. Snip the stitching, resisting the temptation to tear it apart - old, brittle leather will rip as easily as card - and sew the replacement into place using twine from an upholsterer or saddler, passing it through the existing holes.

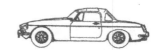

Seat Webbing Replacement

Replacement of a broken seat membrane is referred to in the above section on seat re-covering. Many MGB seats, however, were fitted with straps of Pirelli webbing, and when these break, as they frequently do after a few years, they're relatively easy to replace. This work was carried out on the seats of the immaculate V8 that the author once owned.

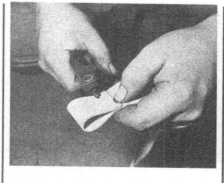

SWR3. We borrowed a fabric hole punch to make the necessary holes in the rubber webbing ...

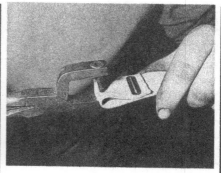

SWR6. A slight modification to the original: instead of cutting a slot, we simply punched another hole just inboard of where the wire would pass through the loop.

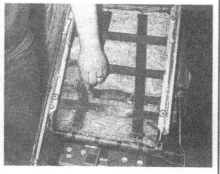

SWR1. This is a typical case of seat webbing disintegration, just at the point where the posterior is most likely to come into contact with the floor beneath! New Pirelli webbing is available from most trim shops.

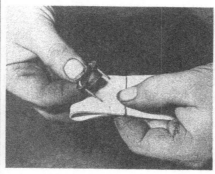

SWR4. ... before passing through new webbing clips that were also available from the trim supplier.

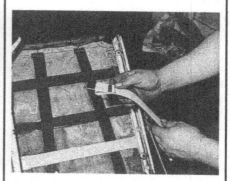

SWR7. Following the same pattern as the original webbing, the new sections were looped under and over as before.

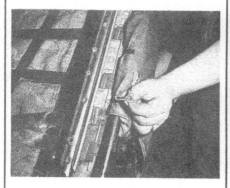

SWR2. Each piece of webbing passes round a rod which is in turn hooked onto the edge of the seat frame with a clip such as this one.

SWR5. The legs of the clips were passed through a fixing plate and then bent over with a hammer.

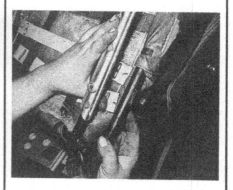

SWR8. Some care had to be taken in ensuring that the loops came in exactly the right place, but then it was just plain sailing.

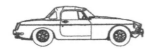

Soft-top Replacement & Tonneaux

You can fit a new soft-top yourself and avoid a nightmare of sags, drafts and flapping vinyl by working carefully and methodically, as shown in the following step-by-step instructions.

The first job, and probably the most important one, is to buy the best soft-top that you can afford. If you can get an original factory soft-top, the advantages are that it is very likely to fit much better than those made by outside concerns, it may be better made and it will be constructed of the correct material. The only disadvantage of a factory fresh soft-top is that it is likely to cost a little more. If you have to buy one from one of the soft-top specialists try, if you can, to avoid buying without seeing first (there are some horribly mis-shapen offerings), and get yourself a soft-top with the clips and stud fastenings already fitted, if possible. The small extra cost saves a lot of work - not to mention the risk of getting it wrong!

Do ensure that the soft-top is (a) the right one for your car, and (b) that it fits, before removing the old one or attempting to alter the new one. The fit can be checked by the simple expedient of draping and smoothing it over the old, erected soft-top, and checking for shape and size. There will be some useful sized overlaps where the manufacturer has allowed for adjustment during fitting.

Toolbox

Tape measure; chalk; awl; drill; screwdrivers (various); craft knife; pop-rivet pliers; contact adhesive; glue-brush; light hammer; scissors.

Safety

Contact adhesive is highly flammable and also gives off dangerous vapour. Read Appendix 1 on 'Fumes' when using volatile adhesives. Always work in a well-ventilated area away from sparks, heat or flames. Don't smoke!

The only soft-tops recommended here are those manufactured by Coventry Hood and Seating Company. Their soft-tops are tailored on the original jigs used to supply the MG factory at Abingdon, and they are available from most MG specialists. These soft-tops are available with or without the header rail - the bar attached to the front of the soft-top which is then clamped to the windscreen frame. Soft-tops with header rails are designed to ensure quick and accurate installation. After many years in which the original high-quality soft-top material was 'N.L.A.', Coventry Hood and Seating put totally original soft-top back into production in late 1991. They can be identified by the unique 'CHS' label stitched to every one. The economy version is still available.

Prior to the reintroduction of the CHS soft-top, in which Moss were instrumental, you could not buy one with a header rail fitted. Installation for this soft-top is estimated at 30-45 minutes, while installation of the soft-top without header rail is estimated at 1-2 hours but could take much longer. These soft-tops are only available in black vinyl, although it is possible through the MG Owners' Club to buy a double-duck (cloth fabric) soft-top which, while non-original, can look most attractive.

Types of Soft-top

The manufacturers used the term 'hood' in their descriptions of the following:
Packaway Hoods 1963-70. These were designed to be folded up and put in the boot, and were used with a 'split in two' type frame which was also stored in the boot when not in use. This system has certain advantages in that the car looks at its most attractive with the soft-top completely removed and the space behind the seats free. In addition, the soft-top material is most likely to be damaged when it is folded and crumpled in the fold-away mechanism. On the other hand, re-erecting the split-in-two frame is difficult to carry out single handed.
Deluxe Hoods 1963-70. These hoods were designed to remain attached to the frame when in the folded-down position. The frame (originally painted grey) remained in the cockpit when in the down position, and when in the erected position appeared complex, cumbersome and a threat to the top of your head!
Folding Hoods 1970-76. These soft-tops also remain attached to the frame when folded down. The Michelotti designed frame (originally painted black) was an improved design which appeared more elegant than its predecessor and allowed for easier operation.
Zip-Down Rear Window Hood 1976-on. These soft-tops are the same as the 1970-76 soft-tops but have a zip-down rear window fitted. All of the 1970-on soft-tops can be used on earlier models as long as they are used complete with the later frame. Folding soft-top frames can and do wear badly, and new ones are available from Moss. These last soft-tops of all are undoubtedly the best of the three folding types, the zip-down rear window providing delightfully draught-free ventilation.

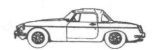

ST1. When working on a Heritage shell, or with new wing panels, the soft-top fitting clips will have to be added. ➡

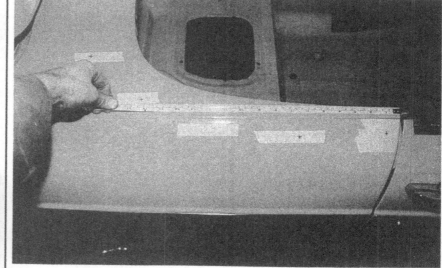

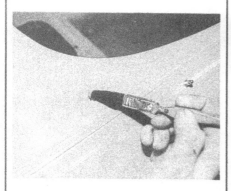

ST2. Graham Macdonald found that the best way was to measure and mark on masking tape the dimensions copied from the donor car.

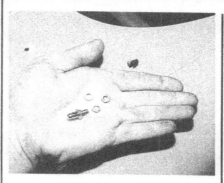

ST4. Each of the soft-top press-stud studs was bolted down with plain washer, spring washer and nut.

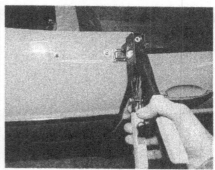

ST6. ... and just behind the B-post the eye clip for taking the hook on the soft-top at this point.

ST3. After drilling, every fresh hole was treated with Waxoyl.

ST5. Towards the front goes this round press-stud clip ...

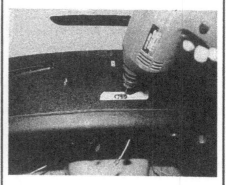

ST7. On top of the dashboard are three tonneau clips ...

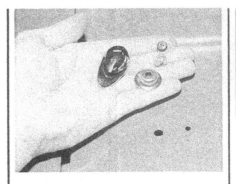

ST8. ... and on the rear deck more clips, including the streamlined shaped clips for the steel bar in the back of the soft-top.

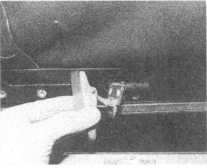

ST11. Header rail clips can become worn and useless. New ones are simply held on with two screws.

ST13. They're folded over and glued down to each other, making a loose tube along the frame - they are not glued directly to it.

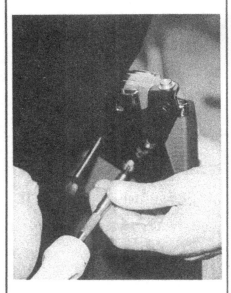

ST9. Fitting a new Tickford hood and frame assembly is simplicity itself. Somewhat strangely, the sockets for the original soft-top frame are left in place (they can now be used for the frame for the small rear tonneau) and the three studs holding the soft-top hinge mechanism to the car are screwed in to the bodywork just behind the B-post. ⬆

ST10. Three small crosshead countersunk screws hold the frame to the header rail. ➡

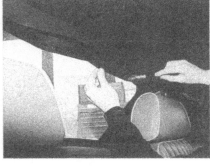

ST12. The new soft-top has to be fitted to the folding frame just above the rear screen using the flaps of material left for this purpose.

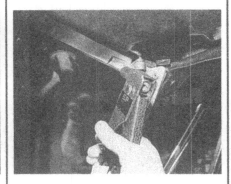

ST14. It's a simple matter to add later-type sun visors to an earlier vehicle, but take great care not to drill so deep that you crack the windscreen glass.

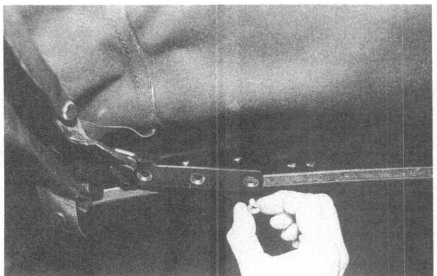

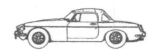

ST15. Here's how to go about fitting the least expensive soft-top that you can buy - one without the header rail already fitted. ➡

ST16. First step is to open the doors, fold the soft-top back, remove the rubber header rail sealing strip and drill off the pop-rivet heads found beneath.

ST17. Lift away the aluminium channel, being careful not to distort it.

ST18. Unscrew the soft-top where it is folded and held down to the ends of the header rail. Only a coat of adhesive stands between header rail and removal of the front soft-top - peel them apart. Rub the header rail down and repaint it to give a smooth finish under the new soft-top.

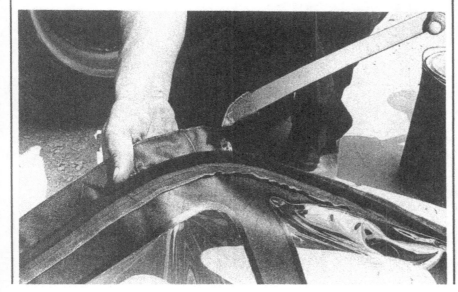

ST19. Slip the steel bar (which clips onto the two chrome 'claws' on the rear bodywork) out from the old soft-top and, right away slide it into the new soft-top - before you forget which way round it goes! ⬅

ST20. Refit the bare header rail to the top of the screen frame.

ST23. Apply glue, with a brush, to the central third of the header rail ...

ST26. Make absolutely certain that the sides of the soft-top line up with the closed door glasses.

ST21. Clip the rear of the soft-top in place, after fitting the soft-top frame (unless yours is of the folding type known as Michelotti, in which case it will be attached to the header rail) ...

ST24. ... and to the corresponding part of the inside of the soft-top.

ST27. Fold back each front corner, apply glue to it and the header rail.

ST22. ... and after folding the front-most part of the header rail back on itself, measure with a tape and mark the centre of the header rail with chalk.

ST25. Pull the soft-top forward, aligning the chalk mark with the windscreen steady bar and ensuring that the soft-top is taut.

ST28. Stretch each corner forwards just enough to get rid of any sags or wrinkles - but not so much that you will need a team of three to close the header rail on a cold day when the material has contracted!

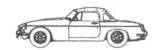

ST29. Fold the draught excluder corners down onto the header rail, pierce them with an awl and fit them into place with the crosshead screw and cup washer removed earlier. ➡

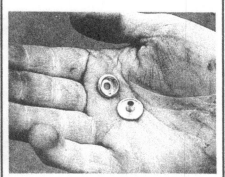

ST34. Snip the surplus hood material around the front frame clips then cut off the surplus with a craft knife.

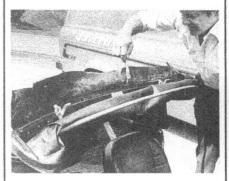

ST30. Glue the flap at the front onto the face of the header rail which sits on the top of the screen frame.

ST32. Pop-rivet it back down then refit the draught excluder rubber ...

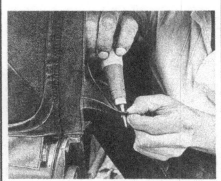

ST35. Press-stud clips, in two parts ...

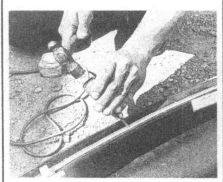

ST31. Glue down the draught strip channel in order to prevent leaks behind the strip itself, remembering to line up the holes with an awl before the glue dries.

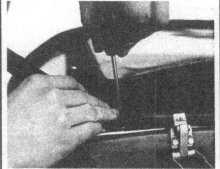

ST33. ... carefully easing it into the channel with the aid of a screwdriver.

ST36. ... have to be fitted to the tags provided one on each side, at the bottom of the window aperture. First, pierce with an awl ...

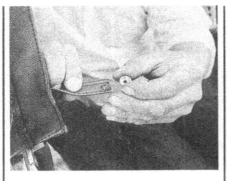

ST37. ... and spread the hollow tube with a centre punch and hammer, using another hammer as an anvil beneath. Although fitting the press-studs with the soft-top in place is awkward, it is the only way of ensuring that they align with the buttons on the car.

ST38. If at all possible, buy a soft-top with the rear clips already fitted. If this is not possible, pierce the cloth as shown on this sample and push the claw part of the clip into place through the material. ➡

ST39. Place the material on the bench with the claws sticking upwards through the material, and locate the retaining plate over the claws before bending them inwards with a light hammer.

ST40. Also available from MG specialists are the Tickford full tonneau cover and the hood cover, shown here.

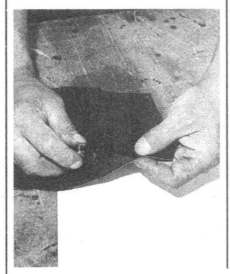

ST41. Early in 1992, Tickford introduced a soft-top fitting service, the cost being around half the price of one of their 'Original Equipment' soft-tops. Here, new soft-tops are constructed by the skilled Tickford/Coventry Hood workforce.

Boot Carpet

BC1. The Moss Boot Carpet kit, though not original, adds yet another luxury feel to the car and consists of a surprising number of ready-cut parts! ⬇

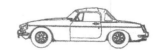

BC2. *The fitted kit looks elegant and allows you to fold up a jacket and put it in the back of the car without fear of it getting dirty.* ➡

Seat Belts

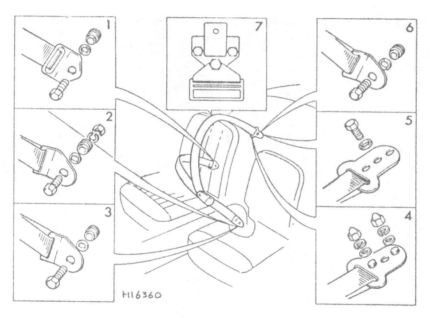

H16360

SB1. *These are the various belt fitting positions for the static type of seatbelt:*
1. sill;
2. drive-shaft tunnel (early cars);
3. drive-shaft tunnel (later cars);
4. wheel arch (early cars);
5. wheel arch first type belt (later cars);
6. wheel arch second type belt (later cars);
7. stowage clip.

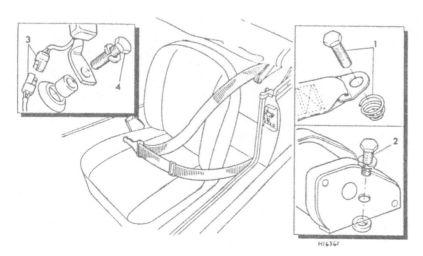

H16361

SB2. *This is one of the inertia reel seat belt types, with wiring connectors shown for USA and Canada cars.*

161

SB3. This is a different type of inertia reel belt fitted to certain cars and, once again, the wiring connections are for overseas cars, and, in this case, also for some UK cars. ➡

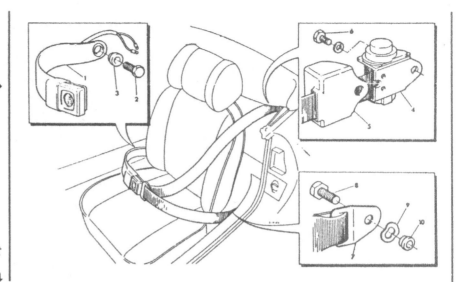

SB4. We fitted new Securon inertia reel belts to the project car, and would strongly recommend the owner does not even consider fitting static type seat belts. ⬇

SB7. With the trim in place, the seat belts were refitted as they had been trial fitted previously ...

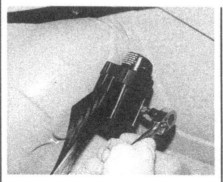

SB5. The seat belts were trial fitted before the trim went in, and it was found that the inertia reel units would only work with the drum at this angle. This is the rear right hand wheel arch.

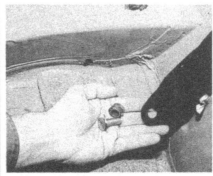

SB6. Don't forget to include the spacers and anti-rattle washers as described in the Securon instructions which you must read carefully and understand.

SB8. ... not forgetting to make the relevant cut outs in the carpets as shown in the carpet fitting section.
FOOTNOTE: Since producing this section the original pattern of inertia real seatbelts has been re-introduced through the efforts of Heritage.

Chapter 6
Mechanical

Introduction

Among some of the uninitiated the MGB has gained a reputation for being difficult to work on. In fact, that is an unfair judgement to make and, although it's true that in some respects the dear old car is a bit of a 'B' to work on in more ways than one, there's nothing difficult about it. Sometimes awkward and time consuming, yes; difficult, no!

Before carrying out any of the restoration jobs listed here, a complete set of tools should be bought or hired - and there will still be money to spare when compared with the cost of having main-dealer work carried out! In addition, a Haynes Owner's Workshop Manual should be regarded as a vital - and inexpensive - part of any toolkit. It gives all the fine detail, dimensions, clearances etc. not included here. This chapter is aimed specifically at the older-car owner who is confronted with dirty, worn and possibly difficult-to-remove components. As a friend of the author's once pointed out: 'You should never despair when mechanical things are a problem to repair. You just have to remember that man made them, and man can take

them apart; so you've got to win in the end!'

This chapter aims to pick out, in advance, the problems you are most likely to encounter.

Safety

THESE SAFETY NOTES APPLY TO THE WHOLE OF THIS CHAPTER.

Abide by the correct safety procedures outlined in Appendix 1. Ensure that the car is raised off the ground in such a way that it cannot topple onto anyone underneath it, bearing in mind the amount of force that will be applied to it, and NEVER rely on the handbrake to hold a car that is on a slope or on ramps. Ensure that whenever possible there are always two wheels remaining on the ground and that they are chocked so that the car cannot move when using jacks or ramps. Use axle stands when working under the car, NOT the jack.

Fitting the Crossmember

The crossmember shown here has been converted to take the

Moss coil-over-shockabsorber front suspension, so you will see a hole in the shock absorber mounting plates where none would normally be found. Other than that, there is no difference and the crossmember fits in the normal way.

You almost never have to replace a crossmember except when building up a new shell.

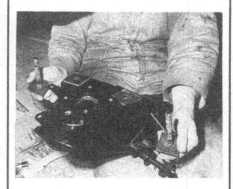

FCM1. Remember to rescue the rubber buffer pads from the donor car - they usually survive intact - or make up new ones from the correct thickness of rubber. The mounting bolts are so sturdy and well protected that they also are invariably reusable. Two rubber pads and metal plates fit beneath the bolt heads; two more sit between the top of the crossmember and the MGB's front chassis rails.

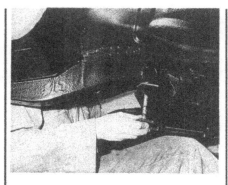

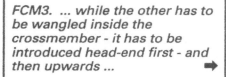

FCM2. Two bolts secure the crossmember at each end. One passes upwards through the extension bracket ...

FCM3. ... while the other has to be wangled inside the crossmember - it has to be introduced head-end first - and then upwards ... ➡

FCM4. ... where a plain washer and lock nut can be attached by hand. At this stage, Graham was sitting on the floor beneath the car supported on axle-stands (the car, of course) with the crossmember held on his knees while the bolts were pushed up from beneath. ⬇

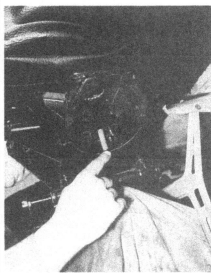

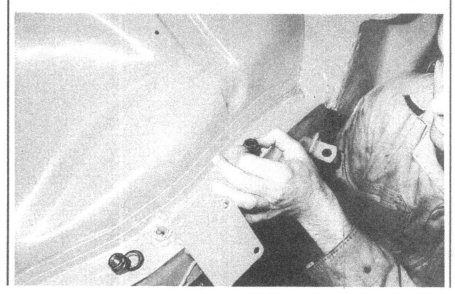

FCM5. Graham used the Sykes-Pickavant torque-wrench to tighten the crossmember nuts to the torque figure recommended in the manual. Copper Ease lubricating grease was smeared along each of the bolts, before fitting through the chassis members, to eliminate the risk of future corrosion. ⬅

Kingpin and Front Suspension

New kingpin bushes have to be reamed to size after being fitted to the stub axle, so when buying a new kingpin and bushes you are strongly recommended to go for an exchange stub axle assembly with the new bushes correctly reamed to size.

Also note that it is almost universally recommended now that MGB owners do not fit standard lower inner wishbone bushes, but that they fit the reinforced ones as used on the MGB GT V8. Only two per side (four per car) are needed because they are twice as long as the eight-per-car standard bushes. They provide more resistance to twisting between the shock absorber arms and the top trunnion and give better handling.

Safety

Observe all the normal safety rules when working beneath a car suspended above the ground - see Appendix 1. Make 110% sure that all the bolts and fittings are connected up - and that none are missed. Ensure that the kingpin clearance and free play are correct (see KFS28) before trying the car on the road. DO NOT DRIVE WITH STIFF KINGPINS BECAUSE STEERING WILL BE STIFF AND UNSAFE. If necessary, have a specialist check it over for you.

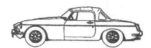

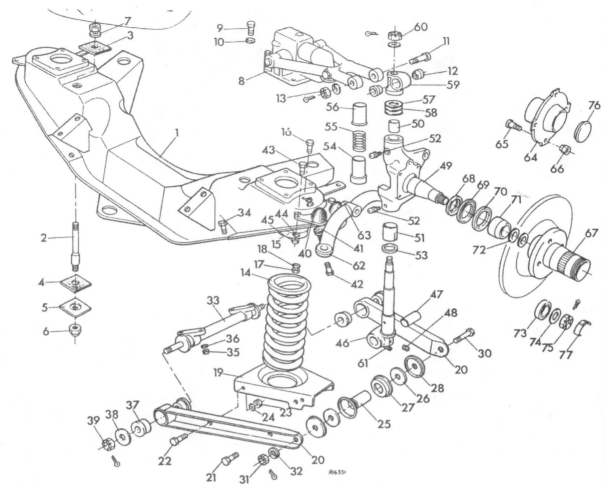

KFS1. The front suspension components (item numbers referred to hereafter in this section).

KFS2. A completely standard front suspension unit. Stripdown will be the reverse of the assembly procedure described in the latter parts of this section. Take very great care when disconnecting the kingpin because of the enormous force contained within the front coil springs. If the engine is in the car, you can place a trolley jack firmly and securely beneath the bottom trunnion and then lower the trolley jack very slowly and carefully whilst supporting the car itself on an axle stand, or you could use the Sykes-Pickavant spring clamps described later in this section. For safety's sake, we chose to use both together!

KFS3. Extracting the old bushes from the inner end of the wishbone arms can be tricky. We applied releasing fluid ...

KFS4. ... then used a pair of spanner sockets - one large and one small - to force the bush right out of the end of the wishbone arm.

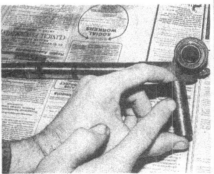

KFS5. To get the last bit out, the bush was gripped in the vice and the arm levered upwards.

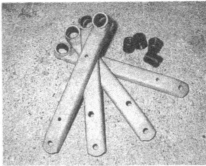

KFS6. Needless to say, new bushes were to be fitted later. The wishbone arms themselves had been sandblasted and were to be painted in Wurth zinc-rich primer and aerosol black Smoothrite.

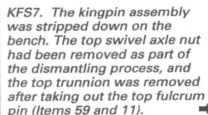

KFS7. The kingpin assembly was stripped down on the bench. The top swivel axle nut had been removed as part of the dismantling process, and the top trunnion was removed after taking out the top fulcrum pin (Items 59 and 11). ➡

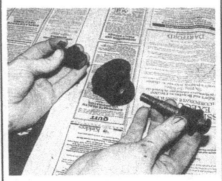

KFS8. This is the fulcrum pin and the old bushes as they come out of the trunnion. The bottom swivel bolt and bush (Items 30 and 47) often wear, and the bush at least should be replaced.

KFS9. The kingpin (Item 46) slides easily out of the stub axle (Item 49).

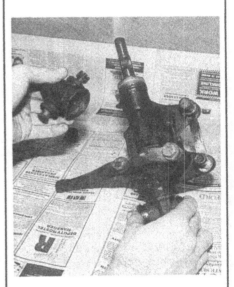

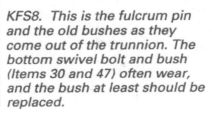

KFS10. This is an example of the wear that can take place in the swivel pin bush ...

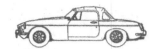

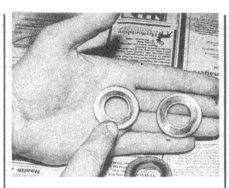

KFS11. ... and of that which occurs in the top thrust washers (Items 57 and 58).

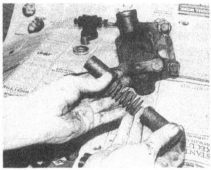

KFS13. Look after these components! Clean them up carefully, paint and grease them ready for re-use.

KFS14. We have long been admirers of XL Component's reconditioned lever arm shock absorbers. Mark Marwood's company, while expanding in other directions, has always retained a specialism in these products, which means that they do a darn good job of reconditioning them!

KFS12. The dust excluders can be extracted from the kingpin by pushing down against the force of the spring and taking all three components out together (Items 54, 55 and 56).

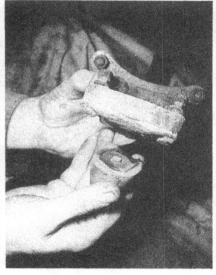

KFS15. The usual fate of aged bump stops! Not only does the bump stop rubber come adrift, but the aluminium packing piece corrodes heavily against the steel with which it comes into contact, and the whole thing expands and buckles. ←

KFS16. Fortunately, Moss are able to supply (as with almost everything else!) new bump stops complete with top and bottom rubbers and new aluminium spacer blocks. ←

KFS17. Their bright zinc-plated mounting bolts finish the job off properly and will cut down to some degree on the resultant corrosion.

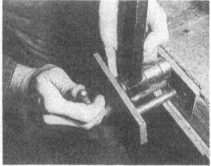

KFS20. A reversal of the previous process (see KFS4) ensured that the new wishbone bushes were pushed fully home. Don't use grease - it rots rubber! Waxoyl is said to be OK.

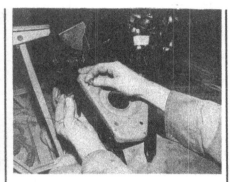

KFS22. Wishbone pans bolt between the wishbone pivots ...

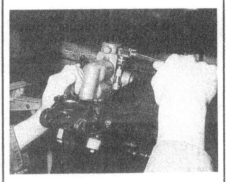

KFS18. The XL front shock absorbers were bolted down into the four large captive nut positions on top of the crossmember.

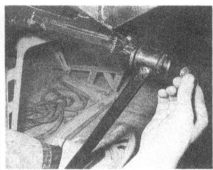

KFS21. The washer nut and split pin (Items 38 and 39) can next be fitted to the end of the wishbone pivots.

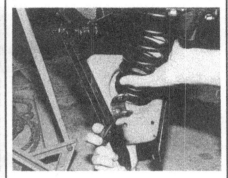

KFS23. ... and the new road springs, also available from XL Components, are inserted between the wishbone pans and their housings in the crossmember.

KFS19. On some Heritage bodyshells there is insufficient clearance between the top of the shock absorber and the inner wing/flitch panel, which means that the flitch panel has to be hammered out of the way to make room for the top of the shock absorber.

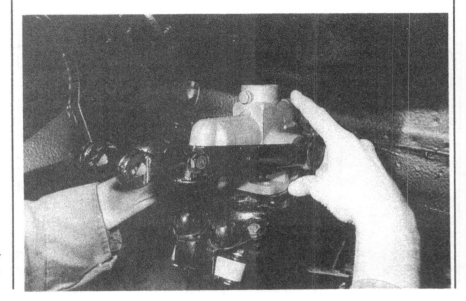

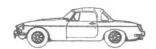

KFS24. Graham has already started to use the Sykes-Pickavant spring compression tools at this point although, strictly speaking, he could have waited until the kingpin assembly had been fitted to the ends of the wishbones. ➡

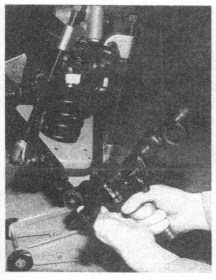

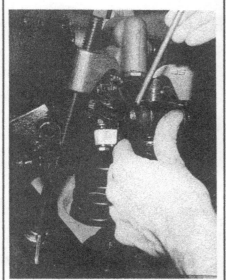

KFS25. He backed off the bolts holding the pivot arms together on the XL Components shock absorber, so that the top trunnion bushes could be inserted more easily.

KFS27. A new split pin - very cheap and very essential!

KFS28. The kingpin top nut, when tightened down to the torque recommended in the manual, should also be fitted with a new split pin. Before doing so you should check that there is no more than 0.002 inches ('two thou') of play, or up and down movement, in the kingpin. Arrange to purchase a whole selection of thrust washers so the the right amount of play can be established. In practice, 'two thou' of play will mean that you can scarcely detect any up and down movement at all but - and this is important - there must be no stiffness when attempting to move the stub axle forwards and backwards through its full steering range.

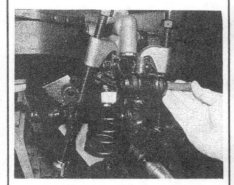

KFS26. A new fulcrum pin was fitted (Item 11) and, when tightened up, the shock absorber bolts were re-tightened.

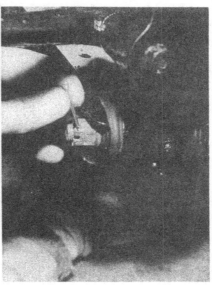

KFS29. More new split pins - this time in the bottom pivot bolt nut after, once again, tightening up to the recommended torque. The trick is to tighten up correctly, and then back off the slot in the castleated nut by the smallest amount possible to expose the hole through which the split pin can be passed before being split open and bent in opposite directions on the other side. See your workshop manual for further details. ⬅

169

Steering Rack & Column

When removing a steering column from a car which is to be rebuilt, make careful note of the positions of all packing washers so that they can be replaced in the same positions. The same applies to any shims that may have been fitted to the steering rack mountings, but which might not have been riveted down as recommended in the manual.

Safety

When fitting a completely new steering column and/or steering rack, and fitting them to a new bodyshell, the correct alignment of column and rack is critical. If you are fitting the energy- absorbing or collapsible type of steering column, and if alignment cannot simply and exactly be guaranteed, you would be strongly recommended to take the job to a specialist engineering shop. Have any work on the steering system checked after completion by a specialist, unless you are a fully trained mechanic.

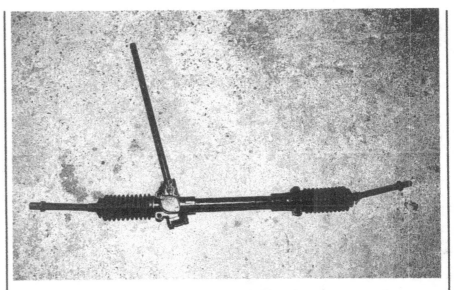

SRC2. XL Components, bless 'em, also recondition steering racks, and it was from them that we obtained a fully rebuilt steering rack to be fitted to the project Heritage MGB. ↑

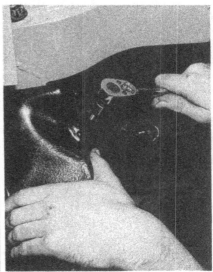

SRC3. Graham started by clearing the threads in the crossmember because they had been clogged when the crossmember was plastic powder coated. ➡

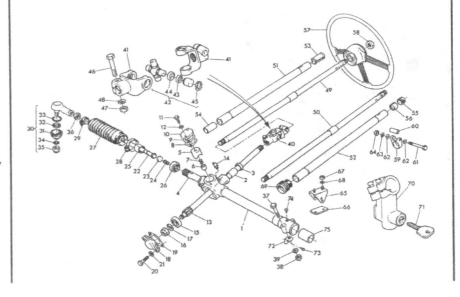

SRC1. This is an exploded view of the steering gear, although you are strongly recommended not to strip down the steering rack yourself. Rather, when it is worn, exchange it for a reconditioned one. Item 70 is the steering lock fitted to later models.

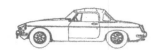

SRC4. The mounting holes in the XL Components rack were slotted, as all of them are but, as a variation on the theme of Orwell's pigs, some are more slotted than others. This feature - the slots not the pigs - will be relevant later.
(Incidentally, it is the slots in the original castings that vary; nothing to do with the work that XL Components carry out on them.) ➡

SRC9. The old felt was pulled out of its steel retainer and a new piece of felt obtained from Moss.

SRC5. The rack is introduced to its mounting brackets from beneath the car - easy to see with no engine in place.

SRC10. It was soaked for 24 hours in lubricating oil before being fitted back into the steering column tube.

SRC7. Graham had previously stripped down the whole steering column assembly for reconditioning.

SRC6. Note that the frontmost mounting is by bolt and nut, whereas the top one is by bolt into captive nut. Don't tighten down at this stage.

SRC8. Play could easily be felt between the steering column and the top bush in the column tube. This was extracted from the column tube. ➡

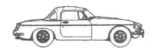

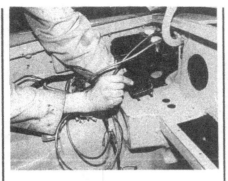

SRC11. The column bottom mounting plate is secured through the bulkhead, and this plate fits on top of the bulkhead before washers and nuts are assembled.

SRC12. Here you can see at the top of this picture the plate referred to in the previous shot, and here is the steering column draught excluder (Item 69) being offered up to the hole inside the driver's side footwell. ➡

SRC13. And with the column in place, and the rack in place - it was found that the universal joint could not be fitted because the two did not line up! It was then that the full amount of movement in the XL Component's rack was taken advantage of. In fact, we had to remove the rack, and file the slots a little longer, but this was done by as little as possible to ensure that the strength was not removed from this part of the rack. If you have to take off more than a few strokes of the file will manage, give up; do not take chances - get specialist advice. The workshop manual refers to shims being available to pack the rack, but these are no longer available and you would have to have them specially made. In our case, up and down movement was not sought, or necessary. ➡

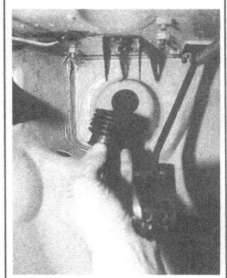

SRC14. A lot more movement was found to be available in the lower end of the steering column, although we had to file out the hole in the bulkhead to enable the column to move quite far enough. ⬅

SRC15. When things were sufficiently lined up, the new universal joint was pushed on so that the fixing bolts could pass through the slots in the steering column and the steering pinion. Line up the holes exactly with the slot. Many a thread has been stripped by those forgetting this necessity!

SRC16. The steering column top mounting position in the lower part of the dashboard.

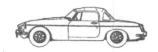

Front Suspension Conversion

The MGB's standard front suspension is one of the car's most obvious Achilles' heels. Among its many failings is the car's inability to soak up low speed bumps, and a lack of adhesion when cornering at speed. One of the problems is that the lever arm front shock absorbers also have to act as the top suspension arm, and they're not really up to the job, allowing too much movement to take place in the wrong directions. Another is that the lever arm shockers themselves are not able to soak up the bumps with the efficiency of a modern telescopic shock absorber. To overcome these problems, Moss Europe have developed a new front suspension system that enables the existing one to be adapted to a more modern format whilst allowing the owner to change back to the original system if he or she should wish to at any time. This is certainly not the case with some of the alternative conversions on offer!

Toolbox

In addition to the normal tools used when working on the front suspension, you will need an electric drill and a sharp, coarse half round file. There is quite a lot of filing to do, so it may be worth while investing in a new file.

Safety

Observe all the normal safety rules when working beneath a car suspended above the ground - see Appendix 1. Make 110% sure that all the bolts and fittings are connected up as shown in the instructions that come with the kit - read the instructions carefully! - and be sure that none is missed.

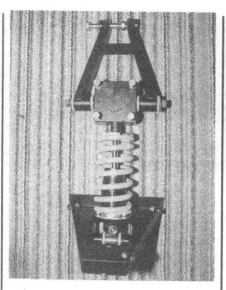

FSC1. *This is the system as it is delivered from Moss with all the components assembled in the correct order.*

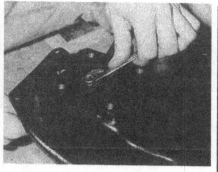

FSC2. *This is the kit broken down into its component parts. Note that Moss strongly recommend the fitting of uprated MGB V8 bushes. (Courtesy: Moss Europe)* ➡

FSC3. *We decided to carry out the conversion work while the crossmember was off the car, but you certainly don't have to do it this way, and the kit can be fitted with the car complete. A dished plate is found inside the crossmember dome, and it can be removed first by undoing the nut and bolt shown here ...* ➡

FSC4. *... then this one - Graham is using a socket spanner out of view beneath the crossmember ...*

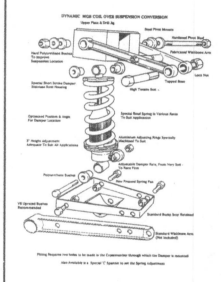

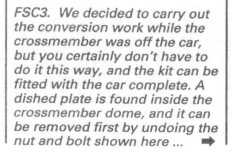

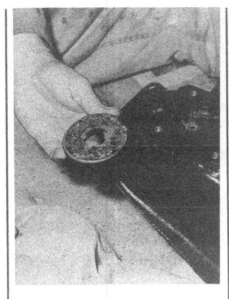

FSC5. ... and then the plate which locates the top of the standard car's coil spring can be taken from inside the crossmember.

FSC6. This plate is part of the kit and also acts as a template for modifying the crossmember. Bolt it down to the crossmember using the mounting points for the old shock absorbers. Then, using the 1/4 in. drill provided with the kit, drill through each of the ring of holes shown here. ➡

FSC7. Remove the template and switch to the larger 3/8 in. bit, supplied with the kit, to enlarge the first set of holes. We used Castrol releasing fluid to keep the drill bit cool whilst it was doing its job - the steel here is quite thick and the drill could easily lose its edge through overheating. ➡

FSC8. With the jagged-edged centre taken away, the hole can be opened out further with the file.

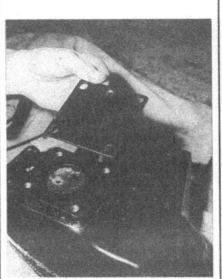

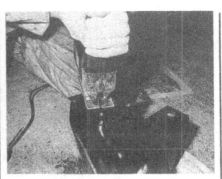

FSC9. In practice, we found it easier to drill one larger hole and then cut around the rest of the opening with a metal cutting blade in the jigsaw. This saved a lot of time and gave a neater result.

FSC10. With the standard bump stops mounted on the crossmember, the pivot mounts can be placed over the former shock absorber mounting holes ...

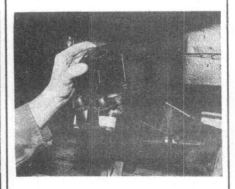

FSC11. ... the upper plate placed over them, and the bolts provided in the kit used to install them.

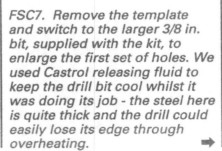

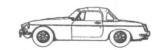

FSC12. Welcome to the real world! We were supposed to pass the top mounting of the new damper through the hole cut in the crossmember but it was quite a lot too small. We used a Black and Decker Power File to quickly sand away the required amount of metal. Wear goggles when working beneath the car.

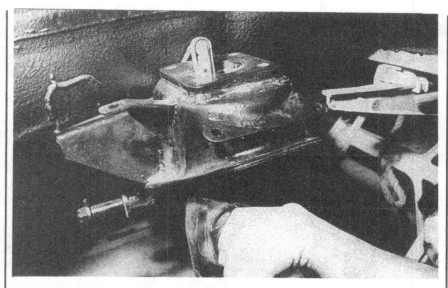

FSC13. Back to Plan A! The shock absorber top mount was installed with the plastic bushes and pivot stud.

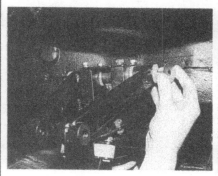

FSC14. New bushes, new wishbone arms, washers and nuts can all be fitted at this stage.

FSC15. The idea is that the pivot stud will stay fixed in place while the wishbone arms and shock absorber pivot on the plastic bushes provided. A grub screw and Allen key are provided to tighten the stud and stop it from turning.

FSC16. The existing wishbone arms are supplemented by a brand new replacement for the bottom spring pan. The new bottom shock absorber bolts to the new pan and the pan is fitted to the wishbone arms in the conventional way.

FSC17. The front stub axle assembly and anti-roll bar link are both connected in the conventional way ...

FSC20. This shop demo. piece shows how the kit looks when it's not surrounded by the car's bodywork. ⬆

In the author's opinion the Moss kit is one of the most worthwhile modifications that you could possibly make to your MGB. Ride quality is very much improved with less bump-thump, more comfort and more positive steering. Turn-in is sharper, steering responses generally are enhanced and steering patter is greatly reduced when cornering on a bumpy road at speed.

FSC18. ... but before tightening everything up, add the separate bridge piece that links and reinforces the top wishbone arms.

FSC19. Damper settings can easily be adjusted by turning the knurled screw on the bottom of the damper, and ride height can also be set with a special 'C'-spanner used to screw the height adjustment rings up or down the damper as required. ➡

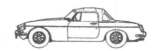

Anti-roll Bar

ARB1. The rubber anti-roll bar bushes have a split in them to enable them to be passed over the bar, and each of the two bushes is fixed to the chassis with a U-shaped strap. ➡

ARB2. A special clip is held to the anti-roll bar with a pair of small nuts and bolts to prevent the bar from moving sideways under load. When you change the anti-roll bar, retrieve the old clips - if they're in good condition - and switch them to the new bar.

ARB5. The anti-roll bar assembly. Item 14 relates to the Roadster; items 18 and 19, 20 and 21 to the GT. Thicker anti-roll bars require different sized bearings (Item 5). ⬇

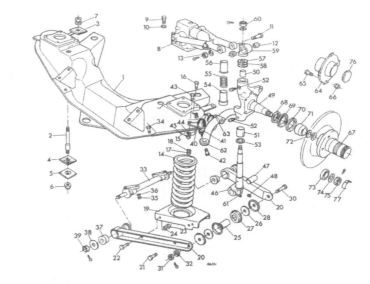

ARB3. The anti-roll bar link bolts to the bottom wishbone and pan on both the conventional and the Moss converted suspension.

ARB4. The end of the anti-roll bar being connected to the link shown in the previous shot.

Many MGB authorities recommend the fitting of a thicker anti-roll bar as a means of improving the MGB's handling. The author tried it to the MGB V8 he once owned and felt that the stiffer bar made the car understeer even more than normal. Instead, stiffer shock absorber settings and a standard anti-roll bar were fitted and, in the author's personal opinion, this provided the best option. It must be said that not everyone agrees with him!

Front Hub, Disc & Backplate

Toolbox

Jack and axle stand; socket set; long extension bar; Rover Special Tools Nos. 18G 284 and 18G 284D - or see text.

Safety

Remember the safety rules when working on a car supported off the ground - see Appendix 1. Securely chock the front wheels in both directions. Don't inhale brakeshoe dust - any asbestos content can cause lung cancer. Always wear an efficient particle mask and dispose of all waste efficiently.

It's not uncommon for the splines on wire wheel hubs to wear and need replacement. One of the symptoms is of wheels that clonk under braking. It has even been known for splines to wear to such a degree that the wheel breaks free under heavy braking and spins on the hub which of course means that there will be no brakes at all on that particular wheel. Don't take chances with worn splines; replace hubs and wheels if necessary. One indication of worn splines is that they will feel sharp when you run your finger along them.

Wheel bearings need replacement if they make a rumbling sound as you are driving along or, when they're stripped down, there is evidence of marks or pitting on the bearing races, or if the bearings make an uncouth noise when you spin them in your hand.

Brake discs should be replaced as a matter of course if they are scored or worn down at all. Braking efficiency relies

upon there being plenty of 'meat' in the brake discs in order to dissipate the heat. The discs shown being fitted in this section are V8 discs from AP Lockheed, and you are strongly recommended to only use genuine AP Lockheed discs as fitted in the factory to MGBs. Specialists such as Moss will be able to supply them off the shelf. Disc will have to be replaced if they have warped. Maximum disc runout is 0.006 in. at outer edge of disc face. Measurements will have to be made by a properly equipped specialist. Subjective symptoms include a "pumping" feeling through the brake pedal when brakes are applied.

You can remove the front hub by disconnecting the front brake calliper, without taking off the flexible hose. This removes the need for bleeding the brakes later. Have ready a stout piece of wire to hang the calliper up inside the wheel arch, so as not to put any pressure on the flexible hose. It must not be stretched by the weight of the calliper left hanging on it. In other respects, dismantling is the reversal of the procedure shown here, except that the hub may have to be levered off with a pair of stout tyre levers.

HDP1. If you're changing the wire wheeled hub, the studs for holding the brake disc to the hub will have to be swapped over. Run a scrap nut down the stud until it is level with the top of the stud ...

HDP2. ... then hammer the stud until it comes free from the hub. You will see that the stud has a set of splines just beneath the head ...

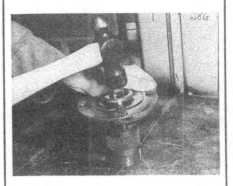

HDP3. ... place each stud in turn into the hub from the back and then hammer very smartly down until the head is completely tight against the back of the hub flange.

HDP4. You can now fit the disc to the hub with new lock nuts tightened to the torque recommended in the workshop manual.

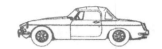

Refer to illustration KFS1. in the section 'Kingpin and Front Suspension' for references to item numbers in the rest of this section.

HDP5. The bearing spacer (Item 71) will fit inside the hub between the inner bearing and the shims.

HDP7. ... and the rollers themselves which are shown here being heavily lubricated with Castrol LM (high-melting-point) grease.

HDP8. Next the oil seal (Item 69) can be carefully fitted to the hub with the lip facing inwards or uppermost in this shot. The space between the bearing and the oil seal should be packed with more Castrol LM grease, and the oil seal itself wiped around with grease. ➡

HDP9. The back plate, sandblasted to bare metal and painted with Smoothrite is shown being fitted ... ⬇

HDP10. ... and the oil seal collar (Item 68), having been wiped all around with grease, is being pushed onto the stub axle.

HDP6. The inner bearing comes in two parts; the outer race which must be pushed or carefully drifted down inside the hub housing, taking care not to mark the surface on which the rollers will run ...

HDP14. ... followed by the bearing retaining nut (Item 75). ←

HDP11. The front hub and disc assembly have been placed on the stub axle and Graham is holding a set of shims (Item 72). Moss can supply packing shims in three different thicknesses; three, five and ten 'thou'; (thousandth of an inch) ATB4240, ATB4241 and ATB4242 respectively. You are supposed to fit the outer bearing retaining washer and tighten the nut. Measure the end float in the bearings, using a dial test indicator. Remove the nut, pull the hub assembly from the axleshaft and reduce the number of shims to produce the required end float. It should be .002 ('two thou') to .004ins. ('four thou'). Clearly, the vast majority of home workshops are not going to have a dial test indicator. You could use the method described later and then take the car to a specialist to have the end float checked to make sure that it is within the accepted tolerances. Read on!

HDP13. Next comes the bearing retaining washer (Item 74), the tab on the washer being aligned with the key way in the stub axle ...

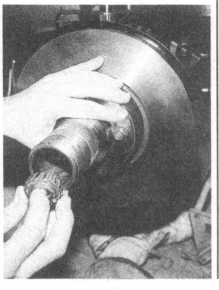

HDP15. The retaining nut should be tightened up to the torque figure given in the workshop manual. The trial-and-error method of obtaining something like the correct end float is as follows: Fit and tighten the hub as shown. If the hub turns freely, dismantle it back as far as HDP11, and take out one or two shims. Reassemble and tighten to the specified torque. If the hub still rotates freely, carry out the same procedure again until there is the beginnings of some resistance to the free rotation of the hub. If you have done this correctly, the end float will be exactly zero. By disassembling the unit again and adding one of the shims with the thickness of 0.003ins. ('three thou'), the freeplay should be just that: 'three thou'. It is essential that you subsequently have the freeplay checked by an engineer with a dial test indicator.

HDP12. After fitting the outer race of the outer bearing (Item 73), lots more Castrol LM grease can be packed in and then the roller bearings added. ➡

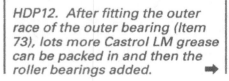

HDP16. Turn the castelated nut until it aligns with the hole through the stub axle which will enable you to fit a new split pin through the hole in the splines in the hub. Bend over the ends of the split pin - always use a new one.

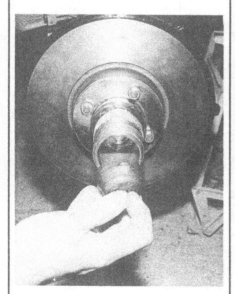

HDP17. Remember to refit the grease retainer cap, after packing it with Castrol high-melting-point grease.

Halfshafts and Rear Hubs

Toolbox

Jack and axle stands; socket set; long extension bar; Rover Special Tools Nos. 18G 284 and 18G 284D - or see text.

Safety

Remember the safety rules when working on a car supported off the ground - see Appendix 1. Securely chock the front wheels in both directions. Don't inhale brakeshoe dust - any asbestos content can cause lung cancer. Wear an efficient particle mask.

Earliest MGBs were fitted with what is known as a three-quarter floating axle, while later cars, including all GTs, were fitted with semi-floating axles. The early type, commonly known as the 'Banjo' rear axle because of the shape of the axle tube, has a different type of halfshaft for the disc wheel models when compared with that used for the later axle - also known as the tube-type axle.

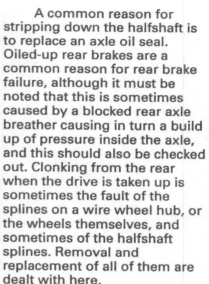

A common reason for stripping down the halfshaft is to replace an axle oil seal. Oiled-up rear brakes are a common reason for rear brake failure, although it must be noted that this is sometimes caused by a blocked rear axle breather causing in turn a build up of pressure inside the axle, and this should also be checked out. Clonking from the rear when the drive is taken up is sometimes the fault of the splines on a wire wheel hub, or the wheels themselves, and sometimes of the halfshaft splines. Removal and replacement of all of them are dealt with here.

It is just about possible to get away without draining the rear axle oil by ensuring that the side of the car that you are working on is raised high enough for the oil to run to the other end of the axle tube. Ensure that the car is not raised so high that it becomes unstable.

Halfshaft removal is not covered here, but it is basically a reversal of the re-fitting procedure that follows. Whilst stripping down, and when you are at the stage reached in illustration HH11, you are supposed to use one of the Rover Special Tools mentioned earlier in order to take hold of the halfshaft and withdraw it from the axle. You will usually find that the bearing is a tight fit in its housing. One way of getting it out would be to temporarily bolt the driving flange to the end of the halfshaft and then fit an old brake drum to the driving flange, back to front, and hammer the old brake drum outwards with a soft-faced hammer. Do not use one of the car's own brake drums because there is a serious risk of cracking the brake drum. An invisible hairline crack could cause the drum to fail in use with possibly lethal consequences. Don't take the risk!

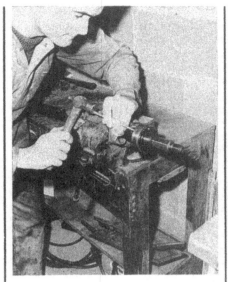

HH1. You can sometimes manage to drift a wheel bearing off a halfshaft and to drift a new one back on again, depending on the range of manufacturing tolerances you happen to encounter. But don't bank on it!

HH2. One of the Project car's new wheel bearings was too tight to get onto the halfshaft ...

HH3. ... so we took it to Nicol Transmission who pressed it on with their hydraulic press.

HH4. This disc wheel halfshaft is just about to be fitted to the tube-type axle on the V8 that the author once owned.

HH5. The halfshaft is just about to be drifted home. It will be necessary to go all the way around the outside of the bearing race and to tap that home once you have introduced the splines on the far end of the halfshaft into the differential unit.

HH6. The bearing cap is fitted with a new oil seal. Be sure to wipe a trace of grease around the inside of the oil seal so that it is lubricated when you first start using the car.

HH7. Use Hermetite before fitting the bearing cap ... ←

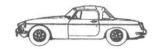

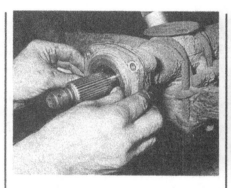

HH8. ... to make sure that there is no risk of oil leakage when the cap is fitted ...

HH11. A smear of Hermitite sealer is wiped around the halfshaft ...

HH14. A smear of Copper Ease type anti-seize compound is wiped onto the collar ...

HH9. ... and held down with the bolts that pass right through the brake back plate.

HH12. ... and onto the collar (see HH24 item 44) ...

HH15. ... and onto the splines inside the driving plate.

HH10. As referred to earlier, the inside of the bearing is now being lubricated, here with oil rather than grease.

HH13. ... before lightly tapping the collar fully home.

HH16. The driving plate is pushed fully home onto the halfshaft, followed by the special axle shaft collar (Item 49) ...

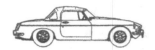

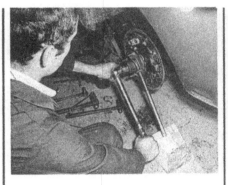

HH17. ... before the halfshaft nut is tightened up to the figure shown in the workshop manual. Quite a lot of force will be required, so note how the hub is locked to prevent it from turning.

HH19. In the case of wire wheeled cars the hub and wire wheel splines are an integral unit.

HH21. ... followed by the halfshaft nut ...

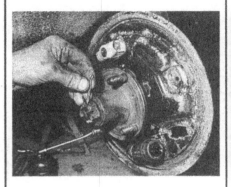

HH18. Use a new split pin to secure the castelated halfshaft nut, bending open the ends of the split pin after fitting.

HH20. Graham fits the axleshaft collar ...

HH22. ... here, the brake drum is in place, but it makes no difference. With an extension on the Sykes-Pickavant torque wrench, the halfshaft nut it torqued up to the figure shown in the workshop manual ...

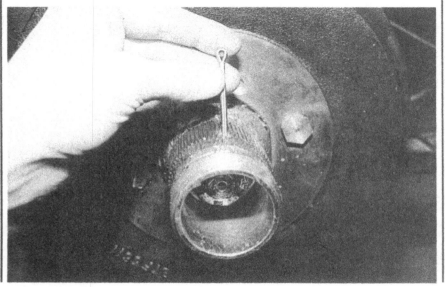

HH23. ... and then a hole in the splines is aligned with the slot in the castelated nut, which in its turn is aligned with the hole through the end of the halfshaft. The split pin is passed right through all of them until, reaching down inside the hub, the split pin is bent back as previously described.

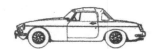

HH24. These are the components used in the semi-floating (tubed- type) rear axle, as fitted to the majority of MGBs. Note that it may be impossible to remove, and it will almost certainly be impossible to replace the differential unit without the use of a special tool. Nicol Transmission rebuilt the project car's differential and fitted it to the axle casing themselves. ➡

HH25. The three-quarter floating (banjo-type) rear axle as fitted to earlier Roadsters. This differential can be unbolted and removed (after pulling out the half-shafts) without the use of a special tool. ⬇

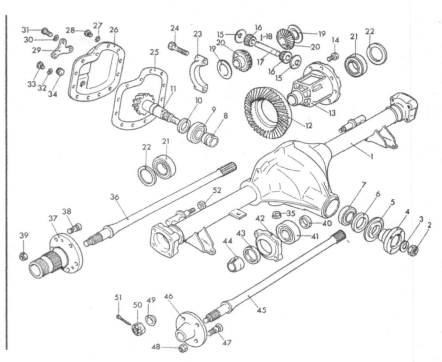

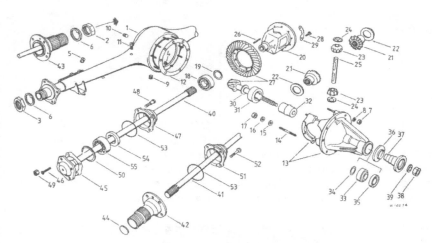

Notes

1.   On both types of axle, the new oil seal should be fitted into place with the lip facing inwards, towards the differential.

2.   When refitting hubs on to wire wheeled cars, make certain that you have the hub marked 'RH' on the right-hand side of the car and 'LH' on the left-hand side of the car, when viewing the car from the rear. The spinners are also marked. If you inadvertently reverse them, you stand a risk of losing a wheel when you are driving.

3.   When refitting the halfshaft to a banjo-type axle disc wheeled car, make sure that you renew the paper washer between the hub and the halfshaft flange.

4.   Banjo-type axle only. The outer bearing face should protrude 0.001 to 0.004 ins. (0.025 to 0.102mm) from the outer face of the hub after the bearing has been pressed into place, to ensure that the bearing is clamped by the axleshaft driving flange and the abutment shoulder in the hub.

5.   Remember to knock back the tab on locking washer (HH25, Item 6)

6.   Tube-type axle only. When having a new wheel bearing pressed onto the halfshaft, remember also to have the spacer pressed on first (HH24, Item 40)

Differential Mini-Overhaul

Clonks from the rear end of the MGB are most often caused by worn universal joints, or could be due to worn halfshaft splines or wire wheel splines. MG enthusiast and engineer, Peter Laidler, offered the following

mods. and checks in the MGOC magazine Enjoying MG some time ago.

You need specialist equipment to properly check wear in the differential and specialist equipment to remove it from the tubed-type rear axle. Our project car's differential unit was rebuilt by Nicol Transmission of Kidderminster, a company specialising in gearboxes and diffs. for MGBs and other British sports cars. Nicol removed the diff. from the axle and reconstructed it with all new bearings and seals, re-setting all the clearances correctly. This is not a job to be tackled by the home restorer, even if you could remove the differential in the first place. But you can do all of the following with the differential still in place.

Peter has devised the following means of testing the backlash in an MGB differential to give a 'rule of thumb' guide to whether it is wear-free, worn or worn out! He suggests removing the rear propshaft flange so that you have the differential flange facing you. You can now grip the differential flange and measure the amount of freeplay in it, starting from a point that you can mark on the differential casing. In Peter's view, and he admits that this is really a subjective opinion based upon his great experience as a motor engineering lecturer, six degrees of turn back in a clockwise direction would be typical of an unworn differential; ten degrees is the norm for a perfectly useable diff., whilst anything over thirteen degrees suggests that a complete overhaul is called for. Alternatively, you can make further marks on the differential casing and measure the distance between them, in which event, he says, the movements quoted would be 4.5mm, 8mm and 10mm respectively.

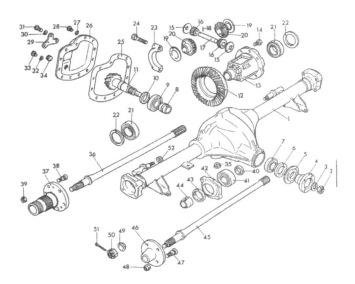

DO1. Peter's mini-overhaul plan is based on the replacement of thrust washers (Item 19) for the differential wheels (Item 20) and thrust washers (Item 15) for the differential pinions (Item 16). ⬆

DO3. After draining the differential oil, the car has to be safely supported above the ground (see 'Safety' in Appendix 1) and the halfshafts removed (see relevant section).

DO2. All these parts can be obtained from Moss. Peter also suggests replacing the roll pins (Item 18) with new split pins. ⬇

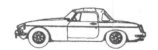

DO4. Now take off the differential casing backplate and the handbrake cable linkage.

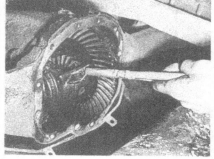

DO5. Turn the differential cage until each roll pin passing through the end of the cage and pinion pin becomes visible. Pull it out with pliers.

DO6. Now the pinion pin (Item 17) can be removed. Do not try to remove the pin by drifting it into the differential casing; you might snarl things up internally. Push or drift upwards, turn the cage until the pin faces you and then pull out with a pair of pliers. ➡

DO7. Now the sun gears (differential wheels, Item 20) and the two planet gears (differential gears, Item 16) can be rotated without the differential casing moving. Turn them to reveal the planet gears ... ➡

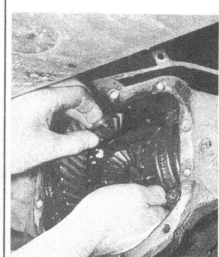

DO8. ... and remove them, one above and one below.

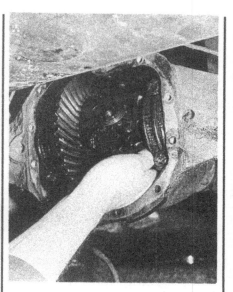

DO9. The new thrust washer will measure .034 in. in thickness. You can bet that the old one doesn't!

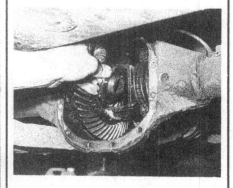

DO10. The sun gears can be removed next. They are fitted on to the ends of the half shafts, which don't have to be fully removed of course.

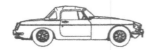

DO11. The thrust washers on the sun wheels are made of fibre (paxolin) and also wear relatively quickly. With all four thrusts worn, the gears are allowed to slip outwards on their bevels which gives more play between them, expressed as a 'clonk'. When they are moved closer in towards the centre, the play is taken up.

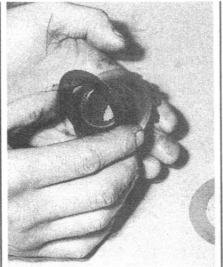

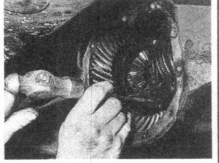

DO12. Believe it or not, reassembling really is the reverse of dismantling!

DO13. You could replace the old roll pins (Item 18) with new, but Peter suggests that it is possible, just possible, for the roll pins to come adrift and cause a major mashing in the differential. Peter recommends drifting in the roll pin and then adding a split pin through the centre of the roll pin and long enough to reach right through the cage, so that the ends can be turned over and tapped down, well out of the way of any differential components. There can be no harm in this latter mod., and it could save a lot of heartache and expense, especially where the virtually irreplaceable V8 diff. is concerned.

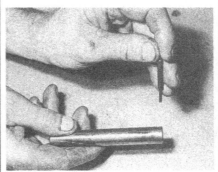

DO14. The pinion pin, a new roll pin with a split pin through the centre of it, ready to fit.

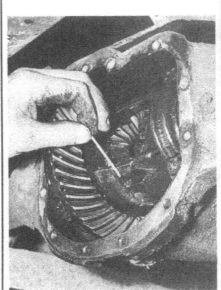

Propshaft and Gearbox Drive Flange

Most workshop manuals seem to give a fairytale method of replacing universal joints. Here's how we renewed them on the MGB.

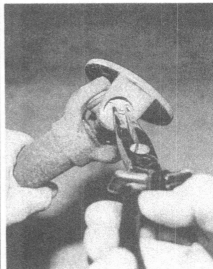

PG1. After drifting the end cap firmly downwards to take the pressure off the circlip, a pair of long-nosed pliers were used ...

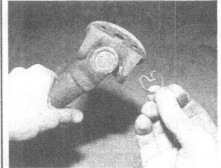

PG2. ...to extract the circlip. Quite a fiddle!

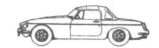

PG3. With all circlips out, the drive flange was placed on the edge of the vice and the yoke hammered downwards to drift the cap halfway out.

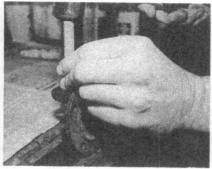

PG6. ... and the other cap drifted out of the yoke. A similar procedure was used to remove the UJ from the other half of the assembly.

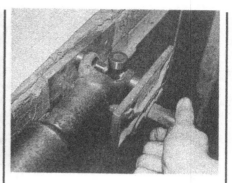

PG9. Then press them home in the vice, using a pair of spanner sockets to get them all the way in.

PG4. It was then grasped with a self-grip wrench and extracted.

PG7. The new UJ kit as supplied by Moss. We dismantled and added a touch more Castrol LM grease, although it wasn't strictly necessary.

PG10. Do the same with the remaining caps ...

PG5. The two halves were separated ...

PG8. Take off the caps with great care so that the needle roller bearings don't spill out onto the floor. Grease will hold them in but don't take chances! Carefully holding down the two caps that are to stay in place at this stage - you could use a rubber band - insert the new caps into the yoke as far as they will go. ➡

PG11. ... then fit the new circlips. These had small holes in them and demanded the use of a pair of circlip pliers.

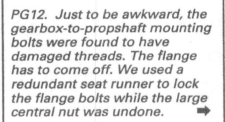

PG12. Just to be awkward, the gearbox-to-propshaft mounting bolts were found to have damaged threads. The flange has to come off. We used a redundant seat runner to lock the flange bolts while the large central nut was undone. ➡

PG14. Moss demonstrated their cleverness by supplying a new set of special bolts and lock nuts and the flange nut was refitted with a drop of Loctite to prevent it from coming undone. ⬆

PG13. And the nut, washer and flange were tapped off their spline. ⬇

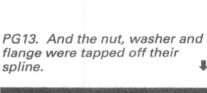

PG15. The propshaft could then be bolted to the gearbox.

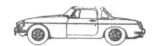

Wire Wheel Conversion

Toolbox

Jack and axle stand; socket set; long extension bar; Rover Special Tools Nos. 18G 284 and 18G 284D - or see text.

Safety

Remember the safety rules when working on a car supported off the ground - see Appendix 1. Securely chock the front wheels in both directions. Don't inhale brakeshoe dust - any asbestos content can cause lung cancer. Wear an efficient particle mask.

Steel wheel axles are about 1½ ins. wider than wire wheel axles and this causes wire wheels to foul the wheel arches if splined hubs are fitted to a steel wheel axle. (It also means that half-shafts are not interchangeable – take note if buying second-hand.)

Moss have come up with a rather brilliant conversion kit which consists, at the rear, of a special splined driving flange, or hub, which moves the wheel centre further inboard and allows even 185 tyres to just clear the wheel arches.

It is possible to convert tubed-type axles from non-wire wheel to wire wheel hubs by changing the driving flanges shown in HH24, Items 37 and 46. The trouble is ...

WW1. ... this is what you get at the rear of the car, especially with wider wheels and tyres. ➡ (We know that these are not wire wheels; they are Moss Minilite knock-on wheels which fit on to wire wheel splines.) In a few cases and with standard width tyres, you can just about get away with it, but in most cases, tyres foul on bodywork.

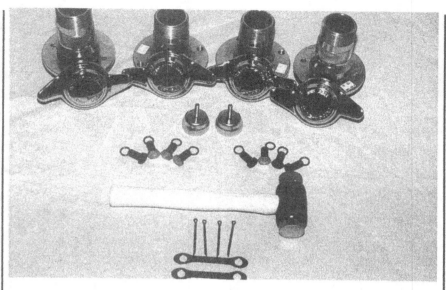

WW2. The complete kit consists of four hubs and spinners, two grease caps (frequently missing from cars in use) a wire wheel spanner and soft-faced mallet, special bolts, spring washers and split pins and full fitting instructions. Read the fitting instructions carefully before and whilst carrying out the work. The instructions in this book for front hub and rear halfshaft removal and replacement should give you a good idea of what is required. ⬆

WW3. The key to the extra clearance gained is in the rear hub. Take a look at the way in which the tapering shoulder at the back of the hub, on which the wire wheel locates, has been moved closer to the mounting flange at the back of the hub on the Moss component (right) compared with the standard item (left).

WW4. The standard hub has bolts which protrude forwards and on which nuts are fitted to mount the brake drum. The Moss hub has threaded holes and special bolts with shallow heads that face the opposite way to the standard ones. This saves the length of the stud and the thickness of the mounting nuts and enables each wheel to be moved inwards perhaps 5/8 in. when compared with the standard units.

Rear Springs, Shock Absorbers and Bump Stops

Toolbox

Set of spanners; jack; axle stands; wheel chocks.

Safety

Observe all the normal safety rules when working beneath a car suspended above the ground - see Appendix 1. Make 110% sure that all the bolts and fittings are connected up - and that none are missed.

SSB1. Before fitting the bump stop to the chassis, lubricate the fitting hole with Waxoyl. Don't use grease, because it causes rubber to go spongy.

SSB2. The bump stop is a hard push onto the mushroom shaped fitting peg inside the wheel arch.

SSB3. A replacement spring is best fitted first at the front spring hanger.

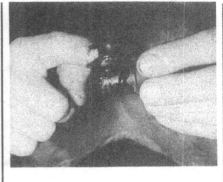

SSB4. Rear spring mountings have pairs of rubber bushes; the front has a metalastic bush pressed into the spring. Waxoyl help the rear bushes slip in more easily.

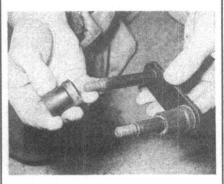

SSB5. The rear shackle pins are fitted with a pair of rubber bushes ...

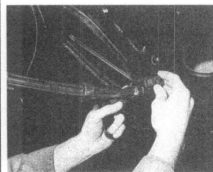

SSB6. ... and the shackle pins can be pushed through the rear chassis mounting point and the rear end of the spring with new rubber bushes fitted.

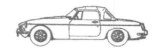

SSB7. The new spring from XL Components had to be jacked-up in the centre to take the weight off the spring so that Graham could carry out the fitting and concentrate on pushing the shackle pins and bushes into place. The shackle plate is next fitted over the inboard bushes - you may sometimes have to use a clamp to push it far enough on to get the spring washers and nuts started on the threads. ➡

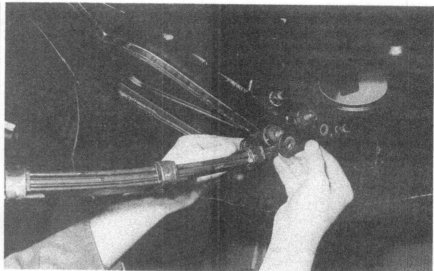

SSB8. New rubber pads were purchased from Moss ...

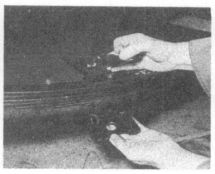

SSB9. ... to fit between the locating plates when the axle was fitted up.

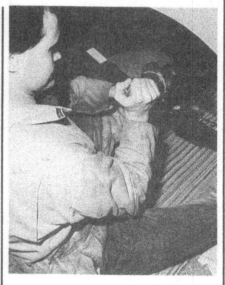

SSB10. With the top rubber pad and top locating plate resting on top of the spring (and both springs fitted to the car!) Graham manhandled the reconditioned axle underneath the car and placed it in position on top of the location plate.

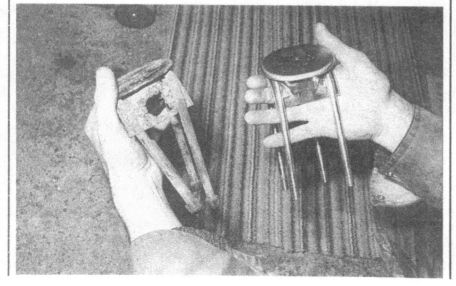

SSB11. Bump rubber pedestals are notorious for rusting out and, you can now purchase bright zinc-plated ones from Moss, along with matching U-bolts, all of which are very resistant to future corrosion.

193

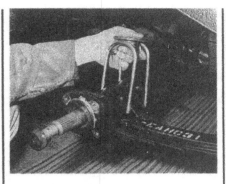

SSB12. The bump stop pedestal and U-bolts were slipped into position through the top locater plates and around the XL Components rear spring.

SSB13. The bottom rubber pad and bottom locater plate were pushed onto the U-bolts ...

SSB14. ... and the shock absorber link and plate added to the sandwich.

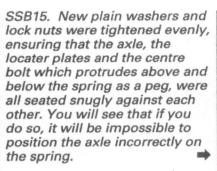

SSB15. New plain washers and lock nuts were tightened evenly, ensuring that the axle, the locater plates and the centre bolt which protrudes above and below the spring as a peg, were all seated snugly against each other. You will see that if you do so, it will be impossible to position the axle incorrectly on the spring. ➡

SSB16. XL Components are one of the country's leading specialists in reconditioned lever arm shock absorbers. One of their replacement units is shown here being offered up to the inner side of the rear inner wheel arch. ➡

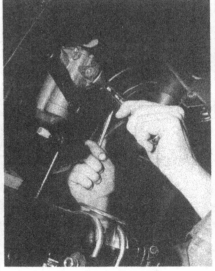

SSB17. They're simply located to the body with a pair of bolts, spring washers and nuts ...

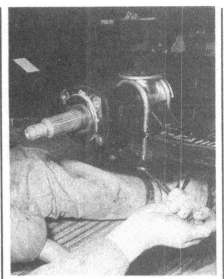

SSB18. ... and the shock absorber link described earlier is passed through the end of the arm and a plain washer, spring washer and nut fitted to secure it.

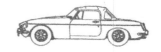

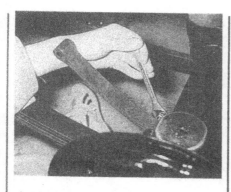

SSB19. Don't forget the rebound strap which bolts onto a special and rather flimsy mounting welded to the rear axle casing...

SSB20. ... and to a bracket on the underside of the body through which a nut and bolt are passed.

Note

When removing the old checkstrap, the nut holding it in place on the bracket on the rear axle frequently seizes solid, and the bracket itself is prone to shearing away. For that reason,

if the nut is in any way difficult to remove, use a nut splitter, or saw through the outer edge of the nut so as to ensure its removal without damaging the bracket. In the past, MGB rear axles have been scrapped because of this bracket breaking off. Now, Moss have put into production a repair kit which enables a replacement bracket to be clamped to the axle tube.

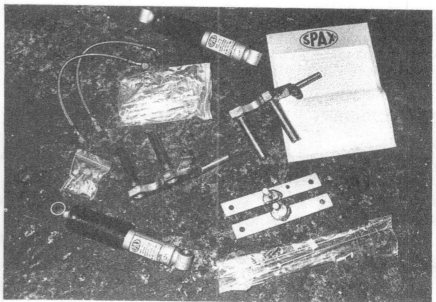

Telescopic Front Shock Absorber Conversion

Safety

Observe all the normal safety rules when working beneath a car suspended above the ground - see Appendix 1. Make 110% sure that all the bolts and fittings are connected up as shown in the instructions that come with the kit. Read the instructions carefully! - and be sure that none are missed.

Great improvements can be made to the MGB's front suspension by retaining the standard front shock absorbers as link arms, but doing away with their shock absorbing ability while replacing them with a pair of Spax telescopic dampers.

TS1. The Spax 'hardware' is zinc-plated for corrosion resistance and alongside the instructions, which you should read carefully before fitting, you will receive a set of braided flexible brake hoses, needed to reroute the brake lines away from the new shock absorbers. ⬆

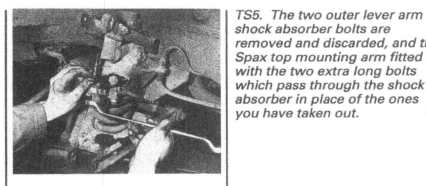

TS5. The two outer lever arm shock absorber bolts are removed and discarded, and the Spax top mounting arm fitted with the two extra long bolts which pass through the shock absorber in place of the ones you have taken out. ➡

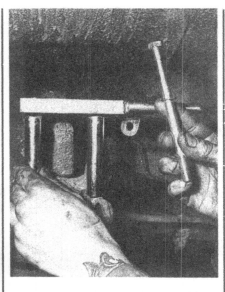

TS2. The king pin has been removed here, which you can ignore. The valve is removed from the bottom of the shock absorber unit ...

TS3. ... and the valve separated from the plug.

TS6. The new bottom shock absorber mounting bracket is fitted through the existing holes in the lower wishbone and pan. New bolts are supplied with the kit.

TS8. In place of the old flexible hose goes a piece of copper brake line, supplied with the kit, and then the braided hose takes up the strain from the mounting on the new top bracket.

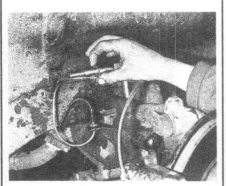

TS4. The valve is discarded, a plug replaced and the shock absorber refilled with fluid so that the spindle is properly lubricated.

TS7. The old flexible brake hose has to be removed; first from the bracket and then from the calliper.

TS9. Place the washer on the top bracket ...

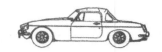

TS10. ... and then offer up the
new telescopic shock
absorber.

RSC1. The Spax rear telescopic
kit is as simple to fit as it
appears here.

TS11. Fit washers, lock nuts
and tighten up. Establish that
the new brake hoses are clear
of all the suspension
components and only then
tighten up. Bleed the brakes in
accordance with instructions in
your Haynes manual.

Telescopic Rear Shock Absorber Conversion

Safety

**Observe all the normal safety
rules when working beneath a
car suspended above the
ground - see Appendix 1. Make
110% sure that all the bolts and
fittings are connected up as
shown in the instructions that
come with the kit. Read the
instructions carefully! - and be
sure that none are missed.**

Fitting Spax shockers to either
the front or the rear end of the
car gives one distinct
advantages in that they can be
adjusted for stiffness, so you
can tune suspension to suit

your own needs.

Stiffer dampers do not only
mean less comfort, they also
give, theoretically, better
roadholding, but there can be a
flip side-literally! If one end of
the car is significantly stiffer
that the other, you may upset
the handling balance to such a
degree that oversteer or
understeer becomes excessive
and the car could become
dangerous. Drive the car with
great care after first fitting one
of these conversion kits, and if
you are not sure of the affect
that you are having on the
handling, have it checked over
by an expert. In general, such
changes as you make will be
beneficial, but they ought to be
part of a package. It's no good
fitting greatly improved, greatly
stiffened dampers to one end of
the car when all of the rest of
the suspension is badly worn
out.

Your best bet is to fit new
dampers, whether they be
reconditioned lever arm units
from Moss or from XL
Components or, telescopic
conversions from Spax, all
round the car at the same time.
Never replace just one shock
absorber; only ever replace
them in pairs.

RSC2. Graham studies the
fitting instructions carefully
before beginning work -
essential!

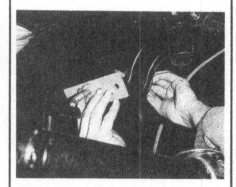

RSC3. The top mounts fit as a
direct replacement for the
original lever arm shock
absorbers.

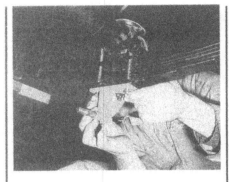

RSC4. The bottom mounts fit to the rear axle U-bolts in place of the original shock absorber link plates.

RSC5. Ensure that all four nuts are tightened evenly so that the U-bolts are pulled down level, and by an equal amount in all four corners. ➡

RSC6. The Spax shock absorber is simply fitted over the mounting pegs in a similar fashion to that shown for the front shock absorbers. This conversion was actually carried out on the project car and has proved to complement the Moss front suspension conversion quite superbly. ⬇

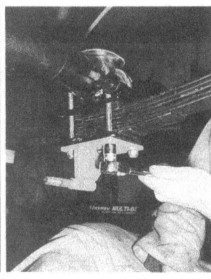

RSC7. You have to crawl underneath the car to adjust the rear shock absorber settings, but then it's simply a matter of turning a screwdriver in the slot shown here. ⬅

Front Brakes

Toolbox

Selection of hand tools; Automec copper brake pipes; Disc brake lubricant. We strongly recommend that only AP Lockheed brake components (fitted as standard to the MGB) are used when overhauling the brakes.

Safety

Unless you are an experienced and practised mechanic, do not work on the braking system by yourself without having someone who is fully trained check everything over after you have completed the work and before using the vehicle on the road. Check the workshop manual at each stage for each procedure.

While the standard MGB braking system is capable and efficient we decided to uprate it in view of the fact that the engine to be fitted would be a little more powerful than standard. The original brakes would probably have coped perfectly well but, where braking is concerned, it's better every time to be safe than sorry. We fitted MGB V8 brakes to the Project car giving even more efficient front brakes and better heat dispersal from the thicker V8 brake discs.

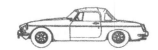

FB1. If just so happened that one of the calliper sets that we obtained was gold, the other silver. We used Smoothrite to make them a matching pair – keep it out of seals, dust plugs etc.

FB2. When bolting on new callipers, always use brand new tab washers. Ensure that bleed screws are at the top – these callipers can be fitted upside down. ➡

FB3. After tightening the fitting bolts the tab washer ears can be knocked over with a drift.

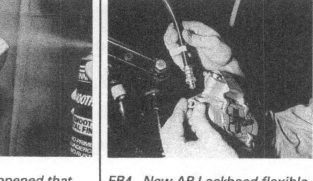

FB4. New AP Lockheed flexible brake hoses can be fitted, but always remember to use a new copper sealing washer.

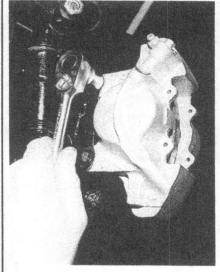

FB5. This special plate is fitted to the bracket on the crossmember ...

FB6. ... before the hose is connected up.

FB7. The thread on the end of the flexible hose can be fitted with the Automec copper brake pipe ...

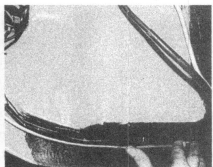

FB8. ... which can easily be bent and routed along the line of the body clips that must be used to hold it in position.

FB9. Just to make sure that the AP Lockheed brake pads would operate without a trace of squealing, Graham put on the slightest smear of Copper Ease to the metal face on the back of the pad. It is essential that you don't use too much Copper Ease and that none of it is allowed to get onto the friction surface or the disc. Use original metal shims if fitted. ➡

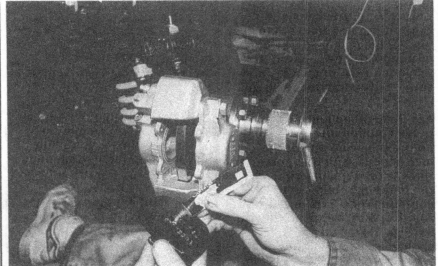

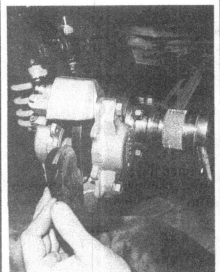

FB10. The pads can be slotted between disc and calliper pistons.

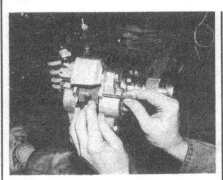

FB11. A pair of clips hold the discs in place ...

FB12. ... and are themselves located with split pins whose ends can be opened out once they have been fitted. NEVER RE-USE A SPLIT PIN; USE NEW!

FB13. It was good to be able to use brakes from the dear old V8 on the Project car, and it took quite a search to find them. As an alternative you could turn to Moss' own uprated front braking kit incorporating V8 AP Lockheed discs and Moss' own twin piston callipers. ⬅

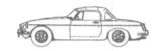

Rear Brakes and Backplate

Safety

Observe all the normal safety rules when working beneath a car suspended above the ground - see Appendix 1. Always have your work checked over by a trained mechanic before using the car on the road and after working on the brakes. Ensure that no oil or grease finds its way onto brake pads or linings. Take very great care not to breathe in any brake dust which may contain asbestos. Wear an efficient particle mask and dispose safely of waste. Ensure that no contamination gets into any of the hydraulic components. Always read the manufacturer's instructions with great care before replacing any of the brake components. Only ever use fresh brake fluid.

RBB1. The components in this exploded view of the rear brake assembly will be referred to later in the text. Note that the brake drum nut (Item 26) relates only to wire wheeled cars. ⬇

RBB2. The brake back plate is held on by four bolts and lock nuts (Items 2 and 3). Graham chose to fit them this way round.

RBB3. We used new AP Lockheed brake components throughout. AP Lockheed are the manufacturers of original equipment MGB brake parts. The assembled brake adjuster (Item 11) was bolted to the backplate with the two nuts and washers provided. Graham had taken the adjuster apart and lubricated all of the internal components with Copper Ease to prevent future corrosion. It's particularly important to lubricate the adjuster wedge (Item 13). ➡

RBB4. The new AP Lockheed wheel cylinder assembly was to be fitted next ...

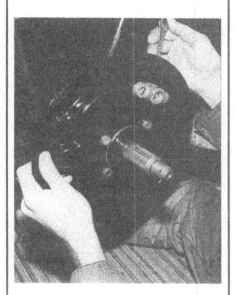

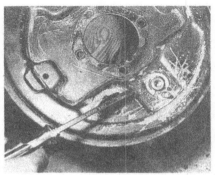

RBB5. ... and was clipped into place with the new retaining clip (Item 20). The "E" cup fitting tool STL 107 is available.

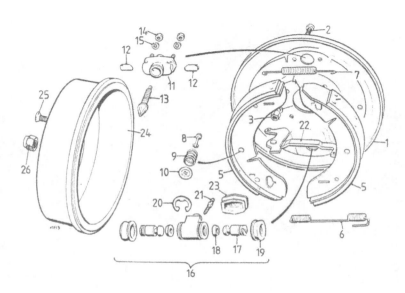

RBB6. Not the same car but the same principle ... the handbrake lever (Item 22) is introduced into the backplate ...

RBB7. ... and a new rubber boot fitted to the back of it.

RBB8. Here an existing adjuster is left attached to the backplate during a brake strip down, and the wedge, having been taken out of the assembly, has been greased ready for refitting.

RBB9. On either side of the wedge, there is a tappet (Item 12) lubricate as previously described and refitted, ensuring that the tapered end of the tappet matches the taper on the wedge.

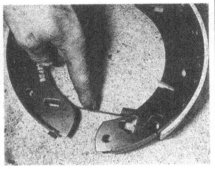

RBB10. You can fit the brakeshoe springs to the brakeshoes whilst they are off the car - note how the bottom spring is fitted to the relevant brakeshoe ...

RBB11. ... and the brakeshoes forced apart and pulled on to the adjuster and the wheel cylinder in turn. ↑

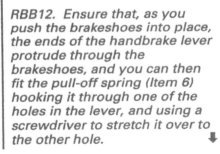

RBB12. Ensure that, as you push the brakeshoes into place, the ends of the handbrake lever protrude through the brakeshoes, and you can then fit the pull-off spring (Item 6) hooking it through one of the holes in the lever, and using a screwdriver to stretch it over to the other hole. ↓

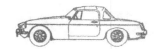

RBB13. Two steady pins (Item 8) - one for each brakeshoe - are pushed through the back of the backplate and through the hole in the middle of the brakeshoe. ➡

RBB14. The spring (Item 9) and steady washer (Item 10) can then be fitted. You hold the steady pin tight against the backplate from the back of it; push the steady washer over the pin and against the force of the spring and twist through 90 degrees.

RBB16. ... before refitting to the car.

RBB17. When fitting new components - this is a new AP Lockheed brake drum going on to the project car - you should slacken the adjuster right off, and also ensure that the handbrake is not connected so that the brakeshoes are 'in' as far as they will go. Occasionally, as happened with us, you can have an inordinate amount of trouble just getting the brakeshoes centralised and the brake drum on!

RBB18. And then you find that it has to come off again and be turned through 90 degrees so that the holes for the brake drum screws (Item 25) line up with the threads in the hub. In the case of wire wheeled cars, the brake drums are held on with four lock nuts (Item 26). ⬇

RBB15. Where a serviceable brake drum is being reused, it can have any shine taken off it with a piece of wet-or-dry paper or silicon carbide ...

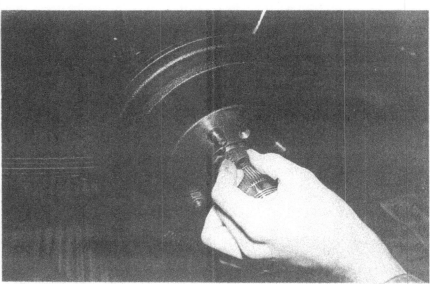

Handbrake Mechanism

HB1. The old mechanism has been removed from the car, and new handbrake and ratchet obtained from Moss (the ratchet mechanism can wear), and new cables obtained from Speedy Cables in London. Ensure, when ordering a new handbrake cable, that you quote the chassis number of your car, and also state whether it has wire or disc wheels, since cable lengths differ. ➡

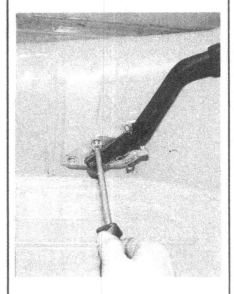

HB2. It is a simple matter to bolt the handbrake mechanism to the bodyshell, which has captive nuts already in place. The handbrake cable is connected to the handbrake mechanism from beneath the car (see HB13).

HB3. The front cable post where the inner cable protrudes from the outer, is bolted into the bodywork through a hole provided at the edge of the transmission tunnel. ➡

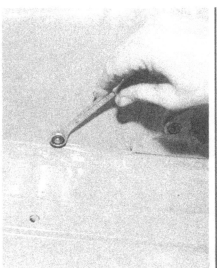

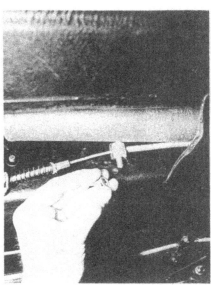

HB4. Graham tightens the fixing nut from inside the cockpit. ⬅

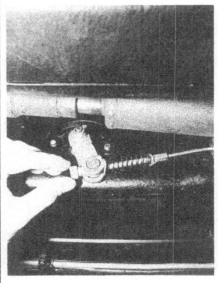

HB5. The cable can then be pulled through and the threaded end passed through the end of the handbrake operating lever, screwing on the special nut provided. At this stage, you should only start the nut off so as to leave plenty of adjustment at the other end of the cable.

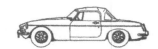

HB6. *The compensator (Items 13 to 18) was retrieved from the donor car and stripped down with a pair of spanners ...*

HB7. *... removing it from the old cable ready for cleaning up, painting and fitting to the new. It does the job of distributing the 'pull' evenly between both rear brakes, and it is essential that it operates freely.*

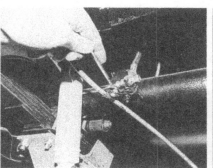

HB9. *... and one that goes on the opposite end of the axle to the compensator.*

HB11. *Clevis pins (Item 25) tend to wear, when they should be replaced with new.*

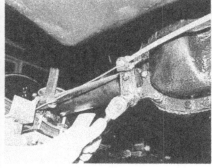

HB8. *Also salvaged from the donor car was this clip that is screwed to the bottom of the battery box area ...*

HB10. *After treatment with Waxoyl the compensator was bolted into place on the axle.*

HB12. *They're secured each with a plain washer and new split pin, the end of which should be opened out after fitting.*

HB13. The handbrake lever, cable and operating mechanism.

Brake Lines and Hoses

Safety

You are strongly recommended to follow the Haynes manual when it comes to working on the braking system, particularly with regard to bleeding the system to remove unwanted air, and with regard to safety. Do not work on the braking system unless you are confident of your own abilities and, in any case, have a qualified mechanic check the braking system over after you have completed your work on it and before using the vehicle on the road. Observe all the normal safety rules when working beneath a car suspended above the ground - see Appendix 1.

BLH1. These are the various single line circuit brake pipes and fittings from 1962 to 1978. The part numbers shown relate to the Moss parts list. (Courtesy: Moss Parts Catalogue) ➡

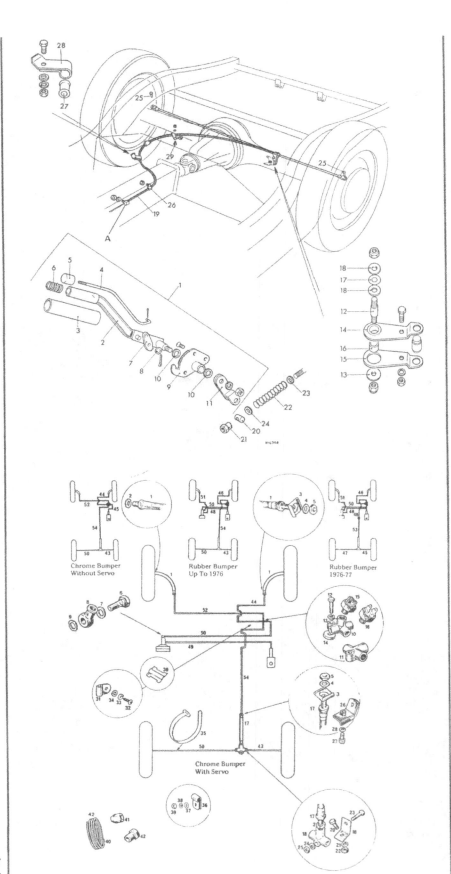

Chrome Bumper
Without Servo

Rubber Bumper
Up To 1976

Rubber Bumper
1976-77

Chrome Bumper
With Servo

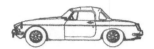

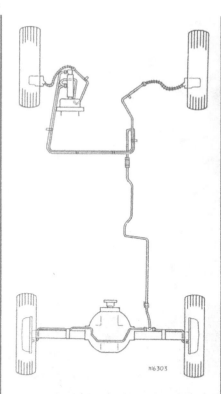

BLH2. This is the later type hydraulic brake layout - left-hand drive shown - with tandem master cylinder and servo.

BLH3. Every classic car owned by the author over the past few years has been fitted with an Automec brake pipe kit, and the project car was no exception, also benefiting from a fuel feed kit and Automec clutch pipe. Automec's copper brake pipes are ready cut to length and correctly labelled, are made of corrosion resistant copper and are easy to bend to the exact contours required. We also use Automec's D.O.D.5 silicone brake fluid because, unlike conventional brake fluid, it does not absorb moisture from the air and does not require changing every few years. In addition, brake wheel cylinders no longer seize when the vehicle is standing because of the internal corrosion. ➡

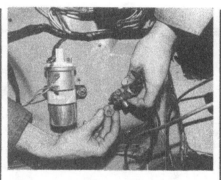

BLH4. The hydraulic brake light switch and three way connection had to be packed out with a thick washer when bolted to the flitch panel ...

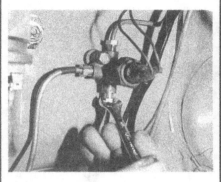

BLH5. ... so as to give clearance for the fitting nuts on the Automec pipes.

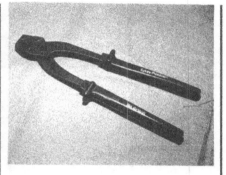

BLH6. Very tight bends in copper or most other bends in steel tubing are most easily carried out with the aid of the Sykes-Pickavant brake pipe bending pliers.

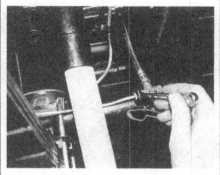

BLH7. The copper brake pipes were continued through to the three-way connection on the rear axle ...

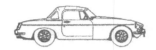

BLH8. ... and with careful bending and clipping to prevent any chaffing between brake pipes and any moving components, connections were taken to the wheel cylinders. ➡

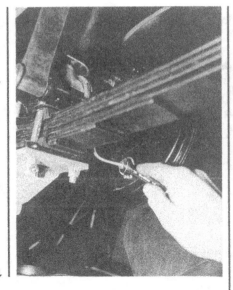

BLH9. From the Wurth catalogue (also from Automec) came these excellent rubber lined hose clips which look good and are an absolute guarantee against rubbing between adjacent metal components. ⬇

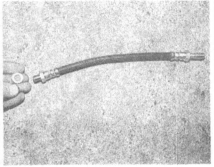

BLH11. No chances taken with flexible hoses! All were brand new ones from Lockheed. Use the correct copper washer when fitting the hose to the wheel cylinder ...

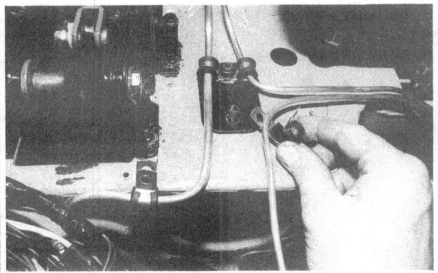

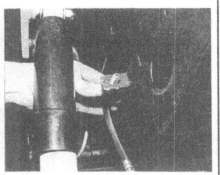

BLH12. ... and then after tightening, the hose can be fitted to its appropriate bracket ...

BLH10. If you make up your own brake pipes or you find that one or two of the Automec ones are a touch too long for comfort, you will have to cut the pipes down and make new flares. Do not carry out this work unless you are fully trained and competent. Graham used a Sykes-Pickavant brake pipe flaring tool. This is a superb professional kit and you may be able to hire one from your local tool hire store.
N.B. Automec recommend contacting them to check that the correct flares are used. Alternatively, they will replace faulty pipework FOC.

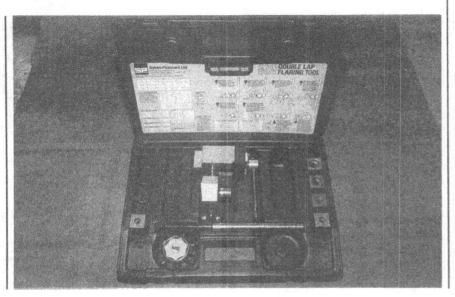

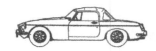

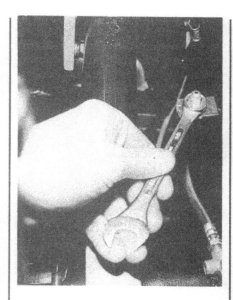

BLH13. ... and in conjunction with the special washer and spring washer, tighten to the bracket with the nut provided, using another spanner to lock the hexagon at the end of the hose in order to prevent it from turning.

BLH14. Very minor brake ➡ bleeding operations can be carried out with a rag as shown here, but major ones, especially with new pipe work, will require a brake bleeding tube from the bleed nipple. Read your Haynes manual for full details.

Master Cylinders, Pedals and Servo

M.G. originally fitted the remote servo with the air control valve uppermost. AP Lockheed now suggest turning it through 180 degrees.

MCP1. The brake pedal box components will be referred to later in this section. Item 1 relates to right-hand drive models; Item 2 to left-hand drive. The clutch pedal works in parallel with the brake pedal shown here. ➡

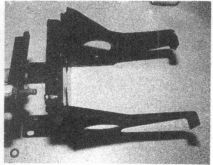

MCP2. All of the project car's pedal box hardware had been stripped down, sandblasted and painted with Wurth zinc-rich primer and black Smoothrite before being reassembled. ⬅

MCP3. The master cylinders - this is the clutch - were fitted with their brake pipe unions prior to fitting to the pedal box.

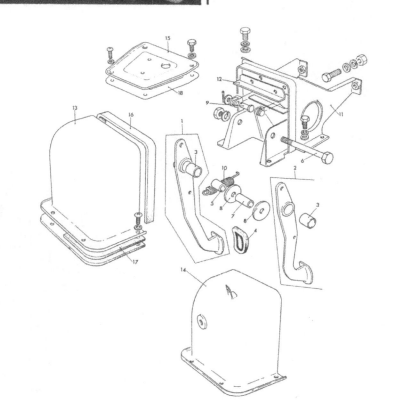

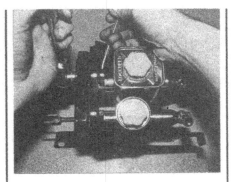

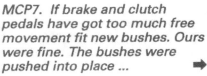

MCP7. If brake and clutch pedals have got too much free movement fit new bushes. Ours were fine. The bushes were pushed into place ... ➡

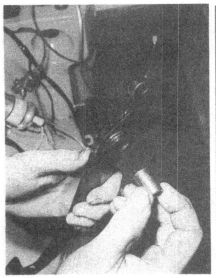

MCP4. The two new Lockheed units are bolted into place ...

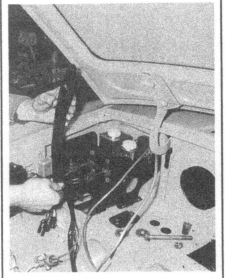

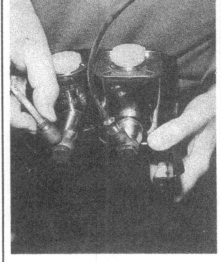

MCP8. ... and the first pedal lowered into place through the aperture in the top of the bulkhead.

MCP9. With the correct sequence of washers and the spacer plates between them, the pivot bolt was inserted ...

MCP5. ... and we found it to be essential to fit the copper brake pipes to the master cylinders before fitting the assembly to the car. ➡

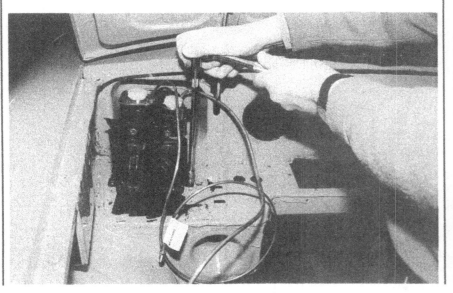

MCP6. With seam sealer beneath the pedestal, the master cylinders were bolted down to the bulkhead. Note that there ain't no room back there to get at the brake pipe connections! ➡

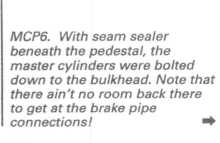

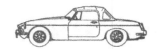

MCP10. ... whilst each part of the assembly was added in turn. It helps - nay, it's essential - to have two people working together on this, one of them inside the car holding the pedals in place and 'jiggling' when required! ➡

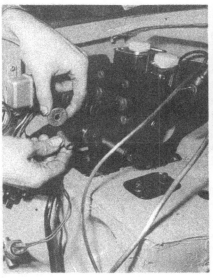

MCP14. ... before screwing the cover down with the correct crosshead screws and spring washers. Note the gasket (Item 17) that goes between box and bulkhead.

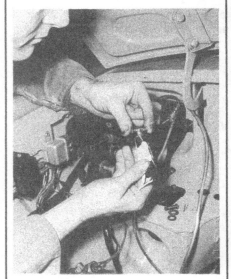

MCP11. With Copper Ease added to each pivot point ...

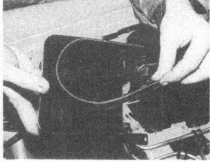

MCP13. Dear old Moss were able to supply new gaskets for the box cover and they were glued into place ...

MCP15. On the 'other' side of the car - depending on whether your car is left-hand or right-hand drive - goes a blanking-off plate. We have to clear the way through to the captive nuts beneath with some careful drilling.

MCP12. ... the top end of the pedals was connected to the master cylinders with clevis pins, washers and new split pins with their ends opened after fitting.

MCP16. In the absence of a gasket, we used windscreen sealer to ensure a watertight seal between the blanking plate and the bulkhead. ⬅

MCP17. Also from AP Lockheed came the servo which was first bolted to the mounting bracket ...

MCP18. ... and then the mounting bracket screwed down to the bulkhead top.

MCP19. Another bracket fits at the nose end of the servo and this had yet to be fitted at this stage. A hole had to be drilled in the bulkhead in order to fit this bracket. The brake pipes ...

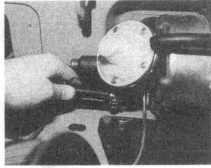

MCP20. ... and the pressure hose to the inlet manifold were fitted at this stage. A one way valve screws into a tapping in the top of the manifold.

Engine Removal

Toolbox

General range of sockets, screwdrivers and spanners. Engine hoist, and preferably a few friends.

Safety

NEVER work or stand beneath an engine suspended on a hoist, or have an arm or hand in a position where it could be crushed. Even the sturdiest of hoists could give way, or ropes or chains could slip. When attaching to the engine, try to use mechanical lifting gear rather than tying ropes. Always have someone with you to lend a hand.

With the engine out of the car ensure that, when working on it, that the block is securely chocked and that there's no danger of it toppling over. Don't trust anything but the stoutest of benches. Hire a purpose-built stand, or work on the floor. If garage roof timbers are used as a mounting for the hoist, ensure that they are REALLY strong. If in doubt, support them on either side of

the car with 4" x 4" timbers used as vertical baulks. Ensure that all lifting gear is sound and efficient. Watch out for trapped hands or fingers - engines rarely come out in one sweet movement - and keep children, pets and yourself from beneath the power unit whilst it is in the air. Make sure that batteries are disconnected. Work away from sources of ignition when disconnnecting the fuel system and store carburettors, which invariably contain petrol, safely out of doors.

Follow your Haynes manual for detailed instructions on engine removal, but here is an overview. Note that the following section shows how to remove the engine and gearbox together, although it is quite possible to remove the engine by itself. For clutch replacement, there is little to be gained by leaving the engine in situ since persuading the engine and gearbox to realign themselves is notoriously difficult on the MGB! It is not possible to take out the gearbox without removing the engine.

On US cars and others fitted with the earlier type of emission control equipment, the air pump air cleaner is removed after disconnecting the hoses and removing the two nuts and washers. The pump itself is removed after loosening the pump bolts and removing the drive belt, then removing the top adjusting link bolt and the mounting bolt, after which the pump is free.

On later cars, the restrictor connection must also be removed from the rocker box cover, and other components removed before the basic engine ancillaries become accessible for removal.

As well as what's shown in the following photographs:
*   Remove the water temperature gauge sender, being careful not to damage the transmission tube. Coil the tube

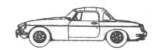

and place the whole unit out of harm's way in the rear corner of the engine bay.

* Drain the engine oil and the coolant, and disconnect all the hoses. If they are to be replaced, you may wish to cut through them with a saw, especially the bottom hose which is difficult to get at.

* Unbolt the oil cooler from the car leaving the hoses in place, disconnect the hoses at the engine end, take out the radiator and shroud complete, and lift all of these components away together. Disturbing the oil cooler connections at the oil cooler can easily cause damage to the cooler and is likely to cause leaks. Use two spanners if you have to remove the hoses to prevent shearing the union from the top of the oil cooler.

* The air cleaners will have to be removed and you may wish to take off the carburettors.

* Take off the oil filter assembly.

* Undo the propshaft bolts at the gear box flange and 'telescope' the propshaft splines backwards and lower the shaft to the ground.

ER2. Disconnect the oil pressure gauge pipe from the engine.

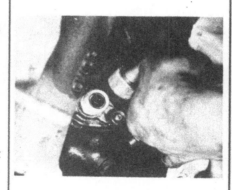

ER3. Earliest MGBs have a cable drive tachometer and this must be disconnected at the engine.

ER1. The first job of all must always be to disconnect the battery or batteries.

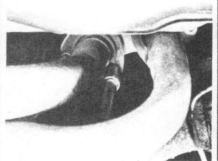

ER4. The exhaust must be unbolted from the manifold ...

ER5. ... and the exhaust pipe clip removed from the bellhousing.

ER6. The gear lever retaining bolts are taken out and the lever removed - this is the earliest model.

ER7. The clutch slave cylinder can be unbolted from the gearbox but the hydraulics left connected and the slave cylinder tied safely out of the way, placing no pressure on the hydraulic pipes.

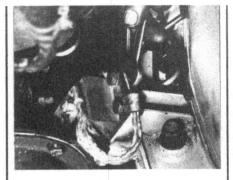

ER8. The engine earth strap and the engine mountings can be unbolted.

ER9. The bolts can be taken from the rear gearbox crossmember and then, when it is lowered to the ground with the aid of a trolley jack, the crossmember unbolted from the gearbox. ➡

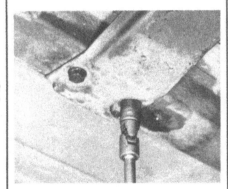

ER10. The engine and transmission being tilted and lifted out of the engine bay. ⬇

Engine Strip

This section shows how to strip a worn engine once removed from the car. If you're lucky enough to own an engine dismantling stand, use it; otherwise do the work on the floor, covering it first with an opened out cardboard box for cleanliness. It is much safer to work on the floor than on the bench from which the engine may topple!

The Haynes Owner's Workshop Manual gives further details on MGB engine stripping. Use the manual in conjunction with this section.

Cylinder Head Removal

This can be carried out with the engine either in or out of the car. The following section contains photographs from a mixture of engine stripdowns; some of them with engine in car; some with engine out. The general principle remains the same.

If you are taking the cylinder head off with the engine still in the car, the first jobs are: disconnect the battery; drain the radiator and block; remove the water temperature gauge sender unit, the heater tap, top hoses, the dynamo or alternator, and the spark plug leads.

CH1. Start by taking off the rocker cover.

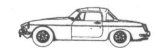

CH2. And then the carburettors and heat shield. ➡

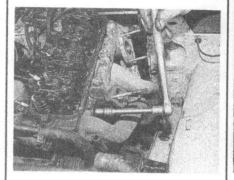

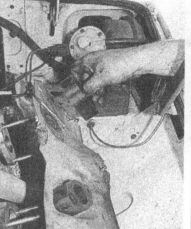

CH6. Lift-off the rocker gear ...

CH3. Take off the manifolds and, if the engine is to remain in the car, you can get away with leaving the exhaust manifold connected to the exhaust pipe and tying it right back against the inner wing.

CH4. Undo and remove the cylinder head nuts and those for the valve rockers ...

CH5. ... following the tightening and loosening sequence shown here. ⬇

CH7. ... and, where shims were fitted beneath the rocker posts, note that they were only fitted to the two centre posts and refit them on reassembly. They were not fitted in all cases. ⬆

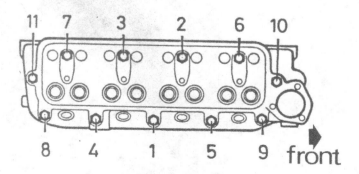

11   7   3   2   6   10

8   4   1   5   9   front ➡

CH8. In a heavily sludged engine you will find it difficult to pull out the pushrods, but persevere! Poke eight holes into a piece of cardboard and number them one to eight. Insert the pushrods into the holes in the order in which they come out of the engine so that they can go back in the same place when rebuilding. ➡

CH9. If the head is totally stuck down and the engine is in the car, replace the spark plugs and turn the engine over on the starter. The compression should help to lift it. Otherwise, use a soft-faced mallet on the thermostat housing casting. Do not hammer a screwdriver or other blade into the gap between head and block. ⬆

CH11. With the aid of a valve spring compressor, you can squeeze the springs tight, remove the collets and withdraw the valves. Keep each collection of valve components together so that it can be reassembled from whence it came. ⬆

CH12. You can best remove the head studs by locking two cylinder head nuts tightly against each other and then turning the bottom nut anti-clockwise with a ring spanner, while keeping the pressure on the top nut with another spanner held in the other hand. ⬅

CH10. Lift the head away, and take care: (a) that you don't get your fingers underneath the head as you lift because it is easy for it to slip back down again and trap fingers between head and block, and (b) that you have the weight of the head supported adequately so that you do not injure your back as you stretch in to the engine bay.

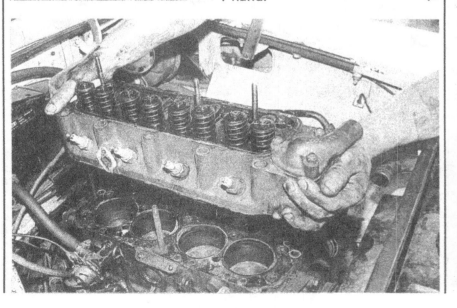

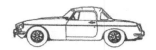

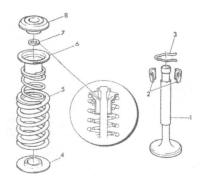

CH13. This is the valve assembly for those engines with double coil springs.

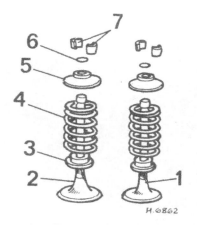

CH14. Valve assembly, single coil spring engines.

H.6862

Engine Block Stripdown

Safety

Do not lift excessive weight by yourself when moving the engine around. Enlist help and use a suitable trolley. Don't work where the engine can topple on you.

This section covers the stripdown of several different engines, some 3-main-bearing;

some 5-main-bearing. The aim is to give the full story of what's involved in restoring an aged MGB engine. Use this section in conjunction with your Haynes manual.

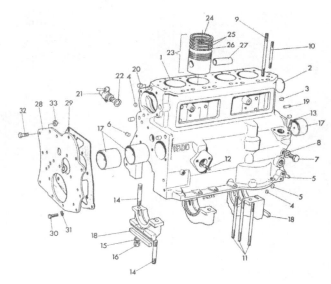

EBS1. The early, 3-main-bearing engine cylinder block components.

EBS2. The early engine's internal components.

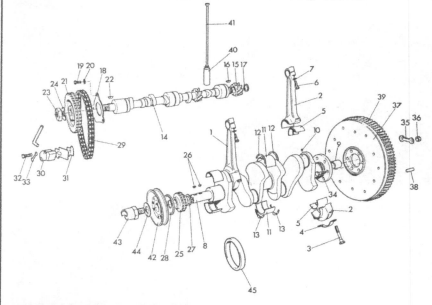

EBS3. Remove the tappet chest covers ...

217

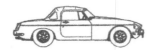

EBS4. ... and reach inside to pull out the cam followers like a set of thimbles. Long-nosed pliers might be useful here.

EBS5. After removing the distributor and the plate found beneath it, secured by a countersunk screw, you can take out the distributor driveshaft. Screw in a 5/16ths ins. UNF bolt and lift out the driveshaft, turning slightly to free the skew gear.

EBS6. Undo the crankshaft pulley nut and pull the pulley away after knocking back the tab washer. If it's impossible to shift, jump to EBS29.

EBS7. Tab washers knocked back, the fan, spacer and pulley can be removed from the water pump, which can be unbolted and tapped free as shown.

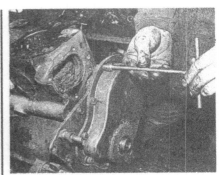

EBS8. A ring of bolts holds the timing chain cover in place; it usually has to be prised off the block.

EBS9. The oil thrower on this earlier engine is fitted with concave side facing outwards. The oil thrower on later engines looks slightly different. The correct oil thrower has to match the correct timing chain cover. Early ones have a felt oil seal; later ones a neoprene seal.

EBS10. Tap back tab washers, undo the bolts and ... ←

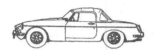

EBS11. ... remove the timing chain tensioner. If it's too tight to remove, screw it back into its housing with an Allen key.

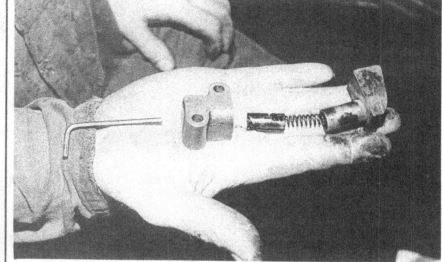

EBS12. Another tab washer ...

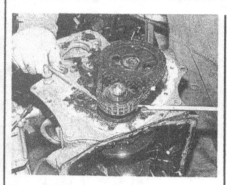

EBS14. ... and both timing chain cogs are free to be levered away.

EBS16. Behind it, the camshaft retaining plate, after which the camshaft can be eased out of the block, or you can leave it until ...

EBS13. ... another nut ...

EBS15. This later engine shows the singe-row timing chain being removed.

EBS17. ... the bolts holding the engine front plate are removed ...

EBS18. ... and the front plate lifted away.

EBS21. ... and the flywheel can be lifted away. Don't let it drop; it's quite a weight!

EBS23. ... and the 5-main-bearing engines rear oil seal retainer can be removed.

EBS19. When taking out the camshaft, it has to be 'jiggled' carefully so that the cams and in particular the skew gear do not damage the white metal bearings inside the block. They rarely wear and rarely require replacement, so look after them! ➡

EBS20. At the back of the engine, tab washers and nuts removed ...

EBS22. More tab washers and more nuts ...

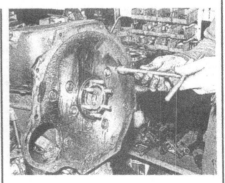

EBS24. In a different sequence, this early engine's backplate bolts are removed ...

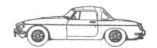

EBS25. ... and tapped free of the block.

EBS26. Wise mechanics do it kneeling down! (It's safer on the floor.)

EBS27. With the innumerable sump bolts removed, the sump can be tapped smartly with a soft-faced hammer and lifted away. ➡

EBS28. Three long bolts hold the oil pump to the block. Lift it away complete. ⬆

EBS29. If it was not previously possible to undo the crankshaft pulley nut, wedge a piece of wood between crank and block, place a socket and tommy bar on the nut, and strike it smartly with a lump hammer. Take care that the spanner doesn't fly off; that the block stays stable and does not topple. ⬅

EBS30. Beneath the oil pump is the oil pump drive which can be lifted with a twisting motion using a pair of long-nosed pliers.

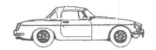

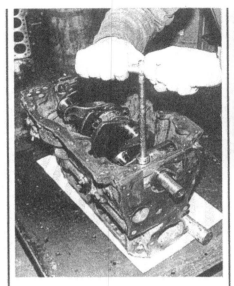

EBS34. Tab washers back; bolts out; big end caps lifted away with the aid of a tap from an engineer's hammer.

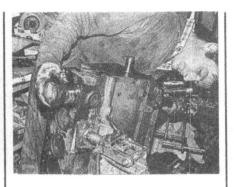

EBS36. Reach up inside the block from beneath with a hammer handle and tap the pistons up and out.

EBS31. Undo all the nuts holding the main bearings in place. Watch out for tab washers! Mark each cap so that it is refitted where it came from.

EBS32. And drift the end main bearings out of the block. You may have to make a special tool which consists of a stout 'bridge' over the bearing cap, a bolt passing through a clearance hole in the top of the 'bridge' and into the thread in the cap, and a nut run down the bolt to bear downwards on the bridge, thus pulling the bearing cap out. ➡

EBS33. The centre main has a semi-circular thrust washer in a recess on each side with another matching pair in the block. Retrieve them all.

EBS35. You can now lift the crankshaft out of the block.

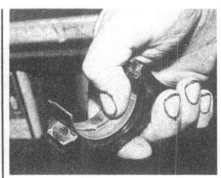

EBS37. Due to the surface tension of the oil, the only way to remove the bearing shell is to slide it out in the direction of the locating lug.

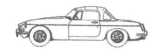

EBS38. Reassemble each con-rod with big end cap - it is essential that they are maintained as matched pairs.

EBS39. Chisel into the centre of each of the core plugs - there is a ledge around the perimeter...

EBS40. ... and lift each one out. This one was really ripe!

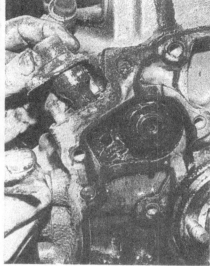

EBS41. On early engines, with the mechanical tachometer drive, undo the nut holding the drive in place at the back left of the engine and lift it away from the block.

Engine Faults

One option open to the enthusiast is to stripdown the engine him or herself, have whatever machining is necessary carried out by a specialist, such as Moss Engineering in Herefordshire (no relation to Moss Europe!), or by Aldon Automotive in the West Midlands, who specialise in MGBs and did such a wonderful job of building the engine featured in the project car. If you take this route, you will have to carefully inspect each of the components in your stripped down engine and decide what you must replace and what you can retain. It would be a good idea to go through the components with someone such as Aldon who will be able to advise on the serviceability of your engine's components.

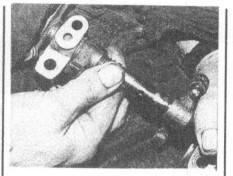

EF1. Pulling against the force of the spring, pull each rocker along the shaft to expose its bearing surface on the shaft, and examine it for wear.

EF2. Check bushes and shaft by taking hold of a rocker and attempting to rock it at 90 degrees from its normal action, i.e. in line with the shaft itself you will probably find excess wear and need to replace the shaft and rebush the rockers.

EF3. Look at the ends of the pushrods and at their mating surfaces on the rockers. Pitting or 'nippling' indicate excess wear, and overhaul or replacement will be called for. Scrap and replace bent pushrods. ➡

EF6. Camshaft bearings are often stained but not often worn. New white metal bushes will have to be pressed in only if the bearings are scored.

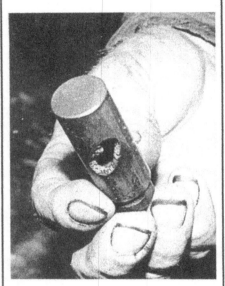

EF4. Look for pitting or wear on the surface of the cam follower, in practise, these are normally scrap. Always replace when fitting a new camshaft.

EF5. Also check for wear on the peak of the cam. You could replace the camshaft or have it reground.

EF7. This is the amount of deflection you get with a new timing chain; any more means wear. ⬆

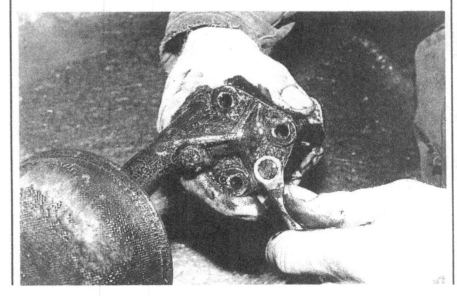

EF8. Take a look at the innards of the oil pump. ⬅

224

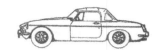

EF9. This is a badly worn outer rotor. Also examine the inside of the outer rotor and the outside of the inner rotor (if you know what I mean!) and look at the peg on the end of the driveshaft where it locates into the slot on the inner rotor shaft. Severe wear can sometimes take place here. Any rebuild should include a new oil pump.

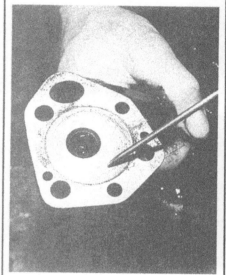

EF10. Scoring on the end plate in particular will cause a loss in oil pressure.

EF12. Not just worn but stepped. Rebore time!

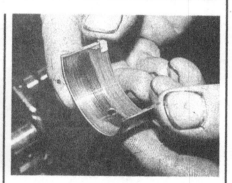

EF14. Unacceptable wear on the bearing shells - through to the copper backing.

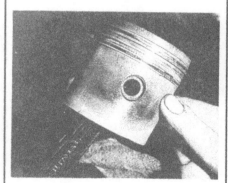

EF11. Dark marks on the side of the piston indicate blow-by caused by worn rings and a worn bore.

EF13. And crank regrind time! Your specialist will be able to measure the crank journals and advise on acceptable wear tolerances.

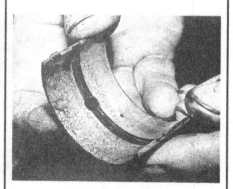

EF15. Even more dire is this complex maze of wear lines in the surface of the shell caused by water getting into the sump oil.

EF16. *Bore wear and bore ovality can only be measured with an internal micrometer or a dial gauge such as this one. More specialist advice required here.* ➡

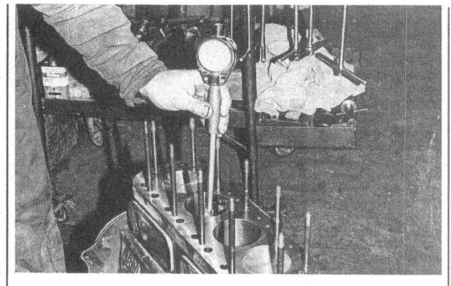

Reconditioning and Big Bore Work

One of the favourite ways of obtaining more power from an MGB engine is to bore it out to 2-litres, and one of the favourite companies for doing this work is Aldon Automotive in the West Midlands who have carried out many such conversions. They also prepare 1800cc engines to various states of tune, all with the common thread that work is always excellently done. The project car's engine was converted to run on unleaded petrol with specially hardened valve seat inserts (see relevant section) and given a mild 'Stage One' tune. It was shown on Aldon's rolling road to have given an improvement in BHP in the order of about 15%. More dramatic, however, is the improvement in torque which gives instant 'urge' at almost any road speed and under almost any conditions.

R&B2. *Aldon's partner Don Loughlin bores the block out to give a new capacity of 1948cc.* ⬅

R&B3. *The bores have to be honed to a 'plateau' finish ...*

R&B1. *An Aldon 2-litre conversion could be an ideal answer for those owners who have a worn engine and were thinking of a rebuild. The extra cost when compared with a standard rebuild is relatively low.* ➡

R&B6. Don lightens a standard flywheel in order to improve acceleration. ➡

R&B4. ... and when checking through a microscope, something resembling a fine screw thread with the peaks smoothed off would be seen! This helps the new piston rings to 'bed'.

R&B7. More of Aldon's high-tech machinery is used to ensure that the crank is perfectly in balance. ⬇

R&B5. The top of the block is skimmed to make sure that it is true and to bring the pistons to the correct height. ⬇

R&B8. Metal is ground away from the heaviest parts until perfect balance is achieved.

R&B9. The flywheel and clutch are assembled together on the balancing machine ...

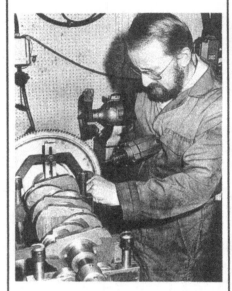

R&B10. ... and small holes drilled in the edge of the flywheel in order to bring things back into balance. Don punches alignment marks on crankshaft, clutch cover and flywheel to ensure that they can be reassembled still in balance.

R&B12. Even the con-rods are balanced on a balancing jig.

R&B13. Where weights are not equal, tiny amounts of metal are ground away in order to ensure thorough balance.

R&B11. Don considers the early split big-end con-rods to be too heavy for tuning. After 1968 the rod shown in the centre was used and, less than a year later, the rod shown right was adopted with a press-fitted gudgeon pin in the little-end. Don prefers the latest of the three.

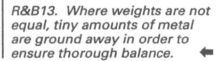

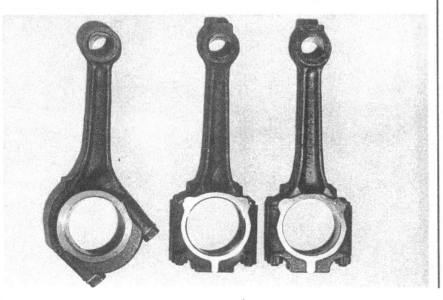

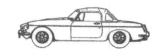

R&B14. On the left is a standard piston and on the right the soon-to-be fitted big bore piston. ➡

R&B15. These pistons have to be honed out to suit the press-fit gudgeon pin. ⬇

R&B16. The gudgeon pin is pressed into place; Aldon prefer not to use heat.

R&B17. Of the two types of timing chain described earlier Aldon fit the Duplex, twin-row type wherever possible. ⬅

R&B18. Spot the difference between the uprated cam (top) and the standard cam below it.

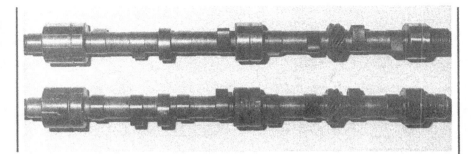

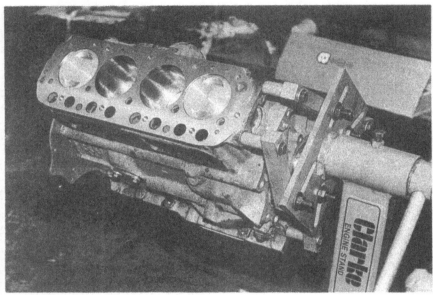

R&B19. The built block awaits the Aldon tuned cylinder head.

R&B20. More capacity and power means more stresses and strain on the clutch. You could choose an uprated one, although the standard AP Lockheed unit is a tough cookie!

R&B21. It is essential that the clutch is fitted with an aligning mandrel otherwise the engine and gearbox will never go back together!

R&B22. An Aldon non-essential optional extra are these core plug straps which prevent even the faint possibility of the core plugs coming adrift.

R&B23. An Aldon competition distributor to round off the performance, so to speak.

Engine Reassembly

This section is intended to form a thorough accompaniment to the Haynes manual, which gives all the technical details you will require. It is also aimed at filling the needs of the enthusiastic restorer. Once again, the safest place to work is on a clean floor surface, although much of this section is shown being carried out on the workbench at engine reconditioner's Moss Engineering in Herefordshire - no connection with Moss Europe. Engineer Don (another Don!) kindly divulges most of his tricks of the trade!

If you choose to have your engineering shop carry out the machining work for you, you will need some or all of the following. Each of the part numbers is clearly identified in the amazingly comprehensive Moss Parts Catalogue or in the parts list available from your supplier.

Engine reconditioners can usually supply pistons and rings, main and big-end shells and, if necessary, camshaft bearings. You will also certainly need a top-and-bottom-end gasket set; oil pump assembly; timing chain tensioner; and new flywheel lock washers.

According to wear, you may well need a rocker shaft or complete rocker assembly; cam followers; valves, valve springs and valve guides (unless you're not reconditioning the cylinder head, new valve springs and valve stem oil seals should be considered an essential); and push rods. Inlet valves do not usually require renewal but exhaust valves are sometimes so badly burned that they do need renewal. However, you may be able to get away with having your machine shop reface the valves and you should certainly consider having the valve seats recut in the cylinder head. At this stage, you are strongly advised to have the cylinder head fitted with valve seat inserts and converted to run on unleaded petrol.

The timing chain - either of the single or Duplex type - is also highly likely to need renewal. On an older engine, there is also likely to be a further list of oddments that you could order at the same time. You will need a new set of core plugs; both oil and grease for reassembly; an oil filter; fresh oil; non-setting sealer such as Hermetite; and almost certainly one or two new studs and possibly the odd pulley; thermostat housing or drain tap that has become damaged. You may also wish to invest in a new water pump.

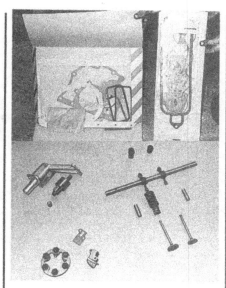

EA1. Before starting work, collect together all the components you think you will need - and keep them clean!

EA2. New core plugs are placed in the cleaned-up block with a smear of Hylomar around them, then struck sharply with a broad drift to force the middle of the convex into a concave, spreading the plug and fixing it in place.

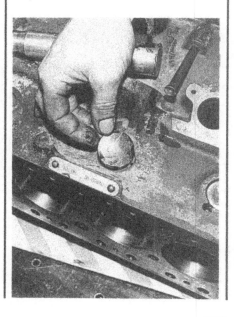

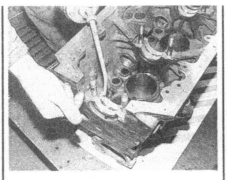

EA3. *After placing the main bearing shells into a block (5 on later engines of course) squirt engine oil on the shell and wipe it around with the back of the index finger, ensuring housings are clean.*

EA4. *The reground crank can be lifted carefully into place.*

EA5. *With webs reground to take new thrust washers, insert the oversize thrusts with the white metal bearing surface facing outwards.*

EA6. *Slide the bottom ones around until they sit with their two ends lying horizontally.*

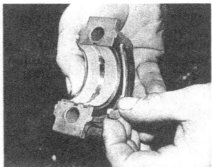

EA7. *The centre cap is assembled with main bearing shell and both thrust washers before being oiled ...*

EA8. *... fitted and torqued down.*

Rebuild Tips!

(1)   Tap the nose of the crank with a soft faced hammer or drift so that it is fully back and measure the gap between the thrust face and the bearing surface on the inside of the crank web. Check that the gap (indicated by the largest feeler gauge that can be slipped in) corresponds to the manufacturer's tolerances. If not, go back to the reconditioner's and complain that either the regrind is out or that the thrust washers supplied are incorrect.

(2)   You can tell if the regrind it too tight - or if you have inadvertently mixed up the big end or main bearing cap - because the crank won't turn after the bearings have been tightened. Check by turning - mind your fingers! - after fitting each bearing in turn. Too loose, and you could have even more problems when you come to use the engine. Slip a piece of thin plastic, around three or four 'thou' thick, between one of the journals and the shell. When you tighten down to the specified torque figure, the engine should be too tight to turn but free to turn without it. If the crank is tight without the plastic in place, check scrupulously that there is no carbon build-up beneath the shells nor a speck of dirt there; that the bearing caps are the right ones (especially important with No. 2 and 4 on the 5-main-bearing engines) and that they're the right way round. The same is true when checking the big-end bearings using the same technics. Each bearing cap is individually machined to fit only in one place - they are not interchangeable or reversible.

If the crank still turns, even with the plastic strip in place, then far too much has been taken off the crank or - less likely - there is a fault with the shell sizes.

EA9. Reinsert the camshaft from the front of the engine, taking care not to damage the bearings.

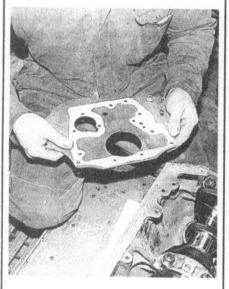

EA10. Fit a new gasket to the front plate and locate the cork seal on top of the front main bearing ...

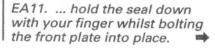

EA11. ... hold the seal down with your finger whilst bolting the front plate into place. ➡

EA12. Hold the driveshaft into the oil pump body with a large dab of grease so that it stays there while the pump is being fitted, and fill the pump with oil before bolting into place. ➡

EA13. The timing gears must first be fitted without the timing chain and made exactly level by the addition or removal of shims beneath the crank nose. Make sure that the woodruff keys (steel guide pegs) are in place on both crank and camshaft noses, and turn them until the crankshaft woodruff key is at the twelve o'clock position and the camshaft at two o'clock. Now place the timing gears into the timing chain in such a position that the dimple on each wheel lines up with the gear wheel centres, as shown. The two gear wheels should now slide straight on, lining up correctly with the woodruff keys, turning the camshaft the smallest amount if necessary to get them to line up. Fit the retaining nut and turn over the tab washer. ➡

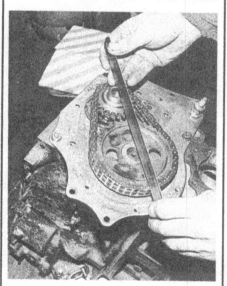

EA14. The Duplex-type tensioner is retracted with the Allen key, fitted and then loosened off once again with the Allen key. Allen key is under blanking plug, held by lock tab.

EA15. The later tensioner - single row type - is simply compressed by hand whilst being fitted. If a plastic tab is fitted (to stop plunger being released) remove after fitting. Then push pad into tensioner block to release plunger. ➡

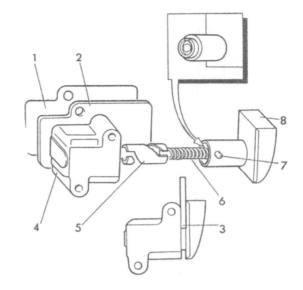

EA16. The early type of timing chain cover incorporates a felt oil seal which has to be dug out and painstakingly replaced if it is to be retained. It is inherently inefficient.

EA17. It is better to retain a later-type timing chain cover which takes a neoprene seal.

EA18. Remember also to replace the crankshaft oil thrower with the later type fitted with the small shoulder outwards. ⬆

EA19. A new oil seal being drifted into the timing chain cover. ➡

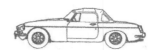

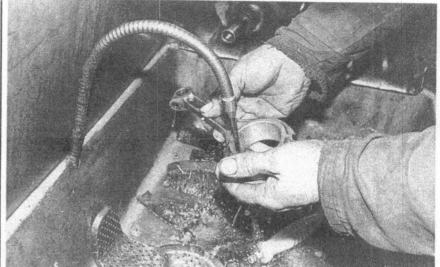

EA20. *Cleanliness is everything when rebuilding an engine and each component should be individually washed and blown out with an air-line. Wear goggles!* ➡

EA21. *One type of piston and con-rod assembly laid out for refitting. Arrows on pistons must point to front of car.*

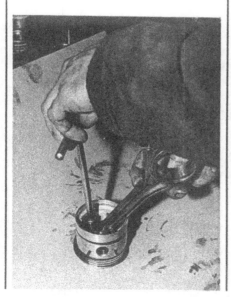

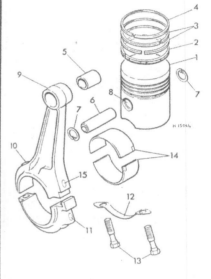

EA22. *Try to match new pistons with new gudgeon pins so that the best fit is obtained. However, if you can't avoid having a tight gudgeon pin, heat the piston in hot water so that the piston expands, allowing the pin to slide in. However, some say that you should only use the gudgeon pins supplied with the pistons ... Use your discretion.*

EA23. *Line up the indentation on the gudgeon pin exactly with the line of the clamp bolt, otherwise the clamp bolt threads can be damaged.* ⬅

EA24. *This is the layout of the fully floating gudgeon pin type of piston assembly. Item 5 is the small-end bush which may be fitted by your machine shop; Items 7 will need to be fitted with circlip pliers. "Press fit" gudgeon pins must be fitted by a machine shop to avoid expensive damage.*

235

EA25. Ensure that the con-rod offsets are correctly positioned; these are Nos. 3 and 4 piston assemblies.

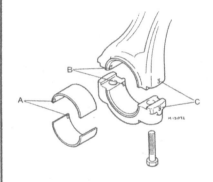

EA26. Ensure that the bearing tabs A fit in the tab slots B, and that the rod and cap numbers at C always correspond.

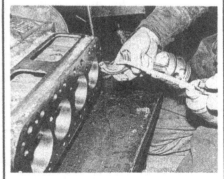

EA27. More lubrication of bearings and piston rings ...

EA28. ... and with the aid of a piston ring compressor, the piston can be sharply tapped into the bore with the handle of a hammer.

EA29. Don't forget to bend over all the bearing tab washers when all have been tightened to the specified torque.

EA30. Replace the oil pump strainer if necessary and fit a new sump gasket.

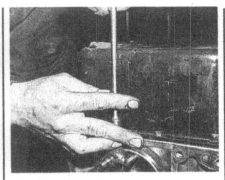

EA31. Fit all of the sump bolts lightly, before tightening any of them down.

EA32. Lubricate the oil pressure relief valve. Always fit a new valve and spring ...

➡

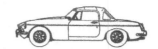

EA33 ... and refit. This is a brand new relief valve and spring.

EA36. Make absolutely certain that you fit new valve stem oil seals. This is the earlier type ...

EA34. The new head gasket will be stamped to show which way round it goes.

EA37. ... and this the later type, and fits unseen, covered by the valve springs, beneath the cotters.

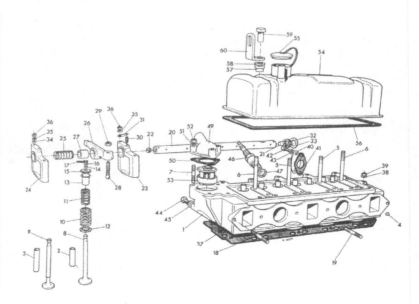

EA35. An earlier cylinder head layout with double valve springs.

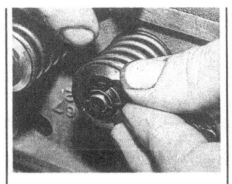

EA38. The valve cotters (early engines only) are held firmly in place with these spring clips. (See EA35 Items 16 and 17)

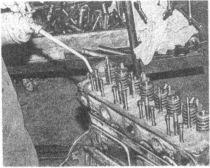

EA40. After fitting the head, camshaft followers and tappet covers fit and lubricate both ends of the push rods ...

EA42. Torque the head and rockers down to the figures prescribed in the manual.

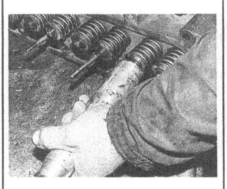

EA39. Finally, give each valve a clout in turn just to make sure that everything is seated properly and that nothing is sticking.

EA41. ... before refitting the rocker assembly, ensuring that each rocker locates with its push rod.

EA43. Don't let the rockers run dry when you start up; lubricate thoroughly.

EA44. Check that number one cylinder is at Top Dead Centre and on the firing stroke i.e. both No. 1 cylinder valves are closed. Now refit the distributor drive so that the slot is in the position shown, with the slightly larger segment to the left. ←

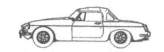

EA45. You will probably have to make your own gasket for the tachometer drive on earliest engines. Cut out a piece of gasket paper, push over the studs and pein a hole in the gasket as shown. This is actually an almost identical MGA engine used for illustration.

➡

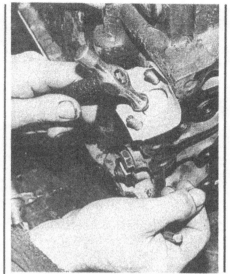

Before, starting up, remove the plugs, fully charge the battery/ies, fill up with fresh oil and turn the engine over on the starter until oil pressure shows on the gauge and oil is circulated throughout the as-yet unstressed engine. If it takes a long time to fire up on the first try, or spits vigorously through the carbs, go back and check the ignition timing from top to bottom, and the firing order - it's a common mistake!

Safety

Have a fire extinguisher handy and fit air filters, just in case of a major spit-back that could cause a fire.

Cylinder Head Rebuild Improvement

Aldon Automotive have a level of expertise in MGB rebuilding and improvement that is second to none. Here, partner Don Loughlin shows what to look for and what Aldon can do when rebuilding an MGB cylinder head.

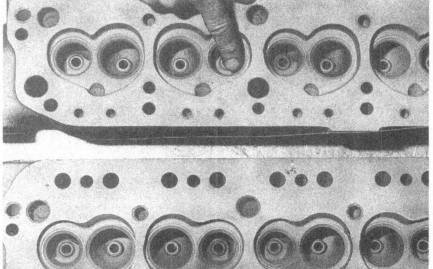

CHR1. The cylinder head at the top is stronger than the one below it. Don points at the two bosses cast in place for air injector ports on cars for the USA. Unused outside the US, they impart greater rigidity and strength. ⬆

CHR2. When cylinder heads crack it tends to be here, on the exhaust seats of cylinders two and three. The upper, pre-1970 head has less smoothed-out combustion chambers than the lower, later and more efficient head. ⬅

239

CHR3. Here, Don is using a template to mark out the exact shape of a revised combustion chamber for one of Aldon's uprated heads. ←

CHR4. He uses this metal working 'router' to form the curved sides of the newly shaped combustion chamber. →

CHR5. The surface is then smoothed out with this flap wheel. ←

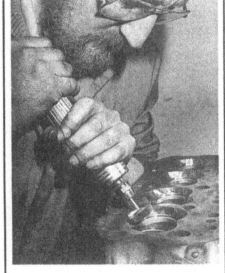

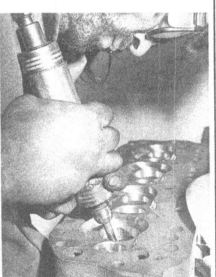

CHR6. The search for improved gas flow continues down into the ports ... →

CHR7. ... and the top of the port is enlarged. ←

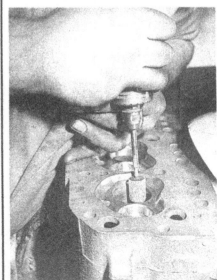

CHR8. The valve seats now have to be recut ... →

CHR9. ... and, after the head is skimmed, Don will measure the capacity of each combustion chamber, grinding out here and there until they are all equal. ➡

CHR10. Aldon use special 'waisted stem' valves to further improve gas flow and, with a larger head size for both inlet and exhaust valves. ⬇

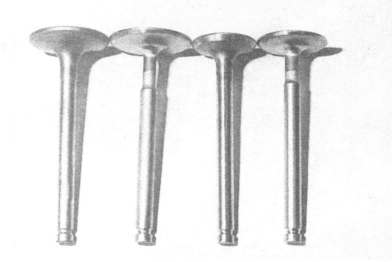

SU Carburettor overhaul

The majority of MGBs were fitted with SU Carburettors, and today the manufacture of the full range of these carbs and all of the components that go into them has been taken over by Burlen Fuel Systems based in Salisbury, England. Fortunately for owners, they offer a complete level of technical support, and also the opportunity to purchase new carburettors, including the larger SUs fitted to the project car and once available from BMC Special Tuning.

Burlen were keen to emphasise that, whilst carburettor overhaul is fully DIY-able, it is vital to work in total cleanliness and with care and patience. Carburettors are precision instruments and do not take kindly to heavy-handed treatment!

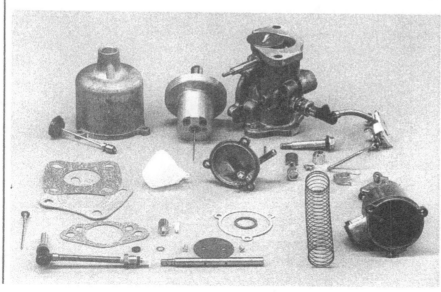

CO1. A Burlen Fuel Systems' kit seen here alongside a dismantled HS4 carb. ⬅

CO2. When putting the HS4 back together again, don't forget to open the split screw end in order to lock the disc in place. ➡

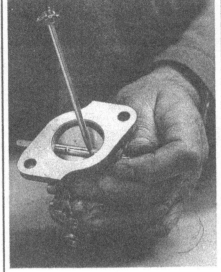

CO7. Ideally, the new needle valve should be fitted with the special Burlen Fuel Systems key, as shown here. However, a 'thin wall' socket spanner will do.

CO3. Having replaced the throttle lever, interconnection lever, tab washer and nut, and tightened them, don't forget to bend the tab washer down to lock the nut.

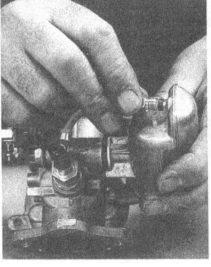

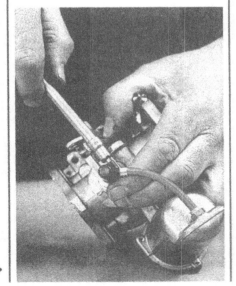

CO8. When refitting the float, be sure to push in the pin so that it is central.

CO5. When fitting the new jet, ensure that the gland nut, metal washer and rubber gland are in the correct order, and tighten in place.

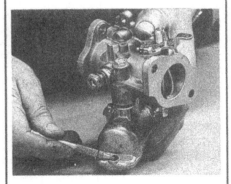

CO4. Before putting the new jet in place, ensure that all of the old rubber gland is removed from the outlet at the bottom of the float chamber.

CO6. If the carbs on your car have a wire jet linkage, push on the new retaining clip with a small socket spanner. Other flat linkages use a small self-tapping screw. ➡

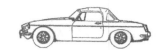

CO9. When screwing down the float chamber lid, replace the alloy tag which includes the carburettor specification number. This is vital to enable the carburettor dealer to obtain the correct parts the next time the carb is serviced. ➡

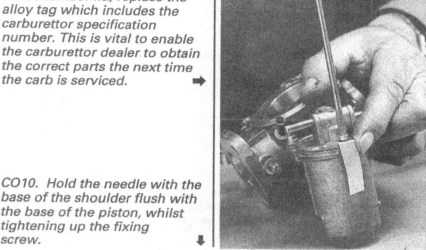

CO10. Hold the needle with the base of the shoulder flush with the base of the piston, whilst tightening up the fixing screw. ⬇

CO12. Don't forget the piston spring when reassembling the suction chamber. Check that the piston lifts and drops smoothly. Early carbs with fixed needles may need the jet centring.

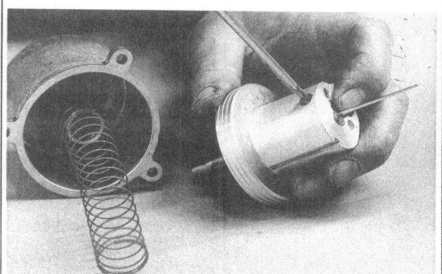

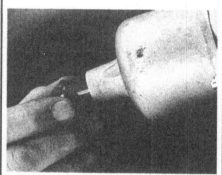

CO13. Finally, replace the damper in the dashpot.

CO11. Take care to line up the keyway in the piston with the tag on the body and, at the same time, ensure that the needle enters the jet.

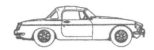

Burlen can supply new SU carbs for American owners to convert to the MGB's original spec - but owners should ensure that, in so doing, they will not be contravening any federal or state laws, particularly in respect of vehicle emissions.

Distributor Overhaul

Complete overhaul of the distributor is generally considered beyond the scope of the DIYer, if only because the sintered bush in the body of the distributor has to be pressed in and then reamered, and most home workshops don't have the facilities. There are one or two checks you can carry out for yourself, however.

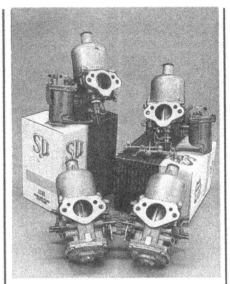

CO14. At the top are a pair of HS4 carbs, complete with linkage. These are a direct replacement for the later HIF type, see below.

CO15. Rather tasty! This pair of HS6 SU carbs is exactly the same as the originals from BMC Special Tuning and is available today from Burlen Fuel Systems. ↓

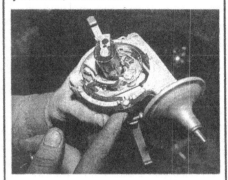

DO1. This is the early 25D4 distributor. Later cars were fitted with 45D4s and then the 45DE4 with electronic triggering.

DO2. Aldon's Don Loughlin sucks on the vacuum pipe. A soft but positive sound should be heard from the diaphragm; if not, it is probably punctured or seized, and a rebuild is called for. ←

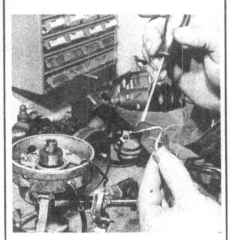

DO3. You could check for yourself that the wiring is in good condition. This V8 distributor's wire has been discovered with almost non-existent sheathing and must have been very close to giving major problems.

DO4. The shaft was also found to be bent, and this was causing the spark timing to be very erratic. ➡

EBD1. One of the delights of working with the new bodyshell is the potential for creating a very attractive engine bay. Here, many of the engine bay components - new and reconditioned; standard and modified - wait ready to be fitted. ⬇

DO5. You need specialist test equipment of this sort in order to be able to check that the distributor is operating satisfactorily. Don plots the advance curve on an Aldon competition modified distributor.

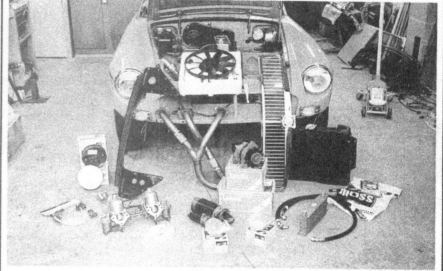

DO6. Aldon can supply rebuilt standard distributors, or mildly modified and improved ones for all models in the MGB range. Since the car's ignition system is in some ways to be regarded as the car's heartbeat, it pays to ensure that it is functioning properly! ➡

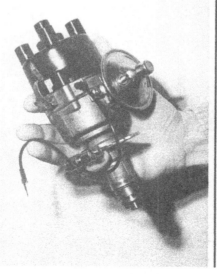

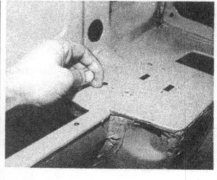

EBD2. It pays not to forget the most mundane details and to refer to the donor car, or another original vehicle, to check that grommets ... ⬆

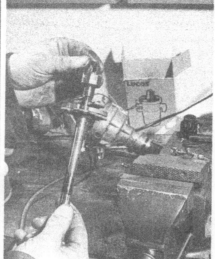

EBD3. ... are preservable or obtainable. Many of the square holes in the Heritage flitch panels can be filled by these plastic 'captive nuts' obtainable from Moss.

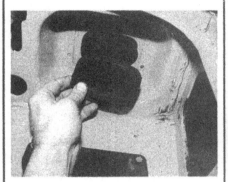

EBD4. This rubber blanking plug was rescued from the donor car and meticulously cleaned up before being fitted to the Heritage shell. It had previously been painted over.

EBD5. It's when you get to this stage that everything starts taking four times as long, as you take the trouble to clean up nuts and bolt heads and to repaint every small component. The end results make it very worthwhile! ⬇

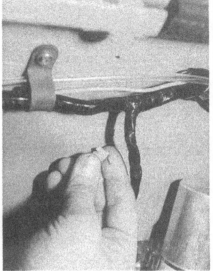

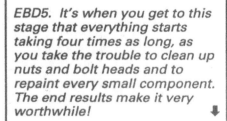

EBD6. Also from Moss you can purchase all the correct engine bay stickers and transfers ...

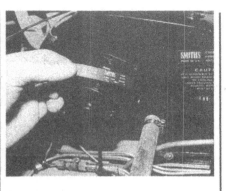

EBD7. ... to go on items such as the heater unit ...

EBD8. ... the washer bottle ...

EBD9. ... the bonnet closing panel, and many other places. Also included are a new Chassis plate ...

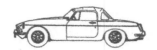

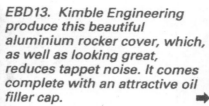

EBD13. Kimble Engineering produce this beautiful aluminium rocker cover, which, as well as looking great, reduces tappet noise. It comes complete with an attractive oil filler cap. ➡

EBD10. ... and Commission Number plate.

EBD11. Ian Harris, an ➡ *enthusiast who is happy to help his peers, will make up Chassis and Commission plates for you to the original numbers - although he does demand proof from the registration documents that he is only dealing with genuine vehicles.*

EBD12. He can also advise on the exact correct positioning for Chassis and Commission Number plates, although with the Heritage shell, since it relates to no particular year of car, you can pick whichever combination you prefer. ⬇

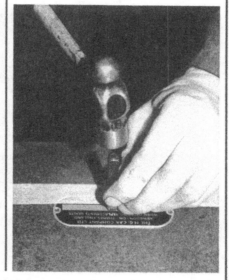

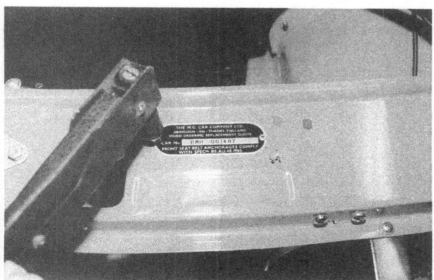

Gearbox and Clutch - Preparing for Installation

The gearbox used in the project car was rebuilt by another company with special expertise in matters MGB - Nicol Transmissions of Kidderminster in the West Midlands. One of the reasons for rebuilding the Heritage MGB around a 1969 model was that it combines chrome bumper beauty with four-syncromesh gearbox excellence. Here's how clutch and gearbox are prepared for refitting to the car.

Safety

Read earlier safety notes about moving and lifting the engine and about working beneath the car. Read Appendix 1.

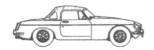

GBC1. *We had a choice between fitting an uprated clutch (left) or a new AP Borg & Beck clutch cover and plate. We chose the latter: the engine is only ten or twelve BHP up on standard and we decided to plump for AP Borg & Beck originality and reliability.*

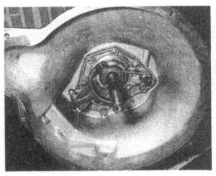

GBC2. *Nicol Transmissions installed the clutch operating forks to the gearbox, and when we got it back to the Porter workshop ...*

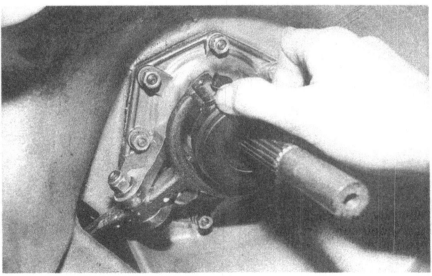

GBC3. *... Graham added Copper Ease to the first motion shaft and clutch splines ...*

GBC4. *... and clipped a new Lockheed release bearing in place. New clutch components are not incredibly expensive; taking an MGB engine out, and 'box', in order to change the clutch is enormous hassle - it pays to renew the clutch when you can.* ↑

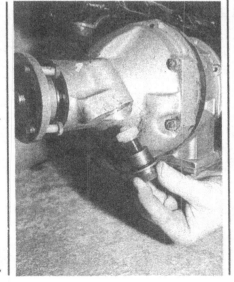

GBC5. *The speedometer drive has to be stripped from the old gearbox ...* ➡

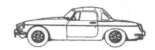

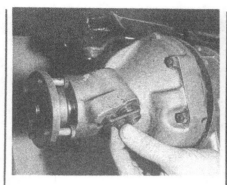

GBC6. ... and held to the new gearbox with the special clamp plate.

GBC9. ... by taking a scrap bolt with the same thread and cutting a slot halfway down its length. Starting from the side of the bellhousing where the thread was undamaged, this sacrificial bolt was screwed with lots of in and out movements and lots of releasing fluid into the thread, chasing it out. It had to be removed several times to clean out the build up of aluminium from the slot in the bolt. It worked perfectly! ⬆

GBC7. Graham used the workshop trolley to introduce the Aldon engine to the Nicol gearbox. Hi there! ⬆

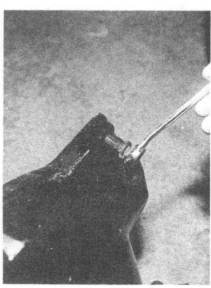

GBC8. The special coarse threads in the gearbox bellhousing, into which the starter motor has to be bolted, had been (quite literally!) screwed up by someone in the past trying to introduce a fine thread bolt. We chased it out afresh ... ➡

GBC10. With the hammer shaft holding the back of the engine up a touch, the gearbox was slipped on. The clutch had previously been fitted with the aid of an alignment tool.

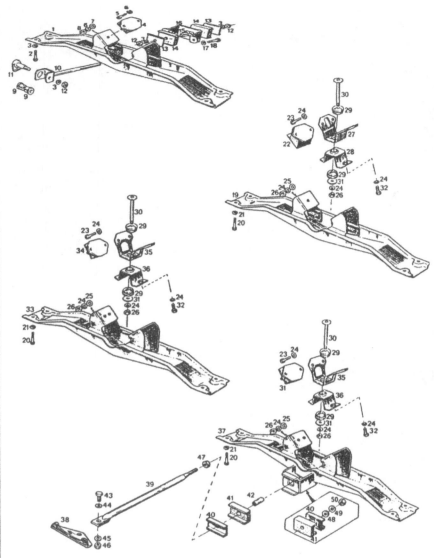

GBC13. ... which enabled the rubber bushes (Item 29) to be forced in.

GBC14. The vertical pin (Item 30) ...

GBC11. In the author's view, the oddest part of the MGB is its gearbox mountings. They were surely never designed for use by man! These are the four different assemblies used during the car's life, running from top to bottom:
Type 1. '62-'67, 3 synchro gearbox Roadster.
Type 2. '65-'67, 3 synchro GT.
Type 3. '67-'64, 4 synchro models up to GHD5341729/GHN5341294. As Type 2 except that part No. 33,34,35 and 36 are different.
Type 4. '75-on. All later models. As Type 3 except that parts No. 37 to 50 are different. (Courtesy: Moss Parts Catalogue) ⬆

GBC12. The rubber bush holes in both upper and lower mounting brackets (Items No. 35 and 36 Type 3) were painted with Waxoyl ...

GBC15. ... was inserted and, on the underside, the plain washer, spring washer and nut was fitted.

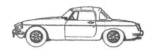

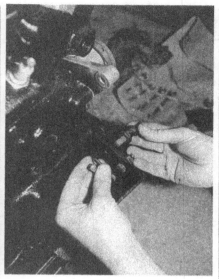

GBC16. *This Porter modification to the crossmember saved the two of us from going loopy! You offer up the newly assembled bracketry to the crossmember and work out which of the two holes in the mounting plate will be used. Another hole is then drilled some way up from the first and turned into a slot with the aid of a jigsaw and metal cutting blade. You can now loosely bolt the assembly, seen in the previous shots, and the rubber gearbox mountings to the gearbox and leave them there until after the engine and gearbox have been inserted into the car. Then, from underneath the car, the crossmember can be added, and the otherwise-impossible-to-fit mounting rubber bolts inserted through the slots freshly cut in the crossmember, everything pushed snugly up into position and, when all eight bolts are in place (nine including the vertical pin!) and the crossmember is tight up against the gearbox mounting, everything can be tightened up.* ↑

Engine - Preparation and Installation

Safety

Read 'Safety' at start of the previous section and in the Appendices.

EP1. *Engine mounting plates are bolted to the block and screwed to the front plate with these countersunk-head screws, necessary to give the required clearance.* ↓

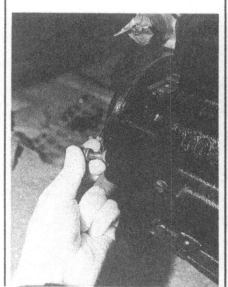

EP2. *The right hand plate also carries the alternator adjuster bracket stud.*

EP3. *Below, the new engine mounting, remanufactured by Moss. Above, the plate designed to stop the engine shifting forward under heavy braking. Ours had been bent back and had to be closed up to give only a quarter of an inch of clearance when fitted to the car.*

EP4. The stud in the centre of the engine mount protruded too far and fouled the engine movement stop. It was a simple matter to file it down a shade.

EP6. There's no need to remove the bonnet if you take off the stay, and tie it fully back, well protected. ←

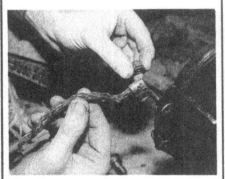

EP5. The earth strap fitted in readiness, with more Copper Ease on the electrical joint.

EP7. Just as a demo., Graham shows how the engine and gearbox have to clear the front panel before being lowered into the gearbox tunnel. Note the homemade bracketry allowing the engine to be lifted off the cylinder head studs. BE SURE TO SUPPORT THE ENGINE ADEQUATELY WHEN LIFTING, AND KEEP HANDS AND FEET WELL CLEAR IN CASE OF ACCIDENTS. ↑

EP8. Later and for real, engine and 'box are slotted fully home - note the bodywork protection ... ←

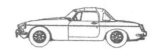

EP9. ... the new trolley jack, specially bought from Machine Mart that morning, was used beneath the car to support and raise the rear end of the gearbox while the front was located on the mountings. ➡

EP10. The engine was raised level and the rubber mountings, already fitted to the engine, were lowered on to their plates in the engine bay.

EP11. Earlier cars have this packing plate to fit beneath the engine mounting on the left hand side - not needed on this Heritage bodyshell!

EP12. The trick is to leave all mounting bolts loose, to hammer the mounting down on its tapering plate so that the holes line up and bolts can be loosely fitted on one side, and then to do the same on the other side. ⬆

EP13. Don't forget to fit the earth strap to one of the mounting bolts on the chassis, and then go round tightening all of the mounting bolts fully. ⬅

EP14. You need to raise the whole car to get the gearbox crossmember in place.

EP17. The crossmember itself bolts into captive nuts in the chassis rails. Not wishing to end this section on a gloomy note, but if these captive nuts have come loose or seized solid in some way, you may have to consider cutting away this part of the chassis rail and letting in a new section complete with new captive nuts.

EP15. Crossmember and crossmember mountings are best assembled as described in the previous section - unless you know something that the author doesn't! It certainly helps to have the rear end of the gearbox lowered down nearer to the ground so that you've got some hope of getting your fingers onto the various nuts and bolts.

EP16. Don't forget the two bolts, holding the gearbox mounting to the crossmember, that go into the mounting through the crossmember from beneath.

EP18. We have used Slick 50 Friction Reducer in engine, gearbox and differential oil for a number of years now. It certainly seems to work - in fact it works so well that we do not recommend adding it to engine oil until the engine has been fully run in. For the first few thousand miles the engine needs its normal quota of friction for bores and bearings to bed themselves in.

Wheels and Tyres

Technically speaking, the term 'disc wheel' refers to all non-wire wheels fitted to the MGB. Thus, the early pattern steel wheel with a ring of small holes and a chrome-plated hub cap, as fitted to the early MGB and

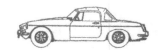

MGC, is a 'disc wheel'; the later Rostyle pattern wheel and the MGB GT Jubilee and V8 wheels are also 'disc wheels'.

Most people prefer the look of wire wheels, although in practice they can be the very devil to keep clean and they tend to go out of true and require more maintenance. The project car was fitted with Minilite knock-on wheels fitted to wire wheel splines. This gives what we consider to be a compromise between the reliability of disc wheels, the quick removal of wire wheels and possibly the only alternative wheel with a truly classic appearance. (For the uninitiated, Minilites were commonly fitted to many sporting English cars of the '60s and '70s.) Today's Minilites, reproduced and sold by Moss, are not made of the very light and very expensive magnesium alloy of the genuine item, but instead are cast in aluminium - which at least makes them affordable!

If wheels make a large difference to the appearance of the MGB, the type of tyres you use will have a greater potential for improving the handling and road holding of your car than any other single modification you can make. Early tyres were not only too skinny for the car's good, they were also made of rubber compounds that have been vastly improved upon by today's modern technology. Early MGBs were fitted with 4J wheels. The largest permissible tyre size for fitting to these wheels is 155/70 14. Where cars were fitted originally with 4½J wheels, the largest permissible tyre size is 165/70 14. Tyre sizes and pressures, as recommended by Michelin, are as follows:

MGB Tourer

4, 4½ or or 5 Rim	155 R14 MX	)	F: 21psi	R: 24psi
	or	)	or, for full load	
4½ or 5J Rim	165 R14 MX	)	F: 21 psi	R: 26 psi

MGB GT

4½ or 5J Rim	165 R14 MX	)	F: 21psi	R: 24psi
		)	or, for full load	
5J Rim	185/70 R14 MXL/MXT	)	F: 21psi	R: 26psi
		)		

MGB GT V8

5J Rim	175 R14 MXV	)	F: 21psi	R: 25psi
		)	or, for full load	
		)	F: 26psi	R: 32psi

The GT V8 model was fitted with a tubeless rim.
Both the Tourer and the GT may have been fitted with either tubeless or tube type rims.

WT1. The Michelin MXT tyres destined for the project car in size 185 70 14 were fitted to the Minilite rims at our local ATS Fitting Centre. ➡

WT2. To save on expense, the project car spare tyre was fitted to a standard wire wheel. Wire wheels, both new and rebuilt are available from most MG specialists, and you can save money by having your own wire wheels reconstructed. They have to be checked regularly for loose spokes and for running 'out of true' and, beyond the obvious faults, it's well worth having this done by a wheel specialist. Tyre specialists ATS recommend that wire wheels have to be fitted with inner tubes - because the spoke holes let all the air out if you fit tubeless tyres! In addition, protective tape has to be placed around the inside of the rim so that the inner tube cannot rub on the spoke nipples. ➡
Important: *Check that it is legally permissible to use a spare wheel of a different type to that of the road wheels in the territory in which you use your vehicle*

WT3. The Michelin MX is Michelin's 'everyday' tyre and is designed to give good grip on both wet and dry roads with a long service life. Reliable, long-lasting - but not especially exciting!

WT4. The MXV is a high speed, high performance, low profile radial with outstanding breaking, precision handling and excellent grip, with rapid water dispersal to prevent aquaplaning at speed. ➡

WT5. The Michelin MXT has replaced the MXL tyre and offers an increased speed capacity over the MXL and is of the latest technological design. It is available in the same low profile aspects as the MXL. As we have discovered on the project car, handling, comfort and, above all, grip on wet or greasy roads are all quite superb! For cars capable of higher speeds, especially the V8 models, Michelin produce their V-rated MXV tyre, also available in low profile types. Check with your local tyre dealer, such as ATS in the UK, for all aspects of current legislation relating to tyre wear, sizes and speed ratings. ➡

WT6. The project MGB - modern Minilites, Michelin MXTs and all. ⬆

Exhaust System

The way in which the MGB's exhaust system bolts to the exhaust manifold is another somewhat eccentric feature of the car. Not only are the mounting nuts difficult to get at, but the studs are notorious for stripping, corroding and shearing. To cure the latter, you will have to remove the manifold and re-drill and tap the threads. As a temporary measure you can, with difficulty, insert a thinner bolt with a separate nut on the far side. If you drill out the hole, you won't be able to re-tap it!

Safety

Do not apply heat to the exhaust system with carburettors still attached to the car because of the fuel that will be contained in their float bowls. Ensure that all fuel and brake lines are safely out of the way before doing so. Read the notes at the start of this chapter, especially with reference to working beneath the car.

ESY1. With the manifold in situ, a welding torch is used to heat the metal around the damaged stud ...

ESY2. ... which can then be worked free and unscrewed with a pair of mole grips. Watch out for hot metal!

ESY3. We decided to fit a Falcon stainless steel system to the MGB. Moss offer several variations on the exhaust theme, and we decided to fit the one that did away with the standard car's exhaust manifold; partly because of the problems described above and partly because the standard manifold is restrictive, while this one improves the gas flow no end.

ESY4. A little brute force was necessary, involving holding the flange in the vice and bending the pipe like mad (but not so far that it kinks!) in order to align all three pipes where they fit the engine, using the standard manifold gasket. Every last bit of this system is made of stainless steel, and it looks as though it could well outlast the car. ➡

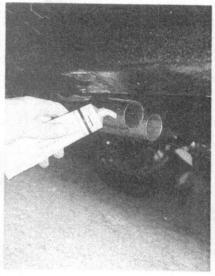

ESY5. Working back along the car, each joint was sealed with exhaust jointing paste ...

ESY6. ... and a set of standard exhaust mounts, obtained from Moss, were bolted to the bodywork.

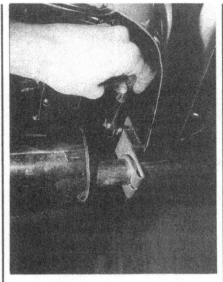

ESY7. This is the rear mount which fits just inside the rear apron. Nothing was tightened until the whole exhaust was in place.

In practice, we found that the exhaust touched in two or three places; so the car was taken to our local independent exhaust centre and classic car enthusiasts, at A44 Service Station in Worcester, where an oxy-acetyline blowtorch and a professional pipe bender were used to ensure a perfect fit.

One additional advantage of the Falcon stainless steel exhaust, quite apart from its almost total resistance to corrosion, is that the exhaust note is really quite sexy and not the awful tinny affair that some stainless steel systems seem to produce. We are also assured that the fitting problems we encountered are not typical.

Fitting SU Carburettors and Associated Components

So many different carburettor set-ups have been used in the

US market that there isn't room to do them justice here. This section concentrates on the basics of fitting the conventional 1½ inch SU carburettors and on what is involved in upgrading to the Special Tuning type 1¾ SUs and improved air filters. The Haynes Manual gives complete strip down details of all the other carburettor types. This section concentrates on restoration.

FSU3. Vibration frequently causes the heat shield to split and you should budget for its replacement.

FSU1. When removing inlet and exhaust manifolds, the stud commonly comes off with the nut. Separate them on the bench and refit the stud properly, otherwise the stud may not go into the block sufficiently when refitting. ⬆

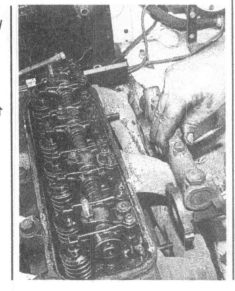

FSU2. The inlet manifold is a separate item, although it shares the same mounting studs as the exhaust manifold.

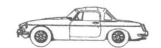

FSU4. Once disconnected from the petrol pipes, return springs, throttle and choke cables, the carburettor assemblies can be unbolted and lifted away as a unit to be dismantled on the bench - though not if you put your arm around the bonnet stay as shown here! The right-hand air filter base is held on with two nuts and bolts; the left-hand with captive nuts on a U-shaped plate which also acts as a bracket for the choke cable. Usually the right hand air filter is also held in place with a U-bracket.

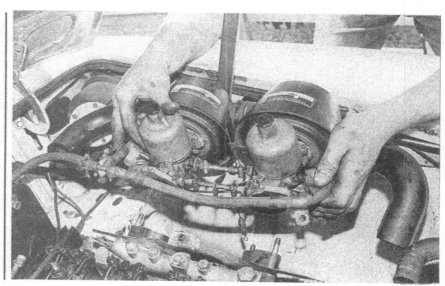

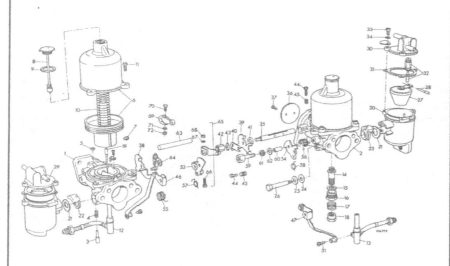

FSU7. This is a super-duper Special Tuning SU manifold - remanufactured by Burlen Fuel Systems.

FSU5. And this is how the various carburettor linkages fit together. There should also be four return springs in all: one for each choke, one for each throttle. ↑

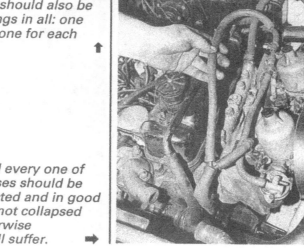

FSU6. Each and every one of the breather hoses should be properly connected and in good condition - and not collapsed internally - otherwise performance will suffer. ➡

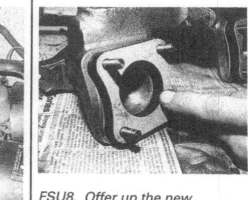

FSU8. Offer up the new emulsion block ...

FSU9. ... and file out the manifold until it fits the shape of the emulsion block precisely.

FSU12. The whole assembly was offered up to the car after the exhaust manifold had been fitted ...

FSU15. The one-way valve for the servo unit was screwed into the top of the manifold with a new copper washer and with Hylomar sealant on the threads.

FSU10. Four nuts and spring washers hold each of the 1 3/4 SUs to the manifold. These carburettors are available brand new as Burlen Fuel Systems/SU Carburettor Originals.

FSU13. ... and it was found that the inlet manifold flanges were a shade too thick. They had to be filed down to exactly the same thickness as the exhaust manifold flanges. If the difference had been great, with therefore a risk of weakening the inlet manifold flanges, special packing shims would have been made and fitted to the exhaust manifold flanges instead. ➡

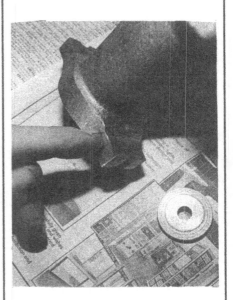

FSU11. A standard manifold gasket is used.

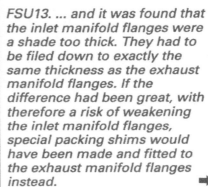

FSU14. New mounting washers spread the load equally and evenly across both manifolds.

FSU16. We made up our own gaskets to fit between carburettors and air filters by holding gasket paper over the flange and tapping lightly with the ball end of a ball pein hammer ...

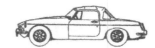

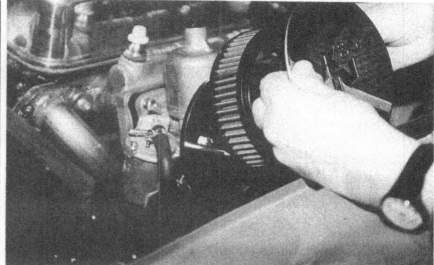

FSU17. ... which cut neatly through the gasket paper in exactly the position required.

FSU18. The gasket was then fitted to the carburettor with non-setting Hylomar ...

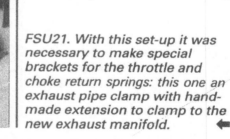

FSU20. K & N filters are demonstrably superior to the original air filters in terms of releasing a measurable 1 1/2 to 2 bhp at the wheels, and last far, far longer. They are usually noisier than standard but are highly recommended. The elements are said to last almost indefinitely. ⬆

FSU21. With this set-up it was necessary to make special brackets for the throttle and choke return springs: this one an exhaust pipe clamp with hand-made extension to clamp to the new exhaust manifold. ⬅

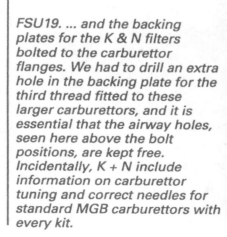

FSU19. ... and the backing plates for the K & N filters bolted to the carburettor flanges. We had to drill an extra hole in the backing plate for the third thread fitted to these larger carburettors, and it is essential that the airway holes, seen here above the bolt positions, are kept free. Incidentally, K + N include information on carburettor tuning and correct needles for standard MGB carburettors with every kit.

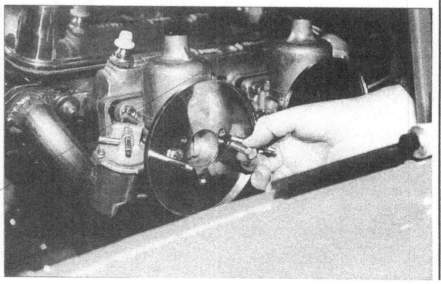

FSU22. It was also necessary to devise a feed for the fuel line to reach the front carburettor. A piece of pipe from the Automec fuel line kit was cut and clamped to the bottom bolt on the carburettor flanges.

FSU24. You can see the way in which more flexible pipe has connected the copper to the carburettor fuel intake. Two more suitable pieces of pipe were cut and shaped to take the fuel overflow from the carburettors ... ➡

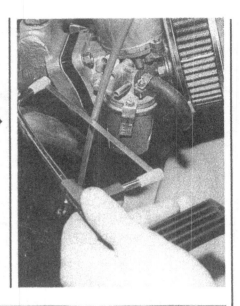

FSU23. The Automec fuel filter was grafted into the system, and some of their flexible pipe used to take a feed from the back carburettor to the new piece of pipe. ➡

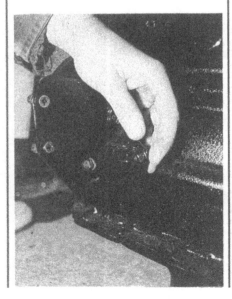

FSU25. ... both of them curving down to reach the bracket on the side of the block and ending up beneath the level of the exhaust system so that any of the fuel that might flow from the carburettors is taken away from any hot spots. ⬅

FSU26. More flexible pipe was used to connect them up.

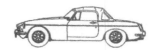

FSU27. The tangled web was completed with fresh crank case breather pipes, and fitted and clipped into place.

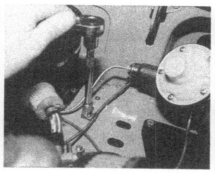

FSU30. ... and both cables were routed into position with body clips.

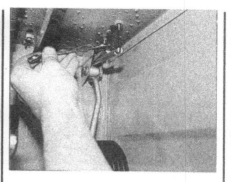

FSU33. Then there was the top throttle stop ...

FSU28. New throttle and choke cables, plus bonnet release pull and speedo cable while we were at it, were obtained from Speedy Cables.

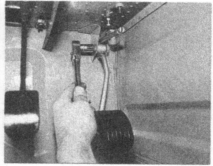

FSU31. The throttle pedal was painted, fitted with a new rubber, rebushed and bolted back into place inside the footwell.

FSU34. ... and the throttle cable mounting to fit inside the large square opening at the back of the flitch panel.

FSU29. We reverted to a Moss choke cable to retain the correct appearance on the dash ...

FSU32. The throttle stop, painted, was screwed back onto the fire wall.

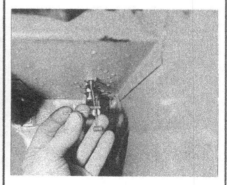

FSU35. The throttle cable inner has to be stripped from its outer, passed upwards through the mounting, and the cable and nipple held in place with a split pin, the ends opened out. The outer is reinserted from above.

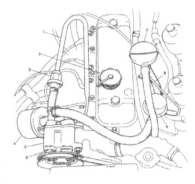

FSU36. This is the earlier, more straightforward emission control system fitted to US cars, with air pump (Item 5) and gulp valve (Item 9).

inside the end-cap but most such repairs seem to fail to effect a permanent cure and the best solution may be to buy a new fuel pump. Burlen Fuel Systems, as well as manufacturing 'original' SU carburettors, do the same with SU fuel pumps. We used one of their units on the project car.

FPR1. The clamp was salvaged from the donor car and sandblasted before being painted, and the clamp rubber was also saved.

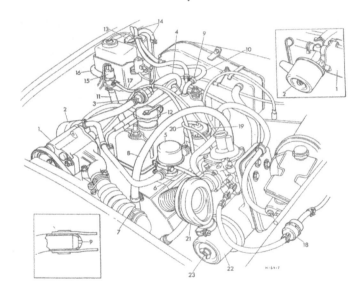

FSU37. Later, the emission control system became a little more interwoven!

Fuel Pump Replacement

After a period of time fuel pumps can, and do, fail; usually going through a period of 'sticking', which can be very temporarily cured by giving the pump a clout with the end of a spanner! A less temporary repair is to clean the points

FPR2. The pump was clamped into place next to the battery box, and the blanking plug was left in place to prevent the ingress of dirt.

FPR3. The non-corroding Automec copper brake pipes were connected to the original special unions which are bolted to the fuel pump.

Fuel Tank Replacement

Safety

Never drain a fuel tank indoors or where the highly flammable petrol vapours can gather, such as over a pit. Store petrol drained from the tank in safe, closed, approved containers. If the empty tank is to be stored, have it steam-cleaned to remove the petrol vapours. Place a damp rag into any openings and keep tank out of

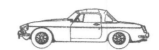

doors for very short term storage. Keep all sparks and flames away from the fuel system whilst working on it.

Before carrying out any major body repairs, it makes good common sense to drain, and remove the fuel tank to a place of safety. The remaining fume-filled tank is especially dangerous, so consider having it properly cleaned out during any extended restoration.

Mild steel or stainless steel fuel tank? The choice is yours. The former are "original" while the latter are very expensive and at the time of writing supply is erratic.

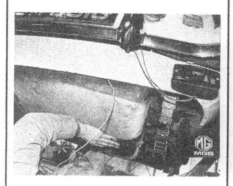

FTR1. MGB fuel tanks invariably corrode and leak from the top, causing a stain to spread down the side of the tank. You should also be able to smell the fuel!

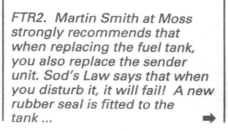

FTR2. Martin Smith at Moss strongly recommends that when replacing the fuel tank, you also replace the sender unit. Sod's Law says that when you disturb it, it will fail! A new rubber seal is fitted to the tank ... ➡

FTR3. ... the sender float passed through the hole and the sender unit mounted with the cut out coinciding with the tag on the tank which ensures that it goes the right way up.

FTR4. A clamp ring is placed in position and tapped round with a drift which wedges the clamp down and holds everything tight and leak proof.

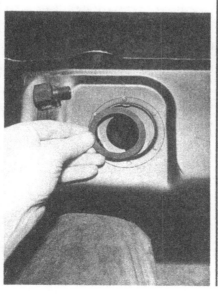

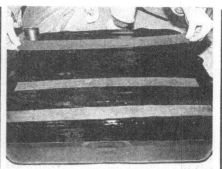

FTR5. Bearing in mind that it is always the top of the tank that rusts out, Graham painted on two thick layers of Waxoyl, then placed the rubber buffer strips on top of that.

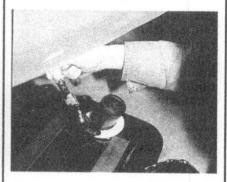

FTR6. More corrosion often occurs around the tank filler neck. The seal used to be of absorbent rubber; now it's non-absorbent, but Graham painted on lots more Waxoyl to be sure.

FTR7. Hands, knees and ... the tank is held up from beneath over the mounting studs beneath the boot floor.

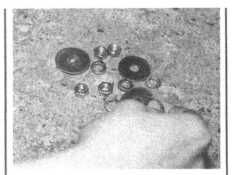

FTR8. If you are working alone, have the (bright zinc-plated or stainless steel) flat washers, spring washers and nuts to hand so that you can ...

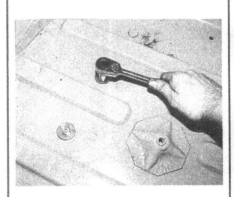

FTR9. ... put several of them loosely on whilst holding the tank in place. Don't yet tighten up. Namrick can supply the fixings used here.

FTR10. You can then go inside the boot and do the same to the bolts that pass down from above.

FTR11. Once all the nuts and bolts are in place - Graham used spring clips on the tank flange for the bolts that come down from above. ➡

FTR12. The rubber grommet joining the tank filler pipe to rear body is fitted, and the short piece of hose connecting it to the tank is tightened up with two large clips.

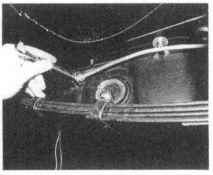

FTR13. The shorter pipe from the fuel pump can now be connected to the tank ...

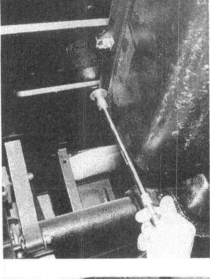

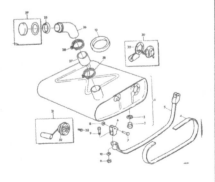

FTR14. ... and the wiring connections made to the sender unit. We then Waxoyled the remainder of the outside of the tank.

FTR15. For a long time, fixing straps for this earlier tank were not available and they have often been replaced by a later-type tank bolted to the floor. Item 5 is the fixing strap and 4 the rubber packing strip.

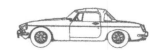

Oil Cooler and Pipework

OC1. If the oil pressure union in the block has been disturbed, replace it with a fresh copper sealing washer. ➡

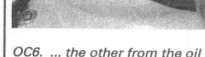

OC6. ... the other from the oil filter housing.

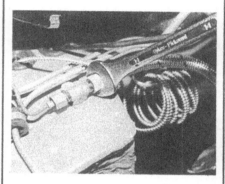

OC2. The braided flexible pipe from the block spanners onto the bulkhead mounted union, to which the oil pipe from the oil pressure gauge is also attached.

OC4. Engines which originally had the hanging down canister type of oil filter can be updated with this fitting from later engines, enabling a disposable oil filter to be fitted.

OC7. Oil cooler hose grommets are split to enable them to be passed over the pipe before they are both introduced into the radiator shroud.

OC3. Oil coolers are still distributed by Serck Marston. The oil cooler bolts down to captive nuts in the lower body.

OC5. New, original-type oil cooler pipes are still available. One runs from a union on the back of the block ...

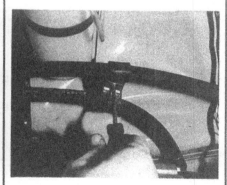

OC8. These rubber ties for holding the pipes together and keeping them neat are available from Moss. Only one was fitted originally; we fitted two, one each side of the radiator shroud for extra neatness.

OC9. *The two pipes connect up to the Serck Marston oil cooler. This single spanner approach is all very well for connecting the pipe loosely; for tightening up - and you have to tighten up really hard - you should place a spanner on the hexagon on the top of the oil cooler to prevent damage as the pipe nut is tightened up.* ➡

CS2. *... and this the improved one fitted to later vehicles. It is an improvement over the earlier one, but if you want to switch you will also have to swap the radiator shroud and the thermostat housing. You could convert the existing shroud if you have good panel beating skills.* ⬇

Cooling System

In Britain, Serck Marston claim to be able to supply a new radiator for just about any make of car. The radiators they build up for the MGB are of the later, more efficient type, but if you want to keep your earlier type of radiator, then they may be able to build a new one using original top and bottom tanks and a new radiator core. Moss certainly list all types of MGB radiator in their catalogue.

Safety

Never attempt to drain a cooling system while the engine is hot. Releasing pressure from the cooling system can cause the water to boil with very dangerous consequences.

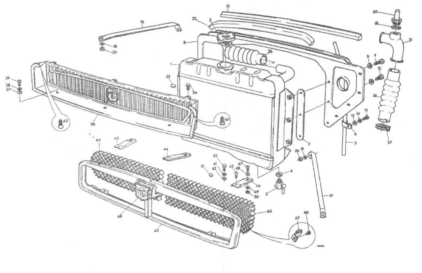

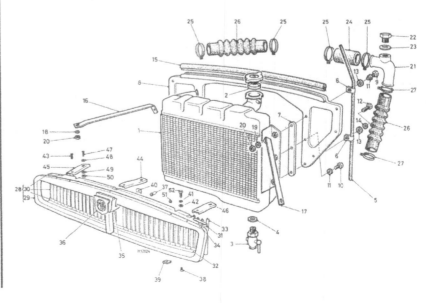

CS1. *This is the earlier type of radiator and associated components ...*

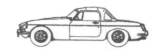

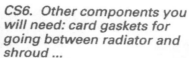

CS6. Other components you will need: card gaskets for going between radiator and shroud ... →

CS3. Someone had fitted an earlier radiator and shroud to the donor car - presumably from a scrap car - so we switched back again. From Bromsgrove MG Centre we purchased a second-hand thermostat housing that goes this-a-way ...

CS4. ... and fitted it with a new gasket and non-setting Hermetite.

CS7. ... and new rubber overflow pipe. The old rots out after just a few years.

CS9. The channel along the top of the shroud was glued up ...

CS5. The heater tap was similarly treated before being bolted to the block.

CS8. The shroud was sandblasted and painted - and then we had to file out some of the holes to get it to line up with the captive nuts.

CS10. ... and the new rubber seal stuck down.

CS11. A line of bolts hold the shroud on each side to the bodyshell...

CS14. We had to make up special brackets to fit on the manifold ...

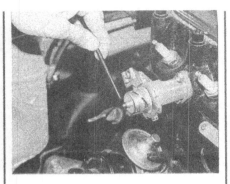

CS17. Speedy Cables again supplied the cable for the heater tap ...

CS12. ... and a vertical row hold radiator to shroud. One longer bolt and an extra nut secures the steady bar to the radiator shroud.

CS15. ... to carry the Moss-supplied heater pipe. Our old one had been irretrievably bent.

CS18. ...which was then connected to the other end of the heater matrix.

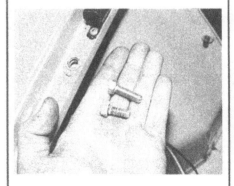

CS13. You may have to take out one of the wing mounting bolts and replace it with a longer one for the other end of the same steady bar.

CS16. A specially curved piece of heater hose connecting pipe to heater matrix.

Footnote

The Project MGB was treated to a new type of product - coolant water that has been specially deionised and combined with anti- freeze and corrosion inhibitors. Produced by Comma, X-stream is ideal for restored cars because, whilst the car is sitting around or undertaking short trips, the X-stream will protect the engine's internals and prevent the usual corrosion and silting-up that takes place.

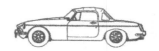

Electric Cooling Fan Conversion

Safety

Disconnect battery/ies before working on the electrical system.

ECF1. The Kenlowe electric cooling fan kit has been around for so long that it has become almost a classic in its own right!

ECF2. Special plastic clamps have to be fitted to the fan body using the fixing supplied in the kit.

ECF3. The instructions leave it to you, the fitter, to decide in detail where everything goes, although the fan has to go in front of the radiator on the MGB. We bolted down one supporting leg facing forwards ...

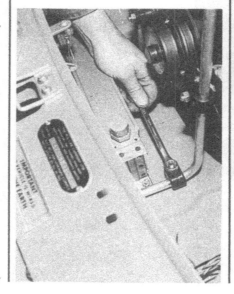

ECF4. ... while on the other side, the supporting leg faced sideways, giving maximum stability between the two of them. The plastic clips are fixed in place on the aluminium support bars with self-tapping screws. Note that the wiring has to protrude from the bottom of the fan motor because that is where the drain holes are also situated. ⬆

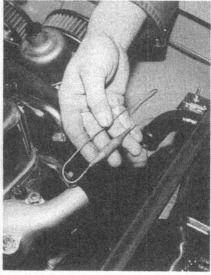

ECF5. The temperature sensor has to be fitted on the radiator side of the top hose with the capillary tube bent back on itself ...

ECF6. ... so that it appears out of the top hose. Kenlowe's Patent tapered seal allows the pipe to come out of the top hose without causing a leak. We used extra sealant and found that the hose clip had to be tightened extra hard for the seal to work, but once it became sealed, it stayed sealed! ➡

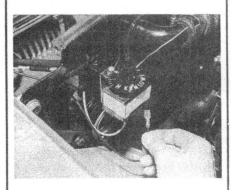

ECF7. We found a pre-existing hole on the radiator shroud on which the temperature control could be mounted, and the wiring was connected up as described in the comprehensive instructions, except that we decided to add an in-line fuse as an extra precaution. This control enables you to set the fan to come on at the right temperature - say, when the temperature gauge reaches 'N'.

ECF8. The strangely named Latex Cushion Company have been making radiator muffs for British cars since well before World War 2. Although it's only needed in really severe weather, this traditionally built and crafted piece of kit looks rather appealing! ⬆

ECF9. The fittings clamp to the radiator grille and can be left on all the year round if you wish, just removing the solid brass knurled nuts to take off the radiator muff; or it can be rolled open and held back with the leather tabs fitted. ⬅

Chapter 7
Electrical

Electrical Components and Loom

Even with a car as relatively unmodified as the MGB has been over the years, changes to the electrical system have been numerous. The Moss Parts Catalogue lists no fewer than 54 different wiring loom sections, depending on the model, the year and the positioning of such fittings as the horn push. Fitting a new wiring loom is a matter of applying method to what you are doing.

The first reaction is to be daunted at the sight of a new loom coming out of the wrapping, but the apparent difficulty of the task can be overcome in two ways. One is by taking great care when removing the old loom; cut the old cables a little way away from each of the components as you remove the loom so that the colour coding on each cable can clearly be seen. You could also make notes and sketches, and take photographs, to show where the old loom has been run. It's far too easy to just pull the old loom out of the vehicle and then find yourself unable to work out where the new one goes when the time comes to fit

it. Perhaps you could insert the new one only as the old one is removed.

Even when you have purchased the correct loom for your car, you must be prepared to make minor modifications to it. If you're fitting a new loom to an existing car, you will undoubtedly come across the situation where someone in the past has changed, say, the alternator or the indicator switch for a different model, requiring the use of different connections. Some examples are given in the following photo sequence.

Safety

Always disconnect the battery/ies before working on any part of the electrical system.

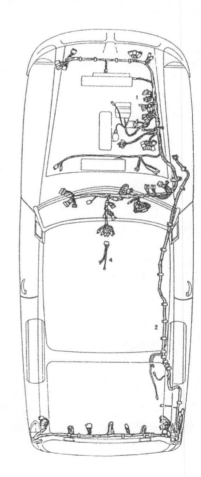

ECL1. These line drawings give some idea of how the main sections of loom have to be routed. (Courtesy: Moss Parts Catalogue)

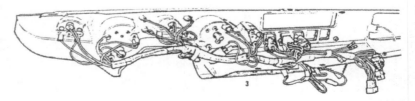

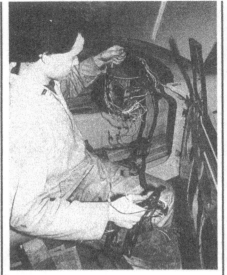

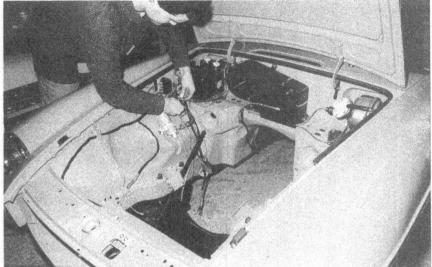

ECL2. 'O what a tangled web we weave,
When first we practise to fit a wiring loom.'
(With apologies to Sir Walter Scott.)

ECL5. Graham Macdonald fits and clips the wiring loom neatly through the engine bay. In many cases you can't work out where it should go until the major electrical components are in place - no problem, of course, if you're rewiring an existing car! ⬆

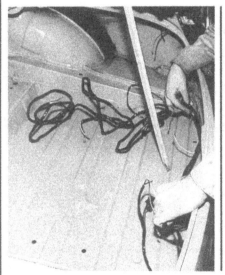

ECL3. Some of the loom clips are fitted to the body shell - slide rubber sheathing insulation over them before bending them over the loom - while others have to be reused or replaced with new. ➡

ECL6. At the fuse box - where the tangle of wires can turn it into a confuse box - you will find the true benefits of having snipped the old wires from the component instead of pulling the connectors off. ⬇

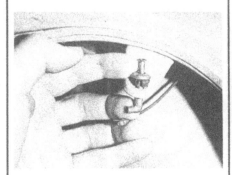

ECL4. When removing the old loom, you will undoubtedly find corrosion-affected switches, which will have to be replaced with new. The Heritage shell provides provision for a boot light switch; we fitted one. ⬆

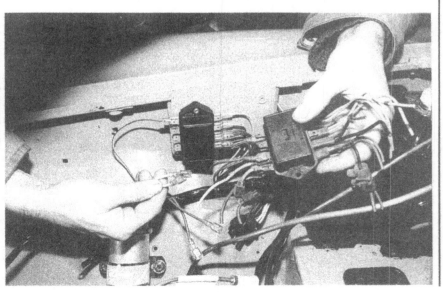

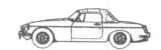

ECL7. In spite of all the preparation in the world, it is inevitable that you will have to carry out some detective work in order to establish what goes where. A purpose-built or home-made test lamp will prove to be invaluable. ➡

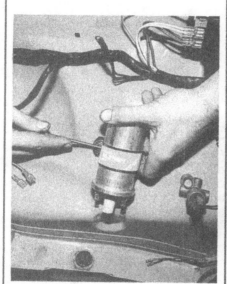

ECL8. New 'OE' (original equipment) Lucas coil doesn't look exactly like the original but undoubtedly works a lot better than an old one!

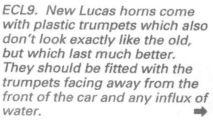

ECL9. New Lucas horns come with plastic trumpets which also don't look exactly like the old, but which last much better. They should be fitted with the trumpets facing away from the front of the car and any influx of water. ➡

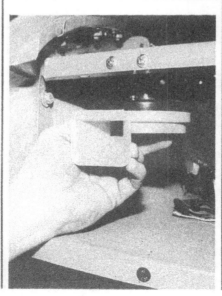

ECL10. After testing, cleaning up and painting, we refitted and re-used the donor car's heater blower unit.

ECL11. As described in the section 'Electric Windows' we fitted the switches to the rectangular slots in the centre console. They were perfect for height, the width had to be filled in a little with strips of plastic cut from a scrap centre console and glued in with model makers plastic glue. ⬅

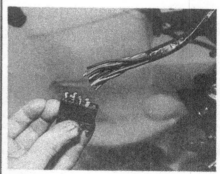

ECL12. Where the loom communicates with the steering column switch gear, the block connector fitted was found to be incompatible with the wiring already on the column. We cut the block connector away ...

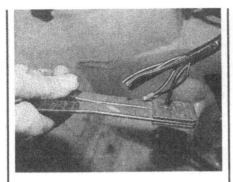

ECL13. ... crimped on new Lucas connectors ...

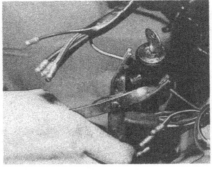

ECL14. ... and used this special tool borrowed from an electrician friend to pull each pair of bullet connectors into their connecting socket.

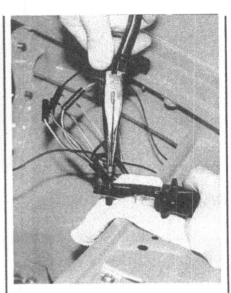

ECL15. Another way of doing the job is to grip the socket firmly in a pair of engineer's pliers, while another pair of pliers holds the bullet connector and pushes it down tightly into the socket. Notice how the car's paintwork is being protected! ⬆

ECL16. The battery boxes can be nasty, festering pits and the source of many problems for your MGB's electrical system. We started by fitting new rubber buffers on which the batteries must rest to reduce shocks to their system.

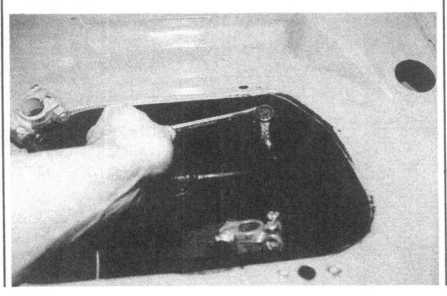

ECL17. Battery cables from the donor car were fitted with brand new battery terminals - use the clamp-type rather than the post-type for greater electrical efficiency ...

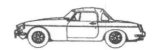

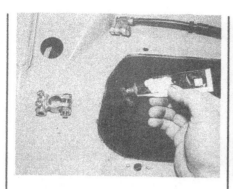

ECL18. ... and apply Copper Ease to each of the connections to improve conductivity and guard against corrosion.

ECL19. Old battery clamps tend to corrode quite heavily, and when fitting the new, don't forget, once again, the rubber buffer strip.

ECL20. Moss have put back into production batteries with the original appearance for just about all models of British sports car made. It's probably less significant in an MGB, with the batteries hidden behind the rear panel, than in any car you can think of!

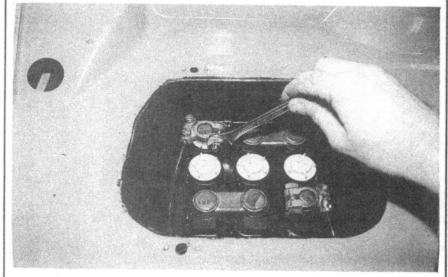

ECL21. Once the battery terminals have been tightened up on to the battery posts, they should be smeared all over with Copper Ease to prevent the furring up that is inevitable. With an older battery, you don't need to buy anything fancy to remove the furring up; disconnect the battery, pour warm water over all of the affected parts, dry off, clean posts and terminals back to shiny metal and then refit with Copper Ease protection.

ECL22. The battery clamp hooks into the eyes in the bottom of the battery box and is intended to clamp the battery down as shown. DON'T ALLOW A SPANNER OR ANYTHING ELSE METALLIC TO TOUCH OR SHORT OUT ANY OF THE EXPOSED METAL PARTS ON TOP OF THE BATTERY.

ECL23. The battery cover - newly manufactured as a Heritage part if you need it - has to be fitted with the correct rubber tubular sealer strip which must be glued around the underside of the cover. ➡

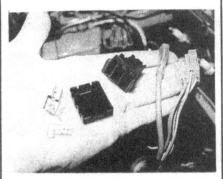

ECL24. Connections on the starter motor have varied over the years. Our new Lucas unit contained instructions for mating the loom to its new connections. Refer to Haynes Manual if necessary.

ECL26. We also fitted a new Lucas alternator to the project car, and it too came with full instructions for fitting the connections up correctly.

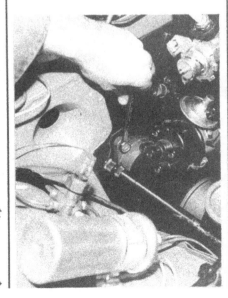

ECL25. The new or replacement starter unit has to be added from beneath the engine bay, and although it's a squeeze, it can be done without any other dismantling. ➡

In the United States it seems that Lucas components are good for a laugh! Road + Track took the Lucas 'Prince of light' slogan and recoined it as 'Prince of Darkness'. This witticism is genuinely funny but it's also, in the author's opinion, completely unjustified. There is not a hint of nationalism in this - Bosch components are at least as good - but the author has found Lucas electrical components to give years and years of excellent service and, at 42 years of age, he has now been driving cars fitted with them for just on a quarter of a century! However, electrical components (in general) are by far and away the largest source of breakdown in cars of any age, and it is for that reason that almost every electrical component on the project car, and certainly every component which is necessary for the safe and adequate running of the car has been replaced with new. You are strongly advised when carrying out an MGB restoration to budget for the replacement of as many electrical components, including smaller items such as lamps and switches, as you can properly afford.

Smart paintwork gives you a good looking car; efficient

mechanical components give you a 'drivers car'; top-class electrics give you a reliable car. And it's no good sitting prettily and broken down on the side of the motorway!

Dashboard and Switch Layouts

The following drawings are intended to provide a guide to the positioning and arrangement of some of the switchgear on the MGB. The drawings work back from the latest to the earliest types fitted.

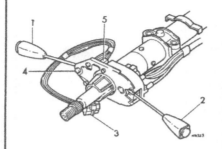

DSL1. Right-hand-drive 1978-79 cars used this steering column switch arrangement.
1. Wiper/washer switch
2. Direction indicator/main beam/horn control switch
3. Multi-plug
4. Wiper/washer switch screws
5. Clamp screw for direction indicator etc switch ⬆

DSL2. Fascia layout, GHN5/GHD5 cars from chassis number 294251 left hand drive.
1. Brake pressure warning light test push switch
2. Retaining clip
3. Panel lamp rheostat switch
4. Retainer
5. Rheostat switch knob
6. Heater blower switch
7. Rocker switch retainer
8. Lighting switch
9. Hazard warning switch
10. Seat belt warning lamp
11. Retainer for seat belt warning lamp
12. Hazard warning lamp
13. Retainer nut
14. Rotary control
15. Retaining nut
16. Rotary control knob
17. Dial assembly
18. Light box
19. Retaining nut ⬇

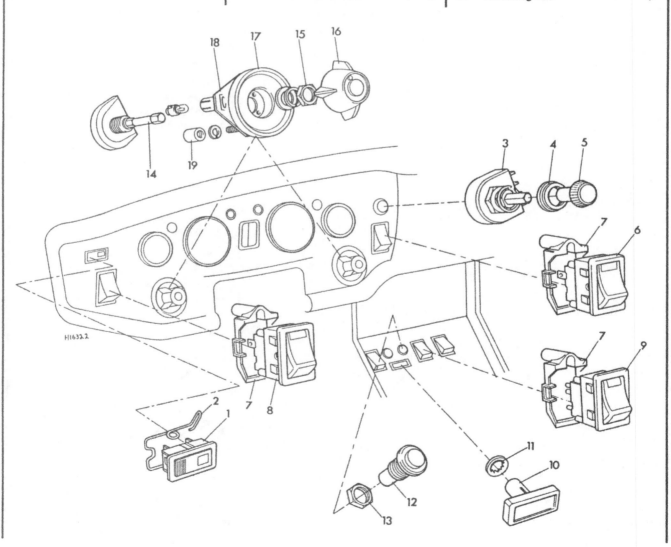

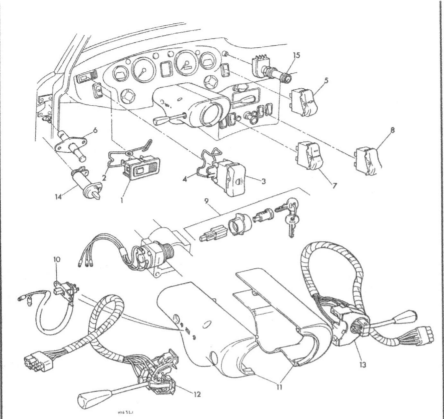

DSL3. *Fascia layout,*
GHN5/GHN4 and GHD5/GHD4
cars, left hand drive.
1.   Brake pressure warning light/test
     push switch
2.   Retaining clip
3.   Lighting switch
4.   Retaining clip
5.   Heater blower switch
6.   Door switch - interior light
7.   Hazard warning switch
8.   Map light switch
9.   Ignition switch
10. Panel light switch
11. Steering column switch cowl
12. Direction indicator/headlight
     flasher   low/high beam/horn
     switch
13. Windshield wiper/washer and
     over-drive switch
14. Audible warning door switch
15. Panel lamp rheostat switch   ←

DSL4. *Fascia layout, GHN5 and*
GHD5 models from vehicle
number from 410002, right
hand drive.   ↓

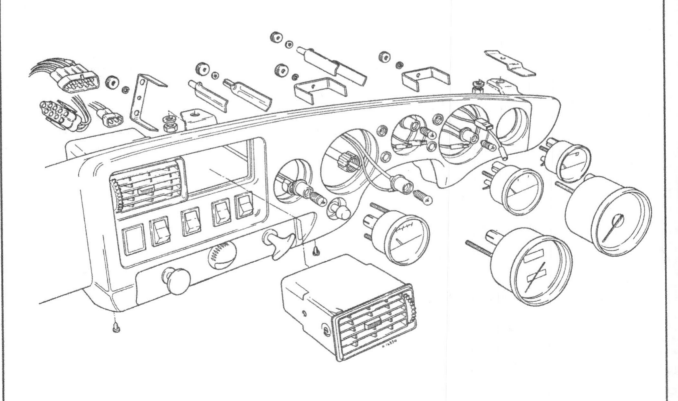

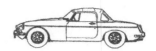

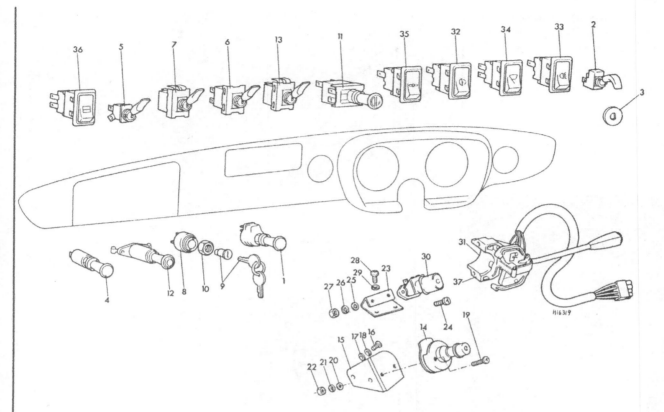

DSL5. Fascia and switch layout, both types fitted to right hand drive vehicles up to chassis number 410001.

1. Panel light switch
2. Overdrive switch
3. Bezel Cars up to and including early GHN5 and GHD5 models:
4. Map light switch
5. Heater blower switch 6. Windscreen wiper switch
7. Windscreen wiper switch (tourer)
8. Ignition/starter switch
9. Ignition switch lock and key
10. Locknut for ignition and starter switch
11. Light switch
12. Heated rear window switch (GT) GHD3 models
13. Light switch
14. Headlight dip switch
15.to 22.   Dipswitch bracket
RH drive models up to and including GHN4 and GHD4 cars:
23.to 29.   Dipswitch bracket
LH drive models up to and including GHN4 and GHD4 cars:
30. Headlight dipswitch GHN4 and GHD4 models:
31. Direction indicator/headlamp high and low beam/ headlamp flasher/horn push switch GHN5 and GHD5 from car number 258001:
32. Fog and spot light switch
33. Light switch

34. Windscreen wiper switch
35. Heater blower switch
36. Electrically heated rear window switch (GT)
37. Direction indicator/headlamp high and low beam/ headlamp flasher switch ↑

Instruments and Gauges

All of the project car's instruments and gauges were overhauled by Renown

Instruments, who made the instrument faces look like brand new, renewed the working bits in the vulnerable oil and water temperature gauge combined unit, serviced and rebuilt all of the gauges and ensured that the speedometer was calibrated properly. They can send you a form to fill in which involves you having to measure the rolling radius of the rear wheels (the height between the ground and the wheel centre), to tell them the differential ratio of your car and the ratio of the speedometer drive gearing in the gearbox. Fortunately, they also tell you how to go about measuring the latter (see 'Gearbox' section for how to find and remove the speedometer drive.)

Safety

Always disconnect the battery/ies before working on any part of the electrical system.

IG1. The reconditioned gauges were totally indistinguishable from brand new. ➡

IG2. The speedometer gauge is held in place with this saddle clamp affixed with two knurled screws from the back of the dashboard. ⬆

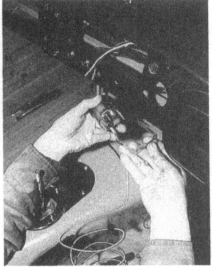

IG4. A similar saddle clamp holds the combined water temperature and oil pressure gauge to the dash ... ⬅

IG3. The speedometer drive is very awkwardly placed and it may be necessary to force it off with a pair of pliers or a self-grip wrench. Before fitting, take great trouble to clean up the thread on both the gearbox and the cable nut, and take care not to cross the threads. ➡

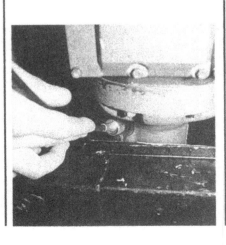

IG5. ... and after passing the sender unit through the bulkhead, not forgetting the grommet in the bulkhead top, the sender unit can be screwed to the block. We coiled and clamped the surplus capillary tube safely and neatly out of the way. ⬆

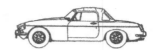

IG6. The tachometer unit is held by two separate clamps. Connect the lamps and wiring before fitting.

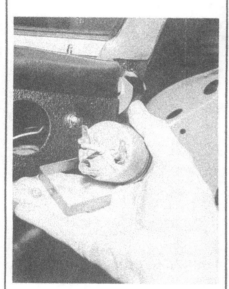

IG7. A single knurled nut holds the fuel gauge clamp in place.

Indicator Switch

IS1. On or off the car, the indicator switch is simply clamped to the steering column.

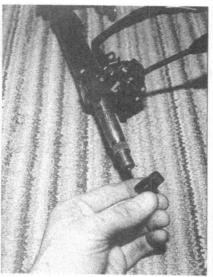

IS2. This spring clip operates the switch-off mechanism on the column. ←

IS3. The donor car's switch cover had grown a patina of age but was made to look like new again with Solvol Autosol metal polish. ↓

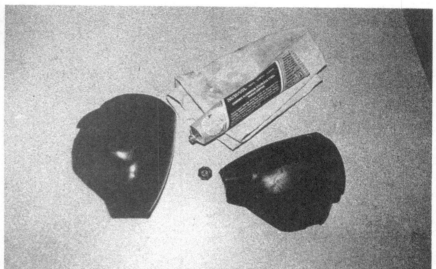

IS4. *The switch cover is held to the column with four recessed self-tapping screws inserted from beneath.* ↑

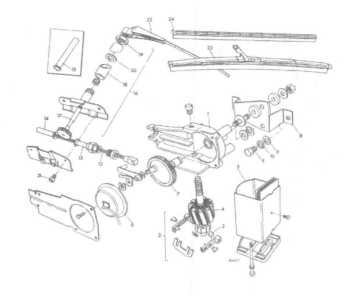

WWM2. *This exploded view is of the single-speed Lucas DR3A wiper mechanism. It is available from Moss and other specialists.* ↑

WWM3. *The two-speed Lucas 14W wiper motor as described here.* ←

Windscreen Wiper Mechanism

WWM1. *The windscreen wiper motor becomes old and lazy even though there may be plenty of life left in the mechanism. Fortunately, Lucas still make the unit and it's quite a simple matter to graft one on to the other.* ➡

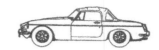

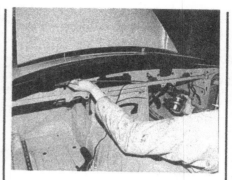

WWM4. After taking off the wiper mechanism drive gear (WWM3, Items 3 and 6) by removing the circlip (Item 4) the gear wheel can be lifted out of the old unit and thoroughly washed clean ...

WWM6. With the correct washers (Items 5) in place, the circlip can be refitted.

WWM7. With the wheelboxes facing 'upwards', as in WWM2 Item 16, the windscreen wiper assembly can be reintroduced to the car from beneath the dash. Transfer the mounting bracket from the old wiper motor to the new.

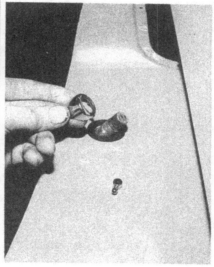

WWM5. ... ready to be packed with grease, fitted to the new unit and for the drive gear to be offered up.

WWM8. Make sure that the solid rubber tube (WWM2, Item 18) has its tapering end facing the right way round beneath the dash. It pays to replace the rubber washer (Item 20) to prevent the ingress of water, and new chrome bezels are available for those regular occasions when they corrode badly.

WWM9. The correct type of windscreen wiper arms, with a chromed finish in this case, are not generally available from motor accessory shops, but all respectable MG specialists should be able to keep them in stock with the correct type of wiper blade.

Windscreen Washers

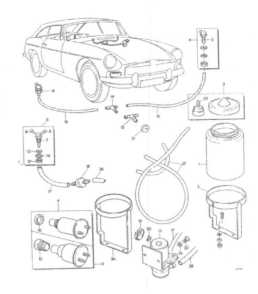

WSW1. These are the windscreen washer components available on early MGBs. At the time of writing, the pump assembly (Item 13) is available; the correct Lucas switch is not.

WSW2. Washer jets are fixed to the bulkhead top with lockwasher and nut provided.

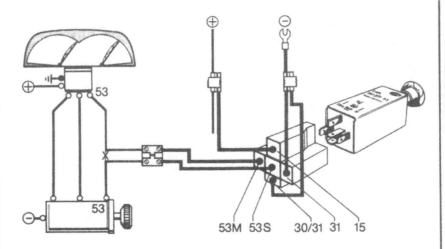

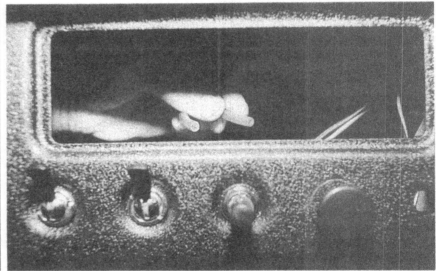

53M 53S   30/31 31 15

WSW3. Two plastic pipes connect up to the hand pump mounted on the dash. The mystery knob on the right is a non-standard windscreen wiper delay control made by Hella and fitted to a 'spare' hole in the dash.   ↑

WSW4. The Hella delay mechanism connects into the existing windscreen wiper wiring as described in the instructions supplied.   ←

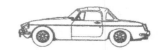

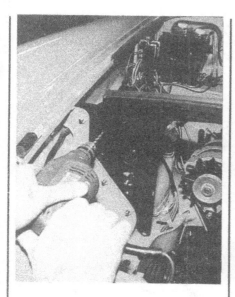

WSW5. We decided that the Heritage MGB would have its washer reservoir mounted on the radiator diaphragm. Different types were used over the years including a 'plastic bag' type hanging on the flitch panel.

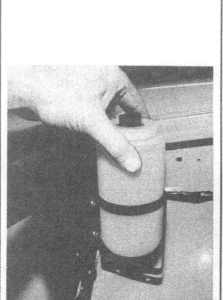

WSW6. The reservoir being slotted into its holder on the engine side of the radiator diaphragm.

Light Units

LU1. All of the MGB's light units can be purchased new except the number plate lamps. Guess which ones were scrap on our donor car! The bulbs were removed after much tugging, tweaking and application of releasing fluid. ➡

LU2. Replacement bulb holders could have come from any similar Lucas units - we took them from two scrap MGB rear lamps by levering back the tabs that held them in the top of the lamp back plates. ➡

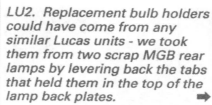

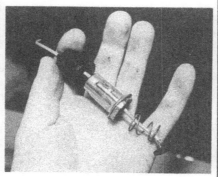

LU3. They were reassembled with the rubber grommet and correct colour cabling from the number plate lamps.

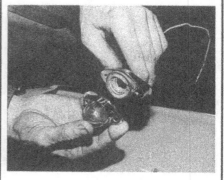

LU4. And then, with plenty of sealer to ensure that this did not happen again, the lamp units were inserted and the tabs bent back over.

LU5. Front indicator and sidelamp units are held in with two set screws built into the units. You may have to use extra sealer, as we did, to ensure a watertight seal between the lamp and wing. ➡

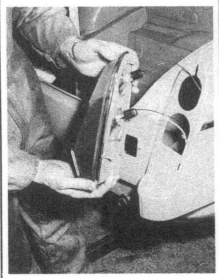

LU6. Three similar threaded set screws are fitted to the back of rear lamp units ...

LU8. Before fitting reversing lamps, threaded spring clips have to be pushed over the mounting holes.

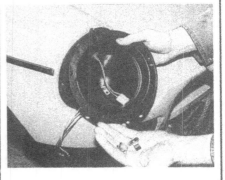

LU10. We could have chosen to use plastic headlamp bowls but they can be the very devil to fit properly and so we stuck with the Lucas pressed steel type.

LU7. ... and to them are screwed these special units with soft rubber washers built in.

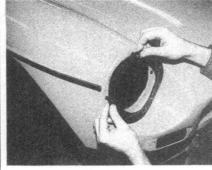

LU9. This rubber seal keeps the mud on the inside of the wing.

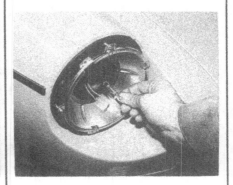

LU11. These came complete with the fittings for sealed beam headlamps ...

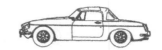

LU12. ... and the Halogen Lucas units simply plugged into the socket on the wiring loom. If you want to convert the headlamps on an existing car, you may find yourself with this minor wiring job to carry out, but you would also be strongly advised to check the condition of all the headlamp wiring and the connections otherwise the extra load demanded by the Halogen lamps may be the straw that breaks the camel's back. In any case, you won't obtain most benefit unless the wires are good and the connections clean. ➡

LU13. Headlamp bezels are a clip fit, easing them on over the top and then pushing, prizing and teasing them on over the bottom.

LU15. ... but you can't buy the correct knob. It is removed by depressing the spring loaded button in the switch stalk through the hole in the bottom of the knob.

LU14. You can buy a new Lucas headlamp switch from Moss ...

Alarm Unit

Top of the range of alarms marketed by Gamma in the UK is an alarm that speaks to would-be intruders, telling them to 'Move away from the car...' when they get too close. For an MGB, that would have been just too much!

Safety

Always disconnect the battery/ies before working on any part of the electrical system.

AU1. The Gamma alarm unit that we chose to fit to the MGB was full of microchip sophistication, but more suited to the nature of the car. It also contains a battery backup so that even if someone disconnects the batteries on the vehicle, the alarm's battery will take over and do its job. ⬇

AU2. The Gamma alarm sensor sends out a microwave beam that can be adjusted to fill the cockpit of the MGB, but is not affected by air movement. Thus, it can be used with a soft-top car or even when the top is down.

AU3. The sensor was to be placed behind the front console, and would be fitted beneath the radio set once that was installed.

AU4. The control box was found a convenient home beneath the dash.

AU5. The Gamma fitter used our Sykes-Pickavant test lamp to identify a source that was 'live' with the ignition turned off. ↑

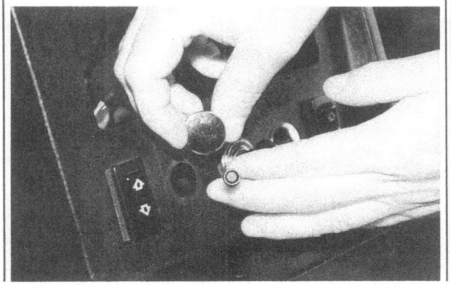

AU6. Almost as important as the alarm itself is this flashing light which tells all and sundry that the alarm is activated. Rather than drill into any integral part of the car, the fitter drilled and mounted the sensor in a prominent position on a switch blanking plate. ←

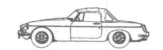

AU7. This is what you call a siren! It comes with its own integral self-recharging battery pack. Where they are fitted, door switches and boot lid and cockpit doors can be wired into the system, and extra switches placed on the bonnet. The unit senses current drain from anywhere in the car and, in addition, there is the microwave movement sensor already described. ➡

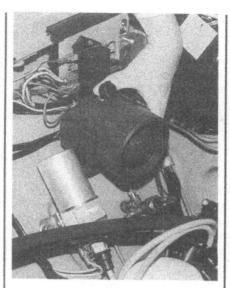

AU8. The remote control that comes with the Gamma alarm causes the car's turn indicator lights to flash on and off once to tell you that the system is armed, and to flash three times when you turn the system off.

AU9. The winking indicator on the dash confirms the status of the system and is a visual deterrent to any would be thief.

Sound System

There's nothing wrong with originality - in fact there's everything right with it if that is what you're setting out to achieve. The V8 I once owned was around ten years old when it came to me, and totally original in every small detail. I was proud to keep it that way. Our Heritage project car was always intended to be a very different animal. In making it a thoroughly modern MGB, we had to fit the sort of sound system that you might find in the very best of any other modern car, Radio Data System (RDS) tuner, high-power, amplifier, remote CD autochanger; it's all here! If you want to fit a simple, unsophisticated '60s style radio and speaker, nothing could be easier, and all you will need will be a small portion of this section. If you want to go all the way, here's how to do it.

Safety

Always disconnect the battery/ies before working on any part of the electrical system.

SSM1. We chose a top-of-the-range Clarion sound system for our project car because of the way in which Clarion has managed to combine a reputation for first-rate quality with affordable prices.

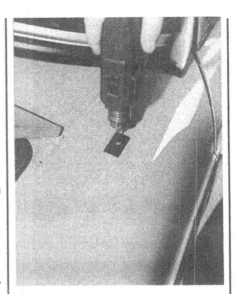

SSM2. Whichever type of aerial you fit - and we chose a Clarion auto electric aerial - remove the mud shield beneath the front left hand wing and investigate how best the unit you have got will fit the fairly generous space to be found. Electric aerials do demand some careful positioning to ensure that they don't come out at a crazy angle because the motor is in the wrong place. ⬅

SSM3. Work out with care where the aerial mounting hole is to be drilled and start off with a small pilot hole, drilling through a piece of tape to help to prevent slipping. ➡

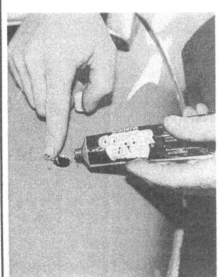

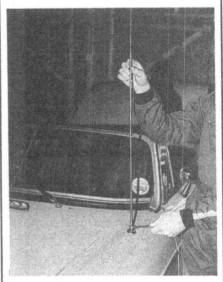

SSM4. After opening out the hole to the size required, it's time for more Copper Ease to give a good electrical contact between aerial and the car's body whilst sealing the bare metal against corrosion. ⬅

SSM5. Clarion fitter Doug Timms adjusts the aerial angle so that it is as upright as possible while still looking 'right', and then the lower end, at the bottom of the motor, is bolted to the inner bodywork with the mounting strap provided with the kit. ➡

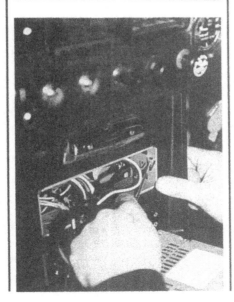

SSM6. The so-called head unit fits into a cage built to a European standard DIN size (DINA-E). A very small amount of plastic has to be filed out from the corners of the hole in the centre console before the DIN-E cage can be fitted and the integral tabs bent over with a screwdriver to hold it firmly in place. ⬅

SSM7. The head unit simply pushes into the DIN-E cage until the spring fixing clips click into position. Special keys provided with the unit have to be used to extract it. The back of the unit is, of course, wired up according to the fitting instructions and with the connectors supplied ➡

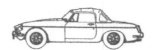

SSM8. One of the best things about the Clarion CRX91R unit, as far as use in a sports car is concerned, is its range of anti-theft facilities. You can unclip the control panel and carry it around in your pocket (leaving the legend SECURITY CODE visible on the set), and you can also programme the unit so that if it is disconnected from the power supply, your own personal code has to be keyed back into it before it will work again. It's a highly desirable piece of kit but it wouldn't be a very smart thief who stole it! ➡

SSM11. We decided to fit a pair of speakers into the quarter panels behind the B-posts. The steelwork was cut out with reference to the speaker templates ...

SSM9 In order to provide more than enough power for the job in hand, Clarion's 334HA four-channel amplifier, giving a total of 120 watts was fitted, screwed to the top of the bulkhead panel on the passenger side. ➡

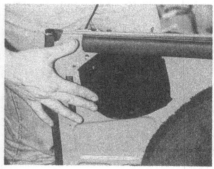

SSM12. ... and the edges of the hole protected with carpet tape.

SSM10. In the boot, Doug fitted the CDC9300 six disc compact disc changer. Six CDs are slotted into a magazine which in turn is slotted into the CD changer. Everything can then be operated whilst on the move from the head unit in the cockpit, without the distraction of empty CD cases littering the passenger seat. Meanwhile the incredible sound quality of CD is kept for you and yours with the autochanger safely under lock and key in the boot.

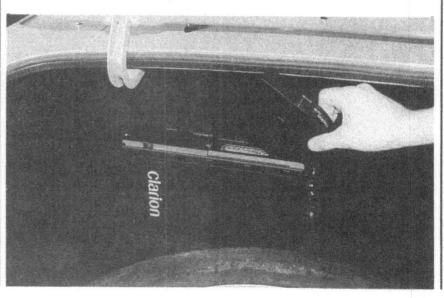

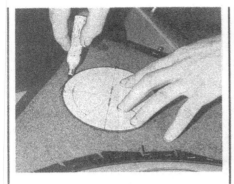

SSM13. The same template, cut from the speaker box, was used to mark the speaker positions on the trim panels ...

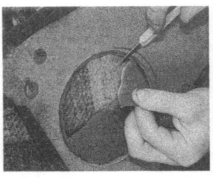

SSM15. The trim was cut out with infinite patience - better to take extra time than to cause extra damage.

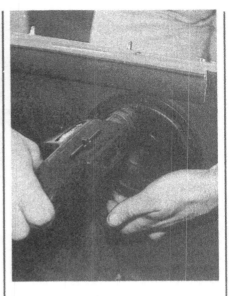

SSM17. Cables from the right hand speaker were run across to join those from the left and all the cables from the rear of the car run to the front. The rear speaker positions were drilled and were then screwed into place.

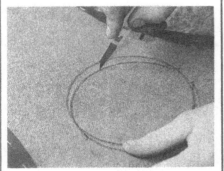

SSM14. ... and Doug found by checking before cutting that the positions needed to be moved a shade. Good practice!

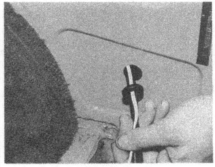

SSM16. Before refitting the trim panels, cables from the CD changer were run from the boot, through this grommeted hole and beneath the carpet on the sills.

NOTE: It is essential that any speakers that you choose to fit here are of the thinnest type possible so that the soft-top mechanism does not foul the speaker as it is folded down. There is very little clearance indeed. If your MGB uses the take- off and put-away type of soft top this won't be a problem, of course.

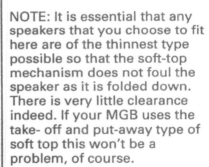

SSM18. There are two places in the doors where speakers can go, and with the Moss trim panels, the front position has been ready scored. It was too small for the type of speaker that we had in mind, however. With reference to the hole in the door shell, Doug has marked out the position for the speaker that we are going to fit. ←

SSM19. Each speaker has two connections on the back of it. It is essential that they are all wired up the same way with no cross-overs between negative and positive terminals. In other words, all the 'positives' must be wired up to the same source, and all the 'negatives'. Otherwise the cones in the speakers will reverberate in a pattern that exactly opposes each other and cancels out much of the sound. ➡

SSM20. After connecting up the wiring, the speakers can be screwed to the door panel after slotting the threaded spring clips on to the door casing - not the door trim - and screwing the speakers down. ➡

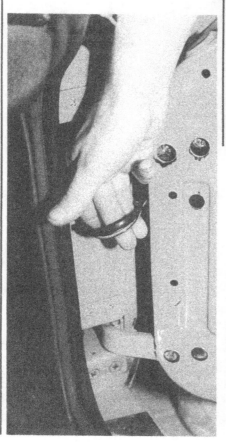

SSM21. As the speaker wires pass through A-posts and door frames they should be protected with grommets. The two holes should not be on a level with each other, otherwise they will tend to push the grommet out as you close the door. Make their heights an inch or two different and the speaker wire will loop gracefully out of the way as the door is closed. ⬅

SSM22. Everything now has to be brought back to the amplifier and head unit and Doug crimps new connectors on to the ends of the cables.

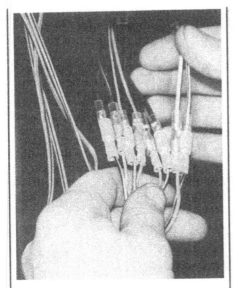

SSM23. It looks like a knitting basket of cable connections but, in fact, everything is thoroughly colour coded, so in theory there should be no problems. A job of this sort is certainly within the abilities of a careful DIYer but it's not something for the ham fisted!

SSM24. The Clarion speakers look most attractive in this modern MGB's setting ...

SSM25. ... and the design of the head unit blends in remarkably well.

Just about everything about this set is amazing! The RDS facility referred to at the start of this section is a feature that seems straight out of the future. When it is turned on, you could be listening to your favourite radio programme, tape or CD but, if a local radio station, wherever you might happen to be, broadcasts a traffic warning message, that message breaks into your listening and tells you what to look out for. If you really don't want it you can turn it off. The RDS tuner also identifies the source of the station that you are tuned into and the CRX91R names the station on the display panel. The Dolby B-tape deck ensures high quality tape listening, but the amplifier plus the CD player mean that is far more pleasant to go and sit in the MGB to listen to your favourite discs than to do so in most people's living rooms! Turned up high, the power of Led Zeppelin seems to make the whole car reverberate with incredible deep bass notes, while the silence in between passages of classical music is almost uncanny. Were MGB's really meant to sound like this?

On Charge!

BAT1. These are quite different from conventional batteries. The plates are coiled and the acid is sealed-in gel. As a result, an Optima battery is smaller, more powerful and can be recharged in an hour without damaging it. It can be mounted at any angle – even upside down! Well, you never know ...

BAT2. When a car stands, its battery can quickly go flat which is irritating and shortens a battery's life. The Exide 12V Charger Battery Saver Plus provides a constant trickle charge from the sun – free and continuous!

Chapter 8
Modifications

Introduction

When the first edition of this book was published in 1982, the aim of most restorers was to attain perfect originality. Since then, more and more people have come to realise that a modified MGB, preferably one that retains the spirit of the original, can make the 'B an even more enjoyable car to own and drive. For that reason, there are many places in this new edition where modifications are treated as a matter of course. Suspension, brakes, tyres, comfort – all are covered in the main body of the book.

For those who wish to go further, I have written a book in conjunction with Dave Pollard, entitled 'MGB Improve & Modify', also published by Haynes.

Therefore, this chapter concentrates on unleaded conversion, engine tuning, V8 conversion and 'de-toxing' the US spec engines. However, on this latter point, it must be pointed out that there are parts of this world where it is illegal to carry out such modifications – it is essential that the owner checks for him or herself – and it is arguable that it is immoral to do so anyway. My personal view is that the heavily encumbered smog-controlled engines are so inefficient that they create extra ozone-damaging CO_2. Don't get me wrong: my politics are firmly on the 'green' side; it's just that I don't believe that the smog controls on the MGB are very good! Best to convert your 'B to run on unleaded fuel, keep it properly tuned and running sweet, and at least the environmental damage we all create will be minimised.

Other books on MGs published by Haynes.

Unleaded Conversion

The project car, whose engine was rebuilt by Aldon Automotive in the West Midlands, has been fitted with an engine converted to run on unleaded fuel. This has involved letting specially hardened valve seat inserts into the cylinder head – a job purely for specialists. Fore more information on the work carried out on this engine, see Chapter 6, 'Mechanical'.

Research carried out by the author some time after producing the first edition of this book, indicates that the cylinder heads produced for US MGBs at some time before 1977 were modified to run on unleaded. The actual date is unclear although the following may provide clues. It is taken from a book, also by the author, on the B-series engine, now out of print.

'The biggest problem in Federalising the B-series was in preventing the valve seats from rapidly deteriorating, since the lead which normally builds up a protective layer on the surface of the valve seat has been removed from US petrol. With the B-series engine, the problem was particularly acute, because it was not at the time

considered possible by British Leyland to machine out the valve seats and insert very hard seats as done on the Triumph TR7 engine, for example. The valves bore directly onto the surface of the casting, and the valve seats were so close together that inserts would have broken into each other. A solution was found by the complex process of adding 1% of tin to the molten iron and then, because the material in direct contact with the mould takes on an unsuitable molecular structure with tin in the iron, excess material had to be cast in place and the outer skin machined off. Then the iron could be induction hardened around the valve seats, itself a difficult operation and one that was only carried out on models bound for the US. In addition, it was found that smaller valves would have less tendency to burn out, and also allow an increase in the size of the water passages in this critical area. Because oil passing through the engine could contaminate the exhaust catalyst, BL took the opportunity to cut down on oil consumption, a problem that had niggled at all pre-1974 cars, with an improved piston and ring pack. Another long-standing problem, the head gaskets, were becoming increasingly prone to failure due to problems experienced by suppliers, who were trying to cut down on the amount of asbestos used. They were upgraded.

'The camshaft was also changed for US cars only, and the valve stems tuftrided for all cars to cut down on wear and contribute to low oil usage. Cylinder head studs were upgraded in specification, and additional water flow through the head ensured by enlarging the passages in the top face of the block. Because of a change in the oil feed hole to the rocker shaft, head gaskets were modified to fit both early and late cars, but the company pointed out that the early-type gasket should not be fitted to 1975-on cars.'

Unleaded Fuel

In the Summer of 1989, the Federation of British Historic Vehicle Clubs published the following information on the use of unleaded petrol in cars, such as most MGBs, that were not built to run on unleaded. The better specialists, such as Aldon Automotive, Moss, Brown and Gammons, M&G International and other major suppliers, will be able to supply MGB cylinder heads suitable for unleaded petrol, or to put owners in touch with those who can carry out the work on the owner's engine.

We are indebted to Dr Matthew Vincent, a research scientist with one of the major oil companies and a Vintage Alvis enthusiast, for this article on the question of using unleaded fuel in older vehicles. 'Before deciding whether to use unleaded petrol in an older vehicle, there are two main factors for the owner to consider:
(1)   Octane requirement
(2)   Exhaust valve/seat metallurgy

1.   Octane requirement
If a fuel of inadequate octane quality is used in a spark ignition engine, detonation or 'pinking' will occur. This may just represent an irritating noise at low speed, but under higher speed and load conditions, when it may be difficult to hear, it can cause piston damage.

Unleaded petrol (Eurograde Premium) is of 95-96 octane quality, as compared with leaded '2 star' which is 92-93 octane and leaded '4 star' which is 97-98 octane. Several oil companies have launched a high octane unleaded petrol which is comparable in octane quality with leaded 4 star.

As a general rule, the older the car, the lower its octane requirement is likely to be. As an example, cars made in the nineteen twenties had compression ratios of about 5:1 to cope with the prevailing petrol, the quality of which was only about 65-70 octane. Certain pre-war supercharged cars may have higher octane requirements than would have been normal at the time, but in general, cars manufactured prior to 1960 are unlikely to encounter problems from inadequate octane quality, if operated with unleaded petrol.

'Classic cars' manufactured since 1960 tend to have higher octane requirements, because vehicle manufacturers took advantage of the better fuel quality available; 100 octane petrol was widely available, for example, during the nineteen sixties. For cars of this era, the octane quality of unleaded petrol may be of greater importance, although with the availability now of higher octane unleaded petrol, this potential difficulty can be overcome.

2.   Exhaust valve/seat metallurgy
Care should be taken with any car, before using unleaded petrol, to check that the exhaust valve seats are compatible with this fuel. If an engine is operated continuously on unleaded petrol, valve seat erosion or 'sinkage' can occur. This problem is associated with valve seats of inadequate hardness, and resistance to oxidation, at very high temperatures (i.e. 750 to 850 degrees Celsius) which may be encountered in the exhaust valve region at higher engine speeds. In the absence of lead salts (which are deposited in the exhaust valve seat region when the engine is run on leaded petrol), erosion of the seat can take place. Inlet valves are

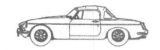

rarely affected, because they operate at much lower temperatures. Light alloy cylinder heads have valve seat inserts fitted, but these may not be hard enough at high temperatures to prevent erosion. Cast iron valve seats, which will be found in the majority of older vehicles, are particularly vulnerable to erosion, or sinkage. Where this happens, tappet clearance will be reduced, and the valves may be prevented from seating properly, resulting in burnt valves and poor performance. In serious cases of seat recession, the exhaust valves may become deeply pocketed, which can have expensive consequences.

The lasting solution to this problem is to fit the engine with exhaust valve seat inserts which are compatible with unleaded petrol, although in some vehicles this may be expensive or difficult to achieve. However, where this modification can be carried out, it will be an effective remedy allowing long term use of unleaded petrol, with no problems from valve seat erosion. There are at least two manufacturers of valve seat inserts in the UK (Brico Engineering of Coventry and TRW of Wednesbury) who can supply suitable valve seat inserts compatible with unleaded petrol. Brico material specifications would be XW 35 for use with 'stellited' valves, or XW 13 for use with plain valves. TRW can, apparently, also supply 'stellited' exhaust valves which are noted for hardness and corrosion resistance. A competent engine machining specialist must be entrusted with the work of fitting valve seat inserts, which is a skilled job.

General points
1. Now that leaded 2 star (94 octane) has been withdrawn from the market, owners of older cars are frequently

concerned about the use of 4 star (98 octane) as an alternative. There is no evidence that use of 4 star will cause any long term problems in engines which normally operate satisfactorily on 2 star. Both types of petrol contain the same amount of lead. The use of 4 star as an alternative to 2 star is greatly preferable to the use of unleaded petrol in an unsuitable engine.
2. Upper cylinder lubricants, of which there are a few proprietary brands available, will have no protective effect upon exhaust valve seats when used with unleaded petrol, and their use cannot be regarded as a substitute for lead in petrol.
3. Proprietary fuel additives, which are claimed to protect exhaust valve seats and thus prevent damage which might otherwise occur with unleaded petrol, are only partially effective. Whilst exhaust valve seat wear rates may be reduced, these additives are unlikely to be completely effective. Manufacturers' claims should therefore be treated with caution, as some valve seat recession may still be experienced when operating with unleaded petrol in an unsuitable engine.'
Author's note: I do not know of a useful petrol additive.

ET1. The leading example of what can be achieved by an MGB in racing trim is 286 FAC, owned and raced by Bill Nicholson who has raced the car for a quarter of a century, clocking up over 250 Class and Overall wins and getting through eight new and highly tuned engines. ⬆

Engine Tuning

Safety

Before carrying out engine tuning, ensure that your MGB's brakes, steering and suspension are adequate for the proposed performance. Take advice from a specialist such as Moss, Aldon or John Hewitt.

The B-series engine is not, by its nature, a high performance engine at all. It is heavy, it has a long stroke, and the 'Siamesed' ports, in particular, place limitations upon it. But it is surprising how much can be done at little cost, especially in the early stages.

The first step to take is perhaps cheapest of all. Before fitting any tuning 'goodies', put your car through a simple

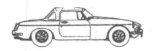

acceleration test. On a really quiet, safe and level stretch of road, take some accurate acceleration figures with a stop-watch and compare your figures with the standard performance figures which I have shown for guidance only (every car has its own individual differences) in the table below.

Then 'tune' the engine meticulously, setting the ignition and carburettor(s) as shown in the workshop manual. (Don't forget to change the condenser, distributor cap and plug leads too, if they look at all ratty). Take your acceleration figures again - you could be pleasantly surprised.

Standard Performance Figures

Speed (mph)		Time in Seconds		
	1960s Rdster	1960s GT	1970s Rdster	1970s GT
30-50 in top	9-9.5	9.5-10	9-9.5	9-9.5
40-60 in to	9-9.5	10-10.5	9-9.5	9-9.5
0 to 50	8.5-9	8.5-9	8-8.5	8-8.5
0 to 60	12-12.5	13-13.5	11-11.5	11.5-12
MPG	28-30	28-30	24-26	24-26

Having set your engine up to a reasonable degree of efficiency in standard form, you can then select from any one of the following 'mild' engine modifications. They have all been tried and tested by John Hewitt, leading MGB racing driver, ex-Formula One mechanic and former owner of The MG Shop in Manchester, and thus one of the very best equipped people in the country to advise on MGB tuning, although his tuning parts company is now run by Moss Special Tuning at Barry Stafford MG Parts in Stockport, Cheshire.

Stage 1

The first step, as suggested by John Hewitt, is to throw away the Cooper's type of air filter and fit a K & N high-flow type of air filter. Any air filter tends to reduce the efficiency of the engine by reducing the amount of air that can readily be drawn through it. However, to run an engine without an air filter at all can reduce its life by a frightening amount, which is OK for short-lived racing engines, but too expensive to contemplate where the engine is to be put to everyday use. Fitting pancake air filters is a retrograde step, according to John, because they can actually lose you around 3bhp from an MGB engine! K & N filters on the other hand give an increase in maximum bhp of 4 to 5bhp,

they only require cleaning - not changing - every 100,000 miles, and they still provide a source of all-important clean air to the engine. The increase in bhp at the rear wheels (and remember that the MGB only develops 60-odd bhp at the wheels: the 95bhp factory figure is given at the flywheel) is a very noticeable difference and is in the same sort of order as fitting a 45 DCOE Weber Carburettor to an otherwise standard engine, but at a fraction of the cost and time involved in setting up.

Having got the air in to the engine more easily, it makes sense to get it out again more

easily as well. John Hewitt recommends fitting an exhaust system without a centre box, or cheaper still, trip down to your friendly local exhaust centre and ask them to substitute a piece of plain pipe for the centre of your existing system if it is basically sound. Now that the air is flowing more freely through the engine, you may gain power by fitting richer needles to the carburettors. Standard MGB needles are No. 5, while No. 6 needles are the next richest. On the other hand, as John points out, earlier MGBs are often on the rich side to start off with, so you need to check the system over very carefully with a Gunson Colourtune or with a CO_2 exhaust gas analyser to find out whether you ought to go to richer needles or not. (Later cars with HIF carburettors often have a 'lean' setting and may well benefit from a richer needle.) In fact, you must set the engine up carefully after fitting these simple modifications because the extra ease with which the air can pass through your engine will have altered the fuel-air ratio on the carburettor settings that you were using before. As a rule-of-thumb, John Hewitt points out that the HS4 and earlier type of carburettor, with hexagonal nut adjustment on the jet would probably need to be richened (screwed anti-clockwise) by one or two flats of the adjuster nut. (Later HIF4 carburettors are adjusted with a screwdriver.) Incidentally, at this stage - or even before it! - copper-cored spark plugs can be recommended. Many racing drivers swear by NGK plugs No. BP6ES for MGBs, or rather expensive platinum-tipped plugs No. BP6EV.

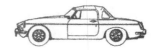

Stage 2

This is the stage where you are not just concerned with making what you have got work better, but you are actually changing one or two simple bolt-on components. The John Hewitt approach is to fit a side-draught Weber or Dellorto carburettor (and appropriate inlet manifold) both of which work on a twin-choke basis. Once again, the improvement in 'input' needs to be matched by 'output', and the best way is to fit a Janspeed 'extractor' exhaust manifold with long centre branch. This is a particularly useful piece of tuning equipment in view of the B-series' 'Siamesed' exhaust ports in the head, because the extra long centre helps to get the extra gases away more quickly. As with Stage 1, a one-box exhaust system is recommended as a way of reducing back-pressure to the engine.

An alternative to the use of a Dellorto is to fit a pair of 1 3/4 inch SU carburettors with KP needles, Blue spring and 0.100 inch jets. This was the traditional way of uprating the B-series engine, and the Burlen Fuel Systems equipment has been put back into production in original spec. They give a more economical alternative to the Dellorto, but they certainly do not give as big an improvement in power, nor do they give the extra throttle 'snap' that a Dellorto set-up will give you.

Stage 3

You can now no longer get away with bolting off-bolting on some external bits, but instead you need to start getting more deeply into the engine. And what's more, the changes made from now on will give extra performance but at the expense of low-range tractability. The Newman 271 camshaft is recommended by John Hewitt as 'a reasonable road cam' (camshafts designed purely with high speed power in mind make an engine highly inflexible and very difficult and frustrating to drive in town traffic), and John also recommends fitting a 'competition'-type distributor at this stage to make the most from the extra power given by the Dellorto, plus Newman camshaft. The competition distributor gives more advance at speeds over 2,200rpm, but less at lower speeds. Incidentally, some competition distributors have a vacuum advance unit and others do not. If you fit one without a vacuum advance, remember to blank off the inlet on the manifold so that no unwanted air is drawn in.

Some people may be surprised that the B-series cylinder head has not yet been the subject of attention. After all, when tuning Minis, the cylinder head is one of the first areas to be modified or replaced. The truth is that the later B-series head is pretty efficient to start off with, so you can gain most by making changes in the areas already mentioned. For owners of early 'Bs, head swaps are the next thing to go for, however. The best heads with the biggest inlet valves are those fitted to engines whose engine number begins with 18V, and the Austin and Morris 1800S engines (although the latter has a slightly lower compression ratio than the MGB). 18V engines partly did away with the Weslake promontory between the valves, and owners of pre-18V engines can use the drawing shown as a guide to cutting a little of it away using a small grinding wheel held in the chuck of an electric drill. The same tool will have to be used to grind a recess in the top of the block when an 18V or 1800S head is fitted to a non-18V block, because otherwise the larger inlet valves will foul the block. When fitting a replacement or re-shaped cylinder head, it would make sense to have the head face skimmed to ensure that it remains true. 0.025 inch can be taken off an MGB cylinder head to give a slight increase in compression ratio, and John Hewitt says that up to 0.050 inch could be taken off, but that would be taking the compression ratio up to the limit imposed by leaded petrol.

Incidentally, post-1975 18V cylinder heads were built with extra 'meat' so that the air injectors used in the US market could be fitted. Of course, the injectors were not fitted in the UK, but the extra metal remains and makes the heads less prone to lifting in the centre, which is a common cause of a blown head gasket on the MGB.

Appetisers

If the tuning bug really gets to you, there is an almost endless range of things you could try doing to your engine. (At the ultimate, what about trying the modification suggested by B-series engine designer Eric Bareham himself back in the 'fifties when he put forward a method of breaking the exhaust port into two halves!) But there is usually one limiting factor, quite apart from the limitations of the weight of the engine and the inefficiencies of its breathing apparatus; and that is cost. The law of diminishing returns works particularly viciously when it comes to

tuning - so much so that you can pay a fortune and end up in a purely speculative, experimental area - with worse performance than you had before if the experiment you try does not work out.

Some modifications which are sure to work out would include lightening and balancing the engine internals, boring the engine out to give a higher capacity (around 1950cc from a 1978), re-working and gas flowing the head, fitting a pair of Dellorto 48s, just using one choke of each and then going on to fit a stronger steel crankshaft to cope with extra power. If you're something of a beginner but you have the money to spend on super-tuning or even going to turbo charging, you will need the specific advice of someone like Brown and Gammons, famous for their MGB racing exploits, or Moss Special Tuning, each of whom can supply all the right tuning bits and tuning advice as well as carrying out the work for you right through from mild to wild.

Building a 2-litre 'B

Chapter 6, 'Mechanical', gives a whole lot more practical information on how Aldon Automotive go about building their 2- litre MGB engines, with additional information on cylinder heads and the suspension and brake modifications that are an integral part of conversions of this sort. In a 1991 issue of Moss Motoring, Moss Special Tuning's Sales Manager, Rick Hockney, wrote the following words of wisdom:

'Please don't forget that handling and brakes need attention before any large increase in power can safely be applied. If you do not feel competent to carry out some of the following, then there are a few specialist companies around who will be able to do the work for you, at a price!

'I have found the key to performance on the B-series engine is the bore of the block. As the humble B-series increased in capacity from 1500 to 1622 and finally 1798, the power increase was out of all proportion to the changes in cc. The secret was unshrouding of the valves in the cylinder head, this enabling the efficiency to increase and thus the power. Carrying this one stage further, the block can be taken out to 1950cc, a mere 150cc but this modification alone gives 15bhp at the wheels at any stage of the tune. The already torquey engine delivers more torque, making this the most popular of all B- series engine modifications. I realise that 1995cc and 2010cc engines have been successfully built by many people, but the 1950cc engine has proved to be relatively cheap to build and very reliable.

'How do I get 1950cc? I can hear you asking - well it's fairly straightforward, but the boring and the decking of the block require great technical skills and this is best left to a specialist. For technical reasons the early MGB three bearing engine is very difficult to build as 1950cc, and the weaker blocks 18B to 18GG should be avoided. It is best to use the 18V, 1972 onwards, block. The bores are carefully machined to suit Lotus 1600 powermax pistons in +0.040 format. At this stage, it is wise to Hydro Test the block to check for porous bores. The Lotus pistons are shorter, gudgeon pin to deck, than the MGB, so the freshly bored and tested block must have material removed from the "deck" to restore the compression ratio. As a rough guide, .009in. (90 'thou') will have to be removed,

but the precise amount will vary from engine to engine. The 18V type con rods have a press-fit gudgeon pin bore line honed to avoid the pin "picking up" in the piston. The earlier type of con rod with a bushed little end will be OK, but watch out for the ones with angular split big ends, as these are notoriously weak in tuned applications. It must not be forgotten that the later blocks have small cutouts at the top of the bores which allow clearance for the larger exhaust valve. When the block is decked these cutouts must be restored, which leaves room for another useful modification. The pocket size can be increased down the bore to 1mm above the top piston ring and across to the head gasket, giving an increase of around 5bhp by allowing the exhaust gases an easier way out.

'I will not go into engine build techniques in this article, but a properly prepared, balanced bottom end is essential if reliability is to be retained at higher engine power outputs.

'The choice of camshafts enters a new dimension with the big bore engine. The higher torque output enables you to select a camshaft one stage hotter than for a normal 1798cc engine. For a 1950cc, but otherwise standard, engine on SU carbs, I would use a Kent 715 cam which gives a very smooth power delivery and peaks at just over 5000rpm. For a more modified engine, but still on SU carbs, I would opt for the Kent 717 which will deliver power to approx 6000rpm. When using a side draught carb either a 717 or 718 cam will remain road usable on a modified 1950 engine, whilst for competition use, a 719 cam allows up to 7500rpm to be used, but will be a bit lumpy at slow speed.

'It is obvious from the above that the whole engine package must be planned in

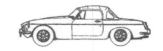

advance, and the appropriate parts selected even if they are not all installed at once. The blend of carb-cam-head is critical to the success of the exercise, but the budget available may influence the final choice.

'The cylinder head has a strong effect on the performance of the 1950 cc engine, and a modified head should be high on your list of priorities. The extra breathing ability of a Stage II head can enhance the tractability, though personally I prefer the stage IV head which improves the mid-range as well as giving a huge dollop of top-end power without loss of bottom-end tractability. Suitable valve springs will be required, and lightened valve gear should be used along with tuftrided rocker shaft, solid spacers and steel end-posts.

'The flywheel will benefit from lightening before balancing is carried out, and a heavy duty clutch is essential to cope with the increased torque. The 1950 engine will require a modified distributor to obtain optimum results, and a suitable unit, available on exchange, will enhance the performance - remember SU carbs need a vac unit type dizzy, side-draught carbs do not.

'So, after all this work what should you expect in terms of power output? A rough idea of bhp at the wheels is as follows:

Std SU's, mild cam, standard head:	75bhp
Std SU's, mild cam, Stage III head:	85bhp
45DCOE, fast road cam, Stage IV head:	105bhp
45DCOE, sprint cam, Stage IV head:	115bhp
48DCOE, race cam, Stage IV head:	125bhp

The last two are really not suitable for town use but can be great fun on the open road. Remember, most MGBs get by with only 55bhp at the wheels.

'Drive safely!'

V8 Engine Conversion - Overview

As you may imagine, fitting a V8 engine into the somewhat crowded confines of the MGB engine compartment can be a very complicated task, although made feasible by the conversion components produced by the V8 Conversion Company. This applies especially to earlier models. That being the case, we have prepared this section as an overview rather than a blow-by-blow account. More work is required than could be described in detail here.

The 135bhp Range Rover engine was fitted by BL, while the earlier Costello versions used the higher output Rover saloon (sedan) units. Both were mated to a standard MGB gearbox and this proved to be the cars' Achilles heel. A far more attractive proposition would be an MGB with a Rover SD1 engine (which has an even higher output but with better fuel economy) and an SD1 5-speed manual-shift gearbox.

The V8 Conversion Company market the parts to enable enthusiasts to fit V8 engines to their MGBs. They make the following points: 'The problems incurred with this conversion vary according to the particular model, but basically the earlier the model the more difficult the conversion. Brief details of some of the problems are as follows:
1)   Mating of the Rover engine to the MGB gearbox by means of a special adaptor plate and crank adaptor (thus utilising the MGB flywheel and starter motor).
2)   Specially fabricating tubular steel exhaust manifold and join pipes.
3)   Body-engine mountings specially made.
4)   Purpose-built engine mountings for the sides of the cylinder block.
5)   Modified steering shaft to clear exhaust and engine mounting.
6)   Bulkhead cut away to clear V8 heads.
7)   Transmission tunnel modifications.
8)   Flitch plates modified to clear exhaust.
9)   Radiator mountings moved forward.
10)   Electric cooling fans required.
11)   Brake pipes rerouted.
12)   Remote oil filtering required.
13)   Changing rear axle ratio.
14)   Recalibrate instruments.
15)   Modify clutch hydraulics.'
To expand on a point raised by The V8 Conversion Company, later cars already have many of the necessary modifications carried out at the factory. Post-1975 cars are already satisfactory in respect of details 3, 5, 6, 9 (and 10, in the USA). The standard gearbox, as fitted to the factory prepared V8s, is not really up to handling the extra power. First gear often stripped its cogs, and the overdrive had to be blanked off from third gear. The Rover five-speed box is far better, and when undertaking a conversion, this is always recommended.

In this section, we show some of the parts fitted by the V8 Conversion Company and some of the optional extras available. You'll also need a V8 or MGC differential to prevent the poor engine from using far too many revs for any given road speed. Don't forget the insurance angle when doubling the number of MGB cylinders.

Many companies will not handle any cars which are non-standard in any way, and most will demand an engineer's report that it is safe. The V8 Conversion Company have no qualms about the safety of their cars, although they cannot help you with the final point ... paying the increased premium! Incidentally, the Heritage bodyshell is capable of being fitted with the V8 engine - which is not surprising in view of the fact that it is the basis for Rover's own 'new-for-'92' MGB V8.

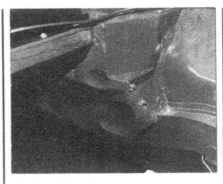

VC3. This picture shows the modifications necessary to the nearside bulkhead of a chrome bumper MGB. Those cars, pre-1975, are the most difficult to convert. After 1975, the same 'V8' bodyshell was used.

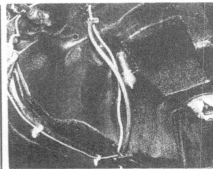

VC4. The gearbox tunnel must be modified to accept the five speed gearbox. This goes to show just how much bodywork, as well as mechanical work, is required, especially on these earlier cars.

VC1. The standard V8 engine in situ. Note the enormous air filters with chambers on their ends, containing temperature sensitive bi-metal strips. These enable the engine to draw heated air from the exhaust manifolds when the engine is cold and cooler air from the engine bay when the engine is warm.

VC2. A nice, pristine engine in the process of being fitted into a late model 'B by the V8 Conversion Company. The radiator mountings, which are well forward compared to earlier models, denote that this is a later '75-on car and thus one of the (relatively!) simpler cars to convert.

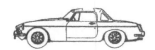

VC5. This is the Offenhauser dual port inlet manifold offered by the V8 Conversion Company.

VC6. Better gas flow is achieved by using tubular exhaust manifolds rather than cast. The shape is very important because of the lack of space for routing. The V8 C.C. supply all of the necessary fittings and gaskets to suit. (Cast manifolds are far harder to obtain, as well as being very restrictive to the engine's efficiency.) All models of MGB, even later ones, require some dressing of the inner wing/flitch panels in order to fit tubular manifolds. ➡

VC7. If you should want to use your original (or rebuilt), four-synchro MGB 'box, then you'll need this gearbox adaptor plate, also available from the V8 Conversion Company. ➡

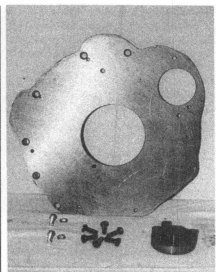

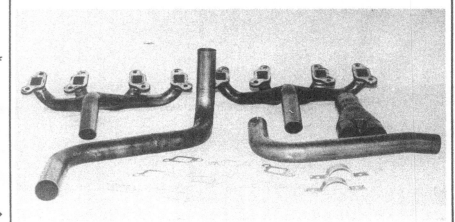

VC8. Cooling the big, eight-cylinder motor is obviously of paramount importance, using these components. Note the twin fans.

VC9. *If you do fit the five-speed SD1 gearbox, you will need another propshaft, crossmember mounts and speedo cable. The V8 Conversion Company can supply their own specially produced propshafts to suit the MGB.* ➡

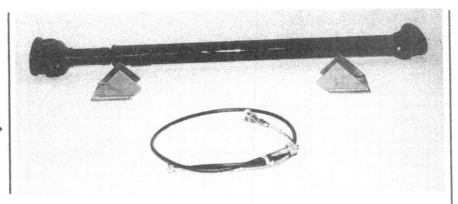

VC10. *More power always requires uprated brakes. The V8 Conversion Company always fit these thicker discs, together with uprated callipers to suit. High performance pads are used.* ⬅

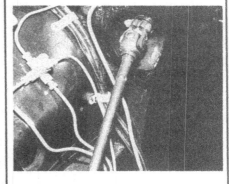

VC11. *The offside bulkhead has to be modified, along with the steering on this chrome bumper model.*

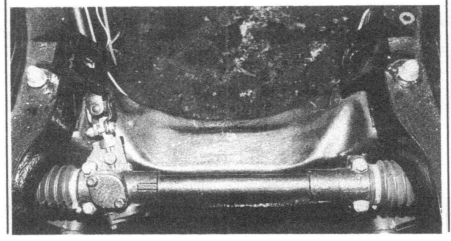

VC12. *Looking further down the same car, showing more of the modified steering system and the revised engine mountings.*

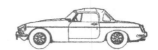

VC13. If you don't want twin carbs (and associated pipework etc), then you can have this single Holley carb instead. ➡

VC14. Made to make your mouth water! An absolutely beautiful, Holley carb-equipped MGB V8 Roadster. Never actually made by British Leyland in the 70s, the V8 Conversion Company have rectified that serious omission by producing the parts for the car you see here. Note that, like the factory cars, the engine fits under the bonnet without the need for a bulge; this is something that not all conversions can boast. ⬇

Warning!

The suspension, wheels, tyres and brakes of the standard MGB are inadequate for the power transmitted by a V8 engine.

Before converting an MGB to V8 engine spec, consult a qualified specialist such as the V8 Conversion Company or Moss specialist tuning to ensure that your car will be capable of safe use.

'De-Toxing' US Cars

Photographs and text by John H. Twist of University Motors in the USA.

North American MGBs were fitted with progressively more strangulatory exhaust emission control regulations which, though initiated for the most commendable of motives, did nothing for the sporting character of the MGB. The North American owner who wishes to 'de-tox' his or her car may gain the following advantages (although nothing can be guaranteed): mileage may be better; acceleration can improve; deceleration too, should be sharper (there will be generally more positive throttle response); there'll be no more 'popping' or red hot converters; the engine looks 'cleaner'; the front spark plug will no longer be hidden from view.

NOTE: De-toxing in some states may be illegal. Responsibility for compliance with the law must rest with the individual owner.

Procedures DT2 to DT14 are for the 1975-80 MGBs.

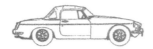

Toolbox

5/16 inch combination spanner;
3/8 inch drive ratchet; 3/8 x 6
inch extension; Allen wrench for
pipe plug; 1/2 inch socket; 5/8
inch deep socket (for injector
bolts); 1/2 inch open-end
wrench; 7/16 inch open-end
wrench; 1/4 NPT tap and tap
wrench; four 7/16 inch bolts;
one 1/4 inch (Allen driven) NPT
pipe plug.

Safety

**Remember when working on or
around fuel systems that
gasoline is volatile and highly
flammable. DON'T SMOKE!**

Before starting, the bonnet
(hood) must be removed or
held aloft with a stick as the
factory slide is too short, and
both fenders should be covered
with large cloths or old
blankets.

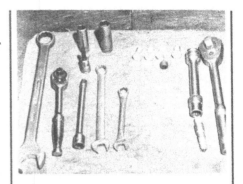

DT1. 'Toolbox' illustrated.

DT2. Remove the two hoses to
the air pump. Remove the long
bolt (1/2 inch wrench) holding
the air pump to the thermostat
cover and remove the bolt from
the adjusting strap (1/2 inch). ⬅

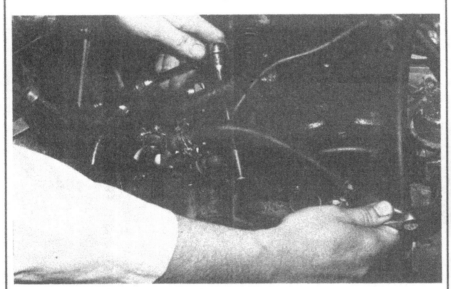

DT3. Remove the pump and the
fan belt.

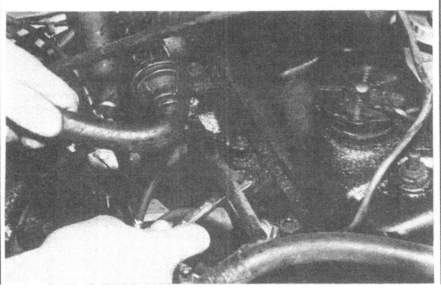

DT4. Remove the four air
injectors with a 7/16 inch
wrench. If the injectors will not
unscrew, cut the tubing at the
injector and use a 7/16 inch
socket. Remove the bolt holding
the injector to the rear right
head nut.

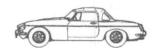

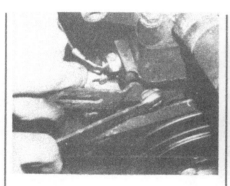

DT5. Remove the air pump adjuster bracket. If this is left in place, and if it should loosen, it could foul the alternator fan. Use a 1/2 inch wrench.

DT7. Hold the tall nut at the thermostat cover with a 1/2 inch wrench to keep it from spinning, and remove the bolt at the top.

DT9. Lift the gulp valve 90° fitting and hoses away. It may be necessary to twist the 90° fitting to facilitate removal.

DT6. Replace the air injectors with 7/16 inch fine bolts or Allen screws, and tighten snugly.

DT8. Remove the thin black vacuum line from the manifold to the TCSA switch on the master cylinder box. Remove the two bolts holding the gulp valve to its bracket (7/16 inch wrench and socket). ➡

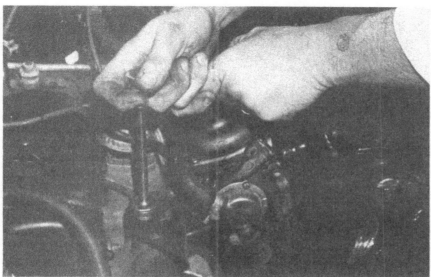

DT10. Remove the bolt holding the gulp valve bracket (15/16 inch socket) and discard the bracket and the thinnest of the two copper washers. Then replace the bolt and one washer snugly.

DT11. Tap the hole from the 90° fitting 1/4 NPT. There will be metal shavings and it's best to grease the tap before cutting the threads so that the chafings will remain on the tap; or, better still, remove the manifold first.

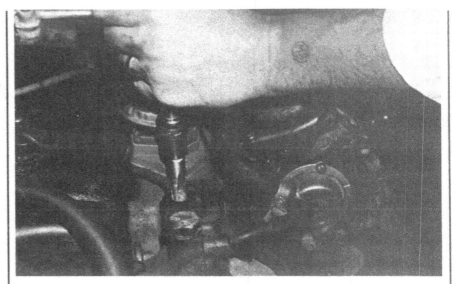

DT12. Fit a 1/4 NPT plug or Allen screw to the hole. To stop possible vacuum leaks, wrap the threads with teflon tape, or use jointing compound.

DT13. Move the vacuum advance line from the TCSA switch directly to the inlet manifold. MGBs fitted with the TCSA switch allow the distributor vacuum advance to work only in fourth gear.

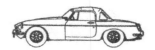

DT14. The later US emission control system.

1. Air pump
2. Air pump air cleaner
3. Check valve
4. Air manifold
5. Gulp valve
6. Sensing valve
7. Oil separator/flame trap
8. Breather pipe
9. Restricter pipe
10. Purge line
11. Air vent pipe
12. Oil fillercap (sealed)
13. Adsorption canister
14. Vapour lines
15. Running-on control valve
16. Running-on control hose
17. Running-on control pipe
18. Fuel line filter
19. Exhaust gas recirculation valve (EGR)
20. EGR valve hose
21. Air temperature control valve
22. Air cleaning case
23. Wing nut retaining air cleaner cover ➡

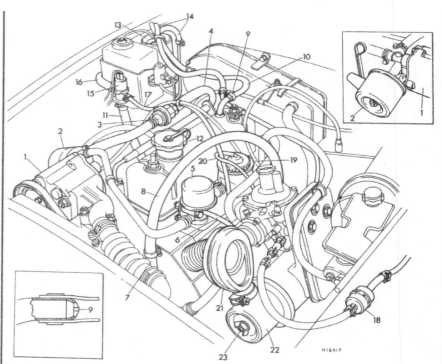

John carries on: 'Further steps, which we don't do, could include removing the EGR line from the EGR valve (top of the manifold) and plugging it. The catalytic converter could be removed but that's best left for an exhaust job in the future. A 1975 (non- Californian) front pipe will eliminate the converter, although the manifold must be removed from the engine to remove the converter from the manifold. The carb can be removed and the spring-loaded valve in the butterfly soldered shut. This allows even faster decelerations.' Steps are as follows:

1. The manifold with the gulp valve and piping are removed.
2. Replace the vacuum fitting with a 5/16 x 1/2 inch bolt (fine) which can be found holding the air manifold to the head, or the air hose clamp to the thermostat cover nut.
3. Tap the centre hole 1/4 NPT. Remove the manifold so as to keep shavings or swarf out of the engine.
4. Use a 15/16 inch wrench to remove the nut from the gulp valve bracket. Replace the nut and the largest copper washer.

5. DO NOT remove or block the hoses to the carbs from the front tappet inspection cover.
6. The detox on the 1968 MGB is the same as for '69-74, except that the 90° fitting in the centre of the intake manifold cannot be blocked, as a Smith's PCV valve is fitted there. Two options: leave a piece of hose on the T-fitting and block the hose with a bolt and hose clamp or, tap the manifold as suggested and instead of blocking it with a pipe plug, fit a 1/4 NPT nipple, about 1 1/2 inch long and reconnect the PCV valve.

Converting to Negative Earth by John H. Twist of University Motors in the USA

Safety

Disconnect the battery/ies before working on any part of the electrical system.

Prior to 1968, virtually all British cars had a positive earth (ground) electrical system. This was the standard in Britain, but the rest of the world was on a negative earth system. Whether due to marketplace pressure, international co-operation, or US Federal law, the British cars 'commonized' their systems with everyone else in 1968.

For the purist, positive earth is a must; but for those wishing to update their sports cars, negative earth is very helpful. Surprisingly, few of the electrical components are sensitive to polarity. Motors sometimes run in reverse (not the starter, but sometimes the heater motor or wiper motor), and the generator and coil need attention to work correctly.

There are stories that positive earth cars corrode more quickly than negative earth cars, which might be correct. But it is more probable that the electrolysis of steel to aluminium in certain cars, such as Healeys, for instance, gave birth to this idea.

Negative earth is now

standard. It is expected. All modern electrical equipment is negative earth.

Suppose that the lights are left on and the battery goes dead. A helpful motorist jump-starts your car for you. The dead short between the two batteries will result in a spark, and there are several chances in a million that the battery will blow up.

If a tow truck with giant batteries jumps your positive earth car backwards, it could ruin your battery, or ruin the voltage regulator.

If you want to install a modern radio or cassette player, it's about impossible to find one set up for positive earth! Therefore, it either has to be isolated for installation, which is a cumbersome task, or it must be powered with a voltage inverter. The inverter is a fascinating unit. It uses the 12-volt positive earth system to create 24-volts positive. The radio or cassette is then powered with 24-volts positive and 'grounded' with 12-volts positive. The net effect makes the 12- volt positive frame 'negative' and the 24-volt positive lead only 12-volts. It's not only confusing, but it's quite expensive, too! In this case, it's far better to change to negative earth.

Procedure

If the car is fitted with a positive earth alternator, go no further, unless you have access to a negative earth alternator which will fit your car!

1)   Reverse the battery(ies). It is usually best to remove the battery from its holder, turn it 180 degrees and reconnect it. Problems will be encountered with the original helmet-style Lucas clamps, as the battery posts are sized (the larger one is the positive post). It is wise to replace the battery terminals on an annual basis anyway. The helmet-style clamps can be melted off the power cables to preserve the length of the cable.

2)   Polarise the Generator. Remove the lighter gauge wire (usually brown w/green, or yellow w/green on early models) from the 'F' (field) terminal on the back of the generator. Now, with a length of wire, flash between the 'F' terminal and a hot (or 'live') lead. The hot lead can be the positive post of the battery, the hot lead on a fusebox, or an 'A' or 'B' terminal at the regulator. Flash just long enough to see a spark. DO NOT LEAVE THIS CONNECTED, even for several seconds! Just flash it a couple of times. Reconnect the proper wire to the back of the generator.

Now start up the car and ensure that the ignition light is working correctly. It must act just as before (light on until about 1000rpm when it quickly dims to naught). Flickering is an indication that the voltage regulator is faulty. If the ignition light should remain on when the car is turned off, IMMEDIATELY remove a battery clamp or the larger wire from the back of the generator ('D' - dynamo). If the condition is ignored, both the wiring harness and the generator will burn up.

The voltage regulator has a certain longevity, and sometimes, if the unit is about ready to fail, the switch in polarity will push it over the edge.

3)   Reverse the coil connections. If the coil is original, then it will be marked CB (contact breakers) and SW (switch). The SW should now be connected to the distributor. In the case of the modern coil, the - (negative) terminal should be connected to the distributor. This allows the spark to jump from the centre electrode to the 'L' on the spark plug.

4)   Test the heater motor. Find the leads on the heater motor, turn the heater motor on and judge the amount of air coming from the heater vents. Then, reverse the heater motor connections and again judge the air flow. Leave the wiring in whichever configuration moves the greatest amount of air.

5)   Test the wiper motor. Ensure that the wiper motor is working properly. Since most wiper systems are gear driven from the motor, it doesn't make much difference which way the motor runs - although the thrust of the armature should be away from the commutator end.

6)   Ammeter/ Voltmeter connections: If the car is fitted with an ammeter or voltmeter, the connections must be reversed.

7)   Fuel Pump: Most of the fuel pumps (SU, Harting, AC) are insensitive to the polarity, but recent SU pumps, as well as some aftermarket units, are voltage sensitive. If you encounter a recent SU pump or transistorised unit, it would probably be best not to change the polarity of the car until another pump is found to work with negative earth.

8)   Clock: Some clocks are sensitive to polarity, some are not. Until you attempt the conversion, you probably won't know!

9)   Tachometer: If the car is fitted with a mechanical rev counter, then obviously this section will not apply. The RVI tach is labelled on its face whether it is positive or negative earth. It is driven by a pulse from the hot side of the coil. Modern tachometers are driven by the pulse from the distributor side of the coil, and are much improved over the older RVI units. Two changes are necessary to make the tach work: a) the wires must be reversed at the 'white wire loop' at the back of the unit; and b) the power and earth

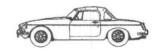

connections must be reversed on the inside of the unit. Disconnect the battery/ies.

a)　The wire in the 'white wire loop' comes from the key switch and travels to the hot (or 'live') side of the coil. Select one of the wires and tag it with two pieces of tape for identification. Then cut the wire between the pieces of tape, and cut the other wire to the same length. Reverse the connections (now there is one piece of tape on each wire), and solder them (remember - this is the power lead for the coil and is unfused). Tape up the connections carefully. When later replacing the plastic block on the back of the tach, ensure that the metal band around the block is carefully positioned. This is a necessary half of the electromagnetic pick-up.

b)　To reverse the power wire and earth wire on the inside of the unit, it is necessary to remove the chrome ring, the glass face, and the glare shroud. The chrome ring is usually removed with great difficulty by prying it with a small screwdriver at the tabs. Then, remove the two screws on the back of the unit that hold the internals to the case, and allow those internals to drop carefully into your hand. DON'T BEND THE NEEDLE! The spade terminal which carried the green or white wire is the power lead. Just next to this is the earth connection. One of the two leads is the resistor. Unsolder the wires and resistor from their positions and reverse them, resoldering the connections. Reassemble the unit after cleaning the glass.

Conclusion

Negative earth is handy for a number of reasons, and converting your pre '68 British sports car is simple. It eliminates the need for isolation of radio units, or for voltage inverters. Most cars can be changed over in about an hour.

Safety Footnote

If any separately fused accessories have previously been fitted, ensure that they are still fused on the correct 'hot' or 'live' power supply side.

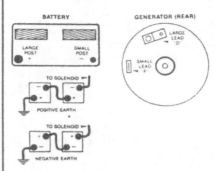

NE1. *Schematic view of the battery and generator connection referred to in the text.*

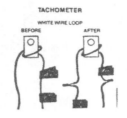

NE2. *Reconnecting the tachometer as described in the text.*

Fitting Contactless Electronic Ignition

Safety

Disconnect the battery/ies before carrying out work on the electrical system.

Fitting a Newtronic Contactless electronic ignition system is a fairly simple means of improving the efficiency of your MGB. The system uses an optical trigger to energise the coil. A slotted disc fitted over the distributor cam revolves between an infra- red light emitting diode and a photo transistor. This is turn, triggers the electronic circuitry to switch off the coil and produce a spark. At high speeds, it allows up to three times longer for the coil to charge than is available with standard points system. This means that there is always a powerful spark, even at high speeds. Obviously, as there are no contacting moving parts, wear and tear are eliminated and thus the timing stays accurate almost indefinitely. By burning the fuel more effectively than any contact breaker points system, the benefits are; reduced fuel consumption, increased power, improved starting, better reliability, less exhaust pollution and smoother running.

CE1. This is the contactless kit needed for a standard 1800cc MGB.

CE2. The old contact breaker points have to be removed in order to fit the contactless ignition. With the points taken out, the base plate can be removed by undoing these two crosshead screws.

CE3. Place the optical trigger in position, using the same crosshead screws. On top of the trigger is the scanning disc, seen here already fitted to the distributor shaft.

CE4. This diagram shows the simplicity of the contactless ignition system. Note that the standard rotor arm is retained. (Diagram courtesy of Newtronic Systems Ltd.) ➡

CE5. Beneath the new base plate, the vacuum advance return spring must be connected.

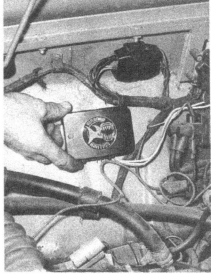

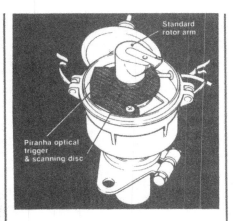

CE6. The kit for the V8-engined MGB is outwardly very similar, but is specific to that particular model.

CE7. The all important 'black box' containing the electronic magic which makes the ignition work, has to be mounted in the engine compartment. It must be mounted away from extreme sources of heat, dirt and moisture. Once installed, the system will require no maintenance. ⬅

Appendix 1: **Workshop Procedures and Safety First**

Professional motor mechanics are trained in safe working procedures, whereas the onus is on you, the home mechanic, to find them out for yourself and act upon them. However enthusiastic you may be about getting on with the job in hand, do take the time to ensure that your safety is not put at risk. A moment's lack of attention can result in an accident, as can failure to observe certain elementary precautions.

There will always be new ways of having accidents, and the following points do not pretend to be a comprehensive list of all dangers; they are intended rather to make you aware of the risks and to encourage a safety-conscious approach to all work you carry out on your vehicle.

Be sure to consult the suppliers of any materials and equipment you may use, and to obtain and read carefully operating and health and safety instructions that they may supply.

Essential DOs and DON'Ts

DON'T rely on a single jack when working underneath the vehicle. Always use reliable additional means of support, such as axle stands, securely placed under a part of the vehicle that you know will not give way. Always leave two wheels on the ground and securely chock them in both directions so that movement is impossible.

DON'T attempt to loosen or tighten high-torque nuts (e.g. wheel hub nuts) while the vehicle is on a jack; it may be pulled off.

DON'T start the engine without first ascertaining that the transmission is in neutral (or 'Park' where applicable) and the parking brake applied.

DON'T attempt to drain oil until you are sure it has cooled sufficiently to avoid scalding you.

DON'T grasp any part of the engine, exhaust or catalytic converter without first ascertaining that it is sufficiently cool to avoid burning you.

DON'T inhale brake lining dust - it is injurious to health.

DON'T allow any spilt oil or grease to remain on the floor - wipe it up straight away, before someone slips on it.

DON'T use ill-fitting spanners or other tools which may slip and cause injury.

DON'T attempt to lift a heavy component which may be beyond your capability - get assistance.

DON'T rush to finish a job, or take unverified short cuts.

DON'T allow children or animals in or around an unattended vehicle.

DO wear eye protection when using power tools such as drill, sander, bench grinder etc., and when working under the vehicle.

DO use a barrier cream on your hands prior to undertaking dirty jobs - it will protect your skin from infection as well as making the dirt easier to remove afterwards; but make sure your hands aren't left slippery.

DO keep loose clothing (cuffs, tie etc.) and long hair well out of the way of moving mechanical parts.

DO remove rings, wrist watch etc., before working on the vehicle - especially the electrical system.

DO ensure that any lifting tackle used has a safe working load rating adequate for the job.

DO keep your work area tidy - it is only too easy to fall over articles left lying around.

DO get someone to check periodically that all is well, when working alone on the vehicle.

DO carry out work in a logical sequence and check that everything is correctly assembled and tightened afterwards.

DO remember that your vehicle's safety affects that of yourself and others. If in doubt on any point, get specialist advice. IF, in spite of following these precautions, you are

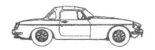

unfortunate enough to injure yourself, seek medical attention as soon as possible.

Fire

Remember at all times that petrol (gasoline) is highly flammable. Never smoke, or have any kind of naked flame around, when working on the vehicle. But the risk does not end there - a spark caused by an electrical short-circuit, by two metal surfaces contacting each other, by a central heating boiler in the garage 'firing up', or even by static electricity built up in your body under certain conditions, can ignite petrol vapour, which in a confined space is highly explosive.

Always disconnect the battery earth (ground) terminal before working on any part of the fuel system, and never risk spilling fuel on to a hot engine or exhaust.

It is recommended that a fire extinguisher of a type suitable for fuel and electrical fires is kept handy in the garage or workplace at all times. Never try to extinguish a fuel or electrical fire with water.

Fumes

Certain fumes are highly toxic and can quickly cause unconsciousness and even death if inhaled to any extent. Petrol (gasoline) vapour comes into this category, as do the vapours from certain solvents such as trichloroethylene, paint thinners and those from many adhesives. Any draining or pouring of such volatile fluids should be done in a well-ventilated area.

When using cleaning fluids and solvents, read the instructions carefully. Never use any materials from unmarked containers - they may give off poisonous vapours.

Never run the engine of a motor vehicle in an enclosed space such as a garage. Exhaust fumes contain carbon monoxide which is extremely poisonous; if you need to run the engine, always do so in the open air or at least have the rear of the vehicle outside the workplace.

If you are fortunate enough to have the use of an inspection pit, never drain or pour petrol, and never run the engine, while the vehicle is standing over it; the fumes, being heavier than air, will concentrate in the pit with possibly lethal results.

The Battery

Never cause a spark, or allow a naked light, near the vehicle battery. It will normally be giving off a certain amount of hydrogen gas, which is highly explosive.

Always disconnect the battery earth (ground) terminal before working on the fuel or electrical systems.

If possible, loosen the filler plugs or cover when charging the battery from an external source. Do not charge at an excessive rate or the battery may burst.

Take care when topping up and when carrying the battery. The acid electrolyte, even when diluted, is very corrosive and should not be allowed to contact the eyes or skin.

If you ever need to prepare electrolyte yourself, always add the acid slowly to the water, and never the other way round. Protect against splashes by wearing rubber gloves and goggles.

Mains Electricity

When using an electric power tool, inspection light etc., which works from the mains, always ensure that the appliance is correctly connected to its plug and that, where necessary, it is properly earthed (grounded). Do not use such appliances in damp conditions and, again, beware of creating a spark or applying excessive heat in the vicinity of fuel or fuel vapour.

Ignition HT Voltage

A severe electric shock can result from touching certain parts of the ignition system, such as the HT leads, when the engine is running or being cranked, particularly if components are damp or the insulation is defective. Where an electronic ignition system is fitted, the HT voltage is much higher and could prove fatal.

Welding and Bodywork Repairs

It is so useful to be able to weld when carrying out restoration work, and yet there is a good deal that could go dangerously wrong for the uninformed - in fact more than could be covered here. **For safety's sake** you are strongly recommended to seek tuition in whatever branch of welding you wish to use, from your local evening institute or adult education classes. In addition, all of the information and instructional material produced by the suppliers of materials and equipment you will be using must be studied

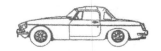

carefully. You may have to ask your stockist for some of this printed material if it is not made available at the time of purchase.

In addition, it is strongly recommended that The Car Bodywork Repair Manual, published by Haynes, is purchased and studied before carrying out any welding or bodywork repairs. Consisting of 292 pages, around 1,000 illustrations and written by Lindsay Porter, the author of this book, The Car Bodywork Repair Manual picks the brains of specialists from a variety of fields, and covers arc, MIG and 'gas' welding, panel beating and accident repair, rust repair and treatment, paint spraying, glass-fibre work, filler, lead loading, interiors and much more besides. Alongside a number of projects, the book describes in detail how to carry out each of the techniques involved in car bodywork repair with safety notes where necessary. As such, it is the ideal complement to this book.

Compressed Gas Cylinders

There are serious hazards associated with the storage and handling of gas cylinders and fittings, and standard precautions should be strictly observed in dealing with them. Ensure that cylinders are stored in safe conditions, properly maintained and always handled with special care and make constant efforts to eliminate the possibilities of leakage, fire and explosion.

The cylinder gases that are commonly used are oxygen, acetylene and liquid petroleum gas (LPG). Safety requirements for all three gases are: Cylinders must be stored in a fire resistant, dry and well- ventilated space, away from any source of heat or ignition and protected from ice, snow or direct sunlight. Valves of cylinders in store must always be kept uppermost and closed, even when the cylinder is empty. Cylinders should be handled with care and only by personnel who are reliable, adequately informed and fully aware of all associated hazards. Damaged or leaking cylinders should be immediately taken outside into the open air, and the supplier and fire authorities should be notified immediately. No one should approach a gas cylinder store with a naked light or cigarette. Care should be taken to avoid striking or dropping cylinders, or knocking them together. Cylinders should never be used as rollers. One cylinder should never be filled from another. Every care must be taken to avoid accidental damage to cylinder valves. Valves must be operated without haste, never fully opened hard back against the back stop (so that other users know the valve is open) and never wrenched shut but turned just securely enough to stop the gas. Before removing or loosening any outlet connections, caps or plugs, a check should be made that the valves are closed. When changing cylinders, close all valves and appliance taps, and extinguish naked flames, including pilot jets, before disconnecting them. When reconnecting ensure that all connections and washers are clean and in good condition and do not overtighten them. Immediately a cylinder becomes empty, close its valve.
Safety requirements for acetylene: Cylinders must always be stored and used in the upright position. If a cylinder becomes heated accidentally or becomes hot because of excessive backfiring, immediately shut the valve, detach the regulator, take the cylinder out of doors well away from the building, immerse it in or continuously spray it with water, open the valve and allow the gas to escape until the cylinder is empty. If necessary, notify the emergency fire service without delay.
Safety requirements for oxygen are: No oil or grease should be used on valves or fittings. Cylinders with convex bases should be used in a stand or held securely to a wall.
Safety requirements for LPG are: The store must be kept free of combustible material, corrosive material and cylinders of oxygen.
Cylinders should only ever be carried upright, securely strapped down, preferably in an open vehicle or with windows open. Carry the suppliers safety data with you. In the event of an accident, notify the Police and Fire services and hand the safety data to them.

Dangerous Liquids and Gases

Because of flammable gas given off by batteries when on charge, care should be taken to avoid sparking by switching off the power supply before charger leads are connected or disconnected. Battery terminals should be shielded, since a battery contains energy and a spark can be caused by any conductor which touches its terminals or exposed connecting straps.

When internal combustion engines are operated inside buildings the exhaust fumes must be properly discharged to the open air. Petroleum spirit or mixture must be contained in metal cans which should be kept in a store. In any area where battery charging or the testing of fuel injection systems is carried out there must be good ventilation, and no sources of ignition. Inspection pits often present serious hazards. They should be of adequate length to

allow safe access and exit while a car is in position. If there is an inspection pit, petrol may enter it. Since petrol vapour is heavier than air it will remain there and be a hazard if there is any source of ignition. All sources of ignition must therefore be excluded.

Special care should be taken when any type of lifting equipment is used. Lifting jacks are for raising vehicles; they should never be used as supports while work is in progress. Jacks must be replaced by adequate rigid supports before any work is begun on the vehicle. Risk of injury while working on running engines, e.g. adjusting the timing, can arise if the operator touches a high voltage lead and pulls his hand away on to a projection or revolving part. On some vehicles the voltage used in the ignition system is so high as to cause injury or death by electrocution. Consult your handbook or main dealer if in any doubt.

Work with Plastics

Work with plastic materials brings additional hazards into workshops. Many of the materials used (polymers, resins, adhesives and materials acting as catalysts and accelerators) readily produce very dangerous situations in the form of poisonous fumes, skin irritants, risk of fire and explosions. Do not allow resin or 2-pack adhesive hardener, or that supplied with filler or 2-pack stopper to come into contact with skin or eyes. Read carefully the safety notes supplied on the tin, tube or packaging.

Jacks and Axle Stands

Any jack is made for lifting the car, not for supporting it.

NEVER even consider working under your car using only a jack to support the weight of it. Jacks are for lifting; axle stands are available from many discount stores, and all auto parts stores. These stands are absolutely essential if you plan to work under your car. Simple triangular stands (fixed or adjustable) will suit almost all of your working situations. Drive-on ramps are very limiting because of their design and size.

When jacking the car from the front, leave the gearbox in neutral and the brake off until you have placed the axle stands under the frame. Make sure that the care is on level ground first! Then put the car into gear and/or engage the handbrake and lower the jack. Obviously DO NOT put the car in gear if you plan to turn over the engine! Leaving the brake on, or leaving the car in gear while jacking the front of the car will necessarily cause the jack to tip (unless a good quality trolley jack with wheels is being used). This is unavoidable when jacking the car on one side, and the use of the handbrake in this case is recommended.

If the car is older and if it shows signs of weakening at the jack tubes while using the factory jack, it is best to purchase a good scissors jack or pneumatic jack - preferably trolley-type (depending on your budget).

Workshop Safety - Summary

1)   Always have a fire extinguisher at arm's length whenever welding or when working on the fuel system - under the car, or under the bonnet.
2)   NEVER use a naked torch near the petrol tank.
3)   Keep your inspection lamp FAR AWAY from any source of dripping petrol (gasoline); for

example, while removing the fuel pump.
4)   NEVER use petrol (gasoline) to clean parts. Use paraffin (kerosene) or white (mineral) spirits.
5)   NO SMOKING!
If you do have a fire, DON'T PANIC. Use the extinguisher effectively by directing it at the base of the fire.

Paint Spraying

NEVER use 2-pack, isocyanide-based paints in the home environment. Ask your supplier if you are not sure which is which. If you have use of a professional booth, wear an air-fed mask fed by a clean air source from outside the building. Wear a charcoal face mask when spraying other paints and maintain ventilation to the spray area. Concentrated fumes are dangerous!

Spray fumes, thinners and paint are highly flammable. Keep away from naked flames or sparks.

Paint spraying safety is too large a subject for this book. See Lindsay Porter's The Car Bodywork Repair Manual (Haynes) for further information.

The Chubb powder-type fire extinguisher is ideal for car or workshop fires. Other types are unsuitable; water can be positively dangerous.

Appendix 2:
Tools and Working Facilities

Introduction

A selection of good tools is a fundamental requirement for anyone contemplating the maintenance and repair of a motor vehicle. For the owner who does not possess any, their purchase will prove a considerable expense, offsetting some of the savings made by doing-it-yourself. However, provided that the tools purchased are of good quality, they will last for many years and prove an extremely worthwhile investment.

To help the average owner to decide which tools are needed to carry out the various tasks detailed in this manual, we have compiled three lists of tools under the following headings: Maintenance and Minor Repair Tool Kit, Repair and Overhaul Tool Kit, and Special Tools. The newcomer to practical mechanics should start off with the Maintenance and Minor Repair Tool Kit and confine himself to the simpler jobs around the vehicle. Then, as his confidence and experience grows, he can undertake more difficult tasks, buying extra tools as, and when, they are needed. In this way, a Maintenance and Minor Repair Tool Kit can be built up into a Repair and Overhaul Tool Kit over a considerable period of time without any major cash outlays. The experienced do-it-yourselfer will have a tool kit good enough for most repairs and overhaul procedures and will add tools from the Special Tools category when he feels the expense is justified by the amount of use these tools will be put to.

Maintenance and Minor Repair Tool Kit

The tools given in this list should be considered as a minimum requirement if routine maintenance, servicing and minor repair operations are to be undertaken.

Ideally, purchase sets of open-ended and ring spanners, covering similar size ranges. That way, you will have the correct tools for loosening nuts from bolts having the same head size, for example, since you will have at least two spanners of the same size.

Alternatively, a set of combination spanners (ring one end, open-ended the other), give the advantages of both types of spanner. Although more expensive than open-ended spanners, combination spanners can often help you out in tight situations, by gripping the nut better than an open-ender.

Combination spanners - 3/8, 7/16, 1/2, 9/16, 5/8, 11/16, 3/4, 13/16, 7/8, 15/16 in. AF.
Combination spanners - 8, 9, 10, 11, 12, 14, 15, 17, 19mm.

Adjustable spanner - 9 in
Engine sump/gearbox/rear axle drain plug key (where applicable)
Spark plug spanner (with rubber insert)
Spark plug gap adjustment tool
Set of feeler gauges
Brake adjuster spanner (where applicable)
Brake bleed nipple spanner
Screwdriver - 4 in long x 1/4 in dia (crosshead)
Combination pliers - 6 in
Hacksaw, junior
Tyre pump
Tyre pressure gauge
Grease gun (where applicable)
Oil can
Fine emery cloth (1 sheet)
Wire brush (small)
Funnel (medium size)

Repair and Overhaul Tool Kit

These tools are virtually essential for anyone undertaking any major repairs to a motor vehicle, and are additional to those given in the Basic list. Included in this list is a comprehensive set of sockets. Although these are expensive they will be found invaluable as they are so versatile - particularly if various drives are including in the set. We recommend the 1/2 in square-drive type, as this can be used with most proprietary torque wrenches. On the other hand, 3/8 in drive are better for working in confined spaces and, if of good quality will be amply strong enough for work inside the engine bay. If you cannot afford a socket set, even bought piecemeal, then inexpensive tubular box spanners are a useful alternative.

The tools in this list will occasionally need to be supplemented by tools from the Special list.

- Sockets (or box spanners) to cover range in previous list
- Reversible ratchet drive (for use with sockets)
- Extension piece, 10 in (for use with sockets)
- Universal joint (for use with sockets)
- Torque wrench (for use with sockets)
- 'Mole' wrench - 8 in
- Ball pein hammer
- Soft-faced hammer, plastic or rubber
- Screwdriver - 6 in long x 5/16 in dia (plain)
- Screwdriver - 2 in long x 5/16 in square (plain)
- Screwdriver - 1 1/2 in long x 1/4 in dia (crosshead)
- Screwdriver - 3 in long x 1/8 in dia (electrician's)
- Pliers - electrician's side cutters
- Pliers - needle noses
- Pliers - circlip (internal and external)
- Cold chisel - 1/2 in
- Scriber (this can be made by grinding the end of a broken hacksaw blade)
- Scriber (this can be made by flattening and sharpening one end of a piece of copper pipe)
- Centre punch
- Pin punch
- Hacksaw
- Valve grinding tool
- Steel rule/straight-edge
- Allen keys
- Selection of files
- Wire brush (large)
- Axle stands
- Jack (strong scissor or hydraulic type)

Special Tools

The tools in this list are those which are not used regularly, are expensive to buy, or which need to be used in accordance with their manufacturers' instructions. Unless relatively difficult mechanical jobs are undertaken frequently, it will not be economic to buy many of these tools. Where this is the case, you could consider clubbing together with friends (or a motorists' club) to make a joint purchase, or borrowing the tools against a deposit from a local garage or tool hire specialist.

The following list contains only those tools and instruments freely available to the public, and not those special tools produced by the vehicle manufacturer specifically for its dealer network.

- Valve spring compressor
- Piston ring compressor
- Ball joint separator
- Universal hub/bearing puller
- Impact screwdriver
- Micrometer and/or vernier gauge
- Carburettor flow balancing device (where applicable)
- Dial gauge
- Stroboscopic timing light
- Dwell angle meter/tachometer
- Universal electrical multimeter
- Cylinder compression gauge
- Lifting tackle
- Trolley jack
- Light with extension lead
- Rivet gun

Buying Tools

Tool factors can be a good source of implements, due to the extensive ranges which they normally stock. On the other hand, accessory shops usually offer excellent quality goods, often at discount prices, so it pays to shop around.

The old maxim 'buy the best tools you can afford' is a good general rule to go by, since cheap tools are seldom good value, especially in the long run. Conversely, it isn't always true that the MOST expensive tools are best. There are plenty of good tools available at reasonable prices, and the shop manager or proprietor will usually be very helpful in giving advice on the best tools for particular jobs.

Care and Maintenance of Tools

Having purchased a reasonable tool kit, it is necessary to keep the tools in a clean serviceable condition. After use, always wipe off any dirt, grease and metal particles using a clean,

dry cloth, before putting the tools away. Never leave them lying around after they have been used. A simple tool rack on the garage or workshop wall, for items such as screwdrivers and pliers is a good idea. Store all normal spanners and sockets in a metal box. Any measuring instruments, gauges, meters, etc. must be carefully stored where they cannot be damaged or become rusty.

Take a little care when the tools are used. Hammer heads inevitably become marked, and scredrivers lose the keen edge on their blades from time to time. A little timely attention with emery cloth or a file will soon restore items like this to a good serviceable finish.

Working Facilities

Not to be forgotten when discussing tools, is the workshop itself. If anything more than routine maintenance is to be carried out, some form of suitable working area becomes essential.

It is appreciated that many an owner mechanic is forced by circumstance to remove an engine or similar item without the benefit of a garage or workshop. Having done this, any repairs should always be done under the cover of a roof, if feasible.

Wherever possible, any dismantling should be done on a clean, flat workbench or table at a suitable working height. Engine dismantling, though, is safer carried out on an engine stand (they can be hired sometimes) or on a large cardboard box opened out to give a clean surface on the workshop floor.

Any workbench needs a vice - the larger the better - and one with a jaw opening of 4 in (100mm) is suitable for most jobs. As mentioned previously, some clean dry storage space is also required for tools, as well as for lubricants, cleaning fluids, touch-up paints and so on, which soon become necessary.

Another item which may be required, and which has a much more general usage, is an electric drill with a chuck capacity of at least 5/16 in (8mm). This, together with a good range of twist drills, is virtually essential for fitting accessories such as wing mirrors and reversing lights. Cordless drills are far more convenient to use and don't carry any electrical risks in use.

Last, but not least, always keep a supply of old newspapers and clean, lint-free rags available, and try to keep any working areas as clean as possible.

Spanner Jaw Gap Comparison Table

N.B. Using a badly fitting spanner – one of the incorrect size, worn or with 'sprung' jaws – can be dangerous.

AF size	Actual size	Nearest metric size	Metric size in inches
4BA	0.248 in	7mm	0.276 in
2BA	0.320 in	8mm	0.315 in
7/16 in	0.440 in	11mm	0.413 in
1/2 in	0.500 in	13mm	0.510 in
9/16 in	0.560 in	14mm	0.550 in
5/8 in	0.630 in	16mm	0.630 in
11/16 in	0.690 in	18mm	0.710 in
3/4 in	0.760 in	19mm	0.750 in
13/16 in	0.820 in	21mm	0.830 in
7/8 in	0.880 in	22mm	0.870 in
15/16 in	0.940 in	24mm	0.945 in
1 in	1.000 in	26mm	1,020 in

Whitworth size	Actual size	Nearest AF size	AF Actual size
3/16 in	0.450 in	7/16 in	0.440 in
1/4 in	0.530 in	1/2 in	0.500 in
5/16 in	0.604 in	9/16 in	0.560 in
3/8 in	0.720 in	11/16 in	0.690 in
7/16 in	0.830 in	13/16 in	0.820 in
1/2 in	0.930 in	7/8 in	0.880 in
9/16 in	1.020 in	1 in	1.010 in

Whitworth size	Actual size	Nearest Metric size	Metric size in inches
3/16 in	0.450 in	12mm	0.470 in
1/4 in	0.530 in	14mm	0.500 in
5/16 in	0.604 in	15mm	0.590 in
3/8 in	0.720 in	18mm	0.710 in
7/16 in	0.830 in	21mm	0.830 in
1/2 in	0.930 in	24mm	0.945 in
9/16 in	1.020 in	26mm	1.020 in

Appendix 3:
MGB's Specifications

Please note that the specifications in this section relate to the MGB upon its introduction. Production modifications are listed separately.

Type designation	MG MGB Tourer MG MGB GT
Built	Abingdon, England, 1962-1980
Engine	Cast iron block and head, pressed steel sump 4-cylinders in-line, overhead valve, camshaft in block Capacity 1798 cc. Bore & Stroke 80.26 x 88.9mm. Maximum power 92bhp (net) at 5,400rpm. 2 SU HS4 1 1/2 in single jet with Cooper paper element air filters.
Transmission	Rear-wheel-drive from front mounted engine. Four-speed gearbox bolted to the rear engine plate. Synchromesh available on top three gears until October 1967, and on all forward gears thereafter. Overall gear rations (1962) 1st 14.21, 2nd 8.66, 3rd 5.37, 4th 3.9, optional overdrive (from January 1963) 3.14. Rear axle of the three-quarter floating type, incorporating a hypoid final drive on early Tourers. Later Tourers and GTs, axle of the tubed semi-floating type.
Chassis	Main structural components: large section three-element side members (sills) and double bulkhead into which torsional loadings are fed via 18 gauge inner wing panels. Wheelbase: 7 ft 7 in
Track	Front: 4 ft 1 in. Rear: 4 ft 1.25 in.
Suspension	Front: independent, coil springs. Rear: helf-elliptic leaf springs.
Steering	Rack and pinion, 3 turns lock-to-lock.
Brakes	Front: Lockheed, discs, 10.75 in dia. Rear: Lockheed, drums, 10 in dia.
Wheels and Tyres	Ventilated pressed steel disc, 4 studs, 4 in width (optional wire wheels). 5.60 x 14 in tyres with tubes.

Bodywork	2-door, 2-seater convertible or fixed- head with very occasional rear seats. Unitary construction of pressed steel 20 gauge outer panels and aluminium bonnet. Pressed on British-made American-designed Hamilton, Toledo and Danby presses at British Motor Holding Group's Pressed Steel Fisher Company's factory at Swindon, Wiltshire, England. GT body assembled at Swindon, but Tourer assembled at Pressed Steel Fisher, Coventry. Body panels joined by spot welding.

Dimensions: overall length: 12 ft 9.2 in; overall width: 4 ft 11.9 in; overall height: 4 ft 1.4 in; ground clearance: 5 in; turning circle: 31 ft; kerb weight: 18.1 cwt weight distribution (dry) 54% front/46% rear.

Electrical System

12 volt 58 amp hr (twin x 6V batteries mounted under rear 'scuttle'). Positive earth Lucas dynamo with Lucas RB340-type voltage regulator. Lucas coil ignition and wiring harness made up to standard Lucas colour coding scheme. Headlamp, Lucas sealed-filament 50-40 watts.

Performance

Maximum speed: 106mph
Speed in gears (approx):
    3rd gear 90mph
    2nd gear 55mph
    1st gear 30mph
Acceleration 0-60mph: 12.2 sec
Standing 1/4 mile: 18.7 sec
Acceleration in gears:
    Top: 20-40mph 9.0 sec; 50-70mph 10.00 sec.
    Third: 20-40mph 5.6 sec; 50-70mph 7.7 sec.
Fuel consumption: 21 to 29mpg.

Appendix 4: Production Modifications and Totals

The Chassis Number (or Car Number) is stamped on a plate which is held on the left-hand wing balance just ahead of the radiator. The engine Number is stamped on a plate found on the right-hand side of the cylinder block.

The Chassis, or Car Number, consists of a code which presents the following information:

1st Numeral indicates make (G = MG)
2nd Numeral indicates engine type (H = 'B'-series engine)
3rd Numeral indicates body type (N = 2 seater tourer; D = GT)
4th Numeral indicates series (1 and 2 = MGA; 3 = 1st series MGB; 4 = 2nd series; 5 = 3rd series. No series changes made after October 1979)
5th Numeral indicates market destination (L = LHD; U = USA)
6th Numeral indicates model year from 1970 (A = 1970; B = 1971; C = 1972, and so on)

Thus: G-HN3 = MG; fitted with 'B'-series engine; Tourer; 1st series MGB. (Also, UK market because no L or U after number.) And: G-HD5UE = MG; fitted with 'B'-series engine; GT; 3rd series MGB; USA; 1974.

There is some confusion over the generic terms 'MkI', 'MkII', 'MkIII', and so on. No cars were ever originally referred to as 'MkI' - first cars were designated '3rd-series' as successors to 1st and 2nd series MGAs, and in any case this designation only came into colloquial use when there was a 'MkII' (officially the 4th-series) to replace it. All cars after October 1969 were known as 5th-series, and are known colloquially as 'MkIII'. However, subsequent production changes have prompted unofficial 'MkIV' and 'MkV' labels to be applied, but the usage of these designations is less than unanimous and so cannot sensibly be applied here. 1975-on cars are generally known as 'rubber bumper' or 'black bumper' models.

Production Modifications

Note: G-HN3, 4 and 5 are Roadsters; G-HD3, 4 and 5 are GTs.

Chassis numbers quoted here are what manufacturers know as 'pure' chassis numbers (i.e. all cars after the number shown are fitted with those parts which relate to the chassis number change point). However, it may well be that, because of production line supply techniques, some cars which appear before the given change point will be fitted with later parts. On the other hand, no cars after a chassis number change point will have been fitted with earlier parts - a point worth bearing in mind when buying or judging Concours cars.

June 1962: MGB Roadster Chassis No. G-HN3 101 Production begins.
September 1962: Cars first released with 3-main-bearing 'B'-series engine of 1798cc. (18G designation, known as 18GA from early 1964.) Front suspension descended from YA, TD, TF, MGA but softer sprung. MGA-type 'banjo' rear axle. Options included: heater, wire wheels, oil cooler (standard for export), front anti-roll bar, folding hood (from G-HN3 19259) tonneau cover (standard for North America).
Early 1963: Laycock overdrive (D-type) available as option.
June 1963: 'Works' glassfibre hardtop available.

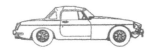

February 1964: Closed-circuit crankcase breathing on engine, now known as 18GA. Chassis No. G-HN3 31021.

October 1964: Chassis No. G-HN3 48766. 5-main-bearing engine fitted, with fully-floating gudgeon pins replacing circlips in pistons. Oil-cooler fitted as standard. Electronic rev-counter replaced mechanical type. Gearbox fitted with larger first motion shaft spigot end and bush in engine crank enlarged accordingly.

March 1965: Chassis No. G-HN3 56743. Fuel tank capacity increased from 10 Imp gallons to 12 Imp gallons. Held by 9 bolts instead of 2 steel straps as previously. Chassis No. G-HN3 57986. Door handles changed from pull-out to pushbutton type externally. Mechanism, locks and door shape also modified.

October 1965: GT launched, Chassis No. G-HD3 71933. Fixed head Coupe with large rear door, more luggage space than Roadster and taller windscreen and window glasses. Presented as '2 + 2' but rear seats adequate only for small children. Styled at Abingdon, 'detailed' by Pininfarina. Salisbury (or 'tube- type') rear axle (not commonised with Roadster).

November 1966: Chassis No. G-HN3 108039. Anti-roll bar standard.

April 1967: G-HN3 132923 (wire-wheeled cars); G-HN3 139215 (disc-wheeled cars). Salisbury (or 'tube-type') rear axle previously fitted to GT commonised with Roadster. However, it should be noted that from G-HN3 123716 to 132922 either a banjo or tube axle is fitted.

October 1967: G-HN4 138401; 'MkII' models (4th-series) G-HD4 139472. Engine numbers 18GD, later 18GG(UK) and 18GF, later 18GH(USA). Engines fitted with emission control equipment (air pumps, check valve, gulp valve, modified cylinder head, modified carburettors and inlet manifolding). Modified engine backplate fitted to all engines from now on. Pre-engaged starter motor replaces 'bendix' type. All-synchro gearbox with optional automatic, as developed for MGC. Gearbox tunnel/toeboard area modified to accept new automatic transmission. Reversing lights fitted as standard. Negative earth alternator (Lucas 16AC type) replaces dynamo. US cars fitted with completely different heavily-padded fascia and dash with glove compartment. Also fitted with energy-absorbing steering column and dual circuit brakes (for which servo not available).

October 1969: G-HN5 187211; G-HD5 187841 'MkIII' models (5th-series); 18GH engines (Federal) now with exhaust emission controls. New recessed radiator grille in black with chrome surround. New smaller steering wheel with 3 drilled aluminium spokes. BL emblems on front wings (except Arab countries where BL then blacklisted!) Rubber inserts on over-riders. Rostyle wheels (wires still optional). Reclining seats as standard, upholstered in vinyl, with longitudinal strips forming ventilated centre panel. Minor fascia re-arrangement. US-style padded- fascia standard for Sweden. Dipping interior rear-view mirror. Optional headrests (from G-HN5 209784 to 258000 and G-HD5 207650 to 258000).

September 1970: G-HN5 219001. Telescopic boot and bonnet stays. Improved ventilation and revised heater. Interior courtesy light. New folding hood (designed by Michelotti) standardised. Interior boot light. More emission control equipment for US market, including engine-driven air pump. Automatic seatbelts standardised on North American tourers from G-HN5 268080.

October 1971: G-HN5/G-HD5 258001. Final engine change to 18V ('V' for vertical) and 18GK(US) types. New fascia with face- level air-vents situated in space where radio previously fitted. New rocker switches and controls. New centre console with ashtray, lift-up armrest with storage space beneath. US fascias still of heavily padded type but with glove compartment. Brushed nylon seat facings. Door-mounted mirror fitted. Collapsible energy-absorbing steering column optional (non-US markets).

May 1972: G-HN5/G-HD5 282420. One-hand seatbelts fitted.

October 1972: G-HN5 294251; G-HD5 296001. New grille with vertical centre bar and black mesh. New padded-steering wheel with slotted spokes. Matching 'upholstered' gear knob. Padded door armrests/pulls. Matt black windscreen wipers. Cigar lighter fitted as standard. Tonneau standard (UK). Heated rear screen fitted as standard on GT. Automatic seatbelts optional, radial-ply tyres standard (UK). Black-spoked steering wheel available on GT (UK only) from G-HD5 320197.

September 1973: G-HN5/G-HD5 328101. Radial-ply tyres standard (all markets). Automatic gearbox option withdrawn. Engine bay/flitch panels commonised with V8. Vertically rectangular rubber over-riders fitted to US cars (G-HN5 339095 to 368081 and G-HD5 339472 to 367803).

September/December 1974: G-HN5 360301/G-HD5 361001, except USA, where G-HN5 363082. GT no longer available in USA. 'Federal bumper' models with large black bumpers front and rear, faired into bodyline at front with heavy steel reinforcement covered by impact resistant urethane padding. Raised ride height. Single Zenith/Stromberg carburettor and further reduced

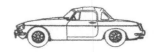

performance (USA). Revised switch layout with BL corporate column controls for wash/wipe. US-style padded fascia commonised to all LHD cars (G-HN5 360301 - on). Hazard warning lights, door mirrors, servo brake assistance all standard. Modified Laycock overdrive (LH- type) with slightly lower (0.82 to 1) step-up ratio. Single 12-volt battery replacing 2 x 6-volt batteries. Catalytic converter added for California cars.

May 1975: Jubilee special to commemorate BL's version of MG's 50th anniversary. 750 cars built, mechanically standard but in British Racing Green with gold striping, head-restraints, tinted-glass, overdrive, V8-type wheels and 175-section tyres. (MGB GT 'Jubilee' chassis numbers interspersed with standard MGBs.)

June 1975: G-HN5 380278/G-HD5 379495. Overdrive fitted as standard.

August 1976: G-HN5 410001. Thicker anti-roll bar at front and anti-roll bar at rear as standard. Electric radiator cooling fan (2 for USA). New fascia/console with electric clock. Lower geared steering (3 1/2 turns lock-to-lock, replacing 3 turn) and smaller 4-spoke steering wheel. Striped fabric seat trim. Gearlever-mounted overdrive switch. Halogen headlights (UK). tinted-glass on GT. Carpet on floor, 2-speed heater fan, lockable glovebox, sealed cooling system with separate radiator catch tank. Pedal pad positions altered to allow, for first time, 'heel-and-toeing'.

April 1977: Inertia reel seatbelt as standard.

January 1978: Twin door-mounted speakers and aerial as standard.

June 1980: Rear foglamps fitted as standard (UK).

October 1980: MGB Roadster and GT-Limited Edition. G-HN5 522581/G-HD5 522422. Last 1,000 cars made (420 Tourers) known as 'Limited Edition'. GTs

finished in Pewter Silver, Tourers in Bronze, both with body stripe. Integral front spoilers, alloy or wire wheels (on Tourer), distinctive badges.

22 October 1980: Last MGB Roadster, G-HN5 523001, last MTB GT G-HD5 523002 produced at Abingdon, Oxford, England.

MGC: Chassis Number Sequences

July 1967 to August 1969 (total built 8,999)

G/CN 101-9099 Roadsters

G/CD 110-9102 GTs

The above comprised:
4,542 Roadsters
4,457 GTs of which
1,403 Roadsters and 2,034 GTs (total 3,437) were for the UK market.

Engine No. prefix is 29G

(Austin 3-litre Engine No. prefix is 29A)

MGB GT V8: Chassis Number Sequences

Early 1973 to late 1976 (total built 2,591)

G/D2D1-101-2903 GTs only.

Virtually all were sold in UK.

USA Cars

1962-67 cars: Almost identical to UK specification cars. Only differences are left hand drive,

and the tail lamp lenses having both top and bottom pieces coloured red. Oil cooler was standard equipment in the USA.

1968 cars: The beginning of the 'Federalisation Era', and regulations from the US government on all cars sold in the US. Emission controls were introduced, as was a padded dashboard, which no longer had a glovebox. Instrument layout was also revised. Oil and temperature gauges were now separate units, with the oil pressure gauge being a unique rectangular shape. Negative ground electricals with alternator were introduced. UK automatic transmission opption was never available in the USA on MGBs, but all-synchro manual gearbox was now standard in the USA as well.

1969 cars: New solid coloured leather seats (no piping), with headrests, were used this year only. Stick-on reflectors were mounted on all four wings, front wings had amber reflectors, and rear wings had red reflectors.

1970 cars: New features included 'blacked-out' grille, fold-down top, and one-piece red and amber tail-lamp lenses. Unlike the UK style tail-lamp lenses with the amber portion at the top, the amber portion is in the centre of the lens. Side marker lamps with built in hazard flashers replaced the previous reflectors, again with lamps on front wings being amber, and red on the rear wings. New steering wheel and vinyl seats were added. British Leyland badge is mounted on both front wings. Split rear bumper is featured this year only. Rostyle wheels replaced disc wheels as the standard wheels, with wire wheels still being optional. New badging for the tailgate, and vinyl inserts in the seats were changes exclusive to the MGB GT.

1971 cars: British Leyland badge on right (passenger) front wing only.

1972 cars: Face level air vents and lockable glove box added to dash. Centre of MG Octagon on steering wheel hub is now coloured red.

1973 cars: New grille introduced, incorporating basic shape of old grille, without vertical bars, but rather black honeycomb centre of grille. MG badge is red and chrome rather than black, red and chrome as in old grille. SU HIF 4 carburettors replace the SU HS 4 carburettors. Armrests are added to inside of doors. Steering wheel has one long cutout in each of the three spokes, rather than the previous series of small round holes. New MGB GT tailgate badge. Pattern of vinyl seats is revised.

1974 cars: Oversized black rubber over-riders are used this year only. Steering wheel spoke cutouts are replaced by filled in recessed area.

1974-1/2 cars: The last of the MGB GTs are imported into the USA. Full rubber bumpers are now fitted, along with single 12-volt battery.

1975 cars: Single Zenith/Stromberg carburettor replaces twin SU carbs. This new carburettor also incorporated automatic choke. 'MGB' badged removed from boot lid. MG badging on front bumper and boot lid are gold and black in colour, as well as centre of MG Octagon on steering wheel hub being coloured gold, in honour of MG's 50th anniversary.

1976 cars: MG badging on front bumper and boot lid changed to chrome and black. Catalytic converter now fitted, and unleaded fuel is required.

1977 cars: Dashboard is revised with larger, modern-style instruments, new four spoke steering wheel, clock, and interior fan now has two speeds. New soft top is featured with zip-out rear window. Pattern of vinyl seats is revised. Front and rear sway (anti-roll) bars are added.

1978 cars: Crankshaft is strengthened.

1979 cars: The 'Limited Edition' package is offererd as an option. Included was special black paint and silver striping, Triumph Stag wheels with MG hubcaps, special steering wheel, and dash plaque. Front air dam is also incorporated into 'Limited Edition' package.

1980 cars: 80mph speedometer is fitted, along with six digit odometer.

1992: New style V8 MGB planned for launch by Rover Group.

MGB Production 1962-1980

	Roadster			GT			
	Home	Export	Total	Home	Export	Total	Grand T
1962	540	3 978	4 518				4 518
1963	3 020	20 288	23 308				23 308
1964	4 321	22 221	26 542				26 542
1965	4 742	19 437	24 179	350	174	524	24 703
1966	4 050	18 625	22 675	2 415	7 826	10 241	32 916
1967	2 749	12 379	15 128	5 276	6 120	11 396	26 524
1968	1 609	15 746	17 355	2 750	5 602	8 352	25 707
1969	2 288	16 762	19 050	3 274	8 938	12 212	31 262
1970	2 841	20 803	23 644	4 466	7 996	12 462	36 106
1971	3 046	19 398	22 444	5 311	6 799	12 110	34 554
1972	4 898	21 294	26 192	7 883	5 291	13 174	39 366
1973	3 034	16 531	19 565	5 760	4 458	10 218	29 783
1974	1 622	17 344	18 966	3 899	5 682	9 581	28 547
1975	1 118	18 848	19 966	4 122	487	4 609	24 575
1976	1 891	23 969	25 860	3 083	615	3 698	29 558
1977	2 262	22 228	24 490	4 065	126 4	191	28 681
1978	2 836	19 170	22 006	5 529	129 5	658	27 664
1979	921	18 976	19 897	3 346	127	3 473	23 370
1980	2 022	8 982	11 004	3 378	46	3 424	14 428
Total	49 810	336 979	386 789	64 907	60 416	125 323	512 112

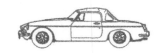

MGC and MGB GT V8 Production

	MGC Roadster	MGC GT	MGB GT V8	Total
1967	189	41		230
1968	2566	2462		5028
1969	1787	1954		3741
1972			3	
1973			1069	
1974			854	
1975			489	
1976			176	
Total	4542	4457	2591	8999

Production Changes

H1. One hundred thousand MGAs were built, but this one is the rarest of all. The DeLuxe MGA was built around the Twin-Cam bodyshell and running gear but with a standard ohv engine. ⬅

H2. One of the very earliest MGBs in all of its uncluttered elegance - a timeless shape. ⬅

H3. By 1965, a much stronger engine was used, but little else was changed. ➡

H4. Leather seats, long-throw gear change, spoked steering wheel and early door trim were still unaltered in 1965.

H6. As far as the cockpit was concerned there was not a change to be seen apart from the improved visibility through the taller windscreen ...

H7. ... but at the rear, there was a tremendous amount of luggage space for a small sports car, and sitting room for two very little people.

H5. 1966 was notable for the introduction of the stylish MGB GT with detailing by Italian design house Pininfarina. ➡

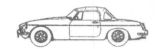

H8. The extra height of the GT certainly did not detract from the car's appearance, and the GT is arguably more aesthetically pleasing than the Roadster. ➡

H9. July 1967 saw the introduction of the powerfully engined MGC. It was slated by the Press at the time but, today, its long torquey engine makes the car a delight to drive. ⬇

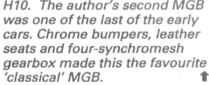

H10. The author's second MGB was one of the last of the early cars. Chrome bumpers, leather seats and four-synchromesh gearbox made this the favourite 'classical' MGB. ⬆

H11. 1969 for the 1970 model year saw the first of the British Leyland-identified models. In practice, several detail touches made the car more user-friendly. This rare automatic MGB was under-rated, and was a delight to drive. ⬅

H12. For the first time, the car's external appearance was subtly changed. Note the 'BL' badges on the wings. ➡

H13. By 1971 further detail alterations included rubber buffers on the bumper over-riders. ⬇

H15. In 1971, MGBs were given face-level air vents. Door pulls are different on this 1972 car.

H14. At around the same time, Ken Costello went into small-scale production with the first MGB GT V8. These non-factory cars wore a large bonnet bulge at first, but later Costello cars managed to fit the whole engine under the bonnet. ➡

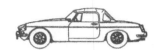

H16. BL jumped on the Costello bandwagon in 1973 with their own V8-engined MGB GT, now one of the great classic cars. ➡

H17. Apart from larger wheels and subtle badge changes, the V8 was indistinguishable from any other GT - until it overtook you! ➡

H18. In the USA and Canada external changes were minimal. This is J.D. Towler's beautifully restored car at his home in Quebec. ➡

H19. 1973 trim was different again, with new steering wheel and switch gear. The old slotted and then 'drilled' steering wheels were dropped because of wealthy ladies with large rings getting their hands stuck in the steering wheel spokes - so the story goes!

H21. The last of the UK chrome bumper 'Bs had number plate lights moved from over-riders to the bumper itself. In the USA large rubber over-riders were fitted.

H22. 1974 for the 1975 model year saw the introduction of the rubber bumper MGB. This was the most dramatic change to be made to the car's appearance throughout its production run.

H20. The last of the chrome-bumper 'Bs had a grille which, at least, had recognisable roots. American 'Bs were becoming really slow! (Photo: S. Glochowsky)

H23. 750 Jubilee models were built in 1975 to commemorate BL's version of MG's 50th Anniversary. Mechanically standard but with gold striping and other detail changes.

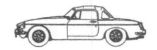

H24. At the same time, V8 MGBs were also built with rubber bumpers and the standardised raised ride height. ↑

H25. The last of the 'standard' MGBs was much like any other rubber bumper car but by now large numbers of detail alterations had taken place. ➡

H26. Last few cars were known as 'Limited Edition' and were given special colour schemes and detail specification changes, including a front spoiler and alloy wheels used on no other MGB. ↓

H27. Ex-Abingdon Press Officer, Peter Franklin, had himself photographed with the last Abingdon MGB to come off the line on 22 October 1980. Remarkably, the company didn't bother to have official photographs taken - how different things are today with Rover Group's Heritage organisation. ⬅

H28. In its August 1991 issue, Car magazine carried a 'MG Shock' story, claiming that Rover Group were planning to put the 'B back into production with a V8 engine in a Heritage bodyshell modified to give a 'Coke bottle' shape. Shape of things to come! ↑

H29. Just over a year later, on 20 October 1992, the MG RV8 was launched at the British Motor Show in Birmingham. ➡

H30. Very little was changed to the basic layout of the car but there was extensive use of leather and burr elm wood veneer on the facia, console and doors. ⬇

The MG RV8

H31. Rover described the changes to the vehicle as 'subtle' but not everyone agrees. Compared with the original car, there are new front and rear wings, moulded bumpers, revised headlamps and tail lamps and a new grille and soft-top. ↙

H32. The 3.9 litre V8 engine provided a claimed top speed of 135mph and acceleration from 0-60mph in 5.9 seconds. While the five-speed gearbox and torque sensing differential make a big difference to the car, Autocar and Motor criticised it for having old fashioned handling. Owners might well consider that to be a part of the car's traditional appeal although the launch price of £26,500 certainly didn't seem very traditional! ⬇

Appendix 5:
Performance Figures

The following performance figures relate to contemporary road test figures of the days when these cars were new ...

UK SPECIFICATION

	MGB 1798cc	MGB 1798cc o/d	MGB GT 1798cc o/d	MGB 1798cc auto	MGB GT 1798cc o/d	MGB 1798cc o/d	MGB GT 1798cc o/d	MGC 2912cc o/d	MGC GT 2912cc auto	MGC Fed 2912cc o/d	MGB GT V8 3528cc o/d
Mean maximum speed (mph)	103	103	101	104	102	105	99	120	116	118	124
Acceleration (sec)											
0-30mph	4.1	4.0	4.0	4.9	3.8	3.5	4.8	4.0	4.4	3.7	2.8
0-40mph	6.2	6.0	6.2	7.1	6.1	5.5	7.0	5.6	6.2	5.4	4.3
0-50mph	8.5	9.0	9.3	10.0	8.7	8.2	9.3	7.6	8.2	7.2	6.4
0-60mph	12.2	12.9	13.6	13.6	13.0	12.1	14.0	10.0	10.9	10.1	8.6
0-70mph	16.5	17.2	19.0	18.5	17.8	16.5	19.1	13.8	14.6	13.6	11.8
0-80mph	22.9	24.1	25.4	26.4	25.4	22.7	28.5	18.0	18.8	17.8	15.1
0-90mph	32.6	35.6	38.1	39.0	36.9	34.5	35.7	23.1	26.3	–	19.0
0-100mph	52.3	–	–	–	–	–	–	29.3	35.8	32.6	25.3
0-110mph	–	–	–	–	–	–	–	40.9	–	–	35.6
Standing 1/4-mile (sec)	18.7	18.9	19.1	19.5	18.5	18.3	19.1	17.7	18.2	18.0	16.4
Overall Fuel consumption (mpg)	21.4	22.0	22.8	25.5	23.7	26.1	25.7	17.5	19.0	22.25	23.4
Typical Fuel consumption (mph)	25	27	26	26	24	28	28	19	20	–	25
Kerb weight (lb)	2072	2128	2379	2144	2379	2289	2442	2477	2615	2600	2387
Original Test published	1962	1965	1966	1970	1971	1975	1977	1967	1968	1969	1973

FEDERAL SPECIFICATION

	MGB GT 1798cc	MGB 1798cc	MGB GT 1798cc	MGB 1798cc o/d	MGB GT 1798cc	MGB 1798cc	MGB 1798cc
Mean maximum speed (mph)	105	104	104	105	94	96	90
Acceleration (sec)							
0-30mph	4.0	3.9	–	–	4.6	5.0	5.5
0-40mph	6.3	6.0	–	–	6.9	7.5	–
0-50mph	9.9	8.4	–	–	10.0	10.7	–
0-60mph	13.6	12.1	12.1	13.6	13.7	14.6	18.3
0-70mph	18.3	16.7	–	–	19.0	20.2	26.5
0-80mph	25.1	23.2	–	–	27.5	29.5	39.0
0-90mph	37.2	32.8	32.8	–	–	–	–
0-100mph	–	–	–	–	–	–	–
0-110mph	–	–	–	–	–	–	–
Standing 1/4-mile (sec)	19.6	18.7	18.7	19.6	19.2	20.2	21.5
Overall fuel consumption (mpg)	28.75	30.0	29.4	24.1	–	–	24.4
Typical fuel consumption (mpg)	–	–	–	–	–	–	–
Kerb Weight (lb)	2308	2220	2220	2345	2250	2380	2275
Original test published	1966	1968	1970	1971	1973	1973	1976

Appendix 6:
Colour Schemes

When purchasing or ordering paint or trim material for your car, the following list of paint and trim colours must be verified as (a) correct and (b) acceptable to the purchaser, by reference to colour samples available from manufacturers or stockists.

Anders Ditlev Clausager has made quite a name for himself in the classic car world! As Archivist to the Heritage Trust, his reputation as a unique source of accurate information is impressive. This is the result of work carried out by him on MGB colour schemes, which first appeared in MG Enthusiast magazine, where Anders wrote:

'The question, "What colour is my MGB?", is one of those that I get asked most often. Surprisingly, despite the great number of learned books devoted to MGBs and MGs in general, I do not think that a complete list of colour and trim options for the MGB has ever been published until now. Of course, I won't claim that the following is the last word on the subject, but I hope it will be of some help to MGB owners and enthusiasts who need to identify a particular shade of colour when they have the car repainted, or who want to make sure that everything is absolutely original.

'The inspiration for tackling this subject really came from Caroline and John Twist of University Motors, Grand Rapids, Michigan, USA, to whom I owe a great deal for their efforts in compiling a list of paint colours. What I have tried to do is partly to combine known paint colours with colours of trim (seats and carpets), hoods and hardtops; also to put the list into historical perspective by arranging it year by year. Actually, much of the information is available in the microfiche parts lists that Rover Group/Unipart still publish for the MGB and MGC, but I have been able to verify the information against the actual production records which have also given reasonably exact dates of when colours were introduced or discontinued.

'In the following, I will go through the colour schemes year by year. But before I start, I must explain that the years I have used are the so-called "model years" which typically run from September one year to August the following year. MG tended to introduce major changes, including new colours, in the period between the summer holiday break and the Motor Show in October. For instance, 1975 model year, which marked the introduction

of rubber-bumper cars - began in September 1974. And although production of the MGB began in May 1962, for a public launch in September we may count all the early cars as 1963 models. This therefore is our starting point:

1963 (from start of production May 1962)
Originally the MGB was available in five exterior colours:

Tartan Red, red trim with black piping or black trim with red piping, red hood

Iris Blue, black or blue trim with pale blue piping, blue hood

Chelsea Grey, red trim with white piping, grey hood

Old English White, black or red trim with white piping, grey hood

Black, black trim with white piping or red trim with black piping, grey hood From around December 1962, a sixth colour was added:

British Racing Green, black trim with white piping, grey hood

1964
Initially, the same colours were offered as in 1963, but in August 1963, British Racing Green (GN.25) was replaced by Dark British Racing Green (GN.29). The period from April to August

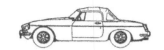

1964 saw the gradual introduction of black hoods which were offered as an alternative to coloured hoods, with all exterior paint colours.

1965
The existing colour range from 1963-64 was continued, but Chelsea Grey was discontinued around March 1965.

1966
With the introduction of the MGB GT we will have to consider the Roadster and GT models separately, as for some years they were not always available in the same colour schemes.

For the Roadster, the previous colour range was continued until around July 1966 when Iris Blue was discontinued and replaced by Mineral Blue, with black or blue trim with pale blue piping, and black hood.

The GT model went into production in September 1965 (as a 1966 model - remember?) and was originally offered in the following colours:

Tartan Red, red trim with black piping or black trim with red piping

Mineral Blue, black or blue trim with pale blue piping

Sandy Beige, black or red trim with white piping

Dark British Racing Green, black trim with white piping or red trim with black piping

Grampian Grey, red trim with black piping or black trim with white piping

Old English White, black trim with red piping or red trim with black piping

Black, black trim with white piping or red trim with black piping

So it can be seen that Sandy Beige and Grampian Grey were unique to the GT, and Mineral Blue was originally only available on the GT, although it was subsequently standardised on the Roadster as well.

1967
Roadster: The 1966 colour range was continued, but coloured hoods were deleted and hoods from now on (right up until 1980!) were available only in black. For Tartan Red and Mineral Blue, red and blue trim respectively were discontinued, so these colours continued with black trim only. In January 1967, a new colour was added:

Pale Primrose Yellow, with black trim with white piping and black hood GT: Also more or less as 1966, but on Tartan Red and Dark British Racing Green cars, the red trim was discontinued, so these cars were only available with black trim. The GT model was also offered in Pale Primrose Yellow with black trim with white piping, from January 1967.

1968
MGB Roadster and MGB GT: Old English White was discontinued and was replaced by Snowberry White, with black or red trim (and black hood). This occurred in approximately January 1968.

During 1968, all coloured trims were discontinued, and were replaced by a new design of seat, in black without contrasting piping. Hardtops (see note at the end of the article) were also now offered in black only. MGC Roadster: This was introduced in October 1967 in the following colour schemes:

Tartan Red, black trim with red piping

Snowberry White, black or red trim with white piping

Black, black trim with white piping or red trim with black piping

Dark British Racing Green, black trim with white piping

Mineral Blue, black (or blue) trim with pale blue piping

Pale Primrose Yellow, black trim with white piping - which were the MGB Roadster colours, but two additional

colours were quoted as "optional extras":

Metallic Riviera Silver Blue, black trim with pale blue piping

Metallic Golden Beige, red or black trim with white piping MGC GT: Similarly, this was available in the MGB GT colours, and the two metallic colours were quoted as standard colours. The complete list was:

Tartan Red, black trim with red piping, or red trim with black piping

Snowberry White, black trim with red piping or red trim with black piping

Black, black trim with white piping or red trim with black piping

Dark British Racing Green, black trim with white piping or red trim with black piping

Mineral Blue, black or blue trim with pale blue piping

Pale Primrose Yellow, black trim with white piping

Sandy Beige, black or red trim with white piping

Grampian Grey, black trim with white piping or red trim with black piping

Metallic Golden Beige, black or red trim with white piping

Metallic Riviera Silver Blue, with black or blue trim with pale blue piping. The blue and red trim options on MGC and MGC GT cars were phased out during 1968, coinciding with the introduction of the new- style seats which were at first always black and no longer had contrast colour piping.

I should also add that some early MGC cars could have been painted Old English White, but Snowberry White soon took over.

1969
MGB and MGC Roadster: The six colours listed above under 1968 for MGC were continued without change, all with only black trim and hoods. MGB and MGC GT: The basic colour range was continued also for these models, and it seems that

for a time the two metallic colours were also offered on the MGB GT, even to the temporary exclusion of the solid colours, Mineral Blue and Sandy Beige. Black trim was the order of the day, except for Metallic Golden Beige cars which were available with a new trim colour, mushroom, as an alternative.

By February 1969, the two metallic colours were discontinued, and replaced by the old favourite solid colours:

Mineral Blue, with black trim

Sandy Beige, with black or mushroom trim

Mushroom trim was only offered until the end of the 1969 model year, and this point in time also marked the end of MGC production.

1970

We are back with just the MGB only, and we have arrived at the introduction of the first "Leyland" colours (which have code numbers prefixed BLVC = British Leyland Vehicle Colour).

Both the MGB Roadster and the MGB GT were available in the following colours: Glacier White, Dark British Racing Green, Blue Royale, Flame Red, Bronze Yellow, Pale Primrose Yellow and Black.

The MGB GT was also available in two additional colours: Bermuda Blue and Antelope (beige). The trim colour on all cars was - you've guessed it! - black.

1971

During a brief period of overlap from July to October 1970 the old colour range was quoted together with the new 1971 proper colours, but for 1971 five old colours were discontinued, so the range was as follows, for both the Roadster and the GT:

Glacier White, Midnight Blue, Flame Red, Blaze, Bronze Yellow and Black - all with black trim

Racing Green, Teal Blue and Bedouin - all with autumn leaf trim

We may note that there is a new trim colour, autumn leaf (brown to you and me). The "Racing Green" is not the same colour as the old BMC colour "Dark British Racing Green" but is a new BLVC colour sometimes called Racing Green'70. Finally, the colour range for the Roadster and the GT is now the same, and would remain so to 1980.

1972

Black trim was discontinued in favour of navy trim - a blue which is so dark it may almost be mistaken for black.

Around July 1971, three new colours were introduced: Green Mallard, with autumn leaf trim; Aqua and Harvest Gold, both with navy trim. In the autumn of 1971 the following old colours were discontinued: Racing Green, Midnight Blue and Bedouin. With these colours, black trim also disappeared for the time being, and in addition to Aqua and Harvest Gold, the following colours were offered with navy trim: Glacier White, Flame Red, Blaze and Bronze Yellow. Teal Blue continued with autumn leaf trim, and Black was offered with either of the two trim colours.

1973

Autumn leaf trim was discontinued around September 1972 and was replaced by ochre trim. Black was offered with either ochre or navy trim; and in a brief period, Teal Blue and Green Mallard may have been available with either autumn leaf or ochre trim.

Also around this time, three new additional colours were introduced: Limeflower and Damask Red, both with navy trim; and Black Tulip, with ochre trim.

By February 1973, Aqua and Flame Red were discontinued.

1974

A new model was introduced, the MGB GT V8, but this was always offered in the same colour range as the two four cylinder models. It may, however, be worth mentioning that early V8 production models were almost all finished in one of three colours, Glacier White, Harvest Gold or Damask Red, all with navy trim, and that the first V8s had either navy or ochre trim. They were also finished in the 1973 colour range.

But with the start of the 1974 model year proper, trim colours were changed from ochre and navy back to autumn leaf and black. Four colours were discontinued, and five new ones introduced, so the complete 1974 colour range was as follows:

Glacier White, Teal Blue, Tundra, Aconite and Bracken - all with autumn leaf trim

Blaze, Harvest Gold, Damask Red, Citron and Mirage - all with black trim

Black - with either black or autumn leaf trim

Note that Glacier White is now offered with autumn leaf trim, rather than black (or navy). There seems to have been an overlap period in the summer of 1973 when the "new" trim colour autumn leaf was offered on cars finished in the old colours Teal Blue, Green Mallard and Black Tulip, and both old and new trim colours on cars in Glacier White, Blaze, Harvest Gold and Damask Red.

1975

The introduction of the "rubber-bumper" model marked the beginning of the 1975 model year (or if you will, the 1974 1/2 model; whatever you call these cars, it makes no difference to the colour range).

Mirage was discontinued with the end of the 1974 model year, and the following colours were also discontinued although they may have been

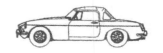

used on some early 1975 cars: Teal Blue, Blaze and Aconite. Two new colours were introduced with a slightly wider trim choice so the range was now:

Flamenco (new colour), Harvest Gold, Damask Red, Citron - all with black trim

Tundra - with autumn leaf trim

Tahiti Blue (new colour), Glacier White, Bracken, Black - all with either black or autumn leaf trim

The Limited Edition (they made 750) GT Anniversary model was finished in Racing Green (which was the 1971 colour) with black trim.

1976
Initially the 1975 range was continued but during the spring of 1976, the following four colours were discontinued: Harvest Gold, Tundra, Bracken and Citron. Three new colours were introduced and trim options were again simplified so the final 1976 colour range was:

Chartreuse (new colour), Glacier White, Damask Red, Flamenco - all with black trim

Brooklands Green (new colour), Sandglow (new colour), Tahiti Blue, Black - all with autumn leaf trim

This was the last year for the V8, but I think that at least one - possibly a few more - of the final V8s had 1977-style trim, see below.

1977
The new trim was two-tone striped brushed nylon fabric, popularly referred to as the "deck chair" upholstery. There were two colour combinations, either orange and brown, or silver and grey. Whereas previously, door trims and other interior liners had matched seat upholstery, all these trim panels were now in black. However, it is important to realise that the new fabric was not used on cars (by now,

Roadsters only) exported to North America and later Japan; these kept to the perforated vinyl seat trim in different colours, and I will deal with these later.

By contrast there were no changes to the exterior paint colours, and the combinations for 1977 for home market (and non- North American export cars - which were very few in number!) were as follows:

Glacier White, Chartreuse, Brooklands Green, Sandglow - all with orange/brown trim

Damask Red, Tahiti Blue, Flamenco - all with silver/grey trim

Black - with either trim option.

However, during 1977 Damask Red was phased out, to be replaced by a new dark red colour, Carmine, which also took silver/grey trim.

1978
No changes to the trim, but the paint colour range was almost entirely new, as follows:

Leyland (Ermine) White, Brooklands Green, Russet Brown - all with orange/brown trim

Vermillion, Pageant Blue, Carmine, Inca Yellow - all with silver/grey trim

Black - with either trim colour

1979
As 1978, except it is possible that Triumph White for a time replaced Leyland White.

1980
As 1978-79, except that Inca Yellow was discontinued and was replaced by a new yellow colour, Snapdragon, also with silver/grey trim; and white cars were now finished in Porcelain White (another name for Leyland White, it seems?)

Production stopped in October 1980, but the 1000 Limited Edition "LE" cars were only released for sale in January 1981. These cars were

finished in two special metallic colours which were picked from the colour range used on the Princess 2 (!) The LE Roadsters were Bronze Metallic (with orange/brown trim), and the LE GTs were Pewter Metallic (with silver/grey trim). These cars were all sold in the home market and should not be confused with the American "LE" model which was Black and of which there were almost 6,700. All LEs were offered with a new style of alloy wheel.

'This brings me to the end of the chronological section of this colour list, but there are a few more points which should be examined. You will notice that I have listed Black throughout the production run, and I believe it was used in all years, but it was not always a standard colour, being at times available to special order only.

'MGB and MGC cars supplied to the Constabulary were often painted in a special colour, Police White, which typically took the darkest trim colour available - mainly black, but in 1972-73, navy. (By the way, Bermuda Blue, which was offered on the MGB GT in 1970, was more often used on Police Panda cars!)

'I have not taken into account special colours, or one-offs, whether for experimental purposes or otherwise - which did happen, even as late as 1978-79, at least if you were in the right position in the BL hierarchy to make such things happen! For instance, from this period I remember a metallic blue MGB GT with rubber bumpers bravely painted in a darker blue colour ... I think the excuse was that it was a styling experiment!

'Hood colours have been listed above, but a word or two on hardtop colours should be added. Hardtops were always extra equipment to special order, and were originally finished in five different colours which could be ordered with

main body colours as follows:

'Cars finished in Old English White, Tartan Red, Chelsea Grey or Black could have hardtops in Red, Black, Old English White or Grey.

'Cars finished in Iris Blue or Mineral Blue could have hardtops in Black, Old English White or Blue.

'Cars finished in British Racing Green or Dark British Racing Green could have hardtops in Black or Old English White.

'But from late 1966 or early 1967, the coloured hardtops were discontinued, and hardtops thereafter remained obstinately black.

'The GT of course could not have a hardtop, but it did have an interior headlining, which was normally grey, except on GTs which were finished in Sandy Beige or Metallic Golden Beige, when the headlining was a matching beige.

'Going from top to toe, so to speak, let us look at carpets. Up to and including the 1976 model year, the carpet colour would usually match the general trim colour (of seats and liners), so on pre-1969 cars you should have red or blue carpets/mats for cars with these trims colours. Afterwards, carpets were black, navy, autumn leaf or ochre, again to match trim. The only exception to the rule was that on GTs in beige with mushroom trim, carpets were brown.

'With the deck-chair upholstery on 1977 or later cars, carpets were black, and thus matched the door trims, and liners on home market cars.

'As mentioned above, North American export models from the period 1977-80 had different trim and trim colours. The paint colour range was the same as for home market cars, except that black was not always available, but the colour trim combinations were as follows:

'White colours (all) - black trim and carpet

'Chartreuse, Damask Red, Flamenco, Inca Yellow, Vermillion, Snapdragon - black trim and carpet

'Sandglow, Tahiti Blue - autumn leaf trim, black and autumn leaf carpet

'Russet Brown, Pageant Blue - beige trim, black and chestnut carpet

'Brooklands Green - 1977: Autumn leaf trim, black and autumn leaf carpet; 1978-80: Beige trim, black and chestnut carpet

'Carmine - 1977: Black trim and carpet; 1978-80: Beige trim, black and chestnut carpet

'On these North American cars, the door trims and liners matched the seat upholstery, and so were black, autumn leaf or beige, depending on the seat colour. On cars with black trim, the carpets were all black, but cars with trim in autumn leaf and later beige had a rather strange combination of black carpet to front footwells, centre tunnel and sills, but autumn leaf or chestnut (brown) carpet to the heelboard and rear compartment shelf behind the seats.

'The chestnut carpet colour is found from late 1977 onwards, probably only in conjunction with beige trim. Chestnut is almost indistinguishable from autumn leaf, the colour it replaced.

'The North American market Limited Edition model of 1979-80 was finished in Black paint, with trim in either black or beige. The North American paint/trim colour combinations are likely to apply also to the MGBs which were exported to Japan in 1980, as these were basically built to Californian specification.

'Component colours is an area where I have much less information, but it is known that the original disc-type wheels, and the painted wire wheels, were finished in silver. The metal fascia panel on the cars which have this, was painted wrinkle (or crackle) black. The engines were originally red, but later engines (from some time in the early 1970s, probably coinciding with the introduction of the 18V-type engines from the start of the 1972 model year) were black. Most transmission, chassis and other mechanical components are likely to be painted black (if they were ever painted at all!)

'Following this article, I have listed all the known exterior paint colours with their code numbers (BMC or BLVC numbers, as well as the reference numbers from the two major paint suppliers, ICI and Ault & Wiborg - useful if you are ordering paint for restoration). But I am tempted to round off this narrative with a true story, told to me by my friend and former colleague Ken Rees, who will be well known to members of the MG Car Club as the Triple-M Register's scribe.

'In the 1970s, he worked for the colour and trim section of the BL styling studio at Longbridge, which looked after the MG range. Now you may not appreciate that it can be a big problem, not only developing and selecting new colours, but also naming them. Anyway, they were having a brain-storming session to name among others the nice new green which would be used on the MGB in 1976. Ken, being well aware of MG's great sporting heritage suggested: "Why don't we call it Brooklands Green?" So someone else, probably a product planner who did not know anything about MG history, replied: "Yes, that's nice. It reminds me of meadows in the countryside." Anyway, for whatever reason, they decided on Brooklands Green.'

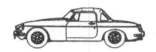

MGB/MGC/MGB GT V8 colours 1962-80: colour names and codes

Name	BMC/BL code	Ault & Wiborg code	ICI code
Black	BK.1		
Black/brown beige colours:	BLVC90,PMA		KE47
Antelope	BLVC7	28040	7984
Bedouin	BLVC4,SAA	28664	7855
Bracken	BLVC93,FME	30096	9427
Bronze Metallic (1980-81 LE)	BLVC370,BMC	34824M/35269M	6759M
Golden Beige Metallic	BG.19	26930M	3006M/2496M
Russet Brown	BLVC205,AAE	31072/32592/ 33669	DD51
Sandglow	BLVC63,AMF	31030	8651/GC20
Sandy Beige (1961-type)	BG.15	23473	6187
- blue colours:			
Aqua	BLVC60,JMA	28002	7932
Bermuda Blue	BU.40	22885	2846
Blue Royale	BU.38	23322/28603	5186
Iris Blue	BU.12	20306	3243
Midnight Blue	BLVC12,JMB	28666	7963
Mineral Blue (MG Blue)	BU.9	18921	3130
Mirage	BLVC11,LMF	30097	7960
Pageant Blue	BLVC224,JNA	31913	FC58
Riviera Silver Blue Metallic	BU.47	26554M	3005M
Teal Blue	BLVC18,JMC	28667	7918
Tahiti Blue	BLVC65,JMP	30788/31692	AF45
- green colours:			
Brooklands Green	BLVC169,HMM	30683	4498/FM45/FD6
Green Mallard	BLVC22,HMD	28895	7925
Limeflower	BLVC20,HMA	28668	7968(?)
British Racing Green	GN.25	21677	8120
Dark British Racing Green	GN.29	24499	9767
(New) Racing Green	BLVC25	28670	7985
Tundra	BLVC94,HMF	30094/32045/ 32777	9424
- grey colours:			
Chelsea Grey	GR.15	17581	2750
Dark Wheel Silver*	GR.36	27177	
M Grampian Grey	GR.12	21175	7087
Pewter Metallic (1980-81 LE)	BLVC377,MMD	35700M/34826M	6766M
Wheel Silver*	BLVC88	29511M	0367B/6040M
Dover Grey*	GR.34	26710	5235
Aluminium*	AL.1	?	?
- red colours:			
Aconite (purple)	BLVC95,KMB	30095	9425
Black Tulip (purple)	BLVC23,KMA	28058	7970
Blaze (orange)	BLVC16,EMA	28665/30545	7864
Damask Red	BLVC99,CMA	20921/30488	4808
Carmine (red)	BLVC209, CAA	29355	9236/FD 32/EE80
Flame Red	BLVC61,CMB	28216/29787	3442
Flamenco (orange-red)	BLVC133,EMC	30789/32137/ 32635	9718/DA63/DA90
Tartan Red	RD.9	20817/32046	3770
Vermillion (red)	BLVC118,CML	32781	FC57/GE40

Name	BMC/BL code	Ault & Wiborg code	ICI code
- white colours:			
Glacier White	BLVC59,NMA	27962/30099	4309
Leyland (or Ermine) White	BLVC243,NMC/ NME	32335/36133	FA78
Old English White	WT.3	32043(1965)/ 24643/18580	2379/2122(?)
Police White	WT.2BLVC1024	24048	HT 49
Snowberry White	WT.4	19303	3012
Porcelain White	BLVC243, NCG/NAF	(numbers as Leyland or Ermine White)	
Triumph White	BLVC206,NAB	24863/31694(?)	3738
- yellow colours:			
Bronze Yellow	BLVC15,FMF	27944	9785/7861
Chartreuse	BLVC167,FMJ	30645	CH76
Citron	BLVC73,FMD	30083	8653
Inca Yellow	BLVC207,FAB	33668/31073/ 32694	DD 50
Pale Primrose Yellow	YL.12	26111	3297
Snapdragon	BLVC235,FMN	31939	GJ 80
Harvest Gold	BLVC19,GMA	28894	791
- others:			
Wrinkle Black (fascia)	BK.2	not known	not known

*These four grey/silver colours are the possible wheel colours which were not necessarily all used on the MGB or associated models. It is unfortunately not clear from the records whether 1962-69 cars had wheels in Dark Wheel Silver, or Aluminium; my guess would be the latter colour. NB: Latest MGBs, those with "VIN" chassis numbers, have their paint codes shown on their chassis number plates.

'In compiling this list, I owe thanks to Mr A.N. Duthie, Colour & Trim Studio, Rover Design; also to Messrs ICI Limited (Paints Division), and Messrs Ault & Wiborg Paints Limited.

'Colour codes of the type "BK 1" are the old pre-1970 BMC colour codes. "BLVC" codes are the post-1970 British Leyland Vehicle Colours. The three-letter codes appearing with most of these are the codes which on 1980 model year cars are stamped on the chassis number plates (or Vehicle Identification Number plates).

'For colours which were available in different shades, there are several numbers listed from paint manufacturers, and MGB owners who are in doubt as to exactly which shade is right for their car, are advised to contact the paint manufacturers who should be able to match existing paint, or supply chips or small samples for comparative purposes.

'Most of the paint colours are also available from American manufacturers of paint, such as Ditzler, Dupont or Rinshed Mason. If American readers have any problems finding the right code number or supplier for these paints, they may contact University Motors Ltd., 614 Eastern Avenue S.E., Grand Rapids, Michigan 49503 (Caroline or John Twist) from where a list of American code numbers is available.

'PS: It should be pointed out that the information appearing in this article does not necessarily apply to MGB cars which were assembled, and painted and trimmed, abroad from CKD kits sent out from Abingdon. In fact, I am certain that the Australian built MGBs had a completely different colour range to anything used in Britain, and this could also be the case for other MGBs built overseas.

Anders Ditlev Clausager.'

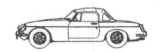

MGC Colour Schemes - All Years. Compiled by Lindsay and Shan Porter

Body exterior and BL Paint Code	Model	Seats	Seat piping	Liners	A. Hood, Tonneau Cover, & Hard Top B. Head-lining	Door Seals	Carpet/Mats
Sandy Beige (BG.15) (GT only)	D	Black	White	Black	B.Beige	Black	Black
		Red	White	Red	B.Beige	Red	Red
		Black	Black	Black	B.Grey	Black	Black
Metallic Golden Beige (BG.19)	N D	Black	White	Black	A.Black B.Beige	Black	Black
		Red	White	Red	A.Black B.Beige	Red	Red
Black (BK.1)	N D	Black	White	Black	A.Black B.Grey	Black	Black
		Red	Black	Red	Grey	Red	Red
		Black	Blue	Black	Grey	Black	Black
		Black	Black	Black	Grey	Black	Black
Mineral Blue (BU.9)	D	Black	Blue	Black	Grey	Black	Black
		Blue	Blue	Blue	B.Grey	Blue	Blue
	N D	Black	Black	Black	A.Black B.Grey	Black	Black
Metallic Riviera	N	Black	Black	Black	Grey	Black	Black
Silver Blue	D	Blue	Blue	Blue	Grey	Blue	Blue
British Racing Green (GN.29)	N D	Black	White	Black	Grey	Black	Black
	D	Black	Black	Black	Grey	Black	Black
	D	Red	Black	Red	B.Grey	Red	Red
Grampian Grey (GR.12) (GT only)	D	Red	Black	Red	B.Grey	Red	Red
		Black	White	Black	Grey	Black	Black
		Black	Black	Black	Grey	Black	Black
Tartan Red (RD.9)	N D	Black	Red	Black	A.Black B.Grey	Black	Black
		Black	Black	Black	Grey	Black	Black
	D	Red	Black	Red	B.Grey	Red	Red
Old English White (WT.3)	N	Black	White	Black	A.Black	Black	Black
		Red	White	Red	Black	Red	Red
	D	Red	Black	Red	B.Grey	Red	Red
		Black	Red	Black	B.Grey	Black	Black
Snowberry White (WT.4 D	N	Black	White	Black	A.Black B.Grey	Black	Black
		Black	Black	Black	Grey	Black	Black
Pale Primrose (YL.12)	N D	Black	Black	Black	A.Black B.Grey	Black	Black
		Black	Black	Black	Grey	Black	Black

N - Roadster
D - GT

Appendix 7: **British and American Thread Systems**

The MGB from 1963-1980 uses Unified National Fine (UNF) in almost all applications, which is completely compatible with American Fine (AF) or SAE threads. A few applications use a Unified National Coarse (UNC) compatible with American coarse threads (some studs into the block and gearcase). There are only a few applications of BSF (British Standard Fine) or BSW (British Standard Whitworth - coarse). The dampers (shock absorbers) use a BSF thread for their filler screws. All Lucas electrics used Whitworth until around 1969 when the change was made to metric.

		Threads per inch		
	BSW	UNC	BSF	UNF
1/8 (0.125)	40	(US) No.5-40		
3/16 (0.1875)	24	(US) No.10-24	32	(US) No.10-32 (0.190 dia)
1/4 (0.250)	20	20 (0.190 dia)	26	28
5/16 (0.3125)	18	18	22	24
3/8 (0.375)	16	16	20	24
7/16 (0.4375)	14	14	18	20
1/2 (0.500)	12	13	16	20

Note: Although the BSW and UNC threads per inch are the same in popular sizes, the angle of the thread differs, and they are incompatible. The BSF and UNF are not compatible either, as the tpi are different for each dia.

Screws used in the MGB are almost all crosshead. Slotted-head screws are simply not acceptable for a good restoration. A popular screw size in the MGB is 2BA (British Association), but that size is fully compatible with the American No. 10-32 screw.

	Diameter-	Threads per in	
2BA	0.185	31.358	(the BA screws use metric pitch)
No.10-32	0.190	32	
4BA	0.1417	38.5	These screws are not as compatible as the
No.6-40	0.1372	40	2BA or 10-32, but are infrequently used.

Except for the interior panels and a very few applications in other places, all the screws are 'machine thread' NOT self-tapping.

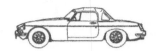

British Standard Pipe

In the applications listed below, BSP threads are used. These ARE NOT compatible with any American threading system, and the proper BSP screws and fittings MUST be used.

Size	Diameter	Threads/inch
1/8	0.3830	28
1/4	0.5180	19
3/8	0.6560	19
1/2	0.8250	14

Uses of BSP on MGB

Radiator drain hole (if fitted)		1/4BSP
Oil Cooler and fittings		1/2BSP
Engine Block:	Sump drain plug	1/4BSP
	Water drain plug	1/4BSP
	Oil hole plug (left side)	3/8BSP
	Oil pressure relief valve	1/2BSP
	Oil outlet (right rear)	1/2BSP
Fuel tank:	Drain (if fitted)	1/4 or 1/8BSP
Fuel line		1/4BSP
Fuel pump:	Banjo bolts	3/8BSP
Fuel line:	at bulkhead	1/4BSP

Most of these BSP applications require the use of BSF/BSW wrenches or the use of a good quality adjustable wrench.

Appendix 8: **British and American Technical Terms**

As this book has been written in England, it uses the appropriate English component names, phrases, and spelling. Some of these differ from those used in America. Normally, these cause no difficulty, but to make sure, a glossary is printed below. In ordering spare parts remember the parts list will probably use these words:

English	American	English	American
Aerial	Antenna	Layshaft (of	
Accelerator	Gas pedal	gearbox)	Countershaft
Alternator	Generator (AC)	Leading shoe	
Anti-roll bar	Stabiliser or	(of brake)	Primary shoe
	sway bar	Locks	Latches
		Motorway	Freeway, turnpike
Battery	Energizer	Number plate	License plate
Bodywork	Sheet metal	Paraffin	Kerosene
Bonnet (engine		Petrol	Gasoline
cover)	Hood	Petrol tank	Gas tank
Boot lid	Trunk lid	'Pinking'	'Pinging'
Boot (luggage		Propeller shaft	Driveshaft
compartment)	Trunk	Quarterlight	Quarter window
Bottom gear	1st gear	Retread	Recap
Bulkhead	Firewall	Reverse	Back-up
Cam follower	Valve lifter	Rocker cover	Valve cover
or tappet	or tappet	Roof rack	Car-top carrier
Carburettor	Carburetor	Saloon	Sedan
Catch	Latch	Seized	Frozen
Choke/venturi	Barrel	Side indicator	Side marker
Clearance	Lash	lights	lights
Crownwheel	Ring gear (of	Side light	Parking light
	differential)	Silencer	Muffler
Disc (brake)	Rotor/disk	Spanner	Wrench
Drop arm	Pitman arm	Sill panel	Rocker panel
Drophead coupe	Convertible	Split cotter	Lock (for valve
Dynamo	Generator(DC)	(for valve	spring retainer)
Earth (elec)	Ground	spring cap)	
Engineer's blue	Prussian blue	Split pin	Cotter pin
Estate car	Station wagon	Steering arm	Spindle arm
Exhaust		Sump	Oil pan
manifold	Header	Tab washer	Tang; lock
Fast back	Hard top	Tailgate	Liftgate
Fault finding/	Trouble	Tappet	Valve lifter
diagnosis	shooting	Thrust beaaring	Throw-out bearing
Float chamber	Flat bowl	Top gear	High
Free-play	Lash	Trackrod (of	Tie-rod (or
Freewheel	Coast	steering)	connecting rod)
Gudgeon pin	Piston pin or	Trailing shoe	Secondary shoe
	wrist pin	(of brake)	
Gearchange	Shift	Transmission	Whole drive line
Gearbox	Transmission	Tyre	Tire
Halfshaft	Axleshaft	Van	Panel wagon/van
Handbrake	Parking brake	Vice	Vise
Hood	Soft top	Wheel nut	Lug nut
Hot spot	Heat riser	Windscreen	Windshield
Indicator	Turn signal	Wing/mudguard	Fender
Interior light	Dome lamp		

Miscellaneous points

An 'oil seal' is fitted to components lubricated by grease! A 'damper' is a 'shock absorber'. It damps out bouncing, and absorbs shocks of bump impact. Both names are correct, and both are used haphazardly. Note that British drum brakes are different from the Bendix type that is common in America, so different descriptive names result. The shoe end furthest from the hydraulic wheel cylinder is on a pivot; interconnection between the shoes as on Bendix brakes is most uncommon. Therefore the phrase 'Primary' or 'Secondary' shoe does not apply. A shoe is said to be 'Leading' or 'Trailing'. A 'Leading' shoe is one on which a point on the drum, as it rotates forward, reaches the shoe at the end worked by the hydraulic cylinder before the anchor end. The opposite is a 'Trailing' shoe, and this one has no self-servo from the wrapping effect of the rotating drum.

Appendix 9:
Specialists and Clubs

The following addresses and telephone numbers were believed to be correct at the time of going to press. However, as these are subject to change, particularly telephone area codes, no guarantee can be given for their continued accuracy.

Specialists

**AUTOMEC EQUIPMENT &
PARTS LTD**
36 Ballmoor,
Buckingham,
MK18 1RQ.
Tel: 01280 822818
www.automec.co.uk
Non-corroding copper brake,
clutch and fuel pipes. Silicon
brake fluid.

BOC LTD
The Priestley Centre,
10 Priestley Road,
The Surrey Research Park,
Guildford,
Surrey, GU2 5XY.
Tel: 01483 579857
www.boc.com
Welding gases and DIY 'Portapak'
gas welding equipment.

BURLEN FUEL SYSTEMS LTD
Spitfire House,
Castle Road,
Salisbury,
Wiltshire,
SP1 3SB.
Tel: 01722 412500
www.burlen.co.uk
All MGB original equipment,
carburettors and fuel pumps –
manufactured, servicing and
repair kits.

CASTROL (UK) LTD
Burmah House, Pipers Way,
Swindon, Wiltshire, SN3 1RE.
Tel: 01793 512712
www.castrol.com
Customer Relations Department
can supply free MGB lubrication
chart and full information on
MGB lubrication requirements.

CHUBB FIRE LTD Chubb House,
Staines Road West, Sunbury-on-
Thames, Middlesex, TW16 7AR.
Tel: 01932 785588
Fire extinguishers for workshop
and car.

CLARION GB LTD Unit 5C,
Interface Business Park,
Binknoll Lane,
Swindon, SN4 8QQ.
Tel: 01793 859560
www.clarion.com
Full range of in-car
entertainment systems.

CLARKE INTERNATIONAL
Hemmall Street, Epping, Essex,
CM16 4LG.
Tel: 01992 565300
www.clarkeinternational.com
Huge range of workshop
equipment – everything from
bench grinders to MIG welders,
spray equipment to power
washers and much more besides.

**COMMA OILS &
CHEMICALS LTD**
Lower Range Road,
Gravesend,
Kent,
DA12 2QX.
Tel: 01474 564311
www.commaoil.com
Motor oil, Copper Ease, X-stream
corrosion resistant coolant.

FALCON EXHAUSTS LTD
Belfield Industrial Estate,
Ilkeston,
Derbyshire,
DE7 8DU.
Tel: 0115 944 0044
Stainless steel exhaust systems.

HELLA LTD
Wildmere Industrial Estate,
Banbury,
Oxon,
OX16 3JU.
www.hella.com
Delay wiper switchgear.

BRITISH MOTOR HERITAGE LTD
Heritage Motor Centre,
Banbury Road,
Gaydon,
Warwickshire,
CV35 0BJ.
www.heritage-motor-centre.co.uk
New MGB bodyshells, technical
information, archivists for the
whole of the BMC range.

HUMBROL LTD
Marfleet, Hull,
HU9 5NE.
Tel: 01843 233525
www.humbrol.com
Plastic re-paint for plastic trim.

K & N FILTERS (EUROPE) LTD
John Street,
Warrington,
Chesire,
WA2 7UB.
Tel: 01925 636950
www.knfilters.co.uk
Advanced performance air
cleaners.

KENLOWE
Burchetts Green,
Maidenhead,
Berkshire,
SL6 6QU.
Tel: 01628 823303
www.kenlowe.com
Electric cooling fans.

**LUCAS AFTERMARKET
OPERATIONS**
Stratford Road, Solihull,
B90 4LA.
Tel: 0121 506 5000
www.lucas.info
Original electrical equipment
used throughout the MGB.

MACHINE MART
(Head Office),
211 Lower Parliament Street,
Nottingham, NG1 1GN.
Tel: 0115 956 5555
www.machinemart.co.uk
The best range of workshop
tools and equipment with outlets
throughout the UK.

METEX CAR COVERS
Holden Fold House,
Holden Fold,
Darwen,
Lancashire,
BB3 0EL.
Tel: 01254 704625
www.cardustcovers.co.uk
Car dust covers.

MG ENTHUSIAST MAGAZINE
Kelsey Publishing Group,
PO Box 978, Peterborough,
PE1 9FL.
Tel: 01959 543530
www.mgenthusiast.com
The independent MG magazine.

MICHELIN TYRES PLC
Campbell Road,
Stoke-on-Trent,
Staffordshire, ST4 4EY.
Tel: 01782 402000
www.michelin.co.uk
Original size and uprated tyres
for MG cars.

MOSS ENGINEERING
Lower Road Trading Estate,
Ledbury,
Herefordshire, HR8 2DJ.
Tel: 01531 632614
(No connection with Moss
Europe or Moss Motors).
Engine reconditioning to a high
standard.

**MOSS EUROPE SPRITE &
MIDGET B, C, V8 CENTRE**
16 Hampton Business Park,
Bolney Way, Feltham, Middlesex,
TW13 6DB.
Tel: 0208 867 2020
www.moss-europe.co.uk
Quality parts and expertise for
MG sports cars.

**MOSS BARRY STAFFORD MG
PARTS LTD**
113-115 Stockport Road,
Cheadle Heath, Stockport,
Cheshire, SK3 0JE.
Tel: 0161 480 6402
Quality parts and expertise for
MG sports cars.

MOSS DARLINGTON
15 Allington Way,
Yarm Road Industrial Estate,
Darlington, Co. Durham,
DL1 4QB.
Tel: 01325 281343
Quality parts and expertise for
MG sports cars.

MOTO-LITA LTD
Thruxton Circuit,
Weyhill,
Andover,
Hampshire,
SP11 8PW.
Tel: 01264 772811
www.mota-lita.co.uk
Classic and modern replacement
steering wheel.

NAMRICK LTD
The Nut & Bolt Store,
124 Portland Road,
Hove, Sussex,
BN3 5LQ.
Tel: 01273 779864
www.namrick.co.uk
Nuts, bolts, washers; a full range
of fixings in plated and stainless
steel.

NICOL TRANSMISSIONS
Coppice Trading Estate,
Stourport Road,
Kidderminster,
Worcestershire,
DY11 7QY.
Tel: 01562 752651
Transmission component
overhaul to a high standard.

SATA
www.sata.com
Rust prevention injection
equipment.

SERCK-MARSTON
2100 The Crescent,
Solihull Parkway,
Birmingham Business Park,
Birmingham, B37 7YE.
Tel: 0121 717 0007
Original equipment oil and water
radiators, number plates.

SECURON (AMERSHAM) LTD
The Hill,
Winchmore Hill,
Amersham,
Buckinghamshire, HP7 0NZ.
Tel: 01494 434455
www.securon.co.uk
Inertia reel seat belts.

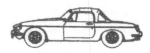

SIP (INDUSTRIAL PRODUCTS) LTD
Gelders Hall Road,
Shepshed,
Loughborough,
Leicestershire,
LE12 9NH.
Tel: 01509 500300
www.sip-group.com
Full range of electric welding and spraying equipment.

SOSNA LTD
Brook Road,
Overross Industrial Estate,
Ross-on-Wye,
Herefordshire, HR9 7QG.
Tel: 08432 663459
Fine quality respray and body preparation.

SPAX LTD
Spax House,
Murdock Road,
Bicester,
Oxon, OX26 4PL.
Tel: 01869 244771
www.spax.co.uk
Telescopic damper conversions.

SPEEDY CABLES (LONDON) LTD
Caerbont Industrial Estate,
Abercrave,
Swansea Vally,
SA9 1SQ.
Tel: 01639 732213
www.speedycables.com
Speedo, throttle, bonnet pull, handbrake cables, etc.

SYKES-PICKAVANT LTD
Unit 4, Cannel Road,
Burntwood Business Park,
Burntwood,
Staffordshire, WS7 3FU
Tel: 01543 679900
www.sykes-pickavant.com
Manufacturers of DIY automotive and industrial service tools and Speedline hand tools.

UNIVERSITY MOTORS
4571 Patterson Avenue,
S E Grand Rapids,
Michigan 49513, USA.
Tel: 001 616 301 2888
www.universitymotorsltd.com
Parts and service exclusively for the MG.

VINTAGE TYRE SUPPLIES LTD
National Motor Museum,
Beaulieu,
Hampshire, SO42 7ZN.
Tel: 01590 612261
www.vintagetyres.com
Suppliers of original pattern classic car tyres.

WURTH UK LTD
1 Centurion Way,
Erith,
Kent, DA18 4AE.
Tel: 020 8319 6000
www.wurth.co.uk
Zinc-rich primer and other workshop equipment.

Clubs

MG OWNERS' CLUB
The world's largest one make car club is not successful by accident! Formed in 1973 and supplying all MG requirements, the club provides a full range of benefits for the dedicated MG enthusiast or the less enthusiastic owner who simply enjoys running an MG for occasional or everyday transport.

Professionally administered from its Cambridgeshire headquarters, the MG Owners' Club publishes a full colour international monthly magazine 'Enjoying MG', supplements packed with adverts for MGs, spares, MG news items and colour catalogues for MG improvements and personal regalia. There are lists of local MG clubs both at home and abroad for members to contact. The club's own insurance department caters for British members' MGs with Agreed Value and was recently expanded to offer cover for members' non MGs and other club members representing other marques for their valued classic cars. Twelve insurers on the club's panel provide first class service, a wide choice of policies and unbeatable discounts due to the size of the club. The MG Workshop handles servicing, repairs, accidents and restorations.

For details of club benefits, free technical advice, recommended supplier lists, workshop manuals, handbooks, and parts lists and just about everything you can think of for over 50,000 members, send or telephone for a free catalogue and booklet.

MG Owners' Club, Station Road, Swavesey, Cambridge, CB4 5QZ. If writing from the United Kingdom, address your envelope FREEPOST and no stamp is required. Telephone 01954 31125 or Fax 01954 32106. For insurance quotations telephone 0480 300023.

MG CAR CLUB:
The MG Car Club was founded in 1930 after John Thornley and others gained the approval of Cecil Kimber for a factory based club. In 1980, its Golden Jubilee was celebrated by the opening of a new headquarters in Abingdon, by the old MG factory.

Today, the MG Car Club's model-based registers and geographically-based centres cater for all MG enthusiasts worldwide. Its members enjoy a wide range of events including social gatherings, concours and motorsport, from lighthearted driving tests to full MG race meetings. For MGB enthusiasts, the MGB Register helps owners get the best from their MGBs. As well as national meetings and rebuild seminars, all manner of MGB enquiries are dealt with, either on a personal basis or via the pages of the club's award-winning monthly magazine *Safety Fast!* For motor racing enthusiasts, the MG car club BCV8 championship provides exciting MGB racing.

Full details of MG Car Club membership, including exclusive and competitive insurance schemes, can be obtained from PO Box 251, Kimber House, Cemetery Road, Abingdon, Oxfordshire, OX14 1FF. (Tel: 01235 555552)

A cavalcade of MG cars passing the original MG Car Co. building after the official opening of the MG Car Club headquarters at Abingdon, Oxon. ➡

The MGOC's impressive club H.Q. shown here as an artist's impression. ⬅